# Management of Technology

## New Directions in Technology Management

### Selected Papers from the Thirteenth International Conference on Management of Technology

EDITED BY

Mostafa Hashem Sherif
Tinton Falls, USA

Tarek M. Khalil
University of Miami, Florida, USA

ELSEVIER
Amsterdam • Boston • Heidelberg • London • New York • Oxford
Paris • San Diego • San Francisco • Singapore • Sydney • Tokyo

Elsevier
The Boulevard, Langford Lane, Kidlington, Oxford OX5 1GB, UK
Radarweg 29, PO Box 211, 1000 AE Amsterdam, The Netherlands

First edition 2007



**British Library Cataloguing in Publication Data**
A catalogue record for this book is available from the British Library

**Library of Congress Cataloging-in-Publication Data**
A catalog record for this book is available from the Library of Congress

ISBN-13: 978-0-08-045115-2
ISBN-10: 0-08-045115-2

For information on all Elsevier publications
visit our website at books.elsevier.com

Printed and bound in The Netherlands

07 08 09 10 11 10 9 8 7 6 5 4 3 2 1

# PREFACE

The 13th International Conference on Management of Technology (MOT) convened during the period of April 3–7, 2004 in Washington, D.C., U.S.A. The theme of the conference was: "New Directions in Technology Management: Changing Collaboration between Government, Industry and University." The Conference chairs were Drs. Tarek Khalil from the University of Miami, John Aje and Frederick Betz from the University of Maryland and the Program chair was Dr. Yasser Hosni, from the University of Central Florida.

Out of more than 550 abstracts that were proposed, the conference team retained 465 from 41 countries as follows:

| Country | Number of contributions |
|---|---|
| USA | 93 |
| Brazil | 62 |
| Canada | 30 |
| Taiwan | 26 |
| India | 23 |
| UK | 21 |
| France | 20 |
| Japan | 20 |
| Finland | 19 |
| Germany | 14 |
| Korea | 13 |
| Philippines | 11 |
| Mexico | 10 |
| Italy | 9 |
| Switzerland | 9 |
| China | 7 |
| Denmark | 7 |
| Austria | 6 |
| Thailand | 6 |
| Columbia | 5 |
| Iran | 5 |
| Madagascar | 5 |
| Malaysia | 5 |
| Spain | 5 |
| Australia | 4 |
| Portugal | 4 |

| | |
|---|---|
| Turkey | 4 |
| Argentina | 2 |
| Egypt | 2 |
| Hong Kong | 2 |
| Netherlands | 2 |
| Pakistan | 2 |
| Slovenia | 2 |
| South Africa | 2 |
| Sweden | 2 |
| Bahrain | 1 |
| Belgium | 1 |
| Bolivia | 1 |
| Ghana | 1 |
| Israel | 1 |
| New Zealand | 1 |

The presentations were arranged into 19 tracks as follows:

| Track Name | Number of Contributions |
|---|---|
| Knowledge management | 48 |
| Strategic competencies for sustainable development | 31 |
| Social impact of technology development | 15 |
| MOT education and research/corporate universities | 22 |
| Innovation and new product development | 50 |
| National systems for technology development | 25 |
| Small business and entrepreneurship/technology incubation | 31 |
| Areas of rapid technology change | 5 |
| Technology foresight and forecasting | 16 |
| Technology transfer/Technology and security | 21 |
| Information and communication technology management | 24 |
| The integration of technology and business strategies | 42 |
| R&D management | 26 |
| Project management | 22 |
| Industrial and manufacturing system technologies/Supply chain management | 16 |
| Virtual organizations and partnerships/E-commerce | 9 |
| MOT in developing countries | 31 |
| Technology alliances, mergers and acquisitions | 17 |
| Theory of technology | 14 |

Clearly, the conference organizers were successful in capturing a snap shot of the state of active research in MOT as it existed world-wide around 2003 and 2004. The full papers submitted to the conference are contained in the proceedings Edited by Y. Hosni, R. Smith and T. Khalil and published electronically in a CD-ROM ISBN#0-9712964-6-4.

Following tradition, we have selected a set of papers from those presented at the Washington D.C. conference for this publication. Although many excellent papers were available for choice, the selection was guided by several factors including originality as well as relevance to current issues of interest. Our aim is to publish a volume to be a handy reference to managers, educators, practitioners as well as researchers in this dynamic and interdisciplinary field. Thus, 61 authors were invited to update their original presentations for another round of reviews. The result of the updates, reviews and selection is this book.

The book is organized around two major themes. The first and the largest relates directly to the conference theme with papers on alliances and collaborations as well as on the use of the Web technology in groupware and group communications. The second theme deals with novel approaches to well-established topics in MOT, such as technology transfer and technology diffusion, business development, impact of technology on social structures, innovations in service, MOT education and technology forecasting. We hope that this collection of papers would further contribute to the mission of the International Association for Management of Technology (IAMOT) in promoting MOT education, research and application.

In closing, the editors would like to express their appreciation for the individual contributors to this volume who accepted to make the many revisions that we requested. Our sincere gratitude goes to Ms. Silvia Rodriguez from the IAMOT secretariat who capably assisted in the preparation of the camera-ready copy and Ms. Julie Walker, from the Business & Management section of Elsevier Ltd., U.K., who guided the publishing process.

M. Hashem Sherif, AT&T, Middletown, NJ.
Tarek Khalil, University of Miami, Florida
September 2005–January 2006

# List of Contents

Preface.......................................................................................v
List of Contents.......................................................................................ix

**SECTION I – ALLIANCES AND COLLABORATION**

1. Success Factors and Hindrances in International R&D Cooperation Programs. The case of IBEROEKA.......................................................................................3
*José Albors, Antonio Hidalgo*

2. Developing Acquisition Strategies Based on Patent Maps..................................19
*Martin Moehrle, Anja Geritz*

3. Technology Transfer Scheme for SMEs in the Graz Region: 10 years of Experience.......................................................................................31
*Franz Hofer, Christoph Adametz*

4. A Knowledge Based View of R&D Collaboration – Experiences of Finnish ICT SMEs.......................................................................................45
*Sami Saarenketo, Kaisu Puumalainen, Kalevi Kyläheiko*

5. Innovating and Developing Mobile Services in University-Company Collaboration.......61
*Juha Nummi, Katja Lahenius*

6. Key Success Factors for Research Institutions in Research Commercialization and Industry Linkages: Outcomes of a German/Australian Cooperative Project...............75
*Thomas Baaken, Carolin Plewa*

7. Upsurge of University Spin-Offs in Japan.......................................................91
*Masayuki Kondo*

8. Creating a High-End Market for Digital Cameras in a "Win-Win" Competitive Environment – The Japanese Experience......................................................103
*Yoshio Sugasawa, Noboru Sugino*

9. Why do some Universities Generate more Patents and Licensing Income than Others? The case of Taiwan ......................................................................119
*Yuan-Chieh Chang, Phil Y. Tang, Ming-Huei Chen, Chun-Yao Huang*

10. Sector-Based vs. National-Based Explanations of the Triptych Governement/Industry/Academic Research in Defense Related R&D Projects: Instances from France, the U.K. and the U.S.A.....................................................137
*Valérie Mérindol, David Versailles*

**SECTION II – GROUPWARE AND WEB INTERFACES**

11. Usability: Providing Better Information System Interaction.................................157
*Simone Bacellar Leal Ferreira, Marie Agnes Chauvel, Marcos Gurgel do Amaral Leal Ferreira*

12. Visualised Indicators of Links in the World Wide Web: Biotechnology and Information Science.....................................................169
*Marianne Hörlesberger, Edgar Schiebel*

13. Perceived Benefits of the use of Web-Groupware for Virtual Teams.......................185
*Lorie Bouchard, Luc Cassivi*

14. The External Linkages of Community of Practice: Integrating Communities Using Internet Technology Forums..............................199
*Dimitris Assimakopoulos, Jie Yan*

**SECTION III – TECHNOLOGY TRANSFER AND TECHNOLOGY DIFFUSION**

15. Technology-Based Investment of German Firms in China- Motives and Nature..........215
*XiangDong Chen, Guido Reger*

16. Industrial Development: Does Technology Transfer Work in the Aircraft Industry?.....233
*Harm-Jan Steenhuis, Erik J. de Bruijn*

17. Technological Capabilities of High Technology Firms in Cross Border Alliances.......249
*Zandra Balbinot, Luiz Paulo Bignetti*

18. Comparitive European Perspectives on the Diffusion and Adoption of Telework Amongst SMEs ........................................................................263
*Keith Dickson, Fintan Clear*

19. Technology Readiness: The Adoption of the Wireless Communication Technology in Finnish ICT and Forest Companies..........................................................277
*Jukka-Pekka Bergman, Jarno Käppi, Sanna Sintonen Taalikka, Petteri Laaksonen*

## SECTION IV – BUSINESS DEVELOPMENT

20. Strategy Formation in Pharmaceutical Drug Discovery........................................295
*Christos Tsinopoulos*

21. Process of Technological Capability Development: Cases From China's Mobile Phone Industry ................................................311
*Maximilian von Zedtwitz, Jun Jin*

22. A Successful Horizontal Cooperation in the Automobile Industry.........................327
*Laure Morel-Guimaraes, Sandrine Aubert*

23. Are Technology and Competition Policies Contradictory?..........................................339
*Kalevi Kyläheiko, Martti Virtanen*

## SECTION V – SOCIAL IMPACT OF TECHNOLOGY

24. ATM & Biometrics: A Socio-Technical Business Model....................................361
*Mario Yanez, Annuar Gomez*

25. The Influence of External and Internal Social Capital on Organizational Growth ........375
*Aino Pöyhönen, Jussi Waajakoski*

26. Social Impact of Technology: A Perspective from Developing Countries................389
*Mohamed Mamdouh Awny*

**SECTION VI – INNOVATION IN SERVICES**

27. Projects in Telecommunications Services..........................................................405
*Mostafa Hashem Sherif*

28. The Development of a Nomological Network to Describe
New and Emerging Technologies in Healthcare.................................................421
*David George Vequist IV, Troy Dunn*

**SECTION VII – EDUCATION**

29. Expanding the Horizon of Japanese Engineers.................................................435
*Chie Sato, Satoshi Kumagai, Junsei Tsukuda, Jun Numata*

**SECTION VIII – TECHNOLOGY FORECASTING**

30. New Methods for Technology Futures Analysis.................................................453
*Alan L. Porter*

31. Managerial Responses to Cognitive Dissonance:
Causes of the Mismanagement of Discontinuous Technological Innovations.............465
*Andrew White, John Bessant*

Author Index.................................................................................................487

# SECTION I

# ALLIANCES AND COLLABORATION

Management of Technology: New Directions in Technology Management
M. Hashem Sherif and T.M. Khalil (Editors)



# 1

# SUCCESS FACTORS AND HINDRANCES IN INTERNATIONAL R&D COOPERATION PROGRAMS. THE CASE OF IBEROEKA

*José Albors, Universidad Politécnica de Valencia, 46022 Valencia, Spain*
*Antonio Hidalgo, Universidad Politécnica de Madrid, 28006 Madrid, Spain*

## INTRODUCTION

The research programs based in cooperation network structures constitute a modality of the international scientific and cooperation policies. The participation of R&D groups from different countries give an international dimension to these networks, and constitute today a frequent international scientific and technological cooperation mode. These networks are especially useful for the accomplishment of scientific and technological objectives, such as technology transfer.

The objective of the IBEROEKA program was to stimulate the technological cooperation between Latin American countries in order to enhance the development of R&D market oriented projects. The program is experiencing an increasing participation as its activity spreads out. The present research presents the statistical analysis of the results of the program, with focus on the technology transfer achievements during its 10 first years of development (1991-2001). Although the general outcome of the evaluation was positive; the basic philosophy of its structure and its asymmetry have proved to be limiting factors in the achievement of technology transfer among its participants. Amongst the participating countries there are great differences such as uneven government support and technology absorption capacity by firms and research organizations, differences in technology markets, etc. This has caused a certain bias in the initial objectives of the program, which calls for a program reorientation.

The objective of this paper will be to examine the potential of international R&D cooperation programs for technology transfer. It will analyse the Iberoeka program outcome. With that purpose, a model will be proposed which will take into account the factors that facilitate the effectiveness of the program, measured by its technology transfer results. Moreover, we will analyse which factors have a hindrance effect.

In order to focus our research, we will describe the context and background of the program. We will review specific literature and propose the theoretical model. Then, we will describe the sample and present the empirical design, with the model and variables used, along with the characteristics of the sample. Finally, attention will focus on the results of the empirical evidence gathered.

## INTERNATIONAL COOPERATION RESEARCH PROJECTS

The international cooperation research programs are based in establishing cooperation networks. These allow multiple interactions and transferences between their associated groups and are especially useful for the accomplishment of scientific and technological objectives, which require the complementarities, or synergies of different capabilities and the participation of heterogeneous actors. Their impact has been analysed and studied by various authors (Bossworth, 1996; Fernández, 1998; Sebastian, 1999; Gómez, 1999; Georghiou, 1998).

These networks are evolving from their consideration as a flexible and effective instrument for international scientific cooperation with consideration given towards the organization of research work for the production of technology and the generation of scientific knowledge (Sebastián, 2001; Callon, 1992; Albornoz and Estébanez, 1998).
The cooperation approach has been pointed out also as a reinforcement tool of the dynamics for the innovation systems of regional or multinational dimension in various European studies (Koschatzky, 2000; Landabaso, 1999).

The proliferation of international research networks has been favored by different programs for promotion of technology cooperation in the international environment. The R&D Framework Program of the European Union it is one of the more relevant instruments due to its mobilization capacity and to the volume of involved financial resources. This Program finances the execution of cooperative European research and development projects. In most of the projects, three or more countries participate, thus constituting international research networks. Moreover, the latest version (VI Framework Program) favours large networks of researchers and integrated projects.

These research networks have become relevant in the processes generating science and technology, as well as its internationalisation. In addition, it substantiates the need for improving knowledge on the motivation, organization, dynamics, efficiency and impact of these programs.

## MARKET ORIENTED R&D INTERNATIONAL COOPERATION

*Eureka and the European Framework Program.* In reference to governing rules in European innovation policy, based on some theoretical assumptions concerning the relationship between the "political systems" and "innovation systems" in Europe, some authors (Kuhlmann, 2000) have speculated about the future European scenario of innovation policies. This scenario is based on an increasingly centralized European innovation policy to the opposite, progressive decentralized regional innovation systems. The European Union Framework Programs objectives are to strengthen the science and technology bases of European industry in order to enable it to become more competitive on international level. These programs respond to the R&D policy objectives over a period of five years.

The European Commission manages and controls these programs closely. After each specific call for proposals, all projects are evaluated and selected by external experts. Participant firms receive up to 50% funding of their budgets, while universities and research institutions may receive up to a 100%. Taking into consideration these attractive conditions, the selection rate is high (in the range of 10 to 20%) and only innovative and experienced firms benefit from the program.

The latest editions of the Framework Programs (V and VI) have stressed the relevance of market orientation. These influences not only project selection but also the follow up by Commission experts. In 1985, in opposition to this centralized scheme, Eureka started a decentralized and bottom up approach. The only fixed structure consists in a Secretariat based in Brussels since the chairmanship is rotating. Financing is variable and the decision on supporting its participants (firms and public research organizations) depends solely on each country. Eureka has 34 country members today with a very ample European geographical spread. After 20 years, 1300 projects have been completed for a total value of over 14 billion €. Two-thirds of the participants are firms and 40% of all participants are SMEs. The EUREKA mechanism, with its flexibility and lack of bureaucracy, matches closely with the industry requirements in Europe. However, declining political and financial commitment on behalf of governments has undermined the value of the initiative and the growth rate has slowed down (Georghiou, 1999).

*The Iberoeka Initiative.* Following specific suggestions from the Latin American scientific background, the Iberoeka program started in 1991 as a CYTED (the Organization for Technology and Science Cooperation for Development of Latin American countries) initiative. Its basic objective was to stimulate the technological cooperation between Latin American countries towards the development of R&D market oriented projects. The experience of Spain and Portugal since 1986 with Eureka was crucial in the establishment of this initiative. 19 countries of Latin America, Portugal and Spain, along the participation of CEPAL, OEA, UNESCO and BID as observers, initiated the original frame agreement.

The philosophy of Iberoeka is based on yielding the initiative of the project's generation to the firms and the research centres of the member countries (bottom up approach). The participants conceive and propose their projects, select their partners, decide the collaboration agreement, and have the sole condition of obtaining results of competitive character. Since each country supports their participants with different financing schemes, this variable geometric approach offers the participants a great flexibility and absolute control of their own initiative (CYTED, 2002).

As it has been mentioned, the projects count on financial support from the countries participating in each project. The coordinating organizations of each country support the firms and approve their participation in the program. A Technical Secretariat provides approval and the Iberoeka label to the projects. Though this label does not follow a technical evaluation, as is the case of Eureka

The program was launched following the same principles of Eureka. Variable geometry, which means that the support from the various participating governments is unbalanced, including the profile of the participating organizations: firms, research organizations, universities, etc. The project is market-led since the participants must seek market objectives. The coordinating entity (CYTED) has only a general support role as coordinator and promoter of the idea.

## Technology Transfer Policies And Models

In order to analyse public technology transfer promotion policies, Bozeman (2000) proposes three paradigms: the market failure technology policy, the mission technology, and the cooperative technology policy paradigm. The programs considered here would fall under the third, which calls for an active role for firms, government, and universities in technology development and transfer. The same author presents a contingent technology transfer effectiveness model, which considers five dimensions.

The transfer object or content and form is scientific knowledge, technological device, process, know-how, and specific characteristics of each of the following: (a) The transfer medium, which is the vehicle by which the technology is transferred, formal or informally, by license, copyright, etc.; (b) The transfer recipient organization or institution firm, agency, informal group, receiving the transfer object as well as its associated characteristics; (c) The transfer agent seeking to transfer the technology considering its characteristics, the context, the type of organization (firm, university or research centre), its culture; and (d) The market demand factors such as price for technology, substitutability, subsidies, channels, market shelters, etc.

The complexity of technology (Singh, 1997) or its radical or incremental nature will have an influence on the organizational capabilities required for its transfer (Hannan and Freeman, 1984), the learning aspects (Bou-Wen Lin, 2003), including transfer efficiency (Chakrabarti, 1976). The transfer agent and recipient are organizations (firm, university or research centre), characteristics, context, and culture play a relevant role in the transfer process (Cohen, 2002; Monjon, 2003). In relation to the cooperative effort of transfer modality, academic literature has reviewed the role of alliances in technology transfer (Chiesa, 1998; Dysters, 1999; George, 1999). Market aspects and technology transfer have been dealt with by numerous authors (Howells,1997; Lynn, 1996: Pelham, 1999; Ottosson, 2002). A school of thought has developed, in the last decade, to deal with technology intensive products and services (Davidow, 1986; Moore, 1995 and 1997; Mohr, 2005).
Based on this we will consider a modified model, which will help us understand the efficiency of the program.

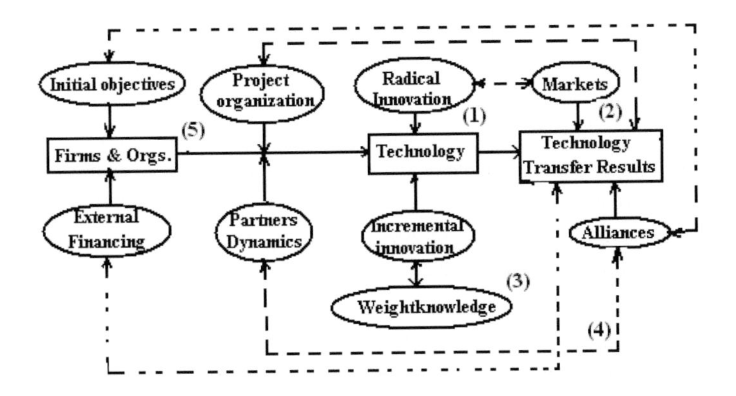


**Figure 1. Technology transfer process in Iberoeka**

The transfer agent and recipient roles were played by participant organizations as well as government agencies. The initial objectives expectations of the participating firms had a significant role. The external financing was a conditioning factor (Hidalgo, 2004) posed by the government institutions coordinating the program. The project organization and its dynamics should be considered under the same group. The transfer object, technology, know how or knowledge was also relevant as the empirical analysis will show. The transfer medium are forms that technology transfer could adopt such as patents, technology alliances, technology exploitation agreements, production licenses, new firm start ups; and development licenses or commercial agreements. It has to be pointed out that many firms joined the program just in order to find technology partners (29,5%) or alliances (34,8%). Finally, the market demand factors also played a relevant role, not only conditioning the process, but also being an objective of many firms joining the program (a 45,9 % intended having access to new markets).

## SURVEY RESULTS

*The Sample - Profile of the Participating Organizations.* A total of 642 confirmed organizations participated in the program: 432 from Spain, 61 from Brazil, 72 from Argentina, 59 from Chile, 37 from Colombia, 34 from Portugal, 34 from Cuba, 18 from Mexico, 19 from Panama, 23 from Uruguay and 10 from Ecuador. Aside from the aforementioned there were other countries that had a minimum participation. The structure of the participants is the following: 74,1% were private firms, 13,3% universities, 7,6% research centres and 5% other organizations such as industry associations, etc.

The profile of the participating Spanish firms has been extensively studied by Aguero (1999), which points out, that it is a young population with 56% of the firms having less than 12 years of existence and 3.8% having less than 5 years. Of them, 50,7% are micro enterprises and only 5.2 % are large firms. It is a relative population of technology intensive firms with an average of 25% university graduated employees and 80% in the range of 1-20 employees. A large number of these firms are exporters (70%) and most of them show a high R&D index activity with 9,8% of them spending more than 15-20% of their turnover in R&D and 14,3% of them spending 10-14%. Moreover, the percentages of R&D dedicated personnel follow the same pattern.

The Spanish firm's replies show a high competitive auto perception, in comparison to their competitors when considering product quality, product price, customer service, market penetration, or technology level. These firms declare an incidence of their innovation activity in their competitive level, which is high in 61,5% of the cases and very high in 24,3% of the cases. A majority of firms (61%) have had previous experience in R&D cooperation with various institutions, universities or other firms, and 40% of them at international level. Only 18% of them have had a previous relationship with their Latin American partners.

The Latin American partner population has a similar size profile with 58% of the firms having less than 50 employees, 20,1% between 50-150 employees and only 17,3% are large firms with more than 250 employees. In particular, the segment of small firms fits the knowledge profile of the Spanish firms. The majority of these small firms develop their work in agro food, information technology, chemical and pharmaceutical industries. In relation to the research organizations, in the case of Spanish universities, which are the most active while medium size research organizations are the majority on the Latin American side.

*Sample Design and Method of Analysis.* The source of empirical evidence for the research was based on the quantitative data collected in a survey carried out with the participant institutions in the Iberoeka projects during 1991-2001, being the analysis unit (firm, organization, university or research centre). The questionnaire was distributed among 733 organizations. A total of 252 surveys were collected, of which 155 were complete, hence 21,11% of the total participant organizations. Considering the percentage of firms, charities and university-R&D centres in the sample, it presents a sampling error of ±7,13% for a level of confidence of 95,5% assuming simple random sampling.

The survey also included customized interviews with 10 participant firms in these projects as well as interviews with officers of the Iberoeka offices in various countries.

The profile of the participant organizations has been determined through the analysis of a set of variables such as location, size, age or technological activity (developer, final user, supplier, researcher, marketer or integrator). The mechanisms of technology transference have been represented by seven variables of dichotomic character such as patents; spin off firms, technology alliances, technology agreements, production or development licenses, or marketing agreements. A composed variable- Technology transfer- was created by adding the technology transfer mechanisms of each respondent. Moreover, the initial objectives of the organizations to join Iberoeka were defined as well by ten dichotomic variables representing the following: development of new products or processes, improvement of existing products or processes, pilot prototypes, knowledge acquisition, management and work quality improvement, access to new markets, industrial alliances and commercial agreements. Two additional sets of variables identified the accomplishment and relevance of those objectives.

In addition, the questionnaire covered the appraisal of the surveyed organizations on final project results such as completion of global project objectives, industrial exploitation,

financial results, marketing results, and final geographical markets reached by the project results. It should be mentioned that these variables were based on 5 point Lickert scales.
The survey also covered the judgement on various items such as: project team performance, critical partners considering their contribution to the project, support of the government Iberoeka offices, reasons for their participation in the program, main barriers for the project completion and project financing. These variables were collected with a mixture of dichotomic and nominal variables. As a result, a preliminary Factor Analysis was carried out with the sample data in order to proceed to a previous assessment and select the critical variables. The analysis was refined later by creating composite variables and proceeding to cluster the sample to classify the results.

*Statistical Analysis- Program Efficiency.* Table 1 shows the first results. Four components were able to show 77,8 % of the variance. The first component (alliance focus) is composed of four variables. These pointed out initial objectives, relevance and accomplishment of the organization related to technology alliances, and the technology transfer results. The second component (incremental innovation focus) is composed of three variables indicating initial objectives, relevance, and accomplishment of incremental innovation (processes and products). The third component (radical innovation focus) is similar but related to radical innovation (pilot plants and new products). Finally, the

**Table 1. Preliminary Factor Analysis**

| | Components | | | |
|---|---|---|---|---|
| Variable | 1 | 2 | 3 | 4 |
| Initobjalliances | 0,857 | | | |
| Relevalliances | 0,834 | | | |
| Accomplalliances | 0,765 | | | |
| Techtransresults | 0,642 | | | |
| Relevincrinnov | | 0,939 | | |
| Initobjeincreminnov | | 0,892 | | |
| Accomincrinnov | | 0,883 | | |
| Relevradinnov | | | 0,886 | |
| Initobjeradinnov | | | 0,843 | |
| Accomradinnov | | | 0,821 | |
| Accomplcommerobjecti | | | | 0,793 |
| Commercproject | | | | 0,756 |
| Projecteamcoord | | | | 0,606 |

Extraction method: Principal Components Analysis.
Varimax standardization with Kaiser
KMO and Bartlett test

| | | |
|---|---|---|
| Sample Adequacy Measure | | 0,719 |
| Sfericity Bartlett Test | Chi-square | 1277,344 |
| | DF | 78,000 |
| | Sig. | 0,000 |

fourth component (Commercial focus) is composed of three variables indicating the accomplishment of commercial agreements, completion of project marketing results, and performance of the project team.

As a second step, and in order to reduce the number of variables, four composed variables were created: Weightincreminnov, adding the results of initial objectives, accomplishment and relevance related to incremental innovation. Weightknowledge, the same concept, but in relation to the development of additional knowledge. Weight alliances, in relation to the development of technology alliances. Finally Weightexploitation, in relation to the consecution of commercial results.

The results of a new factor analysis, considering these composite variables, are shown in Table 2. Five components were able to explain 91,96 % of the sample variance.
Component 1 is composed of firm orientation and results related to technology alliances. The results concern technology transfer, its orientation and results towards commercial exploitation, its return on investment, the level of technology accomplishment and the intensity of the obstacles referred to project financing. This component could define the firm technology transfer and results context. Component 2 is clearly oriented towards knowledge management, the generation through incremental innovation, and its associated barriers (communication). Component 3 is directly related to the frequency of barriers related with partner harmony and financing asynchrony. Component 4 is related to the country location of the firm. As it has been pointed out (Hidalgo, 2004), the Spanish firms had a leadership role in a majority of projects. Finally, Component 5 is concerned with radical innovation and the market barriers related to its commercialisation.

A cluster analysis was carried out with the 5 components resulting from the factor analysis (see table 4). Four clusters were obtained. Table 3 summarizes the results and Table 4 shows the values of technology transfer for the various clusters. It shows that cluster 1 demonstrates the highest values of technology transfer, while cluster 4 exhibits the lowest values.

**Table 2. Factor Analysis**

| | Components | | | | |
|---|---|---|---|---|---|
| Variable | 1 | 2 | 3 | 4 | 5 |
| Weight alliances | 0,915 | | | | |
| Techtransresults | 0,833 | | | | |
| Weightexploitation | 0,720 | | | | |
| ROI | 0,536 | | | | |
| Levtechaccomplish | 0,533 | | | | |
| Barrfinanc | 0,257 | | | | |
| Weightincreminnov | | 0,948 | | | |
| Barrcomm | | 0,178 | | | |
| Weightknowledge | | 0,386 | | | |
| Barrpartners | | | -0,238 | | |
| Country | | | | 0,997 | |
| Weightradinnov | | | | | 0,857 |
| Barrmarkets | | | | | 0,229 |

Extraction method: Principal Components Analysis
Varimax standardization with Kaiser
.(Convergence after 9 iterations)
KMO and Bartlett test

| | | |
|---|---|---|
| Sample Adequacy Measure | | 0,812 |
| Sfericity Bartlett Test | Chi-square | 582,037 |
| | DF | 78,000 |
| | Sig. | < 0,000 |

**Table 3. Cluster analysis (K mean clustering method)**

| | | Frequency | % | Valid % | % Accum. |
|---|---|---|---|---|---|
| Valid | 1 | 38 | 24,20 | 24,51 | 24,51 |
| | 2 | 30 | 19,10 | 19,35 | 43,87 |
| | 3 | 13 | 8,28 | 8,38 | 52,25 |
| | 4 | 74 | 47,13 | 47,74 | 100,00 |
| | Total | 155 | 98,72 | 100,00 | |
| Lost | System | 2 | 1,27 | | |
| Total | | 157 | 100 | | |

**Table 4. Contingency table (techtransresults vs. cluster belonging)**

| | | Techtransresults | | | | | | Total |
|---|---|---|---|---|---|---|---|---|
| | | **0** | **1** | **2** | **3** | **4** | **5** | |
| Clusters | 1 | 3 | 10 | 17 | 5 | 2 | 1 | 38 |
| | 2 | 15 | 11 | 2 | 1 | 0 | 1 | 30 |
| | 3 | 7 | 4 | 1 | 1 | 0 | 0 | 13 |
| | 4 | 50 | 24 | 0 | 0 | 0 | 0 | 74 |
| Total | | 75 | 49 | 20 | 7 | 2 | 2 | 155 |

Phi coefficient =0,712 with p < 0,0001; V Cramer coeff. = 0,412 for p <0,0001

It can be observed how the cluster classification follows an efficiency profile. The cases pertaining to cluster 1 show the highest technology transfer values. In general, as the descriptive analysis pointed out, the program outcome seems to be positive with a large number of cases having reached a minimum technology transfer impact.

*Obstacles that Restrain the Process of Technological Cooperation.* The participants pointed out to the lack of external funding (34.3%), lack of coordination (22.7%) and market changes (17.4%) as the main barriers encountered during the project development. These results show that there was certain alignment among the firms in their cooperative work. The analysis of these obstacles has been carried out by studying the relationships of the variables associated with the final technology transfer results. In addition to those related to the barriers pointed out by the respondents in the survey.

A further exercise (Hidalgo, 2004) analysed the relationship between the initial objectives in the program pointed out by the participants, including the barriers hindering the projects development. Nine variables were utilised in the study to define the possible obstacles to technological cooperation: technology characteristics; market barriers; project partners withdrawal; divergences among the project partners; communication problems; problems related with the type of organization; lack or asymmetry of external financing; legal and IPR problems and other type of barriers.

The results show certain logic. For example, lack of external financing was an obstacle in the case of registering a patent or reaching a commercial agreement to exploit the results of the project. Organizational problems were relevant in the case of completing a commercial agreement of technology alliances (research centers). The technology context was critical again in both cases, the interpretation being the reluctance of firms to share sensible technologies. Moreover, legal problems hinder the start up of new firms and divergences among partners complicate reaching technology exploitation agreements.

The obstacle relative to market changes is the most influential since it affects a greater number of initial objectives: those related to the development of new products; the improvement of existing products; and the access to new markets. The lack of external financing, on the other hand, has a specific incidence in the cases where the organizations consider participating in the Iberoeka projects in order to develop demonstrators or prototypes. Thus, constituting new industrial alliances. This is explained by the need, in this case, of higher investments, which asymmetrically originate from the institutional point of view in relation to external financing. Finally, the problems of communication between partners raise disadvantages when the companies have predicted in their objectives to carry out agreements of commercial cooperation, which require negotiating, and communication skills.

It is interesting to point out that the respondents valued as poor, in 71.5% of the cases the role of universities and research centres. Only in 7.1% of the replies their role was well considered. The reasons were the following: Divergences in R&D focus in universities research centres and firms; Lack of interface connections in the national systems of innovation between firms and universities; Lack of cooperative R&D culture; Absence of incentives for researchers to collaborate in technology programs; and lack of funding and insufficient information about the program.

## Conclusion

The analysis of the survey results confirmed the first conclusion of the program evaluation interviews. The program has a fair performance level. From the respondents judgement it was considered that the program had an 80 % success. More than 20 % of the cases showed a relevant impact in relation to technology transfer. The program unbalance towards Spanish versus Latin American firms appears as a relevant outcome (variable "country"). This is due to the fact that a large percentage of Spanish firms (45%) participate in the program and in a majority of the cases lead the projects. Hence, since in 71.5 % of the cases the role of the universities and research centers was valued as poor, there is also an unbalance in the participating organizations. This fact reflects a significant barrier (variable "organization").

Considering the proposed effectiveness model for technology transfer and its five dimensions, these have a heterogeneous influence in the technology transfer process. The complexity of the technology, its radical or incremental nature has a strong influence in the required organizational capabilities, the learning aspects linked to the knowledge weight or the technology transfer efficiency. Furthermore, market barriers as well as knowledge management associated variables appear correlated with the technology transfer process.

The statistical analysis showed how technology transfer results were linked to the variables related to organizational alliances and exploitation intentions of the organizations. It was found that the modality of the transfer medium (patent, agreement, license, etc.), was correlated heterogeneously to the various obstacles of the cooperative effort. The transfer agent and recipient, the type of organization (firm, university or research centre), its characteristics, context, and culture were found to play a critical role in the transfer process. Moreover, market aspects and associated variables were found to influence the technology transfer process and the type of innovation.

Before closing, there are some things that the economic data could have supported in a better analysis of the surveyed firm context, but these were available for a limited number of firms. Secondly, the initial survey sample defects have limited the sample size, which was initially larger. Finally, further measures of technology absorption could have been estimated by analysing firm parallel developments and training outputs of the program but the authors' involvement in the survey design was too late. As a result, further research should be carried with regards to the roles of research centres, and universities and explicit barriers found by them in the program.

## References


Aguero, E., Suarez, F., Sebastian, J. (1999). Análisis de la cooperación tecnológica de las empresas españolas con América Latina. *Proceedings VIII Seminario Latino Americano de Gestión Tecnológica, ALTEC.* Valencia.

Albornoz, M., Estébanez, M. E. (1998). What do we mean by networking? Selected Latin American Experiences in cooperation. In: *New approaches to science and technology cooperation and capacity building*, edited by UNCTAD, Geneva.

Bossworth, D., Stoneman, P. (1996). *Technology Transfer, Information flows and collaboration.* EIMS 36, European Commission.

Bozeman, B., (2000). Technology transfer and public policy: a review of research and theory, *Research Policy*, **29**,. 627–655.

Callon, M., Laredo, P., Rabeharisoa, V., Gonard, T., Leray, T. (1999). The management and evaluation of technological programs and the dynamics of techno economic networks. *Research Policy,* **21**, 215-236.

Cohen, W.N., Nelson, R.R., Walsh, J.P. (2002). Links And impacts: The influence of public research on Industrial R&D, *Management Science*, **48**, 1-23.

Chakrabarti, A.K., Rubenstein, A.H. (1976). Interorganizational transfer of technology: a study of adoption of NASA innovations, *IEEE Trasnactions on Engineering Management*, EM-**23**, 20-34.

Chiesa, V., Manzini, R. (1998). Organzing for technological collaborations: a managerial perspective, *R&D Management*, **28**-3, 199-212.

CYTED (2002). *Evaluación de los diez años de vida del Programa Iberoeka.* Fundación General Universidad Politécnica de Madrid.

Davidow, W.H. (1986). *Marketing High Technology,* The Free Press, N.Y.

Duysters, G., Kok, G., Vaandrager, M. (1999). Crafting successful strategic technology partnerships, *R&D Management*, **29**-4, 343-351.

Fernández, M.T., Sebastián J., Gómez, J. (1998). La cooperación científica de los países de América Latina a través de indicadores bibliométricos. *Interciencia* **23** (6):328-337.

Georghiou, L (1999). *Strategic Review of EUREKA, Building Europe Innovation Network,* Eureka Secretariat. Brussels.

George, P.V., Farris, G. (1999). Performance of alliances: formative stages and changing organizational and environmental influences, *R&D Management,* **29**-4, 379-389.

Georghiou, L. (1998) Global cooperation in research. *Research Policy,* **27**, 611-626.

Gómez, I., Fernández, M. T., Sebastián, J. (1999). Analysis of the structure of international scientific cooperation networks through bibliometric indicators. *Scientometrics*, **44**, 441-457.

Hannan, M.T., Freeman, J. (1984). Structural inertia and organizational change, *American Sociological Review*, **49**, 149-164.

Hidalgo, A., Albors, J., (2004). La internacionalización de la tecnología a través de los proyectos de innovación IBEROEKA, *Cuadernos de Economía y Dirección de la Empresa*, **20**, 57-82.

Howells, J. (1997). Rethinking the market-technology relationship for innovation, *Research Policy*, **25**, 1209–1219.

Koschatzky, K., Sternberg, R. (2000). R&D Cooperation in Innovation Systems - Some lessons from the European Regional Innovation Survey (ERIS). *European Planning Studies,* **8** (4), 487-501.

Kuhlmann, S., Edler, J. (1999). *Governance of Technology and Innovation Policies in Europe: Investigating Future Scenarios*. Fraunhofer Institute for Systems and Innovation Research. Karlsruhe.

Landabasso, M., Oughton, C., Morgan, K. (1999). Learning Regions in Europe: Theory, Policy and Practice through the RIS experience, *Proceedings* International *Conference on Technology and Innovation Assessment*, Austin, Texas.

Leclerc, M., Gagne, J. (1994). International scientific cooperation the continentalization of science, *Scientometrics,* **31**, 261-292.

Lin, BW, (2003). Technology transfer as technological learning, *R&D Management*, **33**- 3, 327-341.

Lynn, G. S., Morone, J. G., Paulson, A. S. (1996). Marketing and discontinuous innovation: The probe and learn process, *California Management Review*, **38** – 3, 8-37.

Monjon, S. (2003). Assessing spillovers from universities to firms; Evidence from French firm level data, *Int. Journal Industrial organization*, **21**, 1255-1270.

Mohr, J. Sengupta, S., Slater, S (2005). *Marketing of High-Technology Products and Innovations*, Prentice Hall, N.J.

Moore, G. (1995). *Crossing the chasm.* Harper Business, N.Y.

Moore, G. (1997). *Inside the Tornado : Marketing Strategies from Silicon Valley's Cutting Edge*, Harper Business, N.Y.

Ottosson, S. (2004). Dealing with innovation push and market need, *Technovation*, **24**, 279–285.

Pelham, A. M. (1999). Influence of environment, strategy, and market orientation on performance in small manufacturing firms, *Journal of Business Research*, **45**, 1, 33– 46.

Sebastián, J. (1999). Análisis de las redes de investigación de América Latina y la Unión Europea, Proceedings, *VIII Seminario Latino Americano de Gestión Tecnológica, ALTEC.* Valencia.

Singh, K., (1997). The impact of technological complexity and interfirm cooperation on business survival, *Academy of Management Journal*, **40**, 2, 339-367.

Subramanyam, K. (1983) Bibliometric studies of research collaboration: a review. *Journal of Information Science,* **6**, 33-38.

Management of Technology: New Directions in Technology Management
M. Hashem Sherif and T.M. Khalil (Editors)



# 2

# DEVELOPING ACQUISITION STRATEGIES BASED ON PATENT MAPS

*Martin G. Moehrle and Anja Geritz, IPMI – Institute of Project Management and Innovation, Postfach 33 04 40, D-28334 Bremen, Germany*

## INTRODUCTION

Merger and acquisition (M&A) strategies have become increasingly important with a view to securing growth and advantages in competition. More attention is paid to intellectual property rights, like patents or trademarks, especially by technology-oriented companies. Prior to the acquisition of another company an acquisition strategy is needed. One method of developing such an acquisition strategy is the creation and interpretation of patent maps regarding the patent portfolios of different acquisition candidates. For the following paper, results from the semantic analysis of patent texts have been used as a basis for patent maps. Multidimensional Scaling was adapted to SAO-structures in order to map the technological overlap of two companies. The result are patent maps that can be used as a starting point for the deduction of acquisition strategies supporting different acquisition motives, such as diversification or the completion of a company's patent portfolio.

Traditionally, mergers and acquisitions (M&A) have been based on data from management accounting and financial reports. Today M&A are no longer exclusively based on these sources of information, but also rely on proper information about property rights like patents or trademarks. Above all, patents play a fundamental role in the assessment of target businesses for certain M&A-purposes. This paper aims at the development of a patent map to support the M&A-process of deducting strategies and securing informed decisions.

The paper comprises four major parts, of which the first three depict the process of patent mapping (see fig. 1), while the fourth serves to illustrate it.

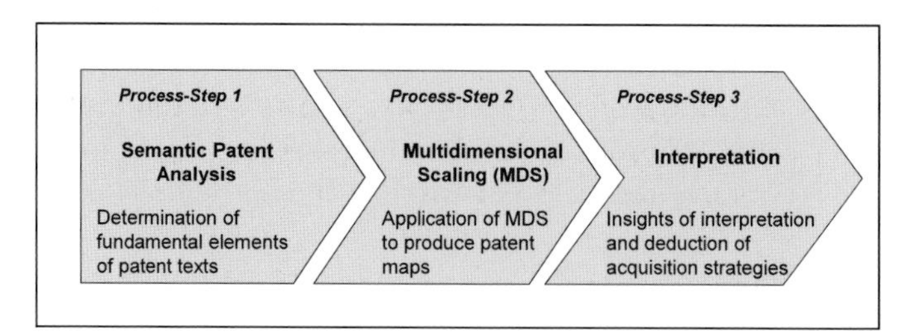


**Figure 1. Steps of developing and interpreting patent maps**

(i) In Part 1 it will be shown how semantic patent analysis is employed to gain data for the development of patent maps. A useful form of semantic patent analysis is based on a four-layer process supported by the commercial software product Knowledgist™ . The output of this process is Subject-Action-Object-structures (SAO-structures) which capture the essential contents of a patent text.
(ii) The use of an empirical standard method known as ordinal Multidimensional Scaling (MDS) of similarity data will be outlined in part 2. The data is taken from a coincidences analysis of SAO-structures in patent sets. Thus a patent map is produced, which can be used to support the M&A-process.
(iii) What types of patent maps may be identified, and how these maps can then be interpreted, will be explicated in part 3.
(iv) Part 4 contains an example of the use of patent maps in combination with M&A-activities. This is to underline the importance of linking technology management with aspects of competitive intelligence and strategic management.

Finally, future tasks concerning the development of patent maps and their institutionalization shall be discussed.

## FUNDAMENTALS OF SEMANTIC PATENT ANALYSIS

In patent mapping a coincidence analysis of patent sets proves to be helpful. To gain the required data a semantic text analysis can be applied. Its main function is the extraction of

SAO-structures from patent texts. A promising approach to semantic patent text analysis is opened up by software technology (see e.g. Krier and Zaccà, 2002; Fattori et al., 2003; Camus and Brancaleon, 2003). The related software is a result of research in Natural Language Processing (NLP), Linguistic Analysis (LA) and Computational Linguistics (CL). Over the past two and a half decades these fields of research have greatly gained in importance. 419 patents related to these subjects were published by the United States Patent and Trademark Office (USPTO) between 1975 and 2002. The protected inventions enable computers to read and process given patent texts with vastly different results. At present, there are several software solutions available on the market. For this paper and the case study introduced later on, the commercial software Knowledgist™ 2.5 by Invention Machine of Boston (MA) was employed. Knowledgist™ 2.5 analyses patent texts by application of a four-layer process (see Invention Machine, 2000; Tsourikov et al., 2000):

- The first layer is termed the *pre-formatter*. Here, the patent text is extracted from a patent document and transformed into plain text. All figures and non-textual elements are eliminated from the patent text. Spelling mistakes can be corrected by means of a dictionary. As a result, the remaining text is divided into single phrases.
- In the next layer, known as *lexical analysis*, these single phrases are examined more thoroughly. The dictionary that has already been used for the correction of spelling mistakes also contains information on possible word classes such as verbs, nouns or prepositions. Every word within the examined phrases is given at least one word class tag.
- The *syntactical analysis* that is performed in the third layer, can be divided into two separate steps. Firstly, it has to be determined whether the tagged word classes form a phrase that corresponds to the rules of English Grammar. This process helps to reduce the number of word class tags attached to words that could not be identified properly by means of lexical analysis. For example, the word 'water' can be either a verb (as in „to water the flowers") or a noun (as in „the water of the Mississippi"). In order to determine the meaning within a phrase syntactical rules are applied. In step 2 statistics are used to find out which sequences of word classes are more common.
- The fourth layer is the so-called *semantic analysis* of given word classes. The final goal being to provide the user with a short structure that contains the technological key findings of the patent text. For this purpose, the main elements of a phrase have to be identified. By application of statistical information the elements subject, action and

- object (SAO-structure) of the phrase are determined. An example of an SAO-structure from a patent text concerning an invention from the automotive
- sector is: „grooves - exhibit - return-flow effect“. This structure captures a single
- key finding from the analysed patent text (see tab. 1 for extracted SAO-structures of US-Patent # 5,516,123). Patents can be represented by several SAO-structures.

These SAO-structures form a good basis for further analysis with empirical standard tools like ordinal Multidimensional Scaling (MDS).

**Table 1. Extracting SAO-structures of US-Patent # 5,516,123 (U-shaped sealing member for sealing a valve cover having an impact absorber)**

| SAO-Structures of US-Patent # 5,516,123 | | |
|---|---|---|
| **Subject S** | **Action A** | **Object O** |
| Clips | secure | beads |
| form of beads | Rest in liquid | tight manner |
| impact absorber | extend to | side of U-shaped profile |
| one bead | Rest off | lid |
| seal of aforesaid type | not transmit | noise |
| thin diaphragm | isolate | noise |
| U-shaped sealing member | Seal | valve cover |
| Zone of sealing strip | attenuate | noises |

## Multidimensional Scaling (MDS) and Measure of Similarity as Means of Generating Patent Map

Based on the data obtained by semantic patent analysis a Multidimensional Scaling (MDS) solution can be applied to generate patent maps. The general approach of MDS is to transform given similarities or dissimilarities into distances. These distances can be mapped in an n-dimensional space and are then easily interpreted by a look at the plot. As the basics of MDS have been intensively discussed in literature (e.g. Borg and Groenen, 1997) only two specific aspects will be analysed in this paper: (i) the measurement of similarities within patents, and (ii) the use of matrices containing sparse data and internal grouping.

*Measures of similarity.* Several similarity measures have been suggested for the purpose of measuring patents (see e.g. Engelsmann and van Raan, 1994), most of them based on binary variables like the Jaccard- or Kulczynski-measure (see Kopsca and Schiebel, 1998).

To introduce a measure that is adaptable to different individual requirements, the aspect of weighing similarities between the entire SAO-structure and single elements thereof had to be taken into account. Equation 1 shows a measure that was used for experimental testing.

The following example will help to explain this measure's construction and meaning: There are two patents from the same field of technology, e.g. automotive; one is filed by a major player in sealing elements (P1), while the other one belongs to the patent portfolio of the third largest manufacturer of gaskets in the US (P2). The user wishes to identify similarities between the contents of these two patents. In the given example his priority is to discern whether there are identical SAO-structures.

$$SM_{ij} = \frac{\alpha \cdot SAO_{ij} + \beta \cdot AO_{ij} + \gamma \cdot S_{ij}}{\min\left(SAO_i ; SAO_j\right)}$$

$SM_{ij}$ = Similarity measure between patents i and j

$\alpha, \beta, \gamma$ = Weight factors

$SAO_{ij}$ = Sum of identical SAO – Structures

$AO_{ij}$ = Sum of identical AO – Structures

$S_{ij}$ = Sum of identical S – Structures

$SAO_i$ = Total Number of SAO – Structures in patent i

$SAO_j$ = Total Number of SAO – Structures in patent j

**Equation 1. Similarity measure PI employed in case study**

Identical AO or simple S-structures are of no superior importance in this analysis. In the example the parameters are 0.74 for identical SAO-structures ($\alpha$), 0.24 for identical AO-structures (β) and 0.01 for S-structures (γ). P1 contains 10 SAO-structures in total, P2 contains 15. The comparison of these patents reveals 1 identical SAO-structure, 2 identical AO-structures and 5 identical S-structures. The entry of this information into equation 1 produces a similarity measure (SM) of 0.127. The scale of measurement ranges from 1: total similarity to 0: no similarity between the two patents. A similarity measure of 1 also denotes total similarity between the patent with the lesser or equal number of SAO-structures and the patent with the greater number of SAO-structures. This can be interpreted as a total overlap of technological problem-solving knowledge.

*Matrices containing sparse data.* Often matrices of patent similarities contain sparse data with isolated internal grouping. Here certain problems had to be solved, because a standard ordinal MDS, as supported by the SPSS-modules Alscal and Proxscal, demands specific matrices for conducting a proper MDS. This was made possible by the implementation of an identifying algorithm introduced by Borg and Groenen (1997). After elimination of the isolated groups within the matrices, one problem remained: First attempts at scaling adjusted matrices by means of the SPSS-module Proxcal revealed signs of degeneration. One way of avoiding this is by use of the Prefscal beta-version. Prefscal is able to unfold the matrices (see Borg and Groenen, 1997) and is designed to avoid degeneration by using a specific stress function (see Busing, 2003).

## INTERPRETATION AND TYPES OF PATENT MAPS

As described above, patent maps can be generated by means of semantic patent analysis and MDS. The question arising now is: What types of patent maps are there, and how does one interpret them? There are three ideal types of patent maps that can be identified (see fig. 2) and linked to acquisition strategies.

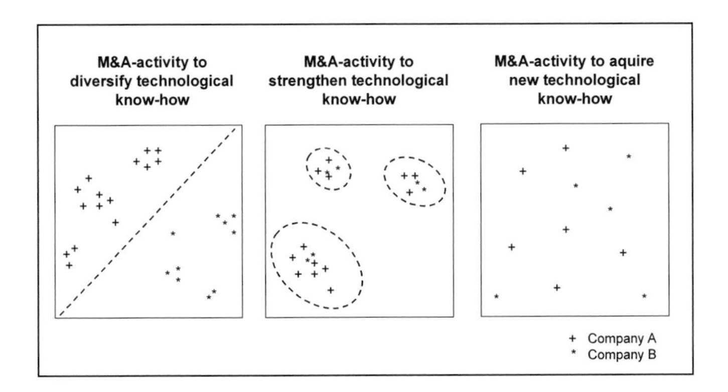


**Figure 2. Different types of patent maps**

The first type shows a clear separation of mapped patents. While the section on the left contains a set of patents from company A, the opposite one contains patents from company B. There is no similarity of SAO-structures between the two patent sets.

Generally, this result indicates a target for an M&A-strategy aimed at completing a certain set of technology. There is no connection between the compared technologies, consequently the acquisition of company B would help to complete the technology portfolio and would support a diversification of technological knowledge.

The second type of patent map clearly shows some clustering. Within the clusters patents from both companies - A and B - can be found, denoting a certain similarity between the patents mapped here. This result indicates that company B would be a potential target, should company A wish to acquire technological knowledge similar to its own - a strategy that serves to broaden and enlarge the current technology base. This can result in a stabilisation of and gain in market shares, also giving wider access to different market segments.

The third type of map shows no common clustering of company A and company B patents. This kind of map allows the conclusion that the targeted company may be an appropriate key to a new technology. On the whole, patent maps can support (i) the targeting and selection of potential M&A-candidates on the basis of different acquisition strategies. (ii) Patent maps can enrich due diligence and become the (iii) foundation of an integration process.

## EXAMPLE: SEALING DEVICES

To give an example, patents of two major players in the field of sealing devices - Freudenberg & Co. KG and Dana Corporation - were compared for the purpose of identifying important patent clusters. Important patent clusters are those surrounding key patents. In this example US-patent # 5,018,749 (title: Slide Ring Seal) was identified as a Freudenberg key patent. This patent is surrounded by patents that require careful examination (see fig. 3). Some of the patents positioned around the key patent belong to the competitor, e.g. patents # 5,915,727 and # 5,865,284. All patents forming the inner cluster were published between 1991 and 2001. They are legally valid. All patents bear a strong connection to the automotive sector.

Within due diligence it is possible to acquire information on the financial status of each patent or an entire field of technology. In addition to publicly available bibliographic information this can provide significant insight into patents bearing a high degree of similarity to the key patents.

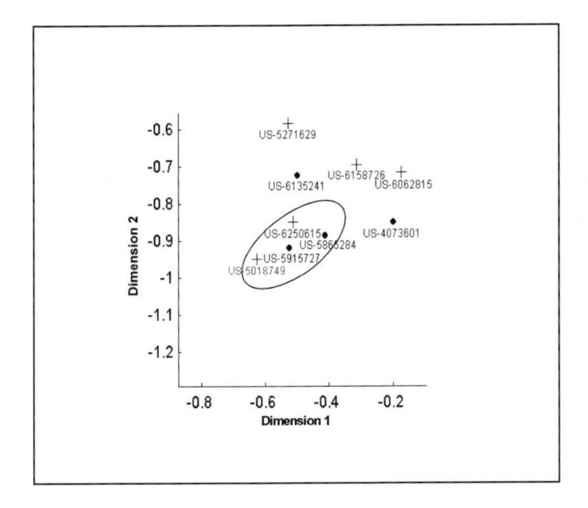


**Figure 3. Sectional results from ordinal MDS with Prefscal**

## Conclusion and Further Research

In M&A there is a need for patent maps that are simple, meaningful and easy to construct. It is possible to implement the results of semantic patent analysis into basic empirical tools such as ordinal MDS. This paper has emphasised and illustrated the use of patent maps generated due to the measurement of similarities between complex SAO-structures in patents. Patent maps can be utilised with a view to various aspects of M&A-activities.

However, some aspects still remain to be examined more thoroughly in years to come, such as the diversity of SAO-structures and their quality. Imminent goals of future research are to generate an appropriate filter that will help to erase irrelevant SAO-structures and to provide a synonym function for the grouping of all SAO-structures capturing the same meaning. Another challenge will be to observe and consider the diversity of different branches implemented in the wording employed to paraphrase identical technical cause-and-effect chains. A further important task will be to merge the calculation of similarity measures, MDS algorithms and the visualisation by means of patents maps into a single comprehensive computer-aided tool. This would speed up the process and help to save valuable time.

One final aspect to be attended to in the future is the measurement of similarity itself: It is necessary to evaluate and test further potential measures in a number of case studies belonging to different technological backgrounds. At this point, there is no evidence that the suggested similarity measure captures connections for all types of comparison. It remains to be established that e.g. connections between patents with a biotechnological background are measured as accurately as connections captured for other comparisons.

On the whole, semantic patent analysis and its utilisation for patent maps and the deduction of strategies for management purposes are promising new aspects in patent analysis and capable of enriching technology management in theory as well as in practice.

## REFERENCES

Borg, I., Groenen, P.J.F. (1997). *Modern multidimensional scaling. Theory and applications.* New York: Springer.

Busing, F.M.T.A. (2003). *PREFSCAL. 3-Way 3-Mode Multidimensional Unfolding through Majorization and Alternating Least Squares of Penalized Stress.* Short User´s Guide to Version 0.91. Unpublished Resource.

Camus, C., Brancaleon, R. (2003). Intellectual assets management. From patents to knowledge. *World Patent Information*, **25**, 155-159

Engelsman, E.C., van Raan, A.F.J. (1994). A patent-based cartography of technology. *Research Policy*, **23**, 1-26.

Fattori, M., Pedrazzi, G., Turra, R. (2003). Text mining applied to patent mapping. A practical business case. *World Patent Information*, **25**, 335-342.

Invention Machine (2000). *Accelerate your speed to Knowledge.* White Paper. Boston, Invention Machine Corporation.

Kopcsa, A., Schiebel, E. (1998). Science and Technology Mapping. A New Iteration Model for Representing Multidimensional Relationships. *Journal of the American Society for Information Science (JASIS)*, **49**, 1, 7-17

Krier, M., Zaccà, F. (2002). Automatic categorisation applications at the European patent office. *World Patent Information*, **24**, 187-196.

Tsourikov, Valery M., Batchilo, Leonid S., Sovpel, Igor V. (2000). US-Patent 6,167,370 (December 26, 2000). Invention Machine Corporation. Priority: US09/321,804 May 27, 1999. Document semantic analysis/Selection with knowledge creativity capability utilizing subject-action-object (SAO) structures.

*Acknowledgements*

We would like to thank Prof. Dr. Patrick J. F. Groenen (Erasmus University, Rotterdam) for his great support in finding a way to scale our patent data and for making some chapters of the second edition of his book (Borg, Groenen published in 2004, Springer) available to us before publication. Furthermore, we wish to thank Frank M. T. A. Busing (University of Leiden) for providing a beta-version of Prefscal.

Management of Technology: New Directions in Technology Management
M. Hashem Sherif and T.M. Khalil (Editors)



# 3

# TECHNOLOGY TRANSFER SCHEME FOR SMEs IN THE GRAZ REGION: 10 YEARS OF EXPERIENCE

*Franz Hofer, Graz University of Technology, Graz, Austria*
*Christoph Adametz, Graz University of Technology, Graz, Austria*

## INTRODUCTION

Easy access to external knowledge becomes increasingly important for enterprises to innovate. R&D institutions, as part of the knowledge-generating infrastructure are ever more involved in the global economy and many recent innovations could have only been achieved through interdisciplinary teams of industrial researchers and scientists from external R&D institutions (Tornatzky, 2000; Business-Higher Education Forum, 2001). However, SMEs especially seem to have problems co-operating with external partners in general and with R&D institutions in particular. Like large scale enterprises (LSEs) they are challenged by shorter product life cycles and more complex business conditions, which lead, in view of restricted internal resources, to the necessity of tapping external knowledge sources (Santoro and Gopalakrishnan, 2001). If this is so apparent, why have most SMEs not established links to relevant partners in their region and beyond it? It is widely acknowledged that trust is one criterion for such links. How can one build trust as prerequisite for successful collaborations between partners like SMEs and R&D institutions, which have different tasks to fulfill, different organizational cultures and other priorities? This article describes one possible way to improve the accessibility of primarily regional knowledge sources for SMEs with sparse or non-existing links to external R&D institutions like universities in order to improve their innovation performance through co-operation. The following chapters comprise an in-depth description of the program "Active Knowledge Transfer" (AKT), which facilitates technology transfer between enterprises (especially SMEs) and R&D institutions in the Graz region with financial support from local government, the city of Graz.

## REGIONAL INNOVATION FRAMEWORK

This chapter gives an overview of the innovation related situation in Austrian, focusing on the Graz region, which constitutes the target area for the program AKT. Austria has about eight million inhabitants, of whom about 10 % have academic degrees. The overall education level is very good; e.g., the performance of Austrian students is on average in the upper third of the participating countries (OECD, 2000). Nevertheless, the overall innovation picture is rather poor (European Innovation Scoreboard, 2002). In almost all indicators, Austria lags behind, but there are signs that through stronger efforts, the gap between the mean European average is closing. Styria, the second largest state of Austria, has a population of about 1.2 million. The main industries are automotive, mining and metallurgy industry, pulp and paper, environmental engineering as well as electronics and I&C related industries. The mining and metallurgy industry is located mainly in the northern part of Styria, whereas the automotive sector is located around the city of Graz, the capital of Styria. In 2002, about 3.67 % of the regional GDP in Styria were spent for R&D activities (GERD), which was well above the Austrian average of 2.12 %. Five of 20 companies with the highest R&D expenditures in Austria are located in Styria. Industry contributed the main part of the R&D expenditures. Their internal R&D expenditures account for about 69.6 % of all R&D expenditures in Styria in 2002 (Adametz and Ploder, 2005). The city of Graz has about 250,000 inhabitants, four universities, and two universities of applied science. The high concentration of HEIs provides enterprises with a highly educated work force. The Graz region, covering the city of Graz and the surrounding area, comprises of about 350,000 people and a wide range of SMEs in different industrial sectors.

*Enterprise structure in the Graz region.* More then 99 % of enterprises in the Graz region are SMEs (with up to 250 employees). Enterprises with up to nine employees account for 87.2 % of the total number of enterprises, 10.3 % have between 10 and 49 employees and 1.9 % have from 50 to 250 employees. SMEs provide about 41 % of all jobs in the region. The importance of LSEs in terms of employment shows the strong influence of the technology sector, especially the automotive industry. Even though their share in numbers of enterprises is almost non-existent, they account for 59 % of jobs in the region. 76 % of all employees work in the service sector, which is at the lower end for urban areas. Thanks to the automotive industry, the production sector with a 20 % share of all employees is strongly represented (Gruber *et al.*, 2002).

## TECHNOLOGY TRANSFER PROGRAM AKT

The Research & Technology Information Unit (FTI), a service provider of Graz University of Technology (TUG), introduced in 1994 a technology transfer program especially designed for SMEs' needs, which was highlighted as an example for a networking initiative with positive effects on regional development (Cooke, 1996). Since 2002, the program is delivered together with the Forschungsservice, the industrial liaison office of UNI Graz. AKT addresses primarily SMEs in the Graz region which do, so far, have no or merely scarce links to external R&D institutions, in the following called co-operation inexperienced enterprises (CIEs). Hanel (1996) segments enterprises according to their use of information sources. Thus, he divides enterprises in three groups, "innovation elite", "enterprises ready to innovate and change" and "conservatives". Building on the explanation used by Hanel, CIEs are largely present in the following two groups, the "enterprises ready to innovate and change", some times called "marginal enterprises", and "conservatives". They not at all or not regularly use R&D institutions like universities as an information source. The overall objective of AKT is the realization of the latent co-operation potential between science and industry in the Graz region. SMEs are especially often skeptical w.r.t. co-operation with R&D institutions. Reasons are, among other things, information deficits of research areas and available services as well as different (organizational) cultures (for more information see Schartinger *et al.*, 2001; McCullough, 2003; Major, 2003). CIEs as the target group are contacted with the aim to initiate and accelerate innovation and research projects in order to strengthen their competitive position. Additional goals are firstly the enhancement of the regional knowledge base aimed at increasing the employment of graduates in regional CIEs in order to increase the innovation performance of enterprises. Secondly, to increase the value added of research intensive services in the region to attract further investment, both human and financial. AKT does not try to further increase the industrial share of university funding by any means. Enterprises that already have well-established contacts to research partners are therefore not part of the target group. The target group consists of primarily SMEs, about 95 % of all enterprises actively contacted from May 2002 until May 2003 have up to 250 employees, enterprises with 11 to 50 employees accounted for 37 % and enterprises with up to 100 employees made up about 83 % of the target group. The line of business is not important, as Asheim (2001) puts it, "*According to Porter, the term high-tech, normally used to refer to fields such as information technology and biotechnology, has distorted thinking about competition, creating the misconception that only a handful of businesses compete in sophisticated ways. In fact, there is no such thing as a low-tech industry. There are only low-tech companies that is, companies that fail to use world-class technology and practices to enhance productivity and innovation.*" The results of an empirical study for Styria[1] (Adametz and Ploder, 2003) show that the co-operation willingness steadily declines with decreasing enterprise size in terms of employees. In general, Styrian enterprises prefer to co-operate with their customers and suppliers rather than with universities to solve a given problem. This coincides with the results of a study on behalf of the European Commission (Enterprise Directorate-General, 2003).

*Support from local government for AKT.* The services offered within the program are free for enterprises due to the financial support from the Department for the Development of Economy and Tourism (A15) of the city of Graz. Additionally to the actively approached enterprises within the Graz region, also enquiries from enterprises located outside the region are handled within AKT. Such enquiries potentially (1) lead to projects with institutions and enterprises within the Graz region and therefore increase the value added in the region and (2) promote Graz and its institutions as easy-accessible and co-operation-friendly knowledge providers. AKT is one of five strategic programs funded by A15. Like other European regions, Graz focuses increasingly on "soft" business support to strengthen the regional economy. It is widely acknowledged that regions which provide "intelligent infrastructure" easy to access and use have competitive advantages in attracting human and financial investment. The strong support from the local government is all the more important when considering that many innovations are generated and realized with the help of different partners, e.g. enterprises co-operating with universities funded by public sources[2].

*AKT – program team.* Although modern I&C technologies enable enterprises to contact researchers and co-operation partners almost all over the world, the regional aspects of innovation related issues like trust and (especially for CIEs) intensive face to face communication still play important roles. Some enterprises, mostly LSEs, make already (extensive) use of the possibilities offered by I&C technologies to establish global research networks. SMEs often lack the possibility to provide enough resources to contact and perform projects with knowledge providers, especially outside their region. Therefore, the main players involved in AKT are situated in the Graz region, close to the enterprises. This has the positive effect that as they are (in general) already well known within the regional community, trust building is easier than it would be for unknown institutions. Founded in 1996 as re-shaped continuation of the former "Ausseninstitut" (Industrial Liaison Office) FTI enables industry to take advantage of the knowledge available at TUG. Its aim is to facilitate

---

[1] The study can be order from michael.ploder@joanneum.at (free of charge, available in German).

[2] cp. "Triple helix", idea introduced by Henry Etzkowitz and Loet Leydesdorff in 1995.

co-operation between industrial enterprises and TUG. FTI employs actually six people, of whom two are full-time employees and the remaining four are part-time employees[3]. Forschungsservice of UNI Graz, the counterpart of FTI, consists of 13 people and is among other things responsible for transfer activities, organization of vocational training for university researchers as well as documentation and evaluation of research activities. Since May 2002, Forschungsservice as representative of UNI Graz is part of the AKT program team to increase the scope of services for enterprises and to enable an interdisciplinary view at enterprise's problems[4]. The AKT program team consists altogether of four people, two of FTI at TUG and two of Forschungsservice at UNI Graz. All team members have academic degrees. The back office staffs of both institutions provide further support.

## AKT Process Description

The general approach of the project team actively contacting CIEs in the region is described as follows: (1) the team contacts and visits the enterprise. (2) If a need for external support is identified and confirmed by the enterprise representatives, the team contacts possible problem solvers (PSs) and checks the capacity and interest for the topic. PSs are not only R&D institutions but also funding agencies, other enterprises or so-called "junior enterprises" (association of students). PSs are institutions or people, which can solve a given problem either alone (e.g. contract research) or in co-operation with the enterprise, which encounters the problem. (3) If the PS and the CIE are both interested in initial collaboration meetings, the team establishes the contact between both partners. The approach of the program aims to overcome barriers concerning co-operation between CIEs and external partners. Before describing the process in detail, main barriers are presented, which can hinder enterprises to firstly get in contact with external R&D partners to secondly solve existing problems and initiate innovation projects. A study performed by Nicolay and Wimmers (2000) shows that about the half of interviewed enterprises wished for a better presentation of services and R&D activities of universities. The lack of information makes it hard to find suitable co-operation partners. The easiest way for enterprises is to turn to well-known customers and suppliers. This is good as first action, but they usually do not have the same resources and knowledge as universities, and therefore the chance for more profound innovations may be missed by not exploiting external knowledge provided by scientists. The lack of knowing adequate funding possibilities as well as restricted human resources and the level of qualification of the staff are additional barriers, which negatively influence the possibility of joint research projects, e.g.

---

[3] For further information regarding FTI's services see www.fti.tugraz.at/de/Folder_eng.htm.
[4] For further information about Forschungsservice see www.uni-graz.at/forschung/.

graduates from universities usually tend to work for large international enterprises, which can be used as springboard for their future career. Therefore, there often is a lack of absorption capability at CIEs level. SMEs, especially the smallest ones, usually do not have their own R&D department or if they have one, it is hardly more than an extended workbench, thus additionally constraining the capability to absorb external knowledge. According to Reinhard (2001) process competence and an innovation-friendly culture are prerequisites for the capability to successfully absorb external R&D knowledge. Enterprises with own R&D departments usually have more contacts to external partners than enterprises without (Nicolay and Wimmers, 2000). This also points to the fact that proprietary R&D activities and the capability to absorb external knowledge positively influence each other. In addition, the PSs can be sources for barriers, e.g. restricted time resources leading to concentrating primarily on larger projects with LSEs, unwillingness of university researchers to co-operate with industry in general, focusing on research topics, which cannot easily be exploited by CIEs because of their low level of absorption capability or the lack of understanding how to present research activities.

*Selecting AKT target group.* The first action is to identify the target group for the program. The only condition is the location of the enterprise: it has to be within the Graz region. The reasons are twofold. Firstly, the financial support of A15 and therefore the local restriction and secondly the necessity of short distances to enable face to face communication (if necessary on an every day level) for building trust between the partners. The majority of selected enterprises are SMEs with scarce or no links to research institutions in the region are part of the target group. Other information like export rate or line of business are not taken into consideration. There is, however, a focus on manufacturing enterprises and knowledge intensive business services. As a basis for the identification of relevant enterprises a database with data concerning Austrian enterprises provided by an external business information provider is used. This database is additionally fed with data from other sources (business catalogues, journals) by the AKT team. A slim version of this database is also accessible online for institutes, staff and students of TUG for their scientific work (e.g. surveys), as source for addresses for job applications or distribution lists for events.

*Getting in contact with the target group.* The next step is to contact enterprises of the target group - of course, not all enterprises of the target group are contacted at once. This active approach is the key feature of the program. Especially SMEs call for an active approach from the part of R&D institutions. This is not only confirmed by our own experience, but also by others (Nicolay and Wimmers, 2000; Tichy and Wulz, 1996). The aim is to arrange a meeting with the top management. Usually two members of the program team attend the meetings at enterprises. Experiences show that the discussed topics are broader the higher the number of participants is and also a possible solution has higher backing within the enterprise because the more people agree to further activities, the higher the chance to overcome possible barriers. Therefore, it is recommended to invite also people responsible for R&D and HR besides the business owner or manager.

*Meeting to identify possible links.* The meeting takes place at the enterprise location, which is positive on the one hand, because it is easier to schedule for the managers of the enterprise and, on the other hand, the program team gets a better impression of the enterprise, the organizational culture, as well as production facilities. After the objectives and services of AKT as well as the enterprise's current activities have been made clear the participants talk about present problems and ideas for future products or processes within the enterprise, where external knowledge or additional human resources could be useful. The whole meeting takes about one and a half hour. Our experience shows that a program team of two operatively active members can meet with about 50 enterprises per year. A semi-structured standardized questionnaire is used to document the meeting with the enterprise representatives. Many standard attributes emerge during the meeting so that it is not necessary to strictly follow the questionnaire. The questions concern innovation related issues like number of graduates employed, patent activities, experiences with funding agencies as well as already existing co-operations. The information gathered during the meeting is afterwards documented in a database. This documentation tool enables the program team to keep track of each enterprise contacted and to analyze relevant data. All records in this database are strictly confidential, even to the funding institution.

*Identifying PSs.* Taking the results of the meeting as starting point, the program team now looks for interested parties that could support the enterprise in solving the discussed issues. The name of the enterprise will not yet be revealed to the possible PSs, because in many cases, the discussed problems are sensitive to the future success of the enterprise and they have to decide which possible partner to choose. The range of external partners to solve a given problem is very wide, but several criteria help to limit the circle of possible partners. The first one arises directly from the problem description, the field of activity. Here it is best demonstrated how important the specification of the problem is, the broader and more general the problem definition the harder it is to limit the area of interest. Not only is it more difficult to get partners from different institutions around one table at the same time, but it is also questionable how CIEs with prior no existing links to external R&D institutions can handle such complex questions. Other criteria checked by the program team are the current capacity of the possible partner and the experiences the members of the program team have made during earlier projects with the partner. These criteria already limit the list of possible partners. The distinction of the competencies of R&D institutions and enterprises as possible PSs in basic respectively applied R&D activities additionally helps to find the right partner. Thanks to good knowledge of the regional enterprise structure and services, it is also possible for the program team to establish contacts between enterprises in order to solve a given problem. Especially LSEs can provide special infrastructure or in-depth knowledge in fields interesting for SMEs. Support through consultants can and is used for certain types of problems, e.g. support of innovation management processes or as moderator in workshops. Riis (2001) says in his article about a manager questioned about differences having students or consultants working in an enterprise, "*[a project with Ph.D. students] should be seen as an opportunity for competence development in the company, and not aimed at providing short-term answers to specific questions and problems*".

*Brokering between CIEs and PSs.* As soon as potential PSs have been identified and have given feedback, the program team contacts the enterprise and a meeting between the possible co-operation partners is fixed, to give them the possibility to get to know each other and to reach a common understanding before further steps are taken. The program team often acts as an "interpreter" during this meeting. Knowing the enterprise representative as well as the invited PS the program team is able to control the course of the meeting.

*Staying in contact.* Independent from the course of the meeting between the enterprise and PS, it is important to stay in touch with the enterprise representatives and the PS to sustain the already built trust and to be considered as reliable support if new problems arise. If a project between them is initiated, the program team can help to overcome difficulties that could occur during the project, e.g. acting as mediator or taking over project management duties. If it does not result in a project, staying in contact means ensuring the possibility for future co-operations. Using I&C technologies is especially efficient for a larger group of recipients to inform them about news and activities. Therefore, FTI introduced an e-flyer in fall of 2002. The recipients are mainly enterprises and R&D institution representatives already contacted within AKT. Sending the e-flyer to people not familiar with AKT to market the program does not make much sense. This is because AKT is a trust building initiative and demands a lot of personal communication to overcome certain barriers – an e-flyer certainly cannot achieve this. Currently the e-flyer has about 2,700 recipients. Due to regular contacts, virtually as well as personally, it is likely that enterprise representatives will remember the services offered and if the need arises contact the program team by themselves to ask for more information concerning certain possibilities or R&D activities.

## SERVICES OFFERED TO CIES

The services offered to CIEs aim at support in innovation respectively R&D intensive activities and raising awareness concerning the positive effects of co-operation with external partners. The range of services and support is not restricted to certain areas, thanks to the variety of possible PSs in the region. The main services are

- Identification of problems on site through enterprise visits
- Establishing contacts to experts at R&D institutions and other enterprises
- Brokering of diploma and doctoral thesis to be commissioned at HEIs
- Brokering of co-operation projects and scientific services
- Information brokerage services (utilizing e.g. TUG library resources)
- Information and consulting w.r.t. vocational training possibilities
- Support in recruiting graduates (for internship as well as full time jobs)
- Opportunity to take part in an annual recruiting fair for SMEs in front of university staff and students

Other universities also offer similar services. The most notable differences concerning other programs with the same objectives are: (1) the relative independence from university marketing goals, even though both FTI and Forschungsservice are organizational units of TUG and UNI Graz. (2) The "information brokerage services", which are free (for the first time in any given year). (3) The annual recruiting fair especially for SMEs and (4) the integration of a non-technical university in the program. Without the financial support of A15, the program team would not have the freedom to choose PSs outside the universities, which would limit the services and therefore the problem solving capabilities offered to enterprises. The mission would probably be to maximize the funding coming from industry and consequently trying to establish projects with SMEs - projects that are usually small in terms of money - would not count for much in the future. The information brokerage service is offered to enterprises with a need for information related to scientific R&D activities. This service is free for the first time in any given year. The task is performed by a person associated to the library of TUG, who is experienced in desk research and has access to nearly all relevant information sources. The service is a "teaser" for enterprises with the goal, that once they have experienced how much their work can be supported just through extensive desk research, they will assign this service also later on, even when it is not free anymore. Because of close interaction with the client, the information broker can look for information like patents and "grey literature" which point in the direction chosen by the client. It is important to note, that the information broker can analyze the collected data just to a certain extent, the interpretation of the papers and literature has to be done by the enterprise. Experience shows, that the service is very well accepted. To give SMEs in the Graz region the possibility to present themselves in front of students and university staff, a recruiting event was installed. This event not only aims at CIEs but also at SMEs, which already have experiences in co-operating with external scientific institutions but encounter problems recruiting graduates. Once a year this event is hosted at TUG. About 10 to 12 SMEs are present to introduce their enterprises. Every lecturer has about 12 minutes to give an overview of the enterprise and possibilities for graduates looking for a job. Additionally the organizer presents five to six enterprises' homepages. Afterwards students, graduates, researchers, and managers have the possibility to get to know each other personally. The feedback from enterprises and students is very positive. This event takes into account that "transfer via heads" is one of the most effective transfer means. Through recruiting graduates sustained links between the graduates' alma mater and the respective company are most likely. The most important recent development of AKT is the integration of Forschungsservice, the liaison office of UNI Graz. The co-operation between FTI and Forschungsservice as representatives of TUG and UNI Graz has led to a broader view of the term innovation. According to the definition of Schumpeter (1911), who was professor at TUG and UNI Graz from 1919 to 1921, the term innovation is not limited to technical areas like product or process innovation but also valid for social ones like new organizational set-ups. The program focus does not any longer lie solely on identifying technical questions and finding technical solutions. Although UNI Graz was already contacted earlier if non-technical questions were identified, the joint enterprise visits additionally help to provide better support as before.

## NETWORKING AND MARKETING FOR AKT

To push the program and make the services available for CIEs, which had as of yet not heard about them, presentation for other intermediaries, are arranged. The objective is to strengthen the links not only between enterprises and R&D institutions but also between intermediaries and institutions in touch with enterprises, which could benefit from the services offered in the program. This has been done since the beginning of the program in 1994 and has proven to be a valuable instrument, where all partners can benefit. For marketing activities like adverts, exhibition stands or leaflet consignment no extensive budget is reserved. The main reason therefore is that AKT is a trust building measure and aims at establishing long-standing relations between enterprises and R&D institutions through a pro-active approach.

## RESULTS SO FAR

The results displayed in this chapter built on the improved data quality since May 2002. It is to be noted that the program scheme in the past did not vary much from today; hence, today's results can be used as reference values for the past taking into account the number of staff devoted to program delivery. From May 2002 to May 2003 the team had contact with 104 companies, of these 68 actively, 36 companies contacted the team in order to find experts in certain fields or to get additional information concerning topics of interests to them. Nine out of the 68 companies responded that a company visit was not necessary because either they had already established contacts to the universities or they were not interested in the services the team has to offer. In almost all cases information concerning areas of activities or contact information of experts could be given. About one third of the contacted companies started projects because of the program team efforts. Projects include consulting or contract research activities, the usage of the information brokerage service, taking part in the annual SMEs exhibition or enterprise-commissioned diploma thesis. Typically, the projects are small scale in terms of money and involved resources, but nonetheless they are important starting points for further collaborations. The quantitative results are also valid for the years 2004 and 2005, where the program did not change regarding services and approach. In the meantime, the scheme was also expanded geographically. Comparing the available results of the expanded project with the above mentioned success rate of the program AWT, 25 to 30 % of the contacted companies starting (small) projects with external R&D institutions, shows that these values are rather similar. Moreover, the efforts have definitely contributed to a broader client base for services offered by local R&D institutions. Furthermore, the good partnership within AKT and the broad knowledge base of enterprises has led to a successful bid for substantial funding from Austrian federal resources for a regional academic incubator called Science Park Graz[5].

*Key criteria for successful knowledge transfer.* Through to the experience in collaborations with enterprises the program team identified the following criteria as crucial for successful collaborations between CIEs and local R&D institutions[6]:

- Honest broker approach (best expert to solve the problem)
- Providing high-quality R&D related information
- Good knowledge of R&D activities in the region
- Good knowledge of R&D related funding possibilities

[5] For further information about the Science Park Graz see www.sciencepark.at.
6 Successful in this context is understood as establishing collaborations between SMEs and external knowledge providers like universities to solve specific problems.

- Support and backing from regional policy
- Keeping in contact with partners
- Continuous support

It does not necessarily mean that fulfilling all these points grants successful collaborations but they positively influence the framework conditions for co-operation projects. The criteria are valid for the context in which AKT takes place. Many of them, if not all, will also be of importance in other regions and for similar projects. To achieve a sustainable success and to get enterprises and R&D institutions together to perform joint projects, a common understanding of the project and long-term commitment from all partners is necessary. Only due to close interaction and co-operation between the funding partner, in this case A15 and the operatively active partners, FTI and Forschungsservice, it is granted, that such a program, which needs time to present results, can be realized, maintained and even given a broader portfolio of tasks.

## CONCLUSION

The program has already proven to be successful. Through the involvement of UNI Graz the services offered to the companies have been expanded and issues can be handled which before were beyond the scope of the program. Due to the increased resources, project management tasks can now be done on a regular basis and customer care efforts have been drastically expanded. Additionally FTI is now implementing a similar program to support SMEs with the aid of the Styrian government and the EU on a broader regional base in co-operation with departments at UNI Graz, University of Leoben and JOANNEUM RESEARCH Forschungsgesellschaft mbH, Styria's largest public research center. The project is based on the same principles as AKT, namely to approach SMEs actively. Stronger than AKT, this project focuses even more on the networking activities between the different intermediaries of the project partners. Due to the expiration of the European Union funding possibilities for investments for Styria with beginning of 2007 and the strong focus on "soft" support initiatives, the chance to continue such non-financial support activities as AKT should be positive. It is the objective of AKT to overcome existing barriers and thus enable enterprises to tap external knowledge. The up-to-now achieved results show that CIEs make use of R&D institutions, if they are being taken by hand and led to partners, which have common research interests and free capacity.

## REFERENCES

Adametz, C. and M. Ploder (2003). Innovationsbericht Steiermark 2003 [Innovation Report for Styria]. Forschungsgesellschaft JOANNEUM RESEARCH mbH, Graz.

Adametz, C. and M. Ploder (2005). Erhebung der Statistik Austria über Forschung und experimentelle Entwicklung im Unternehmenssektor – Vergleich Eckdaten 1998 und 2002 [Industrial R&D: Comparing Data of 1998 and 2002]. Kurzanalyse auf Basis von Daten der Statistik Austria und Eurostat [Analysis based on data of Statistik Austria and Eurostat], Forschungsgesellschaft JOANNEUM RESEARCH mbH, Graz.

Asheim, B. T. (2001). Learning Regions as Development Coalitions: Partnerships as Governance in European Welfare States?. *Concepts and Transformation*, **6:1**, 73- 101.

Business-Higher Education Forum (2001). Working Together, Creating Knowledge: The University-Industry Collaboration Initiative. Business-Higher Education Forum, Washington.

Cooke, P. (1996). Networking for Competitive Advantage. The National Economic and Social Council, Dublin.

Enterprise Directorate-General (2003). Innobarometer 2002 – Innovation papers No 33. European Commission, Luxembourg.

European Innovation Scoreboard (2002). Scoreboard 2002. http://trendchart.cordis.lu/Scoreboard2002/index.html.

Gruber, M., C. Habsburg-Lothringen, K. Moro and S. Pohn-Weidinger (2002). Wirtschaftsbericht 2001 [Economy Report 2001]. Department for the Development of Economy and Tourism, Graz.

Hanel, G. (1996). Typen des Technologienachfrageverhaltens kleiner und mittlerer Unternehmen: ein Segmentierungsversuch als Grundlage für wirtschaftspolitische Maßnahmen [Typologies of Technology Needs of SMEs: Classification as Basis for Economic Measures]. doctoral thesis, Vienna University of Economics and Business Administration, Vienna.

Major, E. (2003). Technology transfer and innovation initiatives in strategic management. *Industry & Higher Education*, Vol. **17**, No. 1, 21-27.

McCullough, J. M. (2003). Technology Transfer: Creating the right environment, *Industry & Higher Education*, Vol **17**, No 2, 111-117.

Nicolay, R. and S. Wimmers (2000). Kundenzufriedenheit der Unternehmen mit Forschungseinrichtungen: Ergebnisse einer Unternehmensbefragung zur Zusammenarbeit zwischen Unternehmen und Forschungseinrichtungen [Customer satisfaction of enterprises with R&D centers: Results of a survey of enterprises regarding collaborations with R&D centers]. Deutscher Industrie- und Handelstag [German Chamber of Industry and Trade], Berlin.

OECD (2000). Programme for International Student Assessment. http://www.pisa.oecd.org/.

Reinhard, M. (2001). Absorptionskapazität und Nutzung externen technologischen Wissens in Unternehmen [Absorption capacity and the usage of technological knowledge in enterprises]. ifo Schnelldienst, 4/2001 – 54. Jahrgang.

Riis, J. O. (2001). University-Industry Interaction: A Means for Stimulating Manufacturing Excellence. Proceedings of The Fourth SMESME International Conference, Aalborg (Denmark).

Santoro, M. D. and S. Gopalakrishnan (2001). Relationship Dynamics between University Research Centers and Industrial Firms: Their Impact on Technology Transfer Activities. *Journal of Technology Transfer*, **26**, 163-171.

Schartinger, D., A. Schibany and H. Gassler (2001). Interactive Relations between Universities and Firms: Empirical Evidence for Austria, *Journal of Technology Transfer*, **26**, 255-268.

Schumpeter, J. A. (1912). Theorie der wirtschaftlichen Entwicklung [Theory of economic development]. Duncker & Humblot. Leipzig.

Tichy, G. and H. Wulz (1996). Beiträge zur Wirtschaftspolitik: Notwendigkeit, Möglichkeiten und Kosten eines Technologietransfers an österreichischen Klein- und Mittelbetriebe nach dem Steinbeis-Modell [Necessity, possibilities and costs of the Steinbeis technology transfer scheme for Austrian SMEs]. AK Vienna, Vienna.

Tornatzky, L. G. (2000). Building State Economies By Promoting University-Industry Technology Transfer. National Governor's Association, Washington.

M. Hashem Sherif and T.M. Khalil (Editors)


# 4

# A Knowledge-Based View of R&D Collaboration – Experiences of Finnish ICT SMEs

*Sami Saarenketo, Lappeenranta University of Technology, Finland* [*]
*Kaisu Puumalainen, Lappeenranta University of Technology, Finland* [**]
*Kalevi Kyläheiko, Lappeenranta University of Technology, Finland* [***]

## Introduction

The aim in this paper is to develop an integrated model that relates a firm's technological capabilities and its knowledge base to possible R&D collaboration. The context of our study, Finland, is among the leading nations in terms of international competitiveness, and was ranked number one in a comprehensive annual study on the competitiveness of nations (IMD World Competitiveness Yearbook 2003). Although Finland formerly used to be best known for its forest and metal industries, it is now also distinguished as one of the leaders in the development of information and communication technology (ICT). Indisputably, the ICT industry in the country is very much driven by Nokia, the world leader in mobile communications. However, an increasing number of small firms are emerging.

[*] Department of Business Administration, Lappeenranta University of Technology, P.O. Box 20, FIN-53851 Lappeenranta. Email: sami.saarenketo@lut.fi.

[**] Department of Business Administration, Lappeenranta University of Technology, P.O. Box 20, FIN-53851 Lappeenranta. Email: kaisu.puumalainen@lut.fi.

[***] Department of Business Administration, Lappeenranta University of Technology, P.O. Box 20, FIN-53851 Lappeenranta. Email: kalevi.kylaheiko@lut.fi.

Technological capabilities and knowledge bases constitute the firm's most critical assets in a high-velocity industry such as ICT. Although marketing and organizational capabilities have their roles to play, these may not have any importance if the technological core of the firm is incomplete. Many small high-technology firms are based on certain product or service innovations, which in turn are based on the knowledge assets the firm possesses. A shorter span of innovation life cycles, a multi-technology environment with higher levels of uncertainty, and escalating costs of R&D all drive both big and small firms to collaborate with each other. From the knowledge-based perspective, we see this R&D collaboration as being driven by the need for enhanced knowledge.

We begin by classifying technological capabilities, and then we offer suggestions as to how these capabilities might be related to the R&D collaboration that firms undertake. We discuss the implications of the nature of the firm's knowledge base: in our view, technology could be considered the sum of its knowledge base and its capabilities. Furthermore, we expect the level and the type of the firm's technological capabilities to be closely linked to its R&D collaboration.

The rest of the paper is organized as follows. The next section elaborates our theoretical framework in the areas of technological capabilities, the nature of knowledge and R&D collaboration. The third section outlines the methodological aspects of our survey in terms of the sampling procedure, the measurement of the variables and the statistical analysis. The key findings from the Finnish ICT industry are then discussed. The concluding section provides a summary of the study and outlines the limitations and managerial implications.

## THEORETICAL FRAMEWORK

*The Technological Capabilities of the Firm.* The paradigm of the resource-based view (RBV) of the firm (e.g., Wernerfelt 1984; Barney 1986; Foss 2000) suggests that a firm's competitiveness is based on its idiosyncratic internal *resources*. The bundling of these resources is then referred to as *capabilities* (Amit and Schoemaker 1993). The RBV further denotes that the resources and capabilities should be valuable, rare, inimitable and nonsubstitutable. Many researchers have emphasized the importance of intangible resources to competitive advantage (see e.g., Kogut and Zander 1992; Deeds et al. 1999).Knowledge-based resources have been found to contribute most to performance in dynamic environments (Miller and Shamsie 1996). However, despite the growing body of conceptual work, empirical research on resources and capabilities is still lacking, and the field has not reached maturity.

The role of technology has been one of the central themes in the study of high-technology small and medium-sized enterprises (SMEs). Its technology strategy has been regarded as one of the most important aspects of any firm's strategic posture, especially in dynamic environments, and it is among the most recognized determinants of the success of new ventures (Zahra and Bogner 1999; Zahra 1996; McGrath 1995). Deeds et al. (1999) note that, *"...to compete and survive, these [entrepreneurial high technology] firms must rely on a steady stream of innovative products."* Our view is that the competitive advantage of high-tech firms is primarily based on their organizational and technological resources and capabilities (see Kuivalainen et al. 2001). However, the relationship between the resources and capabilities and the competitive advantage is often studied in a sequential or "static" manner, without concentrating on the dynamic and complex links between competitive and technology strategies (Zahra et al. 1999). This view clearly disregards the opportunities different technologies can offer the firm in the long run.

Zahra et al. (1999:190) incorporate the following components into the technology strategy: the company's technological posture (i.e., whether it is a follower or a pioneer in a certain technology); technology sourcing (whether to make, buy or co-operate); its technology portfolio (technologies used over time); and its distinctive technological skills and resources (skillful staff). Zahra and George (2002) distinguish between a firm's *potential* and *realized* capacity: it may put a lot of effort into R&D and developing new technologies (potential capacity), but unless it is able to convert this knowledge into innovations (realized capacity) it may not achieve superior performance and sustained competitive advantage in the marketplace.

Bell and Pavitt (1995) made a distinction between 'routine' and 'innovative' technological capabilities across different technological functions. 'Routine' capabilities could be described as *technology-using* skills, knowledge and organizational arrangements, whereas 'innovative' capabilities are those required to create, change or improve products and processes; they include *technology-changing* skills, knowledge, experience and organizational arrangements. To succeed in the marketplace, the firm obviously needs to accumulate and sustain both of these capabilities concurrently.

Another useful classification of technological capabilities is put forward by Costa and de Queiroz (2002), which also reflects both the use and generation of technology. Mere *use* of technology refers to imitation, which is "*the use of technologies developed by external agents and already available in the market*", whereas the *generation* of (new process or product) technology, which is introduced into the market for the first time, represents true innovation.

In their research related to the causal logic of rent generation, Spanos and Lioukas (2001) measured firms' technical capabilities (i.e., competencies that are required when converting inputs to outputs) by looking at the efficiency of production departments, the technological capabilities and infrastructure, and economies of scale and technical experience. They found out that the firm's internal assets have an effect on market performance and thereby on profitability. They also mention that the resource-based view has generally worked well in a managerial context. In our view, there are severe shortcomings, however, as the traditional RBV is basically a static approach. In a dynamic environment such as the ICT industry, in which firms undergo enormous changes, the classification of old-fashioned resources is irrelevant or even misleading. Thus, managing technological capabilities and technologies in a dynamic environment is a challenge for a small firm. We claim that the emerging *knowledge-based view (KBV)* of the firm offers a more promising way of forecasting future success.Learning is considered a fundamental component of longer-term competitive advantage. We now turn our attention to the nature of knowledge, which we also suggest plays an important role in the assessment of R&D collaboration between organizations.

*The Nature of Knowledge.* We claim that it is not only the type and level, but also the very *nature* of knowledge that has an effect on firms' R&D collaboration decisions. Teece and Pisano (1994: 537) interpret firms as generators of *dynamic capabilities,* which help "*in appropriately adapting, integrating, and re-configuring internal and external organizational skills, resources and functional competences toward a changing environment.*" The opportunity window of the firm is always constrained by its existing internal routines and capabilities, thus implying the constraint of *path dependency*. The higher the prevalence of *economies of scale*, the more firms have to specialize in their path-dependent capabilities, and the more vulnerable they become in turbulent markets. On the other hand, the more *complementarities* there are between dynamic capabilities, the more the firm's potential to sustain its competitive advantage can be enhanced. In sum, our knowledge-based view of the firm comprises the following knowledge determinants:

a) *Appropriability regime:* this refers to the question of how easily a firm can protect its ideas from imitation. Appropriability does not only depend on legal protection (patents, trademarks), and the nature of knowledge is perhaps even more important. The more tacit the knowledge is, or the higher the economies of scale, the more appropriate it is.
b) *Complementary capabilities:* these consist of the external capabilities that are needed to complement a firm's own internal capabilities.
c) *Economies of scale and scope (synergies)*: these are exploited when the firm mainly utilizes its own resources/routines and capabilities, thereby building on cumulative learning.
d) *Path Dependency:* this is based on cumulative internal learning mechanisms.
e) *Asset specificity:* this refers to the degree of specificity of knowledge, i.e. can it be used for several or just one purpose.

*R&D Collaboration in ICT Industry.* Particularly in knowledge-intensive industries, there are multiple factors that drive companies to collaborate with others. From the knowledge-based perspective, the basic motive for collaboration comes from the increasing need to exploit the knowledge pool generated by many highly specialized firms. Consequently, we have witnessed a growing trend in the use of non-internal resources through hybrid governance structures such as partnerships, strategic alliances and joint ventures, together known as networks. While these structures are typically linked to many different kinds of firm activities, this study focuses only on R&D collaboration between companies. We define R&D collaboration, following Hagedoorn (2002, p.478), as a *"specific set of different modes of inter-firm collaboration where two or more firms, that remain independent economic agents and organizations, share some of their R&D activities"*.

Some of the major drivers behind the increasing amount of R&D collaboration in the ICT industry include the following:

- Increasingly complex products that constitute multiple different technologies (no single company can have all the required capabilities in all of them);
- Escalating costs of R&D in new high-risk technologies in which the future outcome and importance remain uncertain for a considerable period of time;
- Increasing speed of competition and the importance of time-to-market due to first-mover advantage and the shortening span of product life cycles.

As a result of these forces the manner in which companies carry out innovative R&D activities has been profoundly transformed during the last two decades. While there are multiple reasons why firms aim for collaboration with other organizations, managers should keep in mind the fact that their *"firms must have resources to get resources"* (Eisenhardt and Schoonhoven, 1996). Unless the firm has something to offer in terms of its own technological capabilities, for example, there may be little reason for potential partners to engage in collaboration with it. Consequently, high-profile innovators with the finest technological capabilities should be the most attractive partners, and they could also absorb the most from R&D collaboration themselves (Miotti and Sachwald, 2003).

*Conceptual Model.* In terms of the firm's technological capabilities, we are interested in both the level and the type (generation and innovative). We believe that, in order to attract partners and succeed in R&D collaboration, a firm should have good capabilities at least in one of the two technological types mentioned. Furthermore, as indicated in Figure 1, we expect the nature of the firm's knowledge base to be linked to possible R&D collaboration, although this relationship may be moderated by the technological capabilities in question.

We introduce our conceptual model of technological capabilities, the nature of knowledge, and R&D collaboration in Figure 1 below.

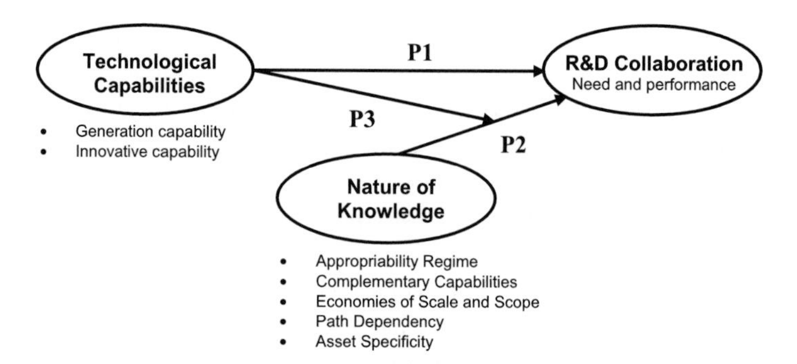


**Figure 1. An Integrated Model for R&D Collaboration**

As far as technological capabilities and R&D collaboration are concerned, the first propositions (P1) of the model are as follows:

- When the level of the firm's technological capabilities is high, it will be easier for it to attract partners for R&D collaboration.
- When the level of the firm's technological capabilities is low, there will be a greater need for external resources through R&D collaboration. However, it will be more difficult for the firm to attract partners because of its poor contribution.

In terms of knowledge determinants, the propositions (P2) of the model include the following:

- The need for complementary capabilities will be positively linked to the need for R&D collaboration.
- Asset specificity will be positively linked to the need for R&D collaboration.
- Appropriability will be positively linked to the need for R&D collaboration and collaboration performance.
- Path dependency will be positively linked to the need for R&D collaboration.
- Economies of scope will be positively linked to collaboration performance.

The third proposition (P3) is that the level of technological knowledge moderates the effects of knowledge determinants on R&D collaboration. Having outlined our conceptual model, we now proceed to explore technological capabilities, the nature of knowledge, and R&D collaboration in Finnish ICT SMEs.

## EMPIRICAL ANALYSIS

*Sample.* The population of interest was defined as small and medium-sized Finnish companies providing value-added services in the ICT sector. These include content providers and software providers for service-platform and management systems. Since there was no single up-to-date sampling frame available for our purposes, the names and contact information of the companies were sought from multiple sources, including the Kompass Finland Database, The Statistical Bureau of Finland database of Finnish companies, IT magazines, and the Internet sites of the companies themselves, and of universities, cities, science parks, incubators, venture capitalists and industry organizations. The data was collected by means of a structured Internet–based questionnaire. A total of 493 companies were identified, and contacted by telephone between November-December 2001. During this phase, 34 companies were found ineligible, and 74 refused to participate in the study. The 385 companies that agreed to participate received an e-mail the next day with the instructions for answering the web-based questionnaire. A reminder message was sent to those that had not sent their responses within two weeks. Of this sample, 123 companies responded, resulting in an effective response rate of 26.8% (123/459) of the eligible target population. This rate could be considered adequate as the questionnaire was rather extensive and the respondents were mainly chief executive officers or managing directors with busy time schedules.

The validity and reliability of the results were secured by several means. For example, the questionnaire was carefully pre-tested in a number of firms. Furthermore, it was targeted at CEOs and managing directors, who are considered the most knowledgeable informants. A comparison of the early and late respondents (with the late respondents being assumed to be similar to the non-respondents) was conducted in order to assess non-response bias (cf. Armstrong & Overton, 1977). No significant differences were found between these two groups, and non-response bias was therefore not expected to have an effect on the results of the study.

*Descriptive statistics and Measures.* The measures for technological capabilities were summated multiple-item scales, taken from Saarenketo et al. (2003). The two scales measure a company's capabilities to create and commercialize new technologies, ranging from 1 (poor) to 5 (good). The first one describes its ability to **generate** novel technologies: this group of capabilities has also been identified by Costa and de Queiroz (2002), and is clearly analogous to '*innovative*' technology-changing skills as discussed by Bell and Pavitt (1995). The second component portrays the firm's ability to frequently introduce new product/service innovations into the market, i.e., to *realize* the underlying technology *potential* in the marketplace. We named this component **innovative** capability. The items are shown in Appendix 1. The overall level of technological capabilities was fairly good: the mean values for generation capability and innovative capability were 3.01 and 3.16, respectively.

**The nature of technological knowledge** was measured by computing principal component factor scores from 13 Likert-scaled items. Since the dimensions were not expected to be orthogonal, oblimin rotation was applied. The rotated factor loadings and the wording of the measurement items are presented in Appendix 2. The means of these standardized factor scores did not differ between companies that had R&D partners and those that did not. The only exception to this was in economies of scope; those currently engaged in R&D cooperation had significantly more economies of scope (synergies).

**R&D collaboration and performance** were measured on 10 items (see the description in Table 1.). Firstly, the current situation was assessed in terms of whether the company had any R&D partners at the time of the study. More than a third (38%) of the respondents mentioned ongoing R&D partnerships. Secondly, the perceived need for R&D collaboration was measured on four five-point Likert-scaled items. Additionally, three items measured the extent to which the company could offer relevant capabilities to prospective R&D partners, and finally, two items measured performance in previous R&D partnerships. The need for technology partners averaged around 3, about one in four companies could not say, while the rest were evenly distributed in terms of those who clearly indicated a need and those who clearly indicated no need. The perceived need for technology partners was significantly higher among those already engaged in R&D partnerships. As many as 80% of the companies stated that they could offer specialized technological skills, innovativeness, and R&D competence to prospective partners. Those already engaged in R&D collaboration had more to offer than the others.

A total of 74 companies indicated that the development of new products had been the objective of current or previous collaboration efforts. Of these, 60% agreed that they had succeeded in this respect, while 19% had not. On the other hand, only 34% acknowledged that they had gained complementary technological capabilities from their partners, and 43% had not. Performance in previous R&D partnerships did not differ across the current R&D cooperation groups.

**Table 1. Descriptive statistics grouped by the existence of R&D collaboration**

| | Current R&D cooperation | | | |
|---|---|---|---|---|
| | No (n=54) | | Yes (n=33) | |
| | Mean | Std. Dev. | Mean | Std. Dev. |
| technology capability: generation sum | 2.95 | 1.11 | 3.06 | 1.11 |
| technology capability: innovative sum | 3.18 | .82 | 3.14 | .87 |
| complementary assets factor score | -.02 | 1.13 | -.14 | .95 |
| asset specificity factor score | -.02 | .97 | -.11 | 1.07 |
| appropriability factor score | .01 | 1.05 | .09 | .95 |
| economies of scope factor score* | -.12 | 1.02 | .35 | .96 |
| path dependency factor score | -.02 | 1.06 | -.08 | 1.08 |
| need partners for developing new products* | 2.55 | 1.22 | 3.30 | 1.07 |
| need specialized technological expertise* | 2.83 | 1.31 | 3.58 | 1.17 |
| need innovativeness | 2.94 | 1.28 | 3.31 | 1.23 |
| need product-development expertise* | 2.51 | 1.12 | 3.39 | 1.09 |
| offer specialized technological expertise | 4.00 | 1.32 | 4.15 | 1.18 |
| offer innovativeness* | 3.92 | 1.24 | 4.48 | .83 |
| offer product-development expertise* | 3.72 | 1.34 | 4.24 | .83 |
| We developed new products during the course of the partnership | 3.40 | 1.31 | 3.68 | .87 |
| We obtained complementary software technological expertise from our partners | 2.76 | 1.13 | 3.17 | 1.17 |

* the group means are different at the 5% significance level (independent samples t-test)

*Analysis.* A correlation matrix (see Table 2) was computed in order to test the propositions (P1 and P2) and determine the relationships between technological knowledge, nature of knowledge and R&D collaboration Both technology generation and innovative capabilities correlated positively with the ability to offer specialized technological skills to prospective partners. The companies seemed to seek complementary capabilities from partners, because generation capability correlated negatively with the need for specialized technological skills. Interestingly, the companies that were better at bringing new products onto the markets (innovative capability) needed more specialized technological skills from partners than their less innovative counterparts. As to the nature of capabilities, the need for complementary assets and the specificity of assets were not significantly associated with the R&D collaboration indicators. Appropriability showed negative correlations with the need for partners in product development, and with the need for innovativeness from partners. The possible moderator effects of technological capability (P3) were examined by subgroup analysis, the subgroups being formed by using three as a cutting value on each capability scale. According to this classification, 21 companies had poor capabilities in terms of both technology generation and innovation, 31 were poor at generation but good at innovation, 13 were good at innovation but poor at generation, and 45 were good at both.

The correlations between the nature of knowledge and the R&D collaboration indicators were then computed separately for the two groups. The first group included companies that had good capabilities in terms of either technology generation or innovation or both, and the second group included companies with poor capabilities in both innovation and generation. Some differences between these two groups were found, although the small sample size of the "poor capabilities" group does not provide a very firm basis for generalization. The need for complementary assets correlated positively with R&D collaboration performance, but only among companies with poor technological capabilities. In the same group, the more specific the assets, the less the companies could offer innovativeness to prospective partners. Furthermore, it was specifically found in the poor capabilities group that the better the appropriability, the less interest there was in exchanging product-development expertise with partners, and the fewer new products were developed in partnership. The more economies of scope a company had, the more it needed partners for product development, but this result only applied to companies with poor technological capabilities. Path dependency was positively associated with the need for specific technology capabilities from partners, but this applied only to companies with good technological capabilities.

**Table 2. Correlations between knowledge and R&D collaboration**

The sub-group correlations are shown on the second (good capabilities, n=45-64) and third rows (poor capabilities, n= 13-17) of the cell.

| | Need partners for the development of new products and services | Need specialized technological expertise | Need innovativeness | Need product development expertise | Offer specialized technological expertise | Offer innovativeness | Offer product development expertise | during the course of the partnership | We obtained complementary software technological expertise from our partners |
|---|---|---|---|---|---|---|---|---|---|
| technology capability: generation sum | .17 | -.18* | .06 | .00 | .36** | .07 | .11 | -.06 | -.14 |
| technology capability: innovative sum | .04 | .22** | .01 | .11 | .19* | .12 | .03 | .07 | -.05 |
| complementary assets factor score | .01 | .17 | .18 | .13 | -.09 | .03 | .06 | .13 | .18 |
| | -.02 | .09 | .10 | .01 | -.06 | .03 | -.04 | .09 | .13 |
| | .08 | .40 | .35 | .60** | -.14 | -.03 | .36 | .48* | .51* |
| asset specificity factor score | -.01 | .10 | .18 | .15 | -.15 | -.09 | .05 | -.17 | -.08 |
| | .04 | .14 | .21 | .19 | -.23* | -.02 | .04 | -.17 | -.10 |
| | -.31 | -.11 | -.09 | .00 | -.29 | -.47* | -.10 | -.06 | .06 |
| appropriability factor score | -.22* | -.18 | -.31** | -.19* | .08 | -.13 | -.16 | -.15 | -.20 |
| | -.20 | -.11 | -.30** | -.07 | .13 | -.03 | -.03 | -.03 | -.23 |
| | -.33 | -.37 | -.42 | -.51** | -.13 | -.42 | -.56** | -.58** | -.15 |
| economies of scope factor score | .07 | -.02 | .02 | .02 | .19* | .31** | .34** | .12 | .22* |
| | .01 | .01 | -.02 | -.03 | .19 | .23* | .35** | .12 | .30** |
| | .45* | .03 | .26 | .20 | .25 | .58** | .41 | .42 | .12 |
| path dependency factor score | .11 | .23** | .18 | .21* | .14 | .08 | .10 | .10 | .06 |
| | .10 | .31** | .12 | .20 | .13 | .10 | .12 | .17 | .08 |
| | .17 | -.06 | .39 | .25 | -.03 | -.18 | -.12 | .19 | .29 |

** Pearson correlation is significant at the 0.05 level. * Pearson correlation is significant at the 0.10 level.

## CONCLUSIONS

The purpose of this study was to develop an integrated model relating the firm's technological capabilities and the nature of its knowledge base to possible R&D collaboration. While we believe that the competitive advantage of high-tech firms stems largely from their technological resources and capabilities, the ability to collaborate with other companies in R&D and other complementary functional areas has become increasingly important. There are multiple factors that drive companies in the ICT industry to pool resources and collaborate with other organizations. From the knowledge-based view, we see this collaboration as being driven by a need for knowledge.

According to our findings, more than a third (38%) of the Finnish ICT SMEs sampled have ongoing R&D collaboration with other organizations. In most cases, the objective of the collaboration effort was the development of new products. While firms certainly have a lot to gain from their partners, it is also important that they have something to contribute to the partnership. Hence, the most technologically capable firms should be the most attractive partners, and should also reap the most benefits from R&D collaboration. Our empirical results partly support this view: the more capable firms had less need and more to offer, but we found no association between capabilities and R&D collaboration performance. As far as knowledge determinants were concerned, companies with more economies of scope had more to offer and also better collaboration performance. On the other hand, the more path-dependent the knowledge, the more need they perceived for R&D collaboration.

Although we found some differences between companies with "good capabilities" and "poor capabilities", the groups were rather similar with regard to their R&D collaboration efforts. Furthermore, the sample size of the "poor capabilities" group did not provide a very firm basis for generalization. The research has further limitations, as the data was restricted to a single country and a single industry. In order to make the results more generalizable, it would be worthwhile to expand the study to cover more countries and more industries. It would also be interesting to find out whether or not similar types of relationships between technological capabilities, the nature of the firm's knowledge base and R&D collaboration would also be found in other high-tech industries. Furthermore, the study was cross-sectional in nature and therefore only provides us with a "snapshot" view of the real-life situations. The firms in the sample were very young and many of them were still in the developmental phase. Researchers should be encouraged to employ a longitudinal research design in order to capture the processes underlying R&D collaboration and performance/sustained competitive advantage. A further limitation in this study has to do with the measurement of capabilities. RBV, KBV and DCV have been and continue to be valuable paradigms for understanding many strategic issues, such as sustained competitive advantage (Schoenecker and Cooper 1998, p. 1140). Still, empirical research is very scarce and dominated by subjective measurement. Clearly, strategy researchers need better measures on which to build research on resources and capabilities in the future.

From the managerial point of view, our study suggests that a focus on the development of superior technological capabilities inside the firm is not enough, and it is becoming increasingly important to accumulate skills in how to collaborate with other complementary, but sometimes also rival, organizations. Finally, it is important to recognize the way how the nature of knowledge that resides within the company may influence performance in R&D collaboration.

## REFERENCES

Amit, R. and P. Schoemaker (1993). Strategic assets and organizational rent. *Strategic Management Journal*, **14**, 33-46.

Armstrong, S. J. and T. S. Overton (1977). Estimating non- response in mailed surveys. *Journal of Marketing Research*, **18**, 263-264.

Barney, J.B. (1986). Types of Competition and the Theory of Strategy: Toward an Integrative Framework, *Academy of Management Review,* **11**, 791-800.

Bell, M. and K. Pavitt (1995). The development of technological capabilities. In: Haque, I.U. (Ed.) Trade, Technology and International Competitiveness. The World Bank, Washington.

Costa, I. and S.R.R. de Queiroz (2002). Foreign direct investment and technological capabilities in Brazilian industry. *Research Policy*, 31, 1431-1443.

Deeds, D. L., D. DeCarolis and J. Coombs (1999). Dynamic capabilities and new product development in high technology ventures: An empirical analysis of new biotechnology firms. *Journal of Business Venturing*, **15**, 211-229.

Eisenhardt, K.M. and C.B. Schoonhoven (1996). Resource-based view of strategic alliance formation: Strategic and social effects in entrepreneurial firms. *Organization Science*, **7**, 136- 150.

Foss, N. J. (2000). Equilibrium vs. Evolution in the resource-based perspective: the Conflicting Legacies of Demsetz and Penrose. In: *Resources, Technology and Strategy: Explorations in the Resource-based Perspective* (Foss, N. J. and P.L. Robertson, eds.), pp. 11-30. Routledge, London.

Grant, R.M. (1996). Toward a knowledge-based theory of the firm. *Strategic Management Journal*, **17**, 109-122.

Hagedoorn, J. (2002). Inter-firm R&D partnerships – an overview of patterns and trends since 1960. *Research Policy*, **31**, 477-492.

IMD World Competitiveness Yearbook 2003. The World Competitiveness Scoreboard 2003, available at: http://www02.imd.ch/wcy/ (accessed: 15th January 2003).

Kogut, B. and U. Zander (1992). Knowledge of the firm, combinative capabilities and the replication of technology. *Organization Science*, **3**, 383-397.

Kuivalainen, O., K. Kyläheiko, K. Puumalainen, and S. Saarenketo (2001). Knowledge-based view on internationalization and effect of product/service types. In: *Technology Management in the Knowledge Area* (Kocaoglu, D.F and T.R. Anderson, eds.), pp. 320-334, PICMET'01, Oregon, USA.

Lefebvre, L., A. Langley, J. Harvey, and E. Lefebvre (1992). Exploring the strategy-technology connection in small manufacturing firms. *Production and Operations Management*,**1**, 269-284.

McGrath, M.E. (1995). Product strategy for high-technology companies – how to achieve growth, competitive advantage, and increased profits. McGraw-Hill, New York.

Miller, D. and J. Shamsie (1996). The resource-based view of the firm in two environments: the Hollywood film studios from 1936 to 1965. *Academy of Management Journal*, **39**, 519-543.

Miotti, L. and F. Sachwald (2003). Co-operative R&D: why and with whom? An integrative framework of analysis. *Research Policy*, **32**, 1481-1499.

Schoenecker, T.S. and A.C. Cooper (1998). The Role of Firm Resources and Organizational Attributes in Determining Entry Timing: A Cross-industry Study. *Strategic Management Journal*, **19**, 1127-1143.

Spanos, Y.E. and S. Lioukas (2001). An examination into the causal logic of rent generation: contrasting Porter's competitive strategy framework and the resource-based perspective. *Strategic Management Journal*, **22**, 907-934.

Teece, D. and G. Pisano (1994). The Dynamic Capabilities of Firms: An Introduction, *Industrial and Corporate Change,* **3,** 537-556.

Wernerfelt, B. (1984). A Resource-Based View of the Firm, *Strategic Management Journal*, **5**, 171-180.

Zahra, S.A (1996). Technology strategy and financial performance: examining the moderating role of the firm's competitive environment. *Journal of Business Venturing*, **11**, 189-219.

Zahra, S.A. and W.C. Bogner (1999). Technology Strategy and Software New Ventures' Performance: Exploring the Moderating Effect of the Competitive Environment. *Journal of Business Venturing*, **15**, 135-173.

## Appendix 1. Components of technological capabilities

| Technological capability items (1=disagree totally, 5= agree totally) In relation to our competitors... | Mean | Median | SD. |
|---|---|---|---|
| **Generation capability** | 3.04 | 3.04 | 1.08 |
| Our products are based on technology developed by our company | | | |
| The company concentrates on developing its own technology | | | |
| The company's core competence is technology-based | | | |
| **Innovative capability** | 3.20 | 3.00 | 0.87 |
| The number of product/service innovations | | | |
| We often bring new products/services to the market | | | |

## Appendix 2. The rotated factor structure of knowledge items

| | Fac1 | Fac2 | Fac3 | Fac4 | Fac5 | Communalities |
|---|---|---|---|---|---|---|
| In the future, we will be more dependent on our technological partners | .80 | | | | .13 | .71 |
| The utilization of our technological core competence significantly depends on other companies operating within the same value chain | .80 | | | .22 | | .68 |
| We are dependent on other companies that supply us with the technology that makes our products/services possible | .73 | | -.16 | -.25 | -.23 | .66 |
| The principal product is a software product that can only be used in specific terminal devices | -.10 | .86 | | | | .72 |
| The products can only be used in specific operating systems | -.13 | .80 | -.11 | | | .69 |
| Our earlier technological choices make us more vulnerable if an abrupt change occurs in the direction of technological development | .35 | .46 | | -.38 | | .55 |
| It is difficult for competitors to adopt the technology we use | | | .87 | | .16 | .76 |
| It is difficult for competitors to imitate our production process | -.21 | | .68 | .18 | -.14 | .62 |
| It is difficult for our partners to adopt our technological knowledge | | -.16 | .62 | -.42 | -.13 | .61 |
| Our technological competence is suited for many types of products/services | | | | .82 | | .68 |
| Our company's technology supports the products/services of many other companies | | -.14 | | .71 | -.10 | .56 |
| Our technological competence is specialized and is hard to transfer to other activities | -.14 | -.17 | | -.21 | .85 | .76 |
| Our earlier choices (for example, technology choices) decisively influence the direction in which our core competence can develop | .30 | .31 | | .13 | .60 | .65 |
| Eigenvalue | 2.61 | 2.09 | 1.64 | 1.30 | 1.01 | |
| % of variance | 20.1 | 16.1 | 12.6 | 10.0 | 7.8 | |
| cumulative % of variance | 20.1 | 36.2 | 48.8 | 58.8 | 66.6 | |

The factors were named as follows:
Fac1: Need for complementary capabilities
Fac2: Asset specificity
Fac3: Appropriability
Fac4: Economies of scope
Fac5: Path dependency

Management of Technology: New Directions in Technology Management
M. Hashem Sherif and T.M. Khalil (Editors)



# 5

# INNOVATING AND DEVELOPING MOBILE SERVICES IN UNIVERSITY - COMPANY COLLABORATION

*Juha Nummi, M.Sc. (Eng.), Researcher*
*Katja Lahenius, Lic.Tech. (Eng.), Researcher*
*Department of Industrial Engineering and Management*
*Helsinki University of Technology, FINLAND*

## INTRODUCTION

This research aims at understanding the forms of collaboration between universities and companies in the wireless cluster in the Helsinki region with respect to innovation and the development of new technologies for mobile services. In this study, the important viewpoint to collaboration, besides the forms of networking, is also the roles of the collaboration partners in innovating mobile services. The local network of technology developers, service providers and equipment manufactures aims to generate new innovations in the mobility of current electronic products and services like electronic banking, computer games, entertainment and edutainment. The mobile services include development of terminal equipment, network elements, software programming and operator services.

The global number of mobile phone users as potential customers for mobile services has increased rapidly and is now over one billion. When the number of customers is growing, also the amount of different mobile services is increasing. Companies developing mobile services operate in an evolving technology area where markets are growing rapidly. Previous research on university-company collaboration shows that the academia can be an important source of new technology for the companies (Bloedon & Stokes, Daniel et al. 2003). According to Bloedon & Stokes (1994) companies have realized the importance of collaborative activities in evolving their core competencies and in making strategic decisions on how to best deploy their research and development (R&D) resources to maintain their competitive advantage. However, here the strategies of big and small companies are different. Santoro and Chakrabarti (2002) found that big companies have knowledge transfer and research support relationships in order to strengthen skills and knowledge for non-core technologies, whereas small firms have them for advancing core technologies.

When Chakrabarti and Santoro (2004) compared Finnish university-company collaboration with university-company collaboration in the USA, they found that collaboration differed in terms of the nature and applicability of the developed knowledge in research projects. Finnish universities tend to be high on the problem-solving type of research because the institutional system in Finland promotes this type of focus, while in the USA, universities are motivated to work more on theoretical knowledge development since reward systems prefer theoretical and more generic types of research (Chakrabarti and Santoro 2004).

University-company collaboration is shown to increase local innovativeness since sources of innovations do not reside exclusively inside the firms, but additionally in the interstices between universities and companies (Powell 1990), and these different sources with different types of knowledge stimulate R&D in companies (Cohen et al. 2002). The useful information sources for companies concerning new technology are university-company research projects, publications and reports of university research, public meetings and conferences, professors' consulting, informal information exchange between universities and companies, recently hired graduates and temporary personnel exchanges between universities and companies (Cohen et al. 2002). The geographical proximity of the universities and companies promotes university-company collaboration and information and knowledge flow (Lindelof & Löfsten 2004).

Cohen et al. (2002) concluded that the most important channels of information flow between universities and companies do not typically follow formal institutional links. According to them, informal collaboration, in addition to formal institutional links, plays an important role in university-company collaboration (Cohen et al. 2002). Informal collaboration is usually based on trust, voluntary and open communication between collaborators. Within organization networks, organizations are linked through formal ties, whereas social networks are operationalized in terms of informal ties among individuals (Granovetter 1985, Uzzi 1990).

In order to increase university-company collaboration, public funding for research and technology development has increased. The National Technology Agency (Tekes) and the Academy of Finland have promoted collaboration between universities and companies by funding technology and research collaboration projects. Although public funding has increased the number of university-company collaboration projects, the changing Intellectual Property Right (IPR) policy of the universities may make the collaboration more bureaucratic and in that way decrease collaboration with companies. To implement the new IPR policy, the universities in Finland have founded innovation centers. These centers manage the research-related IPR contracts for the protection and commercial exploitation of research results. Nowadays contracts are usually made between the company and the innovation center, not between the company and the researchers as earlier. The two main research questions of this study are 1) what kinds of collaboration forms between universities and companies occur in the development of mobile services and 2) how does collaboration work in practice.

## THE FINNISH WIRELESS INDUSTRY

The modern wireless industry in Finland began in the early 1980's when the NMT (Nordic Mobile Telephone) was introduced in the Nordic countries. The next step was the development of the GSM (Global Standard for Mobile Communication) technology in the 1990's and at the same time the liberalization of the global telecommunication industry started, which created the demand for the new technology and reshaped Finnish telecom operating industry (Häikiö 2001). In the late 1990's the Finnish economy was growing rapidly and the information and communication (ICT) cluster was named as the locomotive of the economy.

The wireless cluster, inside the ICT cluster, is mostly concentrated in the Helsinki region, particularly close to the Helsinki University of Technology (HUT) (Tukiainen 2003). Dominant in the Finnish ICT cluster is Nokia. Nokia has nowadays also a strong emphasis on software development and services (Paija 2001). In the Helsinki region there are, besides Nokia, mobile manufacturer Ericsson, the main operators in Finland (like TeliaSonera, Elisa and Saunalahti), venture capitalists, nine universities, three polytechnics and public funding offices such as Tekes, the Academy of Finland and the Finnish National Fund for Research and Development (Sitra).

In the wireless cluster among the industry sector and public funding offices is the academia. The nine universities in the Helsinki region have approximately 50 000 university students. The biggest and oldest university is the University of Helsinki, with about 30 000 students. Helsinki University of Technology (HUT) is the leading technical university in Finland and it covers most fields of engineering including industrial management. The Helsinki School of Economics (HSE) and the Swedish School of Economics (SSE) together are responsible for higher education in business and economy in the Helsinki region. The main difference between these two schools is that the language of instruction in HSE is Finnish whereas the language of SSE is Swedish. HUT has about 14 000 students, while HSE and SSE together have approximately 5000 students.

The transition from analog mobile phones (1G) to multimedia mobile phones (3G) and in the future broadband mobile phones (4G) has changed the companies' geographically constrained strategies to worldwide business strategies (Steinbock 2003). According to Steinbock (2003), the value system of contract manufacturers, equipment manufacturers, platform coalitions, chip and software developers, content aggregators and different service providers is rising and changing (Figure 1). Older companies are forced to globalize their business and new companies must be born global in order to compete in more and more global markets (Steinbock 2003). However, the global markets offer chances for small Finnish companies to provide their products and services worldwide in large-scale markets instead of smaller local markets.

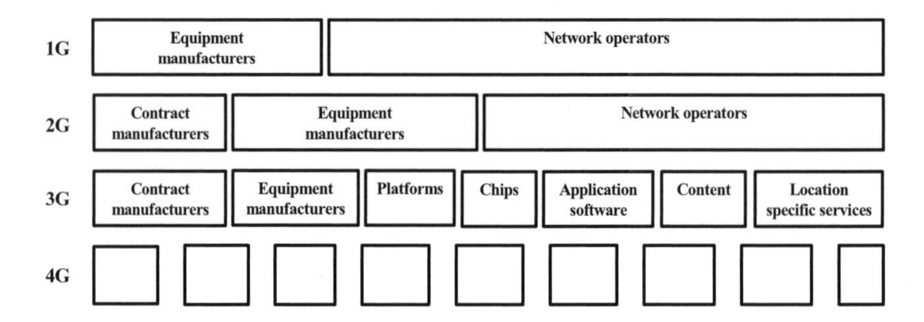


**Figure 1. The Wireless value system and fragmentation in different phases of evolution and specialization of mobile phones. Modified from Steinbock (2003)**

Innovations in mobile services have mainly evolved from the ICT cluster and the big ICT companies located in the Helsinki region. All of the parts in the value chain are important for innovativeness and development in mobile services, because mobilizing the services requires identification of the user of the services, security of usage, and reliability and availability of the services (Paija 2001). The competition between the operators creates an ideal environment for application developers to introduce and test their products. Additionally, the high penetration rate of mobile phones enables large scale testing of applications (Paija 2001).

## MATERIAL AND METHODS

A case study approach (Eisenhardt 1989) was selected as a research method for studying the university-company collaboration in more depth. A case study method is suitable when describing organizational and social phenomena without having control over events (Yin, 1994). The research data was gathered through interviews (N=34). Most of the interviews were conducted by two interviewers and the interviewing time varied from one hour to two and a half hours. In the first 16 interviews, interviewers made notes during the interviews and afterwards the notes were combined. By using notes of several interviewers it was possible to have more objective data than with the notes of only one interviewer. The rest of the interviews were recorded and then transcribed. The data was analyzed with content analysis.

In this study, we used a snowball sampling to locate the active collaborators. We started by interviewing professors and the interviewed professors named their important collaboration partners. We then asked these collaboration partners who their collaboration partners are. This was repeated until we had interviewed all the people mentioned as important collaboration partners. Interviewees represented universities, research institutes and companies. Altogether eight interviewees were professors and researchers of universities and research institutes and 26 were managers from companies. The interviews were conducted between March and June 2002. In addition, background information about the technology itself and the companies was collected from statistics and archive material (the statistical material of Statistics of Finland, annual reports of organizations, etc.).

## UNIVERSITY – COMPANY COLLABORATION

The typical motive for collaboration, both for universities and companies, is to increase the level of know-how and find new perspectives and ideas. The initiative for the collaboration can be made either by the university or by the company. In order to facilitate this collaboration, institutes like HIIT have been established in the interface between the industry and universities such as the University of Helsinki and HUT. HIIT links the ICT and ICT-related multi-disciplinary research of both universities.

The Finnish universities and wireless companies collaborate with domestic and international companies and universities. However, the number of international collaboration partners varied among companies. Some of the companies have a rather large international network of collaborators while some of them haven't actually got any international partners. According to company managers, some EU projects have created collaboration between the small Finnish companies and foreign universities. According to the professors, the universities have just a few international research projects related to wireless technology and the professors share information and knowledge mainly in international conferences, workshops etc.

Company managers saw the international collaboration with companies and universities to be important. Whereas the big companies have active international networks, the smaller companies have usually few personal contacts with company managers and professors abroad. One challenge for the industry is that also small and medium size companies (SMEs) – companies with less than 250 employees - should become more international. The big Finnish mobile phones manufacturer, Nokia, provides for many smaller companies a channel for internationalization. However, it is impossible for all the small companies to have their products embedded into big companies' products. For this reason these companies need to find internationalization channels of their own, which might be challenging especially for companies with young and rather inexperienced employees. Some SMEs, however, have managed to win a global position.

*Collaboration Partners from the Academia's Perspective.* Nearly all the interviewed university professors carried out research in software, but one of them was also involved in electronics research and one professor's research covered human cognitive processes. Collaboration between the companies and the universities is increasing and at the same time company funding has become more important for the universities. The interviewees reported that the strengths of the universities are for instance academic freedom, different kinds of human resources and the possibility to carry out risky basic research projects.

Most of the company partners named by the university professors were big companies. From the academia's perspective, Nokia and the major telecommunications operators are the most important collaboration partners. The small companies do not interest university professors as much as the big companies.

According to the company managers, the development of mobile services acquires more and more inter-disciplinary collaboration. According to the professors, HUT tried to answer the company managers' need with collaboration between different departments within HUT. The collaboration within the university seems to work to some extent, although one interviewee mentioned about problems and another one responded that his unit is not networked with the other departments of the university.

*Collaboration Partners from the Company's Perspective.* All the companies in our sample collaborate with the universities, except one. The collaboration forms and the number of universities as collaboration partners varied significantly between the companies. Based on our data, it is not easy to identify a clear connection between the type of the company and its activity in collaborating with universities or other companies or both. It is easy to understand that SMEs with limited resources cannot maintain active collaboration with many universities but also some bigger companies have rather limited collaboration with the universities.

Almost all interviewed company managers have collaboration with HUT, so it seems to have an important role in the collaboration network. According to company managers, it is easier to have collaboration with the university the know-how of which they know. Because many of them graduated from HUT, they prefer those HUT professors they know as collaboration partners. For some SMEs, HUT was the only university partner. There were only three companies, who didn't have collaboration with HUT. Besides HUT, the University of Helsinki and HIIT were mentioned as important local university partners.

In addition to the universities in the Helsinki region, company managers mentioned the universities in other cities like the Tampere University of Technology and the Lappeenranta University of Technology as important university partners as well. The Lappeenranta University of Technology seems to be surprisingly strong and some of the major companies described it as their most significant university partner, because it was regarded as a flexible collaboration partner with strong know-how in wireless technology. Also the universities of Oulu, Tampere, Jyväskylä and Kuopio were mentioned as collaboration partners.

*The Forms of the Collaboration.* In this study, we found different forms of university-company collaboration. The most common collaboration forms were joint research projects and master theses made in the companies by university students. The professors and the company managers also mentioned consulting and workshops as important collaboration forms. Some of the big companies tried to affect the content of the education to ensure that a university will stay as a source of new employees for them also in the future. While the university representatives recognized mainly the official forms of collaboration, the industry representatives found informal collaboration also significant.

The main collaboration form for university professors was research, which may be either applied or basic research. Master theses made by students in the companies have also been an important part of the collaboration. The university and industry representatives seem to have conflicting perceptions about the significance of the research itself in the collaboration. All the university representatives mentioned the research to be a very significant part of the collaboration while just a few industry representatives found it that important. In this case, the master theses are excluded from the research although they might be regarded as part of it.

The reasons for different perceptions between universities and companies were the different expectations of outputs in the research projects. Companies usually preferred research projects where the focus was to find answers to specific technical problems. However, there were differences between companies. Companies developing advanced technologies with a longer time span were more active research collaborators with universities than service providers and companies developing current technology. These active companies have research projects with universities, where the aim of the research was to find next generation technologies. The objectives of these research projects were broad or some times even unknown.

From the companies' perspective, there were also differences among university professors. The companies which were active collaborators preferred the professors who were active in the field of research, having several research projects going on, while the companies, which were passive collaborators in research projects, preferred professors who did consulting.

It is significant to notice that those four companies, which mentioned research to be an important part of the collaboration, were the companies named by the universities as major partners. For that reason it can be assumed that there are some rather active companies and some more passive ones. The universities don't find the latter ones to be significant partners because of their lack of involvement in research sponsorship. From the passive ones, preferring informal consulting as a collaboration form, professors got information about companies' core-technology more often than in research projects. However, they didn't get funding for the research.

The company managers saw consulting more like informal collaboration whereas the university professors saw it more like formal collaboration. The company managers saw the consulting as ad-hoc help to current problems whereas the professors saw it as work of the collaboration projects. The informal collaboration, like email consulting, seems to be especially important for SMEs because of their lack of resources to participate in research projects. Also market research as one form of consulting is part of the collaboration, being for one operator the most important part of it.

The companies' attempts to affect the content of the university education can be seen also as a form of the collaboration. Although most of the companies have not tried to affect the education, there are some exceptions. A good example was a significant change in the content of the education in the department of computer science at the University of Helsinki in the 1980's. One of the companies in our sample has strongly lobbied HUT in order to create education in its business field. That strongly indicates the company is ahead of the universities in its field of interest.

A typical way to contribute to the education in the university is that company representatives give lectures at the university. So far that has not been very typical in the wireless industry. The industry need is taken into account by a university allowing the industry representatives to express their needs concerning the education and in some cases by increasing the number of students in specific education programmes.

HUT was named as the most important source for new employees when the industry recruits from the universities; however also the University of Helsinki and Tampere University of Technology were named. There are some companies, which recruit only personnel with wide work experience and for that reason they cannot really say from which universities they come from, and a few companies also told that hardly any of their employees have finished any degree, although they may have been studying at some university. According to the professors, especially the students who made their master theses in collaboration projects with companies have been hired to these companies after graduation.

The university professors don't find informal collaboration as important as companies partly because it doesn't bring funding for the academic research. However, it can be quite significant for smaller companies like university spin-offs. These companies have lack of funding to acquire expensive consulting services from consultants. According to the company managers, informal collaboration is usually based on their personal contacts with their former professors. The professors saw important to help these new spin-offs and small companies to develop their technologies and services.

*Funding of the collaboration.* In most of the university-company collaboration projects there is some industry funding. Its share varies but usually it is less than 50% of the entire funding of the project. Usually, the rest of the funding is public funding from Tekes or the Academy of Finland. In some cases, the industry covers all the expenses. In our data, one case was mentioned where one company paid all the expenses although other companies were involved in the same project.

There are also some Tekes projects carried out by the universities, where Tekes covers all the expenses. Thus, public funding is not an absolute precondition for the university-company collaboration, but the volume of the collaboration would be much smaller without public funding. The present funding policy of Tekes seems to be a significant motivator for the universities to find industry partners and transfer know-how to them.

From the university's perspective, also the Academy of Finland which allocates funding for basic research is important for university-company collaboration. Although the industry is not directly involved in the projects funded by the Academy of Finland, ideas for future applied research collaboration may be created in these projects.

*Intellectual Property Rights in the university-company collaboration.* According to the interviewees, IPRs have not been a major problem. This is partly due to the fact that software cannot be patented in Finland and quite many of the companies and the university representatives operate in software. However, companies use their IPRs, especially patents, for trading when collaborating with companies. So the interviewed company managers stated that it is important for their companies to own IPRs in university-company collaboration projects. According to the company managers, the changing IPR policy in the universities may decrease collaboration activity between universities and companies and change the research from focused problem solving to more generic research.

Companies try to protect their core competence against competitors and control the knowledge flow from the companies, so confidentiality between collaboration partners is vital in the collaboration. The company managers stated that they need to limit the scope of collaboration projects and knowledge transfer because of confidentiality although they don't seem to find it as a serious problem in university collaboration. An important question relating to confidentiality is whether the publication of master theses can be delayed. Basically, it is not possible, but in some cases the confidential data have been in non-public appendices.

In any case, some actors find IPRs at least as a source for potential problems and one professor reported that because of written agreements required by the Innovation Center in HUT, he has difficulties in getting projects from the industry. All in all, there are many different kinds of policies related to IPRs and the situation is unclear. Basically, the researcher owns IPRs, but the rights can be transferred to the company or university through contracts.

## DISCUSSION

The focus of the research was to identify the different forms of the collaboration between universities and companies in the mobile services development. For this purpose, eight university professors and 26 company managers were interviewed. The case study method was appropriate for this study. The research questions were answered and the results introduce a picture of what kind of collaboration exists between universities and companies. The snowball sampling method seemed to be the best way to have all the key participants involved in this study. The possible distortion of the sampling, having a too narrowly focused sampling of interviewees, is a limitation of the snowball sampling (Frank and Snijders 1994). To avoid the distortion, we used a set of focal actors instead of one actor when starting the sampling. With a different set of focal actors, we could have different kinds of answers. However, most of the interviewees were top managers in key companies who would be interviewed in any case. Most of the interviewees were intentionally involved in university–company collaboration innovating and developing mobile services as was meant and were thus relevant to the study.

Although the focus in the interviews was on research collaboration between universities and companies innovating and developing mobile services, all the interviewees underlined that the most important role of universities in the wireless industry in the Helsinki region is to be actors, which produce skilled educated people. In addition to education, the role of the different universities varies in research collaboration. From the companies' point of view the most important research collaboration partner is HUT. According to the company managers, reasons for this were HUT's long tradition in industry collaboration. Also many of them had graduated from HUT so they know the professors. In addition, many of their employees were HUT students or graduated from HUT.

The wireless industry consists of a few major companies and plenty of small service and software companies. Our results show that the universities are important collaboration partners to companies; however the collaboration forms between universities and companies vary. The collaboration between universities and companies in the electronics business, like with telecom operators, is usually formal and made in research projects, whereas the software companies are mainly dependent on universities as a source of skilled labor.

Although there were many research projects between universities and companies, the important local impact of the universities is the fact that they supply educated people for companies. Because the technology companies are dependent on the supply of educated work force, they are usually located near the universities. Some of the companies have established new units in the other university cities in order to have access to university research projects and the possibility to employ educated people from these universities.

The motive for research collaboration differed between big companies and SMEs. The collaboration projects between universities and companies focused with big companies on their non-core technologies and with small companies on core technologies. SMEs do not have enough resources to develop their core technology by themselves.

Also the forms of research collaboration differed between big companies and SMEs. While the university representatives preferred mainly the official forms of collaboration, the industry representatives find informal collaboration also significant. Especially managers in SMEs found informal consulting important.

Our results show that the collaboration benefits both parties. The collaboration works although the depth of the collaboration and the number of university partners vary significantly between the companies. The main form of collaboration in mobile service development is applied research and master theses made for the industry. The finding of Chakrabarti and Santoro (2004) that most of the master theses and doctoral dissertations made in university-company collaboration projects in Finland are focused on solving corporate problems is in line with our finding.

In the future, our aim is to focus more on the mobile services. This focusing is needed in order to understand the different roles of actors developing mobile services more deeply. The future research will give answers to the questions of why and how the development of mobile services is mainly concentrated in the Helsinki region and how universities facilitate the innovative capability of the companies.

## ACKNOWLEDGEMENT

We want to thank the interviewees for their positive and open attitude to our research questions and Prof. Eila Järvenpää and Dr. Stina Immonen for their review and support of this paper. This study was conducted in the Local Innovation System (LIS) project funded by Tekes, the National Technology Agency, (40639/01).

## REFERENCES

Bloedon, R.V. and Stokes, D. R. (1994) "Making university/industry collaborative research succeed". Research Technology Management. **37**, 44-48.

Chakrabarti, A.K. & Santoro, M.D. (2004) "Building social capital and learning environment in university – industry relationships", International Journal in Learning and Intellectual Capital. **1**, 19-36.

Cohen, W., Nelson, R. and Walsh, J. (2002) "Links and Impacts: The Influence of Public Research on Industrial R&D". Management Science **48**, 1–23.

Daniel, H.Z., Hempel, D.J. and Srinivasan, N. (2002) "A model of value assessment in collaborative R&D programs", Industrial Marketing Management, **31**, pp. 653.

Eisenhardt, K. (1989) "Building theories from case study research", Academy of Management Review, **14**, 532-550.

Frank O. and Snijders T. (1994) "Estimating the size of hidden populations using snowball sampling". Journal of Official Statistics **10**, 53-67.

Granovetter, M. (1985) "Economic Action and Social Structure: The Problem of Embeddedness", American Journal of Sociology **91**, 481– 510.

term 'marketing' and some marketing ideas start to appear in the research commercialization area (Baaken 2003; Plewa et al 2005; Hoppe 2001). Howard (KCA 2003) mentioned that the increased outsourcing and commercialization of research involves a shift for universities from a science to a user focus. And this shift "requires an increased emphasis on marketing – through networks, application and user focus" (KCA 2003, p. ii).

This paper outlines some key outcomes of the large-scale project 'Science Marketing', namely the analysis of two mirror surveys of research customers. Surveys in Germany and Australia were used to understand how companies that assigned research tasks to research institutions perceive their expectations and experiences as research customers. By analyzing research customers' expectations and perceived performance levels in a three-step process, this paper identifies superior performance factors of German and Australian universities.

In the following section, the application of marketing to research commercialization is discussed, including an introduction to the project 'Science Marketing' and the surveys conducted for this study. Then, the methodology of this study will be described, followed by a discussion of results. Selected findings are outlined in three steps. Firstly, the most important performance factors for customers are identified, leading to a number of key success factors for research institutions. Secondly, differences between expectations and perceived performance levels are discussed to determine customer satisfaction levels. Thirdly, country-specific analysis is followed by a comparison of German and Australian results. This comparison reveals those areas in which each Australia performs significantly better than Germany and vice versa. The paper concludes with an introduction of strategies and an outline of successful instruments, enabling research institutions to perform well in the key components and, in turn, to realize successful research commercialization and industry linkages.

## SCIENCE MARKETING

*Science Marketing Research Center.* The term "science marketing" labels the marketing of science, one part of the marketing activities to be undertaken by universities and other research institutions. Science marketing aims at the usage of marketing principles for the area of science, aiming at a successful commercialization of research competencies, capacities and results from a research institution to its research customers (Baaken 2003).

The key to marketing is a customer and user focus. Marketing the research of research institutions is about meeting a market demand and offering value to customers (Baaken 2003). Such value creation determines a market as the focal action point and an orientation towards customer demand. First, a marketing approach to research commercialization requires the understanding of the market in which exchange between institutions takes place. Based on the potential products and services a research institution has to offer, a market incorporates those companies and government departments willing to pay for these products or services. Second, research institutions are required to orientate their actions towards customer demand. To do so, the identified market has to serve as the starting point for every activity. That means, current and potential customers are the center of action and the customer and their needs and wants have foremost priority.

Based on the positive experiences gained from applying marketing principles to research commercialization at the Muenster University of Applied Sciences, Germany, a Research Center 'Science Marketing' was established. Its aim is to examine whether, how, in which way and based on which criteria companies assign research and development activities to external entities, and to assess the performance and experience they had with research commissions and projects. In addition, the Center aims at using these assessments of research customers to identify and examine best practice models of research providers to develop new strategies and tools to allow universities and other research institutions to benefit from the introduction of marketing to research commercialization.

*The Customer Survey.* This paper details the results of a mirror survey of research customers in Germany and Australia, which was based on the following three key objectives. First, the survey was aimed at revealing the key success components of research institutions from a customer perspective. Key success factors are identified by setting apart those requests made of research providers most important from a customer's point of view. Second, the survey was aimed at determining satisfaction levels of research customers in Australia and Germany regarding the key success factors. Third, a comparison of the German and Australian results was aimed at identifying those areas in which each country performs significantly better than the other.

These three objectives have been converted into three analysis steps for this paper. This conversion is believed to disentangle the research objectives and offer a straightforward structure for the discussion of results.

1. Reveal the most important requests made of research providers to clarify key success factors for research institutions.
2. Determine customer satisfaction levels by comparing expectations and perceived performance levels for the important requests.
3. Compare German and Australian Results and identify those areas in which each Australia performs significantly better than Germany and vice versa.

## METHODOLOGY

Previously, customer focus has been described as the central key to a marketing approach, including the recognition of the customer being the starting point for each activity. Based on this fact, a survey of the customers of research institutions was conducted. The sample for this research was built of experienced research clients in Germany and Australia. The experience in dealing with research institutions was a requirement for the sampling to ensure the expertise of interviewees in the area of this study and, in turn, achieve high-quality results. The fit of interviewees to the sample was reflected in two prerequisites, both tested before starting each interview. First, it was ensured that all interviewed companies are currently or have previously been in contact with a research organization. Second, individual respondents at each company either initiated and/or decided on the assignment of research tasks to external research institutions. In Germany and Australia, 82% and 86% of the interviewees respectively were engaged in both initiation and decision-making, illustrating their high experience as a research client and validity of their responses.

Respondents were identified by several means, including a search of the Internet presence of research and transfer institutions, a search of government grants awarded for research-oriented linkages and snowball sampling, which utilizes referrals of identified members of the target population to identify additional members. Given the perceived value of integrating people from different research institutions and backgrounds for the comprehensive research objective of the Science Marketing Research Center, respondents were not selected based on the research institutes they were dealing with. Therefore, the final sample includes soft and hard sciences. While a degree of heterogeneity in our cross-sectional should be acknowledged, differentiated analysis per research institution or sector was not feasible in this specific study given the limited number of respondents.

The survey was conducted in form of a mirror survey in Germany and Australia and was performed in two steps. First, a series of 105 telephone interviews was conducted in Germany between November 2002 and January 2003 using a structured questionnaire. To achieve the number of 105 interviews, 232 addresses were processed, leading to a response rate of 45%. The target group consisted only of companies experienced with research cooperation with Universities. Following this first step, the questionnaire was translated into English and pre-tested in Australia to ensure the correctness and suitability of the translation for the Australian sample. Following the adjustment of the questionnaire after the pre-test, 100 interviews were conducted in Australia between April and June 2003. Based on 386 addresses processed, a response rate of 26% was achieved. Institutions from different industries as well as institution sizes are integrated in the final interview samples, reflecting each country's market conditions.

As described in the previous section, one research objective was to determine the respondent's satisfaction with a range of requests made of research providers. Satisfaction will be analyzed by assessing differences in expectations and perceived performance levels regarding each request. Based on the disconfirmation paradigm (Parasuraman, Zeithaml et al. 1988), which has been accepted and used by a range of scholars (Eggert and Ulaga 2002; Hennig-Thurau, Gwinner et al. 2002), satisfaction is a feeling based on a comparison between expectations and perceived performance of a product or service. Therefore, respondents were asked to indicate the importance and perceived performance level of research providers regarding each request included in the survey. 34 requests were asked during the interviews, grouped into four clusters, namely (1) general, (2) information, transparency and contact, (3) practical outcomes and customer orientation, as well as (4) management and administration.

Respondents were asked to rate each request on a scale from 1 to 6, with 1 being very important or good performance and 6 being most unimportant or very poor performance. While this scale is uncommon in the majority of the literature, its selection was anchored in the German roots of this project. With a first intention to conduct this survey only in Germany, a system of assessments common in this country was applied. A high degree of familiarity with the scale can thus be assumed in the German sample. A thorough pre-test was conducted in Australia to ensure the easy understandability of the scale also amongst the Australian respondents.

## RESULTS

The three analysis steps for this survey were outlined in the section 'The customer survey', namely (1) to reveal the most important requests made of research providers to clarify key success components for research institutions, (2) to determine customer satisfaction levels by comparing expectations and perceived performance levels for the important requests and (3) to compare German and Australian Results and identify those areas in which each Australia performs significantly better than Germany and vice versa.

Requests made of research providers by their customers were included in the survey, each rated by the respondents regarding their importance and perceived performance. Due to the large number of requests included in the questionnaire and the conduction of the survey in two countries, the discussion of all findings would exceed the limits of this paper. Therefore, the following discussion is brief and outcomes for the second step only describe the constructs grouped under 'general requests'.

*Step One.* The first step was to determine the key success components for research institutions as perceived by their customers. To determine these most important factors, the means of the responses regarding the importance of each request were calculated. Then, a comparison of means was performed for each variable group, leading to a ranking of requests regarding their importance from the customers' perspective. Table 1 shows those requests that are most important for customers when assigning tasks to external research institutions. From a marketing point of view, these requests reflect the key factors of customer demand. Hence, trying to meet customer demand and creating customer value requires the recognition and application of these requests as the starting point for every activity of the research provider.

**Table 1. Key Success Factors**

| GERMANY (D) | Mean | Var. | AUSTRALIA (AUS) | Mean | Var. |
|---|---|---|---|---|---|
| | | | | | |
| Outcome | 1.24 | 0.26 | Competence | 1.21 | 0.27 |
| Competence | 1.35 | 0.25 | Outcome | 1.31 | 0.40 |
| Good cost/performance ratio | 1.59 | 0.54 | Good cost/performance ratio | 1.67 | 0.61 |
| | | | | | |
| Intelligible presentation of results | 1.57 | 0.51 | Intelligible presentation of results | 1.31 | 0.30 |
| Responsiveness/understanding | 1.68 | 0.53 | Personal communication | 1.49 | 0.54 |
| Fast, easy accessibility | 1.71 | 0.62 | Responsiveness/understanding | 1.56 | 0.35 |
| | | | | | |
| Focus on resolving problems | 1.36 | 0.33 | Knowledge transfer | 1.45 | 0.59 |
| Focus on company interests | 1.47 | 0,47 | Focus on resolving problems | 1.54 | 0.48 |
| Focus on company benefits | 1.47 | 0.57 | Focus on company benefits | 1.81 | 0.90 |
| | | | | | |
| Keep Promises | 1.34 | 0.30 | Keep Promises | 1.43 | 0.45 |
| Adherence to deadlines | 1.40 | 0.34 | Adherence to budget | 1.59 | 0.71 |
| Adherence to budget | 1.47 | 0.41 | Adherence to deadlines | 1.67 | 0.61 |

**Var. = variance**

An interesting finding is the similarity of success factors in Germany and Australia, reflecting the similarities between both countries not only in terms of their low-context cultures (Hall 1984) but also in their research and commercialization efforts. For example, national principles and frameworks fostering and guiding the creation and use of intellectual property exist in Australia and Germany (OECD 2003), with very comprehensive policy frameworks, initiatives and reforms in Australia, aimed at leveraging innovation and its impact on economic growth (OECD 2002). Notably, Australia has a smaller number of researchers employed in the business sector (OECD 2002), implying a more substantial reliance on research performed in research institutions.

*Step Two.* Based on the determination of the most important success factors in step one, step two determines customer satisfaction levels by comparing expectations and perceived performance levels for these important requests. Following a questionnaire development workshop and questionnaire pre-test, the term "importance" was used to question respondents about their expectations regarding individual requests. The higher the importance for a customer, the more is expected from the research institution in that respect. Figure 1 shows a comparison of the importance and performance curves for Germany (D) and Australia (AUS) for the first group of requests, namely 'general requests'. The curves show the means of each request regarding the customers' importance and performance evaluation in both countries. The German importance curve was used to rank the requests.

Figure 1 clearly indicates a gap between the importance and performance of research institutions as perceived by their customers. As satisfaction is a feeling based on a comparison of expectations, here shown as the importance curve, and perceived performance, the gap

**Figure 1. General requests. Importance and Perceived Performance**

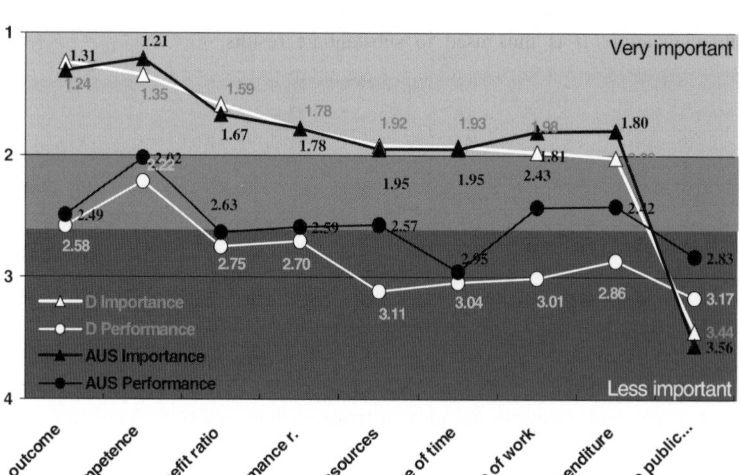

between both curves indicates non-satisfactory performance of research institutions regarding the given requests. Such dissatisfaction is especially critical regarding the most important success factors, detailed in table 1, as these are the key factors on which research customers assigns tasks to external research providers.

The identified gaps between importance and performance curves reveal the importance of this research and indicate a need of research providers to increase customer satisfaction to successfully operate in today's marketplace. As also seen regarding key success factors in Table 1, a similarity between the German and Australian results emerged in both importance and performance curves, especially regarding the most important success factors.

*Step Three.* Step three of this study compares German and Australian results to identify those areas in which Australian research institutions perform significantly better than German institutions as perceived by their customers and vice versa. This identification of best practice areas will be based on a comparison of performance and customer satisfaction levels.

A comparison of performance levels reveals those areas in which German and Australian research institutions perform higher than the respective other country as perceived by their customers, indicated in figure 2 by means of circles. In addition to this comparison of performance, the satisfaction levels of both countries were compared for each request. Customer satisfaction is a key criterion for a successful application of marketing principles to research commercialization. It is thus used to substantiate results of the comparison of performance levels for the identification of best practice areas in this study. As described in step two, satisfaction can be described as the difference between expectations and perceived performance. Figure 2 illustrates this difference by means of lines drawn between the importance and perceived performance curves. Satisfaction levels were generated for every request and were then compared to identify best practice areas for each country.

**Figure 2. Comparison of German and Australian Performance Results**

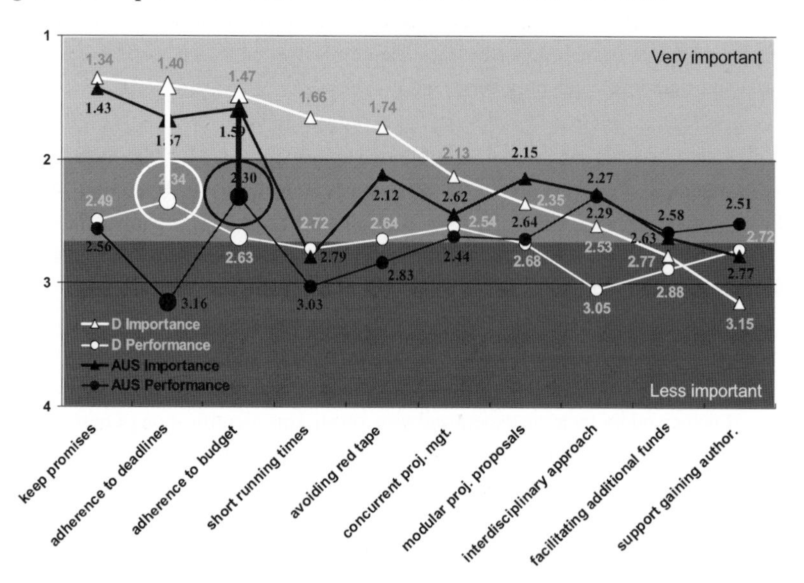


This analysis concentrated on those aspects reported by surveyed customers as being very important and thus on the key areas of customer demand. Given that these areas are the most important factors for research institutions to focus on (refer to step one), the analysis of performance in this step concentrates on those constructs. Comparisons of both performance and satisfaction levels are given in table 2.

Considering the performance and satisfaction levels of all requests included in the survey, the performance of Australian research institutions was rated significantly better than their German counterparts in the following aspects: participation in task selection and definition, inter-disciplinary approach, knowledge transfer, adherence to budget and the intelligible presentation of R&D results. In comparison, German institutions were perceived as significantly better than Australian institutions regarding the following requests: adherence to deadlines, personal communication, focus on company interest and avoiding red tape. Table 2 lists the identified requests together with the respective means of performance and satisfaction level ($\Delta$ pi) in each country.

**Table 2. Identification of Best Practice**

| | Performance | | Δ pi | |
|---|---|---|---|---|
| | **AUS** | **D** | **AUS** | **D** |
| inter-disciplinary approach | 2.29 | 3.05 | 0.02 | 0.52 |
| participation in task selection and definition | 2.14 | 2.43 | 0.20 | 0.40 |
| Knowledge transfer | 2.09 | 2.51 | 0.64 | 0.80 |
| adherence to budget | 2.30 | 2.63 | 0.71 | 1.16 |
| intelligible presentation of R&D results | 2.20 | 2.40 | 0.89 | 0.83 |

| | Performance | | Δ pi | |
|---|---|---|---|---|
| | **D** | **AUS** | **D** | **AUS** |
| adherence to deadlines | 2.34 | 3.16 | 0.94 | 1.49 |
| personal communication | 2.12 | 2.37 | 0.38 | 0.88 |
| focus on company interest | 2.54 | 2.76 | 1.07 | 0.45 |
| avoiding red tape | 2.64 | 2.83 | 0.9 | 0.71 |

Δ pi : performance - importance

The requests 'inter-disciplinary approach' and 'adherence to deadlines' present the most distinct best practice areas in Australia and Germany respectively. As detailed in table 2, the performance of Australian research institutions was rated 0.76 points higher than the performance of their German counterparts for the request 'inter-disciplinary approach'. In addition, in comparison to Germany, Australian research customers showed a very high satisfaction level, as the perceived performance almost meets customers' expectations (Δ pi = 0.2). Regarding the request 'adherence to deadlines', German institutions achieved a 0.82 points higher performance level than their Australian counterparts. While the satisfaction level of German customers for this request requires improvement (Δ pi = 0.94), it is still significantly higher than the satisfaction level of Australian research customers.

## Conclusion and Further Research

Today's research market is characterized by an intensifying assignment of research activities to research institutions by companies and government departments. This paper presented a marketing view on research commercialization and detailed some findings of a mirror survey of research customers in Germany and Australia, conducted by the Science Marketing

Research Center. After an introduction and a brief discussion of the 'science marketing' area, the methodology of the survey was outlined.

Three analysis steps and respective results were given. First, the requests most important for research customers when assigning research tasks to external research institutions were extracted from the data. As detailed in the discussion, these factors are crucial to the successful operation of research institutions and should be seen as the starting point for every activity of a research provider.

Second, a low satisfaction level emerged, indicated by a constant gap between the expected importance curve and the perceived performance curve (see Figure 1). In general, three marketing strategies can be adopted to decrease the illustrated gap between importance and performance and thus to increase customer satisfaction. First, given that the assessment shown in figure 1 accurately reflects the current situation, research institutions have to improve their performance in the relevant areas. Second, if the performance of research institutions is better than the customers' perception of performance detailed here, research institutions have to communication the accurate performance level to their customers. Third, if the importance curve is overstated, customer expectations have to be managed and decreased to a manageable degree.

Third, a comparison of German and Australian performance levels led to the identification of those areas in which one country's research institutions perform better than in the other country as perceived by their customers. These high performance areas will create the base for the second stage of the project 'Science Marketing', during which best practice examples will be identified for each area. These best practice studies in Germany and Australia will lead to the development of strategies and tools to improve performance in the respective other country as well as other countries wishing to make progress in these areas.

To date, few authors have adopted a marketing approach to research commercialization. While these findings and the project 'Science Marketing' are one step into this direction, more and more extensive research is required. Further research may duplicate this survey in other countries that experience a rate of contacts and linkages between research providers and customers. A larger sample size may enable the differentiation between universities and other research institutions, as well as between different types of research institutes and areas. Furthermore, academics and practitioners would benefit from a thorough examination of the willingness and ability of research institutions to adopt a marketing focus in research commercialization efforts.

## REFERENCES

Aijo, T. S. (1996). "The Theoretical and Philosophical Underpinnings of Relationship Marketing: Environmental Factors Behind the Changing Marketing Paradigm." *European Journal of Marketing* **30**(2): 8-18.

Australian Research Council (2001). Mapping the Nature and Extent of Business-University Interaction in Australia. Canberra, Australian Research Council: 71.

Baaken, T. (2001). SMILE Strategisches Marketing in Lehre und Entwicklung. *Die Fachhochschule im Wettbewerb der Hochschulsysteme.* U. Kamenz. Dortmund. **2:** 73-91.

Baaken, T. (2003). Science Marketing. *Applied Marketing: Anwendungsorientierte Marketingwissenschaft der deutschen Fachhochschulen.* U. Kamenz. Berlin, Springer-Verlag: 1051-1066.

Baaken, T. (2003). Strategien und Instrumente im Forschungsmarketing. *Marketing und Kommunikation von Forschung.* B. Mager and H. Hamacher. Koeln, Research Goes Public: 76-81.

Bower, J. (1993). "Successful Joint Ventures in Science Parks." *Long Range Planning* **26**(6): 114-120.

Caloghirou, Y., N. S. Vonortas, et al. (2000). *University-Industry Cooperation in Research & Development.* From Organisational Issues in University Technology Transfer, Indianapolis.

Cartwright, R. (2000). *Mastering Customer Relations.* London, Macmillan.

Cyert, R. M. and P. S. Goodman (1997). "Creating Effective University-Industry Alliances: An Organizational Learning Perspective." *Organizational Dynamics* **26**(4): 45-57.

Desphandé, R., J. U. Farley, et al. (1993). "Corporate Culture, Customer Orientation, and Innovativeness in Japanese Firms: A Quadrat Analysis." *Journal of Marketing* **57**: 23-27.

Eggert, A. and W. Ulaga (2002). "Customer Perceived Value: A Substitute for Satisfaction in Business Markets?" *Journal of Business & Industrial Marketing* **17**(2/3): 107-118.

Engineering, T. W. C. f. A. (1995). *Harness Innovation for Business Success: A Handbook*, The Warren Center for Advanced Engineering, The University of Resarch.

George, G., S. A. Zahra, et al. (2002). "The Effects of Business-University Alliances on Innovative Output and Financial Performance: A Study of Publicly Traded Biotechnology Companies." *Journal of Business Venturing* **17**: 577-609.

Graff, G., A. Heiman, et al. (2002). "University Research and Offices of Technology Transfer." *California Management Review* **45**(1): 88-115.

Griffin, A. and J. R. Hauser (1996). "Integrating R&D and Marketing: A Review and Analysis of the Literature." *Journal of Product and Innovation Management* **13**: 191-215.

Gummesson, E. (2002). "Relationship Marketing in the New Economy." *Journal of Relationship Marketing* **1**(1): 37-58.

Gupta, A. K. and D. Wilemon (1996). "Changing Patterns in Industrial R&D Management." *Journal of Product and Innovation Management* **13**: 497-511.

Gupta, A. K., D. Wilemon, et al. (2000). "Excelling in R&D." *Research Technology Management* **43**(3): 52-58.

Hall, E. T. (1984). *The Dance of Life*. Garden City, NY: Doubleday

Harmann, G. (2001). "University-Industry Research Partnerships in Australia: Extent, benefits and risks." *Higher Education Research & Development* **20**(3): 245-264.

Hennig-Thurau, T., K. P. Gwinner, et al. (2002). "Understanding Relationship Marketing Outcomes: An Integration of Relational Benefits and Relationship Quality." *Journal of Service Research* **4**(3): 230-247.

Hoppe, U. (2001). Marketingkonzeption für Technologie-Orientierte Öffentliche Forschungseinrichtungen: Ein Integraler Ansatz zur Gestaltung der Außenbeziehungen von Außeruniversitären Forschungseinrichtungen. Berlin

KCA [Knowledge Commercialization Australasia] (2003). Forum and Fair of Ideas: Commercialization Discussion Paper. Brisbane, Knowledge Commercialization Australasia

Lee, S.-Y. and X.-Y. Song (2001). "Hypothesis Testing and Model Comparison in Two-level Structural Equation Models." *Multivariate Behavioral Research* **36**(4): 639-655.

Lee, Y. S. (2000). "The Sustainability of University-Industry Research Collaboration: An Empirical Assessment." *Journal of Technology Transfer* **25**: 111-133.

Macure, J. and B. Davies (2000). *Marketing Scientific Results & Services: A Toolkit*. Avalon, NSW, Calibre Communications.

Montgomery, A. J. (1992). Technology Transfer from Universities: Elements of Success. *Innovative Models for University Research*. C. R. Haden and J. R. Brink, Elsevier Science Publishers.

OECD [Organization for Economic Co-operation and Development] (2001). *Science, Technology and Industry Outlook*. Paris, Organization for Economic Co-operation and Development.

OECD [Organization for Economic Co-operation and Development] (2002). *OECD Science, Technology and Industry Outlook 2002*. Paris, Organization for Economic Co-operation and Development.

OECD [Organization for Economic Co-operation and Development] (2003). *Turning Science into Business: Patenting and Licensing at Public Research Organisations*. Paris, Organization for Economic Co-operation and Development.

Palmer, A. (2002). "The Evolution of an Idea: An Environmental Explanation of Relationship Marketing." *Journal of Relationship Marketing* **1**(1): 79-94.

Parasuraman, A., V. A. Zeithaml, et al. (1988). "SERVQUAL: Multiple-Item Scale for Measuring Consumer Perceptions of Service Quality." *Journal of Retailing* **64**(1): 12-40.

Plewa, C. (2005). "Differences in Perceived Benefits from University-Industry Relationships." Paper presented at the Australian and New Zealand Marketing Academy Conference (ANZMAC), Fremantle, 5.-7.12.2005.

Plewa, C., Quester, P. G., and Baaken, T. (2005). "Relationship Marketing and University-Industry Linkages: A Conceptual Framework." *Marketing Theory,* **5**(4): 431-454.

Santoro, M. and A. K. Chakrabarti (2002). "Firm Size and Technology Centrality in Industry-University Interactions." *Research Policy* **31**: 1163-1180.

Siguaw, J. A., T. L. Bakes, et al. (2003). "Preliminary Evidence on the Composition of Relational Exchange and its Outcomes: The Distributor Perspective." *Journal of Business Research* **56**: 311-322.

Siguaw, J. A., P. M. Simpson, et al. (1998). "Effects of Supplier Market Orientation on Distributor Market Orientation and the Channel Relationship: The Distributor Perspective." *Journal of Marketing* **62**: 99-111.

Steenhuis, H.-J. and E. J. De Bruijn (2002). "Technology Transfer and Learning." *Technology Analysis & Strategic Management* **14**(1): 57-66.

Management of Technology: New Directions in Technology Management
M. Hashem Sherif and T.M. Khalil (Editors)



# 7

# UPSURGE OF UNIVERSITY SPIN-OFFS IN JAPAN[1]

*Masayuki KONDO, Yokohama National University, Yokohama, Japan*

## THE NEEDS OF UNIVERSITY SPIN-OFFS IN JAPAN

Many expect that new start-ups will play an important role in Japan in the 21st century. Among the new start-ups, many expect that university spin-offs will lead Japan's high-tech in the 21st century. The number of university spin-offs is increasing rapidly these days in Japan. The Government has launched a plan in 2001 to create 1,000 university spin-offs in the next three years and has taken various policy measures to promote spinning off from universities. There exist several reasons why university spin-offs are needed in Japan.

First, universities are the source of advanced technologies. In Japan university researchers occupy 27 percent of all researchers. From the demand side, there are changes in corporate R&D activities. On one hand, Japanese companies concentrate their R&D resources in target areas to compete in the global market. On the other hand, they need to widen the range of their R&D activities because of technology fusion and new technological developments. Especially in the fields of Pasteur-type research[2], where basic research results can be readily applicable to commercial use, university researchers can play a major role. Biotechnology is one of those fields. More than 80 percent of researchers of health science, which includes medicine and pharmaceutical science, are university researchers in Japan[3]. Within the university sector, more than a half of university researchers in natural science and engineering belong to health science.

Second, university technological achievements need to be commercialized in a faster way to compete in the global market. Time is an important competitiveness factor[4]. Technology transfer needs to be in a short time. From an early stage of technology

[1] This paper is based on Kondo (2002b).
[2] See Stokes (1997) for the classification of research.
[3] See Kondo (2001a).

development, the collaboration between university researchers and company researchers is required. Since technology transfer is done in the form of verbal and nonverbal communication or human transfer rather than in the form of documents in Japan, university spin-off is one of the fastest ways to transfer university technology to industry.

Third, technology frontier is wide and key technologies in the next generation are not foreseen. Existing companies cannot investigate all the possibilities. In addition they are downsizing corporate laboratories to shift their resources to more near-future projects. Thus, university spin-offs are expected to pursue variable technology frontiers to enhance the possibility of Japan's technological competitiveness in the next generation. Technology frontiers could be created from basic research and universities conduct more than a half of basic research in Japan[5].

Regarding the role of universities, Etzkowitz et al. (2000) point out that universities are becoming entrepreneurial, that technology transfer from universities to industry is pervasive in the United States and that university spin-offs are increasing in Europe including the United Kingdom. Jewkes et al. (1969) also argue that universities need to possess public service functions in adition to education and independent research.

This paper, after defining university spin-offs and discussing their types, clarifies some characteristics of Japanese university spin-offs based on the first survey on university spin-offs in Japan, conducted by Tsukuba University and Yokohama University. It analyzes 1) the relation between university spin-offs and their mother universities, 2) founder profiles, 3) the profiles of university spin-offs, 4) difficulties at the time of start up and current difficulties, 5) received assistance from mother universities and public authorities, and so on, comparing with the university spin-offs in Germany. As Albert (1992) names Nippon-Rheinland model compared to Anglo-Saxon model, Japan and Germany have some common features in their economic-industrial structures, such as a close relation between large industrial companies and large banks.

## DEFINITION AND TYPES OF UNIVERSITY SPIN-OFFS

In this paper a university spin-off is defined as a newly founded company that has received some management resources from a university or universities[6]. University spin-offs under

---

[4] See Gates (2000) for the importance of time in business.

[5] See Kondo (2001a).

[6] See Tsukuba University (2001) for the details of the survey. For technology type, our survey distinguishes two types: the case where technology transfer is in the form of patent licensing and other cases.

**Table 3. Relations to Mother Universities at the Time of Foundation**

| Relations | | Ratios (%) |
|---|---|---|
| human resource (a+b+c+d) | | 70.3 |
| | a. human resource only | 32.8 |
| | b. human resource and technology | 17.2 |
| | c. human resource and capital | 1.6 |
| | d. human resource, technology and capital | 18.8 |
| technology (b+d+e+f) | | 62.5 |
| | e. technology only | 25.0 |
| | f. technology and capital | 1.6 |
| capital (c+d+f+g) | | 22.7 |
| | g. capital only | 0.8 |
| no answers (h) | | 2.3 |
| total (a+b+c+d+e+f+g+h) | | 100.0 |

As university spin-offs have some relation with their mother universities before they are founded, they receive some assistance from their mother universities at the time of start-up. Nearly a half (44%) of them received some assistance, from mental supports to the usage of facilities, introduction of customers, intermediation of loans and so on, from their mother universities at the time of start-up. After the establishment of companies, a larger percentage (61%) of them received some assistance from their mother universities.

## PROFILES OF UNIVERSITY SPIN-OFFS

*Profiles of Founders.* Looking at who are heavily involved in the human-resource-related cases of university spin-offs in Japan reveals that a half of them are faculty members and 36 percent are professors (see Table 4). Students occupy nearly a half (47 %), of which nearly a half of them are master course students.

**Table 4. Profiles of Founders**

| Founders | Ratios (%) |
|---|---|
| Faculty | 50.0 |
| of which professors | 36.2 |
| Students | 43.1 |
| of which doctor course students | 12.1 |
| of which master course students | 20.7 |
| of which undergraduate students | 10.3 |
| Researchers/technicians | 6.9 |
| 計 | 100.0 |

This situation is quite different from the situation in Germany, where many of university spin-offs are founded by young entrepreneurs in their early thirties with doctoral degrees. According to ADT et al. (1998), 65 percent of academic spin-offs[17] in technology entrepreneur centers in the former West Germany are founded by students[18]. Those founders are mostly 30 or 31 years old. At least one of the founders possesses a doctoral degree in 32 percent of academic spin-offs[19].

The motives to found university spin-offs vary. The most common motive is to commercialize developed technology (34 %, see Table 5). Then, contributing to society (27 %), commercializing business ideas (18 %) and developing self-competence (11 %) follow. Making a fortune is mentioned by only a few founders as a primary motive (5 %). The similar tendency is found in the motives to start up any company by Matsuda and Shirakura (1997). The most common motive is challenge to his/her own life in Japan according to them.

For a new company, initial public offering (IPO) is a typical milestone of success. University spin-offs in Japan are not exceptions. Those who aim at IPO within 5 years from their foundation occupy 30 percent and those who aim at IPO within 10 years from their foundation occupy another 33 percent. In total, about two thirds (63 %) of university spin-offs in Japan aim at initial public offering within 10 years from their foundation, while a lower percentage, 40 percent, of German counterparts do the same[20].

---

[17] Academic spin-offs include university spin-offs. Some of founders of academic spin-offs have at least diploma, equivalent to master's degree. Academic spin-offs may be from universities, public research institutes or companies and they are R&D-oriented.

[18] This means that a new start-up company is founded by a current student or within three years after founder's graduation.

[19] Many of academic spin-offs the author visited in Germany had one or two staff who had doctoral degrees.

[20] For the comparison of university spin-offs in Japan and Germany, see Kondo (2001b).

**Table 5. Motives**

| Motives | Ratios (%) |
|---|---|
| Practical use of technology | 34 |
| Contribution to society | 27 |
| Commercialization of business ideas | 18 |
| Developing self competence | 11 |
| Making a fortune | 5 |
| Others | 6 |

*Profiles of University Spin-offs.* The size of employees is not large at the time of foundation. In nearly two thirds of university spin-offs (63 %) the number of employees is one to four. The weighted average is 5.2 employees per a university spin-off. The situation is similar in Germany. According to Baranovsky (1999), averagely an academic spin-off in technology entrepreneur centers in Germany starts with three to four employees.

The size of initial capital is fairly large. A half of university spin-offs starts with 10 to 30 million yen[21]. The weighted average is 77 million yen. This large initial capital reflects the facts that 82 percent of university spin-offs in Japan are incorporated as a stock company, whose required minimum capital is 10 million yen. In Germany, according to Baranovsky (1999), the average initial capital is DM 115 thousand[22]. In Germany, the most common form of an academic spin-off is a limited liability company (GmbH), whose required minimum capital is DM 5,000, and a registered legal entity (Gbr), which requires no minimum capital, is fairly common.

Regarding industry sector, most of university spin-offs in Japan belong to manufacturing (45 %). Another one twentieth engage in R&D. Thus, their business look fairy solid, though IT sector is also popular among university spin-offs in Japan (37 %).

## DIFFICULTIES OF UNIVERSITY SPIN-OFFS

Though university spin-offs basically possess technology or other knowledge asset, they lack in other management resources in general. They face various difficulties as a result. At the time of start-up, the largest difficulty they face is finance (25 %, see Table 6). Though several

[21] 1 Euro = 134.0 yen in July 2003.
[22] 1 Euro = 1.95583 DM.

policy measures have been taken in Japan, the issue of financing assistance may be the speed of imbursement, the simplicity of procedures and the flexibility of its usage.

Then, the difficulties that more than ten percent of university spin-offs in university spin-offs in Japan face are staff recruiting (16 %), sales (14 %), the places of offices and laboratories (12 %), and accounting and financial management (12 %). Only a few (2 %) face patent disputes at the time of start-up.

Current difficulties the time of the survey that university spin-offs face are different from those encountered at start-up. Staff recruiting is the most serious difficulty (31 %), which surpasses financing (29 %). Staff recruiting for small start-ups is difficult because of low mobility of qualified workers who prefer large companies and the large company-oriented mentality of students and their families. The situation in Japan is changing and is gradually becoming more entrepreneurial though it takes some time.

**Table 6. Difficulties**

| At start-up (%) | Current difficulties at the time of the survey (%) | changes (% points) |
|---|---|---|
| 1. finance 25% | 2. finance 29 % | **4** |
| 2. staff 16% | 1. staff 31 % | **15** |
| 3. sales14% | 3. sales 13 % | -1 |
| 4. office/lab.12% | 6. office/lab.4 % | -8 |
| 5. accounting/financial management 12% | 5. management 7 % | -5 |
| 6. legal issues 8% | — | — |
| 7. university regulation 6% | — | — |
| 8. procurement 3% | 7. procurement 3 % | 0 |
| 9. patent disputes 2% | 4. patent disputes 9 % | **7** |
| 10. others 2% | 8. others 0 % | -2 |

Note. The numbers before the names of difficulties show the ranking of difficulties.

Though the third most serious difficulty is the same at the time of start-up, that is sales (13 %), the forth is patent disputes (9 %). The issue of patent disputes is not a major difficulty at the time of start-up. However, as a company operates for a while and their activities become visible in the business community, the issue of patent disputes emerges.

The changes in the rank of difficulties from at the time of start-up to now can be understood by looking at the percent changes (see Table 6). Though the issue of financing increased a little, the issues of staff recruiting and patent disputes increased significantly.

Inversely, the issues of the places of offices and laboratories and accounting and financial management decreased their significance. The issue of sales remained almost the same.

Where do university spin-offs go to receive assistance at the time of start-up? In Japan public organizations play an important role in this regard. A little less than a half (45 %) of would-be founders go to public organizations to seek advice and assistance, while one sixth (17 %) go to private organizations. The rest of 52 % do not go to either type of organizations.

Some public assistance measures are very helpful to university spin-offs at the time of start-up. Public finance and incubators are most highly appreciated. Those two policy measures are pointed out as useful by 18 percent of founders.

## Concluding Remarks

This chapter has revealed the following facts:

1) National universities are active in spinning off companies despite their constraints,
2) More than a half of the founders are faculty members,
3) The primary motive is to put invented technologies to practical use,
4) Many of university spin-offs are in manufacturing, and
5) The largest issue is financing at the time of start-up but the issues of staff recruiting and patent protection increase importance later.

Though university spin-off is a relatively new phenomenon in recent years in Japan, more university spin-offs should be created with proper innovation policies taking the number of university researchers and their high technology level into account. The author hopes that university spin-offs will advance innovation in Japan and will contribute to the society as well as to industry as their second most important motive shows.

## References

ADT, FAB, iAi and bigego, 1998, *ATHENE-Projekt, Ausgrundungen technologieorientierter Unternehmen aus Hochschulen und ausseruniversitaren Forschungseinrichtungen.*

Albert, M., 1992, *Capitalism against Capitalism*, Whurr, London.

AUTM, 1998, *Licensing Surve: FY1997.*

Baranovsky, G.., 1999, German start-ups in the fields of high-tech and environment technology (in Japanese and German), in *Contribution from industry, universities and research institutes to start-ups of high-tech and environment technology – The Report of the Conference held in Berlin on October 12-13, 1999* –, Deutsch-Japanischer Kooperationsrat fuer Hochtechnologie und Umweltechnik (DJR), Bonn and Tokyo.

Etzkowitz, H., A. Webster, C. Gebhardt and B. R. C. Tera, 2000, The future of university and the university of the future: evolution of ivory tower to entrepreneurial paradigm, *Research Policy* Vol. **29**, 313-330.

Gates, B., 2000, *Business at the Speed of Thought: Succeeding in the Digital Economy*, Warner Books.

Jewkes, J., D. Sawers and R. Stillerman, 1969, *The Sources of Invention* (Second Edition), MacMillan, London.

Kondo, M., 2001a, Nippon no Kagakugijutsusisutemukozo to Baburukeizaizengo no Henka (The Japanese Science and Technology System and Its Change over Bubble Economy), in: *Proceedings of the 16th Annual Academic Conference of the Japan Society for Science Policy and Research Management*, 184-188.

Kondo, M., 2001b, National systems to create university spin-off venture businesses in Japan and Germany, in: D. F. Kocaoglu and T. R. Anderson (eds.), *Technology Management in the Knowledge Era*, PICMET.

Kondo, M., 2002a, *Daigakuhatsubencha no Ikusei Senryaku (Fostering Strategy for University Spin-Offs),* Chuo Keizai Sha, Tokyo.

Kondo, M., 2002b, Kyutenkaishihajimeta Nippon no Daigakuhatsubencha no Genjou to Kadai (The Current State and Issues of Rapidly Increasing University Spin-offs in Japan), *Venture Review*, No.3, 101 - 107.

Stokes, Donald E., 1997, *Pasteur's Quadrant: Basic Science and Technological Innovation,* Brookings Institution Press, Washington, D.C.

Tsukuba University, 2001, *Daigakutouhatsubencha no Genjou to Kadai ni kansuru Chousakenkyu (Study on the Current Situation and Issues of University spin-offs),* Tsukuba.

Management of Technology: New Directions in Technology Management
M. Hashem Sherif and T.M. Khalil (Editors)



# 8

# CREATING A HIGH-END MARKET FOR DIGITAL CAMERAS IN A "WIN-WIN" COMPETITIVE ENVIRONMENT – THE JAPANESE EXPERIENCE

*Dr. Yoshio Sugasawa, Graduate School of Business, Nihon University, Tokyo, Japan*
*Dr. Noboru Sugino, Graduate School of Business, Nihon University, Tokyo, Japan*

## INTRODUCTION

Digital still cameras (DSC), mobile phones, and mobile information terminal devices are products representative of growth industries in Japan in recent years. All of these products require considerable investment to develop and are in industries where high level composite technical innovation is taking place.

Following trends in DSC as an example, this paper examines what is referred to here as "Win-Win Competition", a type of Japanese competition that takes place during the creative period of new industries which successively and rapidly incorporate new technologies into their products. In a win-win competition, instead of having single winners, there is a group of winners that move in unison side-by-side such as a horizontal line . This paper examines the formation of the winning group, the subsequent process and background of the competition from the time of the growth period to the mature period of the market, during which time a narrowing down of the number of winners will takes place in a decisive showdown resulting from renewed competition among the winners. This paper also examines the structure of the competition and rapid progress in technical innovation.

## THE BACKGROUND THAT CREATED JAPANESE STYLE COMPETITION

The physical formation of the win-win competition, which can be thought of as a type of

Japanese competition, can perhaps trace its origin to the VCR *de facto* standard war, a memorable development in the history of technology in Japan. It was a struggle between the VCR β (Beta) standard, adopted by Sony, and the VHS standard, adopted by Victor and Matsushita Electric. The reason for the downfall of the Beta standard was said to have been due to the delay in the company's "disclosure of its technology".

It was the bitter lessons for the VCR Beta standard group companies during the creative period in the industrial sector where the need to "speed up the development of technology" and to "avoid exposure to development investment risk" were inevitable in Japan. After that incident, companies began to "disclose their technology" and realized that "the formation of complementary relationships in technology" among companies was inevitable. Since then, the disclosure of technology has proceeded in a positive way.

The DSC is said to be the next "crystallization of composite industrial technology" after the VCR. Based on the bitter experience and lessons learned from the VCR competition, the Win-Win Competition can be thought of as applying to conditions where certain conditions apply. This kind of competition applies to industries that can disclose information and reveal their in-house core competence, that require "composite technology, and that need a tremendous amount of development capital during the creative period of the industry."

**Table 1. Producers' Shipments - No. of DSC Units**

| Producer's Shipment＼YEAR | 1999 | 2000 | 2001 | 2002 | 2003 |
|---|---|---|---|---|---|
| Actual Producers' Shipments | 5,088 | 10,342 | 14,753 | 24,551 | 43,408 |
| Under 2MP | 3,434 | 3,834 | 3,383 | 2,476 | — |
| 2MP－3MP | 1,654 | 6,508 | 6,885 | 10,793 | — |
| Over 3MP | — | — | 4,485 | 11,281 | — |

Unit: x1000

Source: Camera & Imaging Products Association

Changes in core technology trends are presented as a parameter in "the development of high resolution image processing devices." The degree of market stimulation resulting from technical innovation becomes clear when the innovative changes we look at them are divided into the four categories as shown below. Table 1 shows the major uses according to pixel number and market category are in the following four areas: (MP = mega pixels).

| **No. of pixels** | **Major use and market category** |
| --- | --- |
| (1) 2MP and under | Toys |
| (2) 2MP – 3MP | Photo printing |
| (3) 3MP – 4MP | High quality printing |
| (4) 4MP and over | Single lens reflex, image processing, professional specifications |

**Table 2. The DSC and SHC Market in Japan**

| Producer's Shipment＼YEAR | 1999 | 2000 | 2001 | 2002 | 2003 |
| --- | --- | --- | --- | --- | --- |
| SHC | 32,391 | 32,483 | 27,392 | 23,104 | 15,617 |
| DSC | 10,342 | 14,753 | 4,485 | 24,551 | 43,408 |

Unit: x1000

Source: Camera & Imaging Products Association

We will now consider the backdrop to the dramatic decline in demand after its release of the 2MP (Mega Pixel) DSC, which was said to have image quality in no way inferior to the silver halide camera (SHC). Production of SHC decreased significantly from 2000 onwards. Table 2 shows an about-face in the direction of the SHC and DSC market scale after peaking in 2002.

**Table 3. Functions and Performance of Models Selected by JCII as Groundbreaking Cameras**

| YEAR / Company Name | | 1999 | 2000 | 2001 | 2002 |
|---|---|---|---|---|---|
| M | Storage Media | Compact Flash | — | Compact Flash | SD Card Multi-Media card |
| | Total number of pixels | 2.7MP | — | 4.95MP | 1.96MP |
| C | Storage Media | Compact Flash | Compact Flash | Compact Flash | CF Card Micro Drive |
| | Total number of pixels | 2.11MP | 2.11MP | 4.11MP | 11.1MP |
| N | Storage Media | Compact Flash | Compact Flash | Compact Flash Smart media | — |
| | Total number of pixels | 2.74MP | 3.34MP | 4.94MP | — |
| S | Storage Media | Compact Flash Smart Media | — | Memory Stick | — |
| | Total number of pixels | 2.11Mp | — | 5.02MP | — |
| F | Storage Media | Smart Media | Compact Flash Smart Media | — | Smart media Micro Drive |
| | Total number of pixels | 2.30MP | 3.40MP | — | 6.17MP |
| O | Storage Media | Compact Flash | Smart Media | Compact Flash Smart Media | — |
| | Total number of pixels | 2.11MP | 3.34MP | 4.95MP | — |

Source: Japan Camera and Optical Instruments Inspection and Testing Institute (JCII)

However, the ( - ) section, where there is no data, was prepared the same as for the previous year.

Changes in the technical innovation and resolution efficiency (including the development of high performance lenses) of image processing devices from 1999 to 2002, said to be the period of innovation in the DSC, are shown in Table 3. The dramatic increases in the pixel number from 1998 to 2003 are summarized below according to year, revealing the following changes:

1998 → Market investment in 1.5MPCCD (Charged coupled devices)
1999 → Market investment in 2MP – 2.5MPCCD
2000 → Market investment in 3MP – 4MPCCD (a temporary return to 2MP)
2001 → Market investment in 4MP – 5MPCCD
2002 → 6MP – 10MP
2003 → Market investment in Super CCD, CMOS

There was a change brought about by the sudden expansion of the market with the release of 2MP and then with the product shift to the use of 3MP, which was said to be excessive in terms specification needs. As a result, a slowing down as an indication of a change in the pace in development can be seen. This indicates hesitation by the industry attributable to the favorable response of customers.

## THE ALIGNMENT OF PRODUCTION VOLUME AND SALES VOLUME

DSC is presently positioned in an industry sector where technical innovation is particularly rapid and product development to improve the performance of pickup devices, the core component, is continuously in progress. Already future development plans are clear and the road map has been worked out in detail. Innovation in plant facilities and technological innovation is necessary to achieve the objectives and the period for achieving that is directly linked to the development of the next generation products and the period the products are released in the market.

The product life cycle and sales plans are not driven by customer needs. Instead, innovation continues largely influenced by the development of core components that will enhance the degree of the product's completion and their supply situation.

In other words, we have come to an age where the development of next generation core component technology and its achievement are directly linked to the new product release phase. Accommodating the time cycle required for technical innovation in production technology during this period, new products are released on a continuous basis about every eight to nine months.

A delay in the development or production of components can cause a shortage in stock or the loss of the market to a competitor, resulting in a sudden pile-up of dead stock. In that sense, "a side-by-side type of competition in development of technology can be quite frightening."

Even when manufacturers accept risk, because the rewards are meager, they establish ambitious, solid plans aiming at strict observation of the market investment phase for next generation models.

However, they keep drawing up production and sales plans for new products in response to the development cycles of these components. In the case of DSC, manufacturers could not keep up with the sudden increase in market demand and as a result, while they aimed for a situation where production volume equals sales volume (the sell out model), the resulting situation was: production □ demand and demand □ sales.

Although it was a "well-received product," it was manufactured in "limited supply." The reason that this shortage eventuated was due to a number of factors: the core technology was shared, "the product specifications were almost the same," "the release periods were roughly the same," and "technical innovations were basically the same." Again, it was a case of a side-by-side race where all the competitor companies lined up and moved together in the same direction at the same pace.

This is one of the major reasons why in this paper production volume rather than production demand was used to get an idea of trends.

## MARKET PROJECTIONS

To predict future market trends, we will next present a summary of trends in DSC prices and specifications.

*Current Prices.* Prices: From results of a DSC market survey, we believe that there is a demand (expectation) for prices within the $100 - $200 range. However, retail prices are actually around the $400 range, so there are still many people who feel that the price is too high.

Results of a survey on price consciousness indicate that a price range of from about $300 to $500 is expected the market sector with high resolution needs. However, there is also a latent demand among a sector who want to take photos simply so that they can see them on the spot, without keep them as a record and this group feels the investment value in the DSC to be worth about $100 to $200 from the viewpoint of their frequency of use (value) and purposes.

The memory-capacity purposes to accommodate IT to replace the usage needed in SHC with DSC and the immediate use purposes that are believed to be sought in mobile phones with camera are currently in a latent state. We believe that this situation will continue for a further two to three years. This chaotic situation is believed to be characteristic of the period of market creation. For manufacturers, these areas of demands are critical issues that cannot be ignored.

*Requirements for Image Quality and the Future Outlook.* In the short term, there has been rapid progress in the development of high resolution and the miniaturization of charged coupled devices (CCD), which are image pickup devices. There is a view that "2MP is required for photo prints" and "the standard for high vision television is 2MP," so 2MP image pickup devices were considered a condition for the dissemination of the DSC and that to surpass that level would be a technological hurdle.

There was definitely a brief period when it was believed that competition in the development of the DSC would settle at 2MP – 3MP. That it did exist is a fact. However, during the development boom of customized IC, as was also the case when during its dissemination phase multifunction IC "that could do anything" was developed, not much technical innovation was required and there was little change in cost. In the long term in an age where further miniaturization is demanded, even what might be initially considered excessive specifications, can be favorably accepted by demand groups. In the DSC, 3MP was accepted with less hesitation than 2MP. Of course, a precondition for acceptance is that there is no difference in price.

*Dissemination of DSC Image Pickup Devices and Trends.* The following are estimates of DSC ownership rates according to each DSC specification (estimates for the August 2003 period):

(1) 1MP – 2 MP Owners 30%
(2) 2MP – 3MP Owners approximately 30%
(3) 3MP – 4MP Owners just under 20%

These figures are good bases for a landslide move towards high quality pictures and this is a measurement that captured a brief moment in the market. In the market, by the summer of 2003, divergence in the two demand groups in the ownership ratio range from 1MP and 2MP could be perceived and anything above this level in high quality pictures was called "mega pixel". The sudden shift in the market in this direction that took place subsequently is now well-known. Furthermore, in product lines with high resolution of 3MP and above, including replacement demand, the market is making a dramatic shift to the DSC (according to our test calculations in October 2003, an estimate of just under 80% of buyers).

At the time 2MP and then 3MP appeared in the market, the scale of the market began to expand at a rapid rate. In the DSC market, it is likely that growth will slow down in the replacement demand sector from a level of over 60%.

As far as trends in high quality pictures go, in terms of satisfying the majority of demand, that objective has more or less been achieved. Consequently, we do not believe that there is a need to exceed 4MP. On the other hand, depending on the outcome of efforts to reduce the cost of image pickup devices, we could anticipate further advances in the development of high quality pictures.

There is another reason for the widespread prevalence of DSC which is another important factor its competitiveness. That is the development and release of printers for producing hard copies. Being able to load the images onto a computer and use a printer connected to it to do print outs, using even, for example, A-4 size printing paper, quality that allows the printout to be viewed as a photo can be maintained. This is another factor in the expansion of the market. With further development of interface functions in computers, it will continue to be an important factor.

*Requirements on Speed of Processing and the Future Outlook.* Compared with the SHC, the time lag, due to the processing time of the release time lag (the time lapse from the moment the shutter button is pressed until exposure begins) is one aspect that is perceived to be somewhat bothersome. There is a demand in development to shorten this time lag and incorporate high speed processing. These issues have already been resolved in top of the range models with the conversion from CCD to CMOS. (Widespread introduction in general models is yet to occur.) The question is by how much will manufacturers be able to cut the cost of CMOS and whether it will be enough to incorporate it into general models. This will depend on future development, but it is possible.

*Requirements on Weight and Shape and Future Development.* The Japanese have an expression "lighter, thinner, shorter and smaller", which is often a goal applied to product development. The drive to make the SDF lighter and more compact describes exactly where the current trend is. Small enough to "fit in a polo shirt pocket and light enough not to feel the weight" describes the desired requirements. For men, the demand is for a mobile phone with an attached camera that can fit comfortably in the back pocket of a pair of jeans.

In technical innovations to satisfy these demands, development is currently underway on an ultra small zoom lens, an auto focus system, and a system to stabilize the camera and prevent it from shaking. However, the functions required in a mobile phone with a camera are not just for a camera alone. The development of additional functions in mobile phones depends on what course development takes in the future and rapid progress in making them lighter and more compact cannot be predicted.

*Requirements on Interoperability with other Devices and the Future Outlook.*

- The number of people making prints on home printers across every generation is high, with over 40% to 50% doing so.
- The percentage of people using computers as a place for storing image information

is believed to be over 80%.

- Where electric transmission is concerned, the percentage of people transmitting images via e-mail is believed to still be just under 40%.

Whatever the case, the distinction and differentiation of mobile telephones is an issue in the future development of technology and a factor that will stimulate further demand. Improved operability and improved functions through the evolution in transmission technology are desired.

*Requirements on Technical Innovations in Time Availability of Batteries and the Future Outlook.*

- There has been rapid progress in carbon nanotubes and other innovations in technology. The DSC's system itself is advanced and energy efficient. Since a reduced power consumption design was developed in 2002 for CCDs and other devices, the battery issue is considered less of a problem. Nevertheless, having to recharge or replace batteries, like batteries in a watch, is perceived as troublesome, and it is clear that demands in this area will follow trends in mobile phones with cameras and attention should be paid to those trends.

*Factors Differentiating the DSC from SHC and the Future Outlook.*

- There is a demand for a system structure that can take full advantage of being able to take and view photos on the spot.
- There is the advantage of not needing to take film to developers and, in particular, it does not have the disadvantages of cost or troublesome operations.
- On the whole, transmission peripherals have not yet been developed for SHC. Continuous efforts to secure superiority in tools for loading image information onto computers are essential.

## BACKGROUND AND ANALYSIS OF COMPETITION IN THE WIN-WIN COMPETITION

Participation in the Win-Win Competition has many requirements. It demands market creation, publicity, market penetration, technical innovation introduced in a timely way while reading market demands, expertise in technology and development, ample development investment funds to provide the market with newly developed products smoothly and continuously, and management ability. The pace of technical innovation is so fast that it is hard to imagine that funds required for development investment and for the product life cycle could be recovered for one-off products.

Keeping in mind as their goal for the time being "the development of a product that was compact, reasonably priced and had the same functions and performance as the SHC," the competitor businesses drew up a plan as if it was the most natural course for them to take. However, just to get to the stage of the product concept (goal) requires enormous development investment (in people, things, money), and capital investment for technological development, product development, and mass production must be carried out in several stages.

(1) After going through several stages of product development, the companies were able to get a rough idea of "the product concept as the goal to attain". In terms of differentiation from the SHC, they eliminated the negative image aspects of the SHC, such as its limitation in resolution, and with superiority achieved over the SHC in "lightness (convenience), compactness and a low price," DSC sales began to increase suddenly. However, the creation of the market did not suddenly occur through the superiority of the product alone.

The success was due largely to the creation and readiness of the environment, thanks to the large scale adoption of IT by society in general. This included the widespread prevalence of computers (cheaper, faster, and with greater memory capacity), printers for home use at a low price, and the rapid incorporation of an infrastructure to enable electric transmission of image information.

(2) "Preparation of the infrastructure and development of related and peripheral devices were undertaken in the same period (timely) in line with market needs and purposes." In other words, technological innovation by electronics manufacturers, power companies and computer manufacturers, including innovation that was coincidental, were all highly advantageous for DSC manufacturers and a confirmed factor in making them winners.

*Use of Win-Win Competition as a Strategy and Tactics.* As can be expected, it is only natural that there will be companies that use the strategy of skipping market entry through early stage short-life products, leaning instead towards capital investment for the development of next generation models, as they keep their technical expertise in tact. However, the higher the level of product completion and market readiness, the faster the pace quickens and the amount of funds needed for plant investment and development investment become enormous.

It goes without saying that it is extremely difficult to recover capital in the short term and make a profit solely on products that have been positioned as short-life products at the time of investment. Product development based on this type of competition using the "front runner" technique (outrunning competitors by getting in the race early) and aiming for a short-term solitary run through product investment does at time reap rewards.

In addition to the method of "skipping" the initial stage entry mentioned above, there are other means of reducing investment until the development of the target product that the company has set as its goal for the time being is reached. For example, there are companies that avoid exposure to risk through decisions and policies in matters such as procurement and will, for example, procure components (important core components) and OEM, refusing to develop them in-house. All of these methods may experience some success but it is generally short-lived and does not result in significant outcomes.

The sorting of the winners from the losers does not take place at this stage. The competitors remain on a level playing field, and by postponing the decisive show-down until the next generation products, become part of a "competition" where it is extremely difficult to discern any kind of differentiation at all. To use a direct translation of a colloquialism, they are like a row of Japanese "dango" dumplings skewered on a bamboo stick. Stuck together, shoulder to shoulder, they move forward in a horizontal line.

(3) "Technical innovation and market growth" during the period of the creation of the new market results in synergy effects where the competitors follow each other toward "the rapid changes of rapid growth," that is, "group technical innovation and market creation."

*Factors and Changes Brought about by Win-Win Competition.* Electronics manufacturers already had VCR lens technology but at the time did not yet have optic technology to accommodate 2MP. Therefore, Sony arranged for Leica to supply the VCR lens while Matsushita obtained it from Zeiss. At the same time, in addition to CCD technology, optical manufacturers had a shortage in technology and facilities for miniaturization mass production of home electrical appliances and devices.

It was in this kind of environment that companies made a choice made to cooperate. As mentioned earlier, in addition to avoiding exposure to risk and as a tactic for short-life product lines, deciding which companies to cooperate was also an important issue. Insofar as possible, companies sought to build complementary relationships for component technology necessary in the composition of their products. The main criteria for establishing complementary relationships are as follows:

(1) During the market creation stage, the more manufacturers entering the market, the more the market is stimulated. Having lots of "companions" joining the market also helps in establishing de facto standards.
(2) During the period when the scale of the market is expanding rapidly, and there is pressure to satisfy the market with the supply of products, there is a belief that this kind of environment does not give rise to antagonism between competitors. This is a problem attributable to a Japanese mentality in regard to competitors, i.e. companies have little awareness of other companies as their competitors.

(3) The rapidity of technical innovation accelerates technical obsolescence, so investment efficiency is very low. Because the outlook for investment recovery is hard to predict, it is necessary to devise measures to spread development investment risk.

(4) It is a market where the road map for development of products and final development specifications can be envisioned to some extent. Investment development and expenses to prepare the development and manufacturing environment are required in a number of stages to prepare for technological development and its development environment. Therefore, idea and decision to avoid risk resulting from investment in short-life products and to survive through external procurement are also major factors.

(5) The concept of give-and-take is established. In other words, for complementary cooperation in technology and production equipment to take place, the existence of mutual benefits is a condition. In selecting partners in a relationship of cooperation, the need to choose a partner who will not become a competitor in the near future and inhibit development through use of patents or other means is a restricting factor in the choices that can be made.

(6) The continuous and consistent creation of know-how in technical innovation is not very important. Rather, the possibility of temporary cooperation which does not result in the outflow of core technology is important. On the other hand, there are also circumstances where the possibility of continuous cooperation is also required.

## CONDITIONS FOR CONTINUING A WIN-WIN SITUATION AS EXPERIENCE THROUGH DSC

The DSC market is in the period of market creation. Supply cannot keep up with the rapidly increasing demand. The environment where DSC itself is right in the middle of technical innovation is a fundamental condition for Win-Win.

*Supply of High Resolution Lenses for Electronics Manufacturers from Optic Manufacturers.* The underlying reason for handling all types of high resolution lenses, such as chromatic aberration and astigmatism types, has been based on market demands for lenses to "have minimal distortion, be light and compact" and there is a need for aspheric surface lenses. Electronics manufacturers, to avoid loss of time and investment including know-how in plant equipment and technology, have been procuring them externally. As this was a measures to overcome mentioned earlier, the existence of a technological barrier in being able to accommodate 2MP.

Among electronics manufacturers, the majority of those that have entered the DSC market already possess the technology for animated images. However, to keep from falling behind in the competition in the development of DSC and to overcome in one shot the two hurdles of achieving the high resolution that is in demands in still images and to make the units more compact and lighter, external procurement was a problem that could not be avoided.

Furthermore, almost all electronics makers have yet to perfect the image processing technology inside cameras in areas such as auto focus, auto exposure and auto white balance. Therefore, from a strategic point of view, the plan to procure internal image processing technology for cameras was a critical business issue.

*Supply of High Pixel Image Pickup Devices by Electronics Manufacturers to Optics Manufacturers.* The production of image pickup devices such as CCD, where semi-conductor manufacturing technology is also used, and high pixel CCD is in the throes of rapidly evolving technology. In addition, the manufacture of minute parts is dependent on the renewal of plant equipment where further miniaturization is taking place.

The purpose behind the miniaturization of plant facilities that optics manufacturers are promoting is to avoid exposure to investment risk in pickup devices (considered a short life item) which are evolving rapidly. Furthermore, as they try to ascertain the goals in development technology that must be achieved in the future to avoid falling behind in high resolution DSC development, they consider external procurement to secure essential core parts (believing that further innovation is going to take place) as being very important.

With technology constantly evolving, electronics manufacturers are also in the position where they have to recover their capital investment in plant equipment as quickly as possible, where obsolescence occurs at a rapid pace.

## Trends in Technological Development Hereafter and the Future of Win-Win Competition

How image quality with originality in the image quality develops is an important factor in determining the future direction Win-Win Competition will take. In component technology, product development in the following three core technologies is already underway. However, improvement will not be limited to image quality alone but will be undertaken in areas of acceleration, such as high speed shooting efficiency and high responsiveness can be expected to progress at a rapid pace.

(1) incorporation of a 4-color filter

development of a CCD which incorporates Super Hole-Accumulation Diodes (by Sony) and a commitment to supply it

(2) development of a CMOS sensor for DSC (by Canon) and its incorporation into in-house products.

(3) development of a Lateral Buried Charge Accumulator and Sensing Transistor Array (LB-CAST) using a Junction Field Effect Transistor as a sensor (by Nikon) and its incorporation into in-house products

While conditions for a Win-Win competition can be expected to continue, those manufacturers who fall behind in the development of core technology and who, in a bid to survive in the Win-Win race, may not possess core technology but may enter into relations with manufacturers who can supply. Consequently, the competition will become more and more uncertain. In the present circumstances where cut-throat competition to drive prices down even further is expected, they will have to establish survival plans as assembly manufacturers or withdraw from the Win-Win competition entirely

## SUMMARY

The Win-Win Competition framework where a narrowing down of members of the winning group is expected to occur as time goes on in the course of rapid progress in technical innovation. Win-Win Competition may simply be thought of as a business game that is like a bicycle race where "no one is looking for a decisive victory or defeat in the short term." It may be considered a process that has as its purpose of "stimulation of the market" or "creation of de facto standards." It is not a process that will have one winner but a group of winners where they will obtain appropriate, respective profits.

This kind of system is a short-lived arrangement in many cases during the market creation phase. However, it is a system that can be expected to be continued on an ongoing basis during the period when a "balance in supply and demand" and a "balance in competition in development of technology" are being established, as well as during the period when complementary relationships for core technology and other purposes are being established between companies.

Already electronics manufacturers have established lens processing technology and have also begun to acquire internal camera image processing technology. At the same time, they have already completed development of the most suitable image pickup devices for cameras. However, there is no indication of dissolution of alliances between companies. In regard to trends in the supply of component parts embodying the latest core technology, electronics manufacturers have made their position clear, but optics manufacturers have yet to give a clear indication.

It is not understood whether this slight difference is a problem related to time or whether it should be viewed as a difference in the market orientation of electronics manufacturers inclined toward mobile phones and mobile terminals, while optics manufacturers are inclined toward the DSC. Nevertheless, in view of the market scale, it is easy to imagine that an overwhelming number of manufacturers will be inclined toward mobile terminals.

In the area of mobile terminals, composite technology greater than that for DSC is required and development investment on a huge scale will be needed. Acceleration in competition to develop that technology is also expected. At the same time, of course, the market is expected to be huge, on a scale never before experienced. On the other hand, in the computer market, although the process is not the same, Microsoft has moved away from Linux and there has been a demand in the installation market for all kinds of devices to make operating systems compatible across the board, and a strategy for an alliance with TRON (The Real-time Operating system Nucleus) has already begun to take shape.

Win-Win Competition from hereon will bring about a change in competition dynamics, with a narrowing down of winners for a period. With the entry of manufacturers that have developed new technology, however, the ongoing possibilities will be enormous as the base of the industry area expands and the market grows to a stupendous size.

## REFERENCES

Brenner, M. S. (1996). Technology intelligence and technology scouting. *Competitive Intelligence Review,* **7**, 20-27.

Coburn, M. M. (1999). *Competitive Technical Intelligence: A guide to design, analysis, and action.* American Chemical Society, New York.

Fleisher, C. S. and B. E. Bensoussan (2003). *Strategic and Competitive Analysis: Methods and Techniques for Analyzing Business Competition.* Prentice Hall, New Jersey.

Herring, J. P. (1999). Key intelligence topics: A process to identify and define intelligence needs. *Competitive Intelligence Review,* **10**, 4-14.

Paap, J. E. (2002). Competitive Technical Intelligence. (Unpublished documents originally provided in California Institute of Technology Executive Program, *Managing technology as a strategic resources.*)

Sugasawa, Y. and N. Sugino (2005). In: *Management of Technology: Key Success Factors for Innovation and Sustainable Development* (L. Morel-Guimaraes, T. M. Khalil and Y. A. Hosni, ed.) pp. 219-236. Elsevier, Oxford.

Management of Technology: New Directions in Technology Management
M. Hashem Sherif and T.M. Khalil (Editors) 


# 9

# WHY DO SOME UNIVERSITIES GENERATE MORE PATENTS AND LICENSING INCOME THAN OTHERS?: THE CASE OF TAIWAN

*Yuan-Chieh Chang*[1], *Phil Y. Yang*[2*], *Ming-Huei Chen*[3] *and Chun-Yao Huang*[1]

[1] *Institute of Technology Management, National Tsing Hua University, Taiwan*

[2] *International Business Department, Central Taiwan University of Science and Technology, Taiwan* [3] *Graduate Institute of Technology and Innovation Management, National Chung Hsing University, Taiwan*

## INTRODUCTION

In the rise of knowledge-based economy, a main concern of many governments today is how to make the best use of the academic knowledge base to foster innovation and economic competitiveness. Policymakers assert that the long lag between discovery of new knowledge at Higher Education Institutions (HEIs) and its use by companies could seriously impair a country's economic growth. Therefore, changing the structure and function of HEIs has become a crucial task to facilitate knowledge flows into new sources of industrial innovation (Etzkowitz and Leydesdorff, 1997).

It has been increasingly acknowledged that HEIs are capable of making a large number of discoveries with the potential to be immediately commercialized. Various institutional and organizational innovations can be found in academia, such as the devolution of intellectual property (IP), the establishment of technology transfer/license offices, spin-offs, and incubators. Inspired by the U.S. *Bayh-Dole Act of 1980*, Taiwan enacted the *Science and Technology Basic Law* (STBL) in the late '90s, and so were Japan and Korea. The Law allowed HEIs to own patents that were created from government research grants, and removed pertinent restrictions on a more decentralized licensing policy. It is expected that academia ownership and management of IP would accelerate the commercialization of new technologies and promote economic development and entrepreneurial activity.

Prior researchers have tried to assess the effects of the *Bayh-Dole Act* on changes in market-oriented research (Thursby and Thursby, 2002), patenting and licensing (Mowery and Ziedonis, 2002), spin-offs (Shane and Stuart, 2002; Di Gregorio and Shane, 2003), and regional economies (Jaffe *et al.*, 1993; Zucker *et al.*, 1998). Moreover, Mowery and Ziedonis (2002) argued that the *Bayh-Dole Act* has contributed to the rapid emergence of new high-technology firms and fast growth of U.S. economy. However, little research has been done to examine patenting and licensing activities in economies that newly enacted technology transfer laws and regulations like the STBL. Do these countries follow the same IP protection and technology transfer pattern in the U.S.? The paper sets out to answer the question by paying special attention to the academies in Taiwan.

## Conceptual Background

*Towards a new HEI regime.* Recently, most worldwide HEIs have experienced funding cuts or stagnation from national or regional government sources (Geuna, 1999). This has also pushed Taiwanese HEIs to diversify their funding sources to fill up the declining funding share from government since 1999 (Table 1). It is worth noting that HEIs received a significant increase of funding from non-profit R&D organizations after the STBL was enacted. Moreover, through the incentive and subsidy system in HEIs, faculty members have increasingly engaged in the disclosure, protection and commercialization of their intellectual capital, making it work in more tangible forms.

Social scientists have noted that the social functions of universities have shifted from scholarly training and knowledge creation to wealth creation (Etzkowitz and Leydesdorff, 1997). HEIs nowadays play a multiple role that responsible for teaching, research, service, and innovation. This makes the knowledge-generating process of universities more inter-disciplinary, cross-institutional and application-oriented in nature (Gibbons *et al.*, 1994). McKelvey (1997) suggested that a dual transformation of universities in terms of institutional dimension and cognitive dimension. Specifically, universities knowledge-seeking activities are increasingly moving from a *scientific-government environment* or a basic scientific environment to a *scientific-economic* environment.

**Table 1. Sources of research funds for HEIs**

| Year | Industry (Million NT$)(A) | % (A/D) | Government (Million NT$)(B) | % (B/D) | Others* (C) | % (C/D) | Total (Million NT$)(D) |
|---|---|---|---|---|---|---|---|
| 1997 | 448 | 2.4 | 17,351 | 94.7 | 529 | 2.9 | 18,328 |
| 1998 | 596 | 2.8 | 20,244 | 95.1 | 451 | 2.1 | 21,291 |
| 1999 | 1,048 | 4.7 | 19,075 | 85.9 | 2,081 | 9.4 | 22,204 |
| 2000 | 916 | 3.9 | 20,483 | 86.3 | 2,340 | 9.9 | 23,740 |
| 2001 | 744 | 2.9 | 21,705 | 85.8 | 2,843 | 11.3 | 25,292 |

**Note: Others could be non-profit R&D organizations and foreign organizations*

*Source: The series of Indicators of Science and Technology from 1998~2002*

Industrial economists adopt the "market-oriented" model to analyze HEIs. The model considers academies as one of the major actors in the process of economic development. HEIs not only have to reflect more scientific and technological needs of the society, but also have to co-operate with firms, becoming the suppliers of applied knowledge (Geuna, 1999). Furthermore, the market model supports that the government should not be the only sponsor for HEIs. Universities are encouraged to actively seek funding from different sources in the competitive contract research and technology market (Howells et al., 1998). Therefore, HEIs have to demonstrate the social and economic benefits of their research in order to compete for diversified sources of funding.

*Establishment of Technology Transfer Infrastructure.* Many governments now devolve IPs derived from government-funded researches to HEIs on the assumption that the technology development gap can be bridged. The U.K. *Patent Act of 1977* and the U.S. *Bayh-Dole Act of 1980* stand as the pioneering legislations. Subsequently, other governments followed suit by promoting similar legislation such as in Japan, Korea, and Taiwan. Specifically, Taiwan's government enacted the STBL in 1999. Some science and technology (S&T) policy researchers claim to adopt "new public administration", such as Technology Transfer Offices and incubator facilities, that increases the efficiency of HEIs' operation and economic effectiveness (Etzkowitz, 2002).

Prior to establishment of the STBL, the National Science Council (NSC), a cabinet-level agency in charge of scientific development, was the sole government agency claiming IP rights on behalf of HEIs in Taiwan. Establishment of the Law has laid out fundamental principles and directions for the country's technological development. Specifically, Article 6 of the STBL allows universities and research institutes to fully or partially claims and commercializes the IPRs derived from government-funded research. The subsequent reform further specifies the distributed shares of licensing revenues among implementing institutes, inventors, and government funding agencies are 40%, 40% and 20% respectively.

We argue that the current institutional environments of burgeoning entrepreneurial HEIs provide the opportunity to adjust organizational structure and function that are beneficial to economic development. Universities are now much more likely to manage and patent intellectual property created on campus than they were in earlier periods of their histories (Shane, 2004). A direct consequence of policies to grant universities titles to inventions and requirements for disclosure and exploitation has been the creation of the technology transfer office (TTO) or an equivalent office to file patents and to deal with licensing agreements of third parties. Thus:

> *Hypothesis 1A: Establishment of technology transfer infrastructure is positively associated with HEI's wealth creation.*
> *Hypothesis 1B: Establishment of technology transfer infrastructure is positively associated with HEI's knowledge creation.*

*University-Industry links.* The triple helix regime modeled from the relations of university–industry-government, explaining that university, industry and government are intertwined in innovation networks (Etzkowitz & Leydesdorff, 1997). The shifting of universities functions towards economic creation has blurred institutional boundaries with other network actors.

Specifically, the evolution of university business incubators from isolated to networked entities indicates that traditional linear university–industry linkages have been replaced by interactive network linkages. Furthermore, due to the increasing complexity of scientific advancement and technology development, the equipment and facilities are usually too expensive to be afforded by any single party (Druilhe and Garnsey, 2001). In particular, modern technology tends to become obsolete easily so that industry-academia sharing of research equipment and facilities is believed to be a cost-saving approach.

With many governments now operating under much tighter fiscal policies, academic researchers have to seek diversified funding sources and develop mechanisms of technology transfer and commercialization to fulfill their mission of creating maximum fundamental research results with limited government research funding (Beath *et al.*, 2003). Faculties cultivate industry contacts to ensure good employment prospects for students, keep curricular up-to-date in some disciplines and obtain financial or in-kind support to reinforce and expand their research capabilities beyond what would be allowed by core funding (Shane, 2004). In responding to these transformations, the university-industry interaction has changed from previous arm's-length, short-term, and informal transaction to institutional, long-term and formal partnerships (Geisler and Rubenstein, 1989).

Not only do university-industry links augment research capacity to enhance knowledge creation, but also HEIs play an assistant role to achieve firms' legitimacy. Several studies indicate that budding firms attempt to enhance their legitimacy by identifying themselves with elite research universities (Shane and Stuart, 2002). Firms engaged in university-industry collaborations can incorporate the skills and knowledge needed into academic curricula; therefore, the legitimacy of the firms and the technologies was heightened. Moreover, firms that cooperate with HEIs capitalize on their advantages of technology development and transfer in low cost and flexible production (Feldman *et al.*, 2002).

The transition to less dependence upon government funding support will drive HEIs' relationship with industry more towards business partnership. To convince researchers to identify inventions that might be candidates for licensing, HEIs often publish information or hold conference for their researchers to explain the benefits that can result from identifying new inventions for licensing (Smith & Parr, 2003). The paper argues that the establishment of university-industry collaborations broadens HEIs' participations in applied technology, and the economical potentials of near-market technology bring HEIs more wealth creation. Thus, we hypothesize:

> *Hypothesis 2A: Establishment of university-industry links is positively associated with HEI's wealth creation.*
> *Hypothesis 2B: Establishment of university-industry links is positively associated with HEI's knowledge creation.*

*Pattern of Academic Licensing.* The theory of Resource Dependence (Pfeffer and Salancik, 1978) points out that no organization is self-sufficient and the need to acquire resources in order to develop its activities creates dependence between the organization and external actors. The nature and extent of this dependence is determined by the volume of the resources required for what constitutes the core activity of the institute (Sanz-Menéndez and Cruz-Castrol, 2003). As the share of industry research funding to total research funding is steadily enhanced, we expect that industry funding will play a crucial role in determining the development and utilization of academic research portfolio.

Fundamental to this perspective of resource dependence theory is the notion that an organization's economic actions are embedded in social networks. The triple helix regime explains that university, industry, and government are the important actors in research networks (Etzkowitz and Leydesdorff, 1997). There is a new balance between structural integration and functional differentiation in which university, industry and government are relatively autonomous but overlapping, with each taking the role of the other (Etzkowitz, 2002). The research networks of university, industry, and government tend to alter the pattern of academic research activities.

Enactment of the STBL empowers HEIs to make decision on licensing and licensee fully according to their own judgment. We argue that university-industry links provide the industrial partner the priority to acquire the license they demand. Ownership of the patented invention remains with the HEI while the firm funding the research retains the right (or option) to license the patent on a precedent basis. Thus:

> *Hypothesis 3A: Industry research funding positively moderates the influence of university-industry links on HEI's cooperator/sponsor license.*

Collective learning in regional development is similar to the concept of knowledge sharing in industry networks, which refers to exchange, assemble, integrate, and deploy knowledge across organizational boundaries. Porter (1998) pointed out that geographical concentration facilitates the interchange and flow of information between firms even though information-flows rivalry is still maintained. An industrial center generates positive externalities related to the transmission of knowledge among firms with geographical proximity (Baptista and Swann, 1998). The perspective of knowledge spillover verified that innovative activities of businesses tend to occur in the proximity of research institutes (Link *et al.*, 2003). Jaffe *et al.* (1993) investigated the citations of university patents and found that citations tend to come from the localized firms, as the extent to which knowledge spillovers are geographically localized. The regional impacts of research institutes depend on whether these institutions can provide complementary knowledge inputs to the internal innovation efforts of businesses (Henderson *et al.*, 1998).

Under the development of knowledge-based economy, academias, especially research universities, are being asked to be responsible actors for regional economic development and employment creation (Diez, 2000). The encouragement of university-industry cooperative project is set to advance patent application and technology transfer through the participation and sponsorship of research development by industrial sector. The OECD survey (2003) shows that European public research institutions tend to file most of their patents in their home states, and that fewer academic patents are filed at European level or overseas. The domestic industrial partners who support funds in developing university-industry cooperative projects have the higher possibility being rewarded as the licensee.

Once the HEIs are increasingly integrated into regional economy as one of the key drivers, we expect that the academic licensee tend to be domestic rather than foreign. Moreover, the higher cost and insufficient understanding of foreign patent application also limit the geographical scope of academic licensees.

> *Hypothesis 3B: Industry research funding positively moderates the influence of university-industry links on HEI's domestic license.*

## METHODOLOGY

*Questionnaire Design.* We developed a questionnaire based on previous research to test our hypotheses. The contents of the questionnaire consist of fours parts: (1) IP infrastructure establishment, (2) licensing activities, (3) university-industry research linkages, and (4) economic creations in HEIs. The questionnaire was pre-tested by interviewing the IP administrators in 10 different HEIs. Based on the feedbacks, we modified the questionnaire to clarify the questions that were difficult to interpret.

*Survey Scope and Response Rate.* Since this paper focuses on the study of the economic potential that embodied in Taiwan's HEIs, it utilizes the universities and colleges listed in Directory of Higher Education Institutions, Ministry of Education of Taiwan. Telephone inquiries were applied in order to construct a complete survey list of the IP managements in the HEIs. Ultimately, the study surveys 122 HEIs including 56 universities and 66 colleges. The questionnaires are mainly addressed to the director/chief of R&D offices or of Technological Co-operation offices in HEIs.

Three rounds of surveys were conducted and all the four investigators were designated for a follow-up study. For reducing non-respondent bias and increasing response rate, the third wave questionnaires were sent by express delivery to the non-respondents who ranked in the top ten HEIs in patenting activities according to the statistics of NSC. Missing values in the questionnaires were filled through telephone interviews and email contacts. Ultimately, 60 questionnaires were received, 2 were non-usable and 58 were valid. The overall response rate of the survey is 48%.

*Data Analysis.* The paper investigated main technology transfer and commercializing activities of HEIs between 1997 and 2001. Being in the early stage of development, Taiwan's HEIs generally do not own spin-offs or start-ups. We focus on the wealth and knowledge creation in the category of economic creation.

Wealth Creation: Licensing incomes and royalties are used as a proxy for technology commercialization, representative of the level of wealth creation. The natural logarithm of license incomes and royalties was calculated as the first dependent variable.

Knowledge Creation: Patent grant is the primary concern because this is the category of IP that has been the target of most recent policy reforms aimed at fostering greater commercialization by HEIs. The number of domestic and foreign patent grants was calculated as the second dependent variable.

*IP Infrastructure.* IP infrastructure is measured as TTO or equivalent office established in the sample period. Here dummy variable represents as "1" if unit establishment happened within the sample period; and "0" if did not.

University-industry link: We calculate the major research links between HEIs and industry partner in the sample period. The strength of the links is measured by looking the number of contract research projects, joint research projects, and joint research centers.

*IP Exploitation.* The number of licenses was used as the measurement of IP exploitation in the sample period. Based on the identity of licensee, the licenses are calculated as cooperator/sponsor licenses and domestic licenses respectively.

## RESULTS

The average, standard deviation, and correlation coefficient for each variable are shown in Table 2. The results of a modified Kolmogorov-Smirnov Goodness-of-Fit test support the validity of the univariate normality assumption. It shows that the establishments of university-industry links, TTO, medical school, and state-owned university are significantly correlated with wealth creation ($p < .05$). While the universities with establishments of TTO, co-research project, and research center participation are significantly correlated with knowledge creation ($p < .05$).

We regressed IP infrastructure establishment, university-industry links, wealth creation and knowledge creation while adding control variables in Table 3. TTO establishment, contract research, co-research project, and research center are employed as the independent variables. Licensing income and patent grant are conducted as the dependent variables respectively. Specifically, Model 1 and Model 4 described the possible relationships between TTO establishment, licensing income, and patent grant. Model 2 and Model 5 explained the significance after the entry of control variables. Also, Model 3 and Model 6 investigated the possible relationships between contract research, co-research project, research center, licensing income, and patent grant. The regression results show that the establishment of TTOs has a positive and significant impact on HEIs' wealth creation and knowledge creation before (model 1: β= .29; model 4: β= .16) and after the entry of control variables (model 2: β= .21; model 3: β= .19; model 5: β= .09; model 6: β= .07). Hypothesis 1A and 1B are thus supported.

**Table 2. Descriptive statistics and correlations[a]**

| Variable | Mean | s.d. | 1 | 2 | 3 | 4 | 5 | 6 | 7 | 8 | 9 | 10 | 11 | |
|---|---|---|---|---|---|---|---|---|---|---|---|---|---|---|
| 1. Wealth creation | 1.22 | 3.88 | | | | | | | | | | | | |
| 2. Knowledge creation | 2.14 | 6.22 | .45*** | | | | | | | | | | | |
| 3. Tech. transfer office | 0.38 | 0.49 | .29** | .16* | | | | | | | | | | |
| 4. Contract research | 4.45 | 2.05 | .16* | .15 | .03 | | | | | | | | | |
| 5. Co-research project | 4.76 | 20.64 | .32** | .15* | .10 | .12 | | | | | | | | |
| 6. Research center | 0.74 | 2.50 | .47*** | .46*** | .17* | .08 | .07 | | | | | | | |
| 7. Medical school | 0.09 | 0.28 | .28** | .07 | .15* | .36*** | .24** | .01 | | | | | | |
| 8. Business school | 0.84 | 0.36 | .14 | .11 | .05 | .05 | .09 | -.28** | .07 | | | | | |
| 9. Government funding | 15.83 | 3.18 | .40*** | .31** | .41*** | .25** | .26** | .27** | .06 | .22** | | | | |
| 10. Industry funding | 12.67 | 3.34 | .37*** | .29** | .41*** | .24** | .25** | .27** | .06 | .21** | .39*** | | | |
| 11.Ownership | 0.29 | 0.46 | .25* | .01 | .31** | .25** | .25** | .07 | .28** | .02 | .28** | .27** | | |
| 12.HEI type | 0.43 | 0.49 | .28** | .24** | .20* | .16* | .20* | .11 | .09 | .01 | .58*** | .57*** | .20* | |
| 13. IP exploitation | 0.27 | 1.09 | .30** | .03 | .15* | -.03 | .16* | .04 | .06 | .11 | .12 | .12 | -.02 | .13 |

*[a] N = 174 (58 cases multiplied by three periods), * p < .05, ** p < .01, *** p < .001*

In Table 3, Model 3 shows that research links with industry are important to wealth creation than in model 2. Co-research project and research center establishment have significantly positive influence on creation of licensing incomes. The number of contract research projects shows positive but not significant correlation with the licensing income. Moreover, Model 6 shows that university-industry links are important to knowledge creation than in model 5. Joint research projects and research centers have a significantly positive influence on patent grants. Again, contract research shows positive and insignificant influence on patent grants. The HEIs with substantial research links with industry create more opportunities of licensing and patenting. Hypotheses 2A and 2B are generally supported.

Table 4 reveals the influence of university-industry links on cooperator/sponsor license and on domestic license. Model 1 presents that university-industry links have positive and insignificant influence on cooperator/sponsor licenses. However, the interactions of industry research funding and contract research or research center participation have significantly positive impacts on cooperator/sponsor licenses, thus partially supporting Hypothesis 3A. Similarly, model 3 presents that all university-industry links have positive and insignificant influence on domestic licenses. However, the interaction of industry research funding and co-research project has significantly positive impacts on domestic licenses, thus generally supporting Hypothesis 3B.

**Table 3. Effects of IP infrastructure and U-I links on economic creation[a]**

| | **Wealth Creation** | | | **Knowledge Creation** | | |
|---|---|---|---|---|---|---|
| **Variable** | **Model 1** | **Model 2** | **Model 3** | **Model 4** | **Model 5** | **Model 6** |
| IP infrastructure | | | | | | |
| Tech. transfer office | .29*** | .21** | .19** | .16* | .09$^{+}$ | .07+ |
| U-I research links | | | | | | |
| Contract research | | | .03 | | | .06 |
| Co-research project | | | .14* | | | .14* |
| Research center | | | .30*** | | | .46*** |
| Controls variables | | | | | | |
| Medical school | . | .29*** | .16* | . | .06* | .11* |
| Business school | . | .17* | .11$^{+}$ | . | .14$^{+}$ | .07 |
| Government funding | | 2.63*** | 2.17*** | | 1.22* | .65* |
| Industry funding | | 2.45*** | 2.02*** | | 1.08$^{+}$ | .46* |
| Ownership | | .11 | .04 | | .15* | .25** |
| HEI type | | .07 | .05 | | .09 | .05 |
| Model F | 15.28 | 19.05 | 23.47 | 4.49 | 9.74 | 18.89 |
| Adjusted $R^2$ | .18 | .63 | .72 | .16 | .38 | .62 |

[a] *For all models, N= 174 (58 cases multiple by three periods), standardized coefficients are shown.*

$^{+}p < .10$; $*p < .05$; $**p < .01$; $***p < .001$

**Table 4. Effects of funding sources and research links on pattern of licensing[a]**

| Variable | Cooperator/sponsor license | | Domestic license | |
|---|---|---|---|---|
| | Model 1 | Model 2 | Model 3 | Model 4 |
| U-I research links | | | | |
| Contract research | .09 | .30 | .01 | .06 |
| Co-research project | .06 | .72 | .71*** | 2.01*** |
| Research center | .01 | 1.06 | .05 | .11 |
| Interactions | | | | |
| Industry funding × | | | | |
| Contract research | | .48* | | .13 |
| Co-research project | | .62 | | 2.72*** |
| Research center | | 1.09* | | .09 |
| Controls variable | | | | |
| Government fund | .07 | .06 | .08 | .01 |
| Model F | 6.73 | 8.24 | 16.94 | 17.92 |
| Adjusted $R^2$ | .34 | .46 | .54 | .61 |

[a] *For all models, N= 174 (58 cases multiple by three periods), standardized coefficients are shown.*

$^{+}p < .10$; $*p < .05$; $**p < .01$; $***p < .001$

## Discussions and Conclusions

The function of academic research has long been promoting knowledge creation. Knowledge so created in HEIs should be shared to enhance the public welfare. However, the "wealth creation" that originates from academic research results tends to be exploited for private interests of universities, professors, or industrial partners. This incurs substantial doubts that commercialization of university knowledge could deteriorates the nature of university knowledge base. This study, an initial step in this direction, indicates IPs management and research linkages of HEIs have been boosted since 1999, upon enactment of the STBL. It has expanded previous work on the links between IP management, research networks, and economic potential in terms of knowledge creation and wealth creation. The empirical results demonstrated that the management capability and university-industry partnership have

Management of Technology: New Directions in Technology Management
M. Hashem Sherif and T.M. Khalil (Editors)



# 10

# SECTOR-BASED VS. NATIONAL-BASED EXPLANATIONS OF THE TRIPTYCH GOVERNMENT / INDUSTRY / ACADEMIC RESEARCH IN DEFENCE RELATED R&D PROJECTS: INSTANCES FROM FRANCE, THE UK AND THE USA.

*Valérie Mérindol & David W. Versailles*[1]
*Research Centre of the French Air Force*

## INTRODUCTION

For decades, the explanation of Defence decision processes occurred in the general framework of the military industrial complexes. This system can be described as a web of interactions within stable relations where the ministries of Defence played a leading role due to their three-part function as the sole client (monopsony), the resource allocator through the discretionary budget and as the industrial operator (State- owned defence-related industries). The cuts in military budgets at the end of the Cold War era and the tremendous rise in

[1] The authors are grateful to Didier LeGall and to Hashem Sherif for the support received in the preparation of the manuscript. Ideas expressed in this communication are those of the authors and neither commit the French ministry of Defence nor the French Air Force.

equipment costs have challenged the leading position of the States in the Defence/Security related issues. Today the model of the military industrial complexes does not apply anymore as such and governments have to find out new interactions with the industry and with the world of academic research. This contribution elaborates on knowledge-based explanations of the various interactions. As Drucker (1993) suggested the main challenge to Defence policies relates to the capacity to self-transform, abandon obsolete knowledge and the related practices and learn to create new paths to innovate and improve knowledge productivity. This challenge dominates the management of R&D for the time-being, the agenda becoming highly difficult for the ones working at the same time under the constraints of a technologically-intensive environment and with the pressure of the return on investment logic related to the commercial markets. This double phenomenon explains why the industry and the administration do move at different speeds on their respective learning paths. The defence industry has wide latitude to amend its R&D projects because their budget is largely self-financed and depend directly on the initiative of the industry. Interactions in the economic process are now featuring an open network of actors where the government's influence is diluted. At least in Europe, the military has lost vis-à-vis the other administrations most of its ability to direct R&D according to its view on potential threats. Today in Europe, this open network includes non-coordinated national states with European industrial companies each following their own strategies. The stable relationships of the past are no longer stable and the old closed networks have been replaced by open networks of parties that each pursue its own strategy without coordination with the other parties. Innovation results from a complicated arrangement of a market process and of non-market institutional features (Romer, 1993).

Considering the sums dedicated to weapons acquisition and their relative importance in the budget of any country that wants to sustain its own armed forces, we want to contrast national and sectoral systems of innovation in order to understand the specificities of Defence-related issues of innovation. Huge reforms have affected Defence-related organizations in the last decades yet all policy objectives remain specific in the various countries. All actors now experience new relationships to fulfil their various tasks. France, the UK and the USA still devote an important part of their national budget to Defence and the reform processes do not endorse the same options. Even though France has not modified its basic defence strategy, several organizational reforms induced by inter-services and budgetary rationalisation have affected the French ministry of Defence (MoD) and, more specifically its Procurement and R&D agency (called DGA). The USA have made deep cuts in their Defence budget and in the format of the armed services but the main outline of the military-industrial complex still holds. The UK has completely reorganized its MoD, with the most spectacular decision being the split of the MoD Defence and Research agency DERA into a public Laboratory (DSTL) and a private company called QinetiQ. This contribution will elaborate on the recent evolutions in the USA, France and the UK in order to explain that the difference between sector-based and national-based explanations of Defence-related innovation processes has faded away. We will stress that the explanation can benefit from the appraisal of knowledge exchanges as they are now analyzed by knowledge-based economics.

Following Kline and Rosenberg (1986), we reject the 'linear' view of innovation processes, and portray technology policies as a nexus of feedback loops involving scientific, technological and design activities, engineering, research and practice. When analysing these interactions in the scope of knowledge-building, it becomes possible to improve the study of the governance of innovation by taking into account the tacit parts of knowledge-production. The issue of governance in project management has become central because the boundaries between civilian and military activities, between public and private sectors portray very loose dichotomies. At first glance, these characteristics may give the impression that our contribution about innovation takes place on the basis of organizational and individual skills, while we are explicitly concerned with *knowledge*. The economic agents in the R&D process all feed their decisions on procurement, schedules, optimal levels of (public) expenses, industrial policies through networked activities that overlap the military and civilian sectors. The opposition usually arises between two types of explanations: national and sector-based systems of innovation do not account for the same interactions and knowledge networks. This paper will focus on networking around innovation and technology policies. We make the point that 'knowledge engineers' (as Nonaka coins them, for instance 1995: 49-50) play a key role as facilitators of knowledge creation, coping dynamically with both the assets and the skills of all actors to the national systems related to the production of Defence/Security programs. Yet in making the point that 'experts' play a major role both in the industrial process and in policymaking, we still need to point out the dynamics related to the skills and assets in the industry and in the administration.

The analysis carried out through this contribution builds upon the notion of localized technological knowledge and suggests that the exchange of technological knowledge is not a spontaneous process. The theme has been developed several times (Antonelli 2003; Guilhon 2001; DiBiaggio 1999) and relates to the literature dedicated to quasi-markets for technological knowledge. The emergence of markets for knowledge results from a complex institutional process with a strong collective character. Management of knowledge depends on individual behaviours embedded in organizational constraints and in socio-economic contexts (Rooney and al., 2003:12; 13). Knowledge can be grasped at both the individual and collective levels. At the micro level, knowledge is rooted in a trial and error process (Boland, 2003; Popper, 1972) confronting individuals through reception and diffusion instances. At the collective level, the main problem relates to the elaboration of the language and of the paradigms necessary for living and behaving efficiently together. Collectively, creation and diffusion of knowledge imply to take into account three dimensions: time (history), space and institutional interactions. This amalgam between the knower and his environment is a reality and has to be taken into account to interpret the "architecture" of knowledge inside a national and regional dimension.

The acquisition of external knowledge and its recombination with internal R&D activities is affected by the broad evolution of the general context of the technological markets. Defence-related technologies depend on knowledge blocks the specialization of which favours the blooming of knowledge markets. Consistently with the current literature on knowledge management, it happens that the analysis has to pervade the cognitive logic of the situation giving birth to the results of innovation.

Our arguments will address first the new organization of the triptych State – Science - Industry and then will characterize the industrial organization between the State and the industry. We will not address specifically the aspects related to the various aspects of the third member of the triptych. The first part of this communication will focus on the importance of the evolution of knowledge and expertise boundaries among the actors committed to Defence technological innovation. Specifically we address the new specificities of Defence- and Security-related activities: military-industrial complexes, boundaries among public-private, public-public and private-public realms of intervention (depending on who endorses the initiative in the process). The second part of this communication will refer to new tools in network analysis. They make possible the confrontation between the relevance of national-based and sector-based explanations of Defence innovation. An examination of knowledge processes will be developed in this paper and we will conclude that international and sectoral invariants in the Defence R&D now greatly overlap each other. The originality of national-based and sector-based explanations of innovations in Defence industries now fades away and both explanations merge together.

## KNOWLEDGE-PRODUCTION FRONTIERS AND THE TRIPTYCH STATE-SCIENCE-INDUSTRY

Elaborating complex and novel arms systems rests on a continuous interaction between the administration, the industry (engineers) and scientists (for instance academics). This interaction takes place from the earliest stages of the research and development phases on, because the actors to the process all occur to master knowledge and series of data necessary to the elaboration of complex programs: technical knowledge, operational knowledge, financial data, program management, etc. Technological innovations are generated and introduced into the programs in elaborating upon the variety of competencies and the localized sets of knowledge making the originality of each participant to the program (Antonelli, 2003). The generation and introduction of such innovations appear therefore as the result of complex alliances among different groups of agents who value local complementarities and knowledge convergence. The alliances always rest on alliances of actors, shaped broadly by the conditions of the various technological markets. The main issue deals with access to the information and knowledge mastered by the actors in the triptych (Pollock, 2002; Barzelay and Thompson, 2001), and with the production of knowledge and the management of their boundaries by each and every agent in the triptych. This section will first describe the specificities of Defence sectors (1.1) and then investigate new national forms for the interaction among public and private actors (1.2).

*Defence sector specificities/recurrent and new features.* Elaborating a complex program requires knowledge and data that are not exclusive to firms and networks of firms but that pervade the whole system, including clients, suppliers, and partners (Heraud & Cohendet, 2001). Thus, external knowledge is an important input in the process of producing the new knowledge. The boundaries among their knowledge sets become therefore difficult to grasp – if ever possible to identify. Interdependence arises from the dissemination of heterogeneous (disparate) knowledge among the actors so that knowledge complementarities support the emergence of new technological assets. Market transactions play only a trivial / partial role in the understanding of such a phenomenon. As Antonelli (2003) points out, knowledge interactions remain much more relevant, because they convey a variety of actors and institutions that represent all branches of the triptych administration/industry/science.

The traditional economic literature on the topic invokes the existence of costs of exclusion. Knowledge and information are deeply embedded in the various actors of the triptych; their production and transmission are not managed at the level of the whole group, but rather in bilateral relations. Here arises exclusion traditionally in the form of intellectual property rights. Like in civilian commercial markets, monopolistic control of knowledge not only prevents uncontrolled leakage (and hence the dissemination of knowledge), it also precludes further recombination of the alliances among the actors who master the relevant knowledge. This makes the notion of exchange slightly more complicated when dealing with knowledge, because the reasons, the content and the context of the exchange differ within each (bilateral) interaction. These imbrications lead to potential competition between the participants to the triptych, and hence to voluntary restrictions on knowledge transfer. This framework reveals clearly that the counterpart to the costs of exclusion lies precisely in the duplication of expenses (in turn incurring a social cost). Complementarities of knowledge present quickly another problem: its indivisibility in the framework of the program. Altogether, these arguments explain the alliances in the various Defence/Security-related technological areas after the reorganization held in the 1990s both in the USA and in Europe, even though the general framework of relationships is no longer stable.

Let us illustrate the complexity of the current triptych administration / industry / science by focusing on the role that the French national office dedicated to the development of research in the aeronautic sector (ONERA) plays in the industrial process. It functions at the same time as an expert for evaluation on behalf of the French MoD and as an independent research institute cooperating with the private industrial firms in the development of the programs (Mérindol, 2005). The issue of positioning ONERA inside the French innovation system relates directly to the position of its expertise in the process of elaborating aeronautic programs. The ambiguity arises when setting up the very same ONERA expertise as constitutive of actions led at the same time by private and public interests which happen to evolve sometimes inconsistently one with each other. In the USA, military laboratories represent the pool of expertise enabling the Department of Defence (DoD) to direct and prescribe the technological options in the armament programs, and they represent at the same time a duplication of the capacities present in the industry (Gansler 1995). If some inconsistency is to occur, it does not take place inside the Pentagon as is the case which ONERA, but inside the military-industrial complex broadly stated.

These elements characterize the Defence sector. When Defence expands into Security, the role of production and transmission of knowledge cannot remain particular to the defense sector. This is a common feature to all knowledge-intensive sectors and relates to the importance of user communities in the innovation process. The only specificity of the

Defense-related areas (production, research, etc) lies in the specific role of the State because of the monopoly of the exercise of the armed force. The State is therefore the only client of military technological programs, even though the broader concept of Security makes it possible to enlarge the content of the so-called Defence monopsony. This evolution tends to extend the notion of public good and to increase the interest for the development of a specific research about the nature of the collective action mobilized by the dynamic of innovation (Romer, 1993). At the same time, even if the notion of 'public good' holds in the realm of Defence/security issues (non-rivalry, non-excludability), the ideal form of 'pure' public goods disappears progressively with the transformation of the concept from Defence into security. Defence represents one of the very few instances of pure public goods, because the clause of indivisibility applies more than in any other field.

To some extent, the appropriation of security by the actors (individuals, firms) benefiting from it services can occur, and therefore non-excludability and the collective character of consumption might help differentiating it from the various functions of Defence and Security. 'Pure' public goods relate to the characters of their collective consumption (non-rivalry) and it is difficult to conceive an individual appropriation of Defence services as such. When dealing with Security as an extension of Defence in the realms that it did not pervade before in the economy and in the society, it becomes compulsory to invoke that the recent evolution of the various threats and constraints has induced an evolution of the position of the State in the innovation process: obviously new 'global' responsibilities, new intervention modes in the economy, new competencies are now required. But the main difference between Defence and Security on one side and security on the other side shows off when differentiating between the services associated in every day life for the individuals and the firms: as a part of a global strategy, the interactions inside the triptych proceed from a pure public good (as much as Defence and Security) whereas the services associated to the implementation of security do not (for instance the services provided by private contractors and mercenaries). The interactions between the State and the other actors to Defence-related R&D arise in the process of the constitution of the elements (mainly knowledge) required to build up the basics for a strategy.

*New national forms for the interaction among public and private actors.* Broadly stated, the evolution of the frontiers between the private and public sectors are induced by the reduction of Defence budgets and the repositioning of the ministries in charge of Defence among the institutions. The reforms brought into the national systems of innovation since the beginning of the 1990s have put the expertise of the State as a user under question. The privatization of UK Defence evaluation and research agency (DERA) has drained "internal" pool of expertise of the MoD in a very different way as it has been separated into two organizations: the MoD agency called DSTL (Defence science and technology laboratories) and the private company QinetiQ. The issue about expertise relates to the fact that DSTL now comprises only 25% of the R&D personnel of the former DERA. The separation of DERA into DSTL and QinetiQ has been justified by the insufficient knowledge and technology transfers from DERA to the industry, and especially to the first level contractors in the programs (James & al, 2003). This situation contrasts sharply with the USA, where the Pentagon retains a wide variety of scientific and technological competencies in the military labs. In the USA, the efforts to streamline are borne by the industry. This illustrates that the frontier between public and private sectors does not show the same picture in all countries, which is somehow trivial, yet a specific separation always exists between the actions prepared for the public and private interests.

Three major arguments make it possible to apprehend the public-private separation. They refer to the new importance of the production of knowledge and information in the emergence of innovation and in the economic process (Petit 1999: 43-6). The situation is related to major changes which appeared during the 1990s in the Defence area. The consequences of these changes in the international context have led to a different appreciation of the relations inside the triptych State/science/industry. Let us elaborate on some points to explain this evolution.

- The first point relates to the emergence and diffusion of the information and communication technologies (ICT). This phenomenon does not affect deeply the problem of the appropriation of knowledge. New organizational paths using the ICT are needed, setting up the conditions of a better and sooner mobilization of a greater amount of knowledge and data. This means the development of appropriation abilities that are better suited to the new technologies. The nature of competencies, the organizational paths, the communication ways have to follow consistently. In the various countries, ICT use varies greatly. In the USA, ICT use by the acquisition services of the DoD happens to be one of the true improvements of the acquisition reform, with the constitution of many technical and financial data bases, shared by the public and private actors (Lebowitz, 2000; Chinworth, 2000). In the United Kingdon, ICT use is still limited inside the MoD according to the National Audit Council (NAO, 2002). The French situation is not any better and mainly focused on the procurement processes.

- The second point deals with the rise in the qualifications in the industry, whatever the sector. In the Defence-related industries, as in other knowledge-intensive sectors, these abilities are essential because they represent a condition necessary to take advantage of the innovations and of the new technology opportunities (DiBiaggio 1999). In the Defence sectors, this phenomenon reveals also that the partnerships between the State, the world of the scientists and the industry has evolved because all individuals have achieved higher standards. What are the required competencies? How to generate them? How to use and coordinate all of this in the elaboration of armaments industrial programs? This issue is central to inquire the coordination between public and private actors: the intensification of the relationships between the industry and the military depends directly on the technical and commercial expertise the public agents will be able to demonstrate on behalf of the user [the State] (Merindol 2003).
- The third point is concerned with globalization which has modified the scale and strategy of the actors in the area of knowledge production. The activities of the State must therefore adapt to maintain its ability to master and re-use knowledge and this holds as a goal in the definition of the strategy. Internationalization of R&D makes the management of knowledge and data more strategic and more complex, because the relationships take place inside open networks. Having there the data available for the Defence/Security programs makes it possible to evaluate the weaknesses and strengths of the national innovation system and, as a consequence, to identify the challenges to attain efficiency in technical R&D and product innovation. Determination of the sectors appropriate for the programs efficiency requires a deep knowledge of markets and technology. This situation not only makes obvious the importance of firms and industrial groups in the triptych, it does also suggest that these industrial actors are in the best place to bring together the needs and the underlying technologies (Metcalfe & Georghiou 1998). Just because their activities are organized and coordinated at an international level, industrial groups are in a position where grasping the uses and opportunities of the technologies is possible, and efficient. This is the reason why the traditional border line between private and public sectors becomes loose.

What appeared as a general tendency for the Defence sector disappears because each country makes up now a specific position for the borderline between public and private responsibilities. Even the very notion of responsibility does not entail the same content in the various countries considered when dealing with public and private actors. The Foresight Science & Technology actions developed in the UK and in the USA around the military rely on a narrow collaboration among private and public actors, which are mobilized both in the public decision processes and in the coordination of public policies. The industry now plays a crucial role in making up the policy related to military R&D processes (Mérindol, 2003). In particular, in such a period of important public reforms, incentives have become really high for the industry to collaborate with the administration to promote new public actions on one side, new public and private behaviours on the other one. The US and UK reforms in Defence acquisition policy show that the collaboration with the industry is now considered as the best way for the State-user to learn the practices consistent for managing complex systems facing an instable socio-economic context (Chinworth, 2000). The culture and habits prevailing inside the French administration are based on a concept of strong internal public expertise for policymaking. The French situation contrasts sharply because the public-private parternerships are somehow limited (Mérindol, 2005).

## KNOWLEDGE-BASED EXPLANATIONS OF DEFENCE INNOVATION NETWORKS

*National-based explanations contribute to Defence-related innovation.* The most important element considering the Defence industrial base relates to the end of the so-called monopsonies. The USA remains the only country where a military industrial complex works within a stable framework of relations between State-science-industry (Versailles, 2005). In fact, this complex can be considered as an emanation of the Pentagon: there is no such thing as a necessity to coordinate through specific actors because the DoD plays its part as a user and as a partner in the industrial policies mainly through the federal budgets.

This situation clearly diverges from the one existing in France and the U.K., where civil ministries are traditionally in charge of this kind of intervention in the economy. As a consequence, European industrial groups have to use and invent innovative organizational ways to interact with the States still retaining sovereignty capacities such as France or the UK. The problem comes from the budget, because these States cannot afford the armaments as easily as they used to do it in the past, and are now akin to sacrifice the preparation of long-run investments in order to appropriate the acquisition budgets in the short-run. This is not a matter of ideology, but rather a manifestation of budgetary pragmatism and intertemporal arbitration. The situation becomes only more difficult with the States that avoid deliberately "of the shelf" appropriation. On the industry side, this situation becomes uneasy because companies rely on governments for orders. If the governments only want to afford "of the shelf' components, the industry will not be able to generate the benefits and returns allowing for R&D and new products. They will have to connect to the networks of the US military-industrial complex that remains the only source of important R&D budgets. Firms, whatever their size and technological niche on the market, need to finance R&D investments and want to account returns on investments. The science part of the triptych remains dependent on the budget introduced by the other actors and cannot but adapt because the opportunities to self-financed activities are scarce if even possible.

Over the last decade there have been several new concepts emphasizing the systemic characteristics of innovation. Defence-related activities used to relate easily to the concept of national system, but this concept and its analytical framework do not meet easily the current evolutions of Defence and Security. The concept has evolved, as it is described by Lundvall *et al.* (2002): its logic passed from a combination of production-related arguments towards the relationships contributing to competence building. It is worth focusing on the arguments developed by Lundvall *et al* (2002) because their argumentation contains all the points relevant for the discussion of the issue. Even though some points mentioned by Lundvall *et al* can be endorsed easily, the reasons for the relevance of the national-based arguments in Defence-related innovation do not meet those mentioned by the authors: the reference seems easy, actually, because Defence and Security relate systematically to national strategies. How is it then possible to argue in favour of national-based explanations? All explanations of Defence and Security specificities actually cope with the close relationship between R&D, competence building and production.

Lundvall *et al* (*cf.* 2002: 214) refer to the impact on innovation of a specific combination of economic policy, economic interdependence, and economic change. Considering Defence R&D or innovation in respect to this argument, the reference to national systems might be disputed. On the one hand, the clear link to a main national authority, namely the ministry of Defence, seems at first glance easy to grasp because of the various macroscopic elements driving the innovation process related to Defence and Security. On the other hand, according to the authors, this concept has been raised in the theory in order to depict the systems made up to overcome the extreme division of the policy institutions and policy analysts committed to the public decision processes, and therefore providing innovation policies with a specific consistency at a national level. In such a sovereignty area as Defence, the usefulness of the concept 'national system' might be loose in comparison with the other realms of its application, which at least conflicts the authors' explanation. At first glance, and in reference to the arguments developed by Lundvall *et al* (2002) themselves, a close analysis of both the structure of the system (the outputs and the related competences) and of the institutional set-up (interaction between production, innovation, learning and rationality of the agents) make Defence a dedicated case enforcing the notion of national system of innovation.

One who wants to understand it needs in reality to link together three different points. First, institutions are to be focused on as organizations committed to the promotion of science and technology, and therefore shaping innovative activities. Second, bottom-up flows of information from the end-user to the producer introduce in Defence-related areas asymmetrical linkages as a consequence of the status of State as a customer [monopsony], funder and operator. Third, even though commercial home markets might be open, Defence-related markets always remain relatively closed and protected. Long-run learning interactions and a multi-lateral system of trust relationships inside the triptych government / industry / academic research represent true prerequisites in order to develop and maintain the Defence industrial base with respect to the length of the Defence programs. Any State around the world being committed to Defence and Security functions by nature, the reference to a national system of innovation might not surprise, because of the need of a specific national consistency. In reality, the reference to national-based explanation of Defence R&D seems tautological or at least trivial.

*The transformation of Defence innovation: the sector-based explanations.* Deepening the analysis of Defence-related R&D makes it compulsory to investigate the details of learning and competence building, because the various people representing the State in its different functions need to cover efficiently all required parts (Versailles, 2005). As pointed out by Lundvall *et al.* (2002: 224-5), it has become most important to address the various components of the new context coined out as 'learning economy': speed of learning, new forms of co-operation and competition, new forms of governance. Not only do networks as such become the object of economic analysis (as referred to by Lundvall *and al*, 2002: 224-5), but they have also become a tool intended to deepen the understanding of interactions. Here the arguments in favour of the concept national system of innovation join the results provided by the sociology of social networks, grasping some social elements related to the innovation processes around a legitimate national mobilization of efforts and a coordinated policy effort. Is this truly different from a sector-based system? In Malerba words (2002: 247), "a sectoral system has a specific knowledge base, technologies, input and demand". Defence-related activities (for instance the Defence industrial base) perfectly correspond to that concept either.

As a matter of definition, a sectoral analysis (or a sector-based demonstration) mainly refers to the role of non-firms organizations, to knowledge and learning processes, to the wide range of relations among agents. The transformations of the sectors may be appraised in the various respects of their boundaries, of their actors, of their products and of their structure(s). The various points which characterize the sectoral analysis perfectly account for the framework of Defence and Security. Despite the fact that Defence-related activities entail a broad heterogeneity in experience and competencies, the cognitive and organizational analysis makes it obvious that public and private actors of the sector exhibit convergent and consistent aspects. This is an instance of the relevance of the analysis of Defence and Security as a sector. The main processes raised by Malerba (2002: 249) perfectly apply to Defence and Security and provide us with another framework, which enlightens specific aspects of the interactions between the actors of the triptych.

Here the main point making the national-based and sector-based interpretations convergent comes up. The sector based analysis does insist on the fact that learning, behaviour and capabilities are 'bounded' by the technology, the knowledge base and the institutional context in which all these heterogeneous agents act and react. Dealing with Defence-related activities, this convergence relates to the way institutional settings emerge from the interaction between public and private actors in charge of Defence programs. The convergence originates in the interactions evocated here between public and private organizations, which all make up the conditions of emergence of a similar range of learning patterns, behaviour and organizational forms. According to Malerba (2002: 251), a sectoral system roots in five building blocks: knowledge base and learning processes; basic technologies, inputs and demand with key links and dynamic complementarities; type and structure of interactions between firms and non-firms organizations; institutions; processes of generation of variety and of selection. Dealing with the Defence and Security innovation, it is possible to find international invariants at each of these levels. Public-public interaction refers to the relationships between the various servants in charge of representing the functions of final user, of program specifications writer, of regulator making up the various aspects of industrial and public policy. Even if the national answers can diverge from country to country according to the specific cultures and traditions, all these functions do exist in any country and manifest the standard functions of the States. Private-public interaction refers to the ways the industry negotiates and adapts to the specifications and regulations edited by the administration. It also evocates the different propositions made up by the industry in order to confront successfully to the invitations to tender. Dealing with Defence and Security innovation, the clue to the convergence of sector-based and national-based explanations lies in the fact that the international invariants in Defence-related innovation patterns, which are constitutive of the sector-based description, complement exactly the boundaries of the related national systems.

How is it then to be distinguished between the characterizations of Defence innovation as a national-based and a sectoral-based system? It might be even possible to dispute whether we need to distinguish between both explanations. Malerba (2002: 255) argues that firms are the key actors in sector-based systems because they focus on users and suppliers, the role of the users being 'extremely important' in several sectors. Defence-related innovation can be characterized by close relationships between supply and demand, knowledge and competencies interacting in various ways. The embedded-ness of the various (public and private) actors makes obvious that the state is at least as much a key actor as the 1st level contractor in the Defence-related industrial process. Public actors occur to contribute as much to the patterns of innovation as the firms and the very same cognitive and organizational process makes up the patterns of the sector-based and national-based characterization. In the end, the demarcation between both conceptual contributions mainly depends on the issue at stake, which remains closely associated to the policy objectives under consideration. Sector-based and national-based explanations merge into a broader explanatory apparatus which covers together all aspects of the topic.

## CONCLUSION

Inquiring knowledge production becomes relevant to grasp the relationships inside the triptych State – Science – Industry, which reveals the necessary overlapping of the expertise domains. Up to a certain point, such an overlapping could be interpreted under the light of complementarities between the (knowledge-) assets involved, or could sketch the enumeration of the specialized technological inputs to a productive system.

Our point in this contribution was to exemplify that the production and management of knowledge in Defence-related areas relates now to a complex social distribution. Places where the relevant knowledge is created are multiplying and this very situation makes the reference to a sector-based or national-based reference highly difficult. This contribution has discussed both the sector-based and the national-based explanations of Defence and Security interactions. It has explained that the originality of both concepts is fading away because of the specificities of Defence activities: international invariants in public-public and public-private interactions relating to the sector and the national originalities overlap. Defence- and Security-related policies need to be assessed with respect to both conceptual frameworks which provide us with a systematic explanatory apparatus of the interactions between the government, the industry and the world of academic research.

## REFERENCES


Antonelli, C. (2003). *The economics of innovation, new technologies and structural change.* Routledge, London.

Barzelay, M. and Thompson F. (2001). How acquisition workforce adds value. *Acquisition Review Quartely*, winter, 31-44.

Boland, L. (2003). *The foundations of economic method, A Popperian approach.* 2nd edition, Routledge, London.

Chinworth, M.W (2000). Acquisition Reform in the United States : Assessing change. *Defense Analysis,*. **16** (2), 165-184.

Cohendet, P., A. Kirman and J. B. Zimmermann (2003). Emergence, formation et dynamique des réseaux. Modèles de la morphogénèse. *Revue d'économie industrielle*, 103 (2èmes et 3èmes trimestres), 15-42.

Conseil général pour l'armement, (2002). *Rapport d'activités 2000-2001*, ministère de la Défense, France.

DiBiaggio, L. (ed) (1999). Economie de la connaissance. *Revue d'économie industrielle,* 2em trimestre.

Dunne, J.P. (1995). The defense industrial Base. in *Handbook of Defense economics.* (K. Hartley and T. Sandler ed.), Handbook in economics **12**, vol. 1, 399-456.

Drucker, P.F. (1993). *Innovation and entrepreneurship : practice and principles.* Harper Collins,

Gansler, J. (1995). *Defense conversion, transforming the arsenal of democracy.* Cambridge Univ Press.

Guilhon, B. (2001). *Technology and markets for knowledge.* Kluwer academic press, Boston.

Héraud, J .A. and P. Cohendet, (2001). *Etude comparative entre le processus de diffusion de l'innovation issue des projets militaires et le processus de diffusion issue des projets civils*. Research project financed by the French Defense Minister (unpublished).

James, A. D., D. Cox and J. Rigby (2003). Testing the boundaries of public-private partnership : the privatisation of the UK Defence Evaluation & Research Agency. communication to the seminar *R&D Management*, july, Manchester.

Kline, S.J. and N. Rosenberg (1986). An overview of innovation. In The positive sum Strategy (Landau R. And Rosenberg N. eds.), National Academy Press, Wahington.

Lebowitz, J. (2000). CESA, the COTR Expert system aid. *Acquisition review quartely,* Summer, 131-142.

Lundvall, B.A, B. Johnson, E. S. Andersen and B. Dalum (2002). National systems of production, innovation and competence building. *Research policy*, **31** (2), 213-231.

Malerba, F. (2002). Sectoral systems of innovation and production. *Research policy*, **31** (2), 247-64.

Mérindol, V. (2003). Expertises, savoir-faire et réseaux. In *La recherche et la technologie, enjeux de puissance* (Versailles, D. W, Mérindol V. and Cardot P) Economica, Paris.

Mérindol, V. (2005). Defense RDT&E and Knowledge Management : A new inquiry into Public and public-private Coordination. *Defense and Security Analysis*, vol 21 (2), june, 159-177.

Metcalfe, J.S. and L. Georghiou (1998). Les deux piliers des politiques technologiques : équilibre et évolution. *Science technologie Industrie*,OCDE, **22,** 85-113.

Mowery, D.C (1998).The changing structure of the US national innovation system: implications for international conflict and cooperation and cooperation in R&D policy. *Research Policy*, **27**, 639-654.

National Accounting Office (2002). *Ministry of Defence : implementation of integrated project teams*. Report by the comptroller and auditor general, London.

Nonaka, I. and H. Takeuchi (1995). *The Knowledge Creating Company. Oxford* University Press, New-York.

Petit, P. (1999). Les aléas de la croissance dans une économie fondée sur le savoir. *Revue d'économie industrielle*, **88**,.41- 66.

Pollock, N. (2002). Knowledge management in acquisition and program management (KM in the AM and PM). *Acquisition review quartely*, winter, 47- 66.

Popper, K. R. (1972). *Objective knowledge, An evolutionary approach*, Oxford university press, London.

Romer, M.P. (1993). Implementing a national technology strategy with self-organization industry investment boards. in *Brookings papers: microeconomics 2,* 345-399.

Rooney, D., G. Hearn, T. Mandeville and R. Joseph (2003). *Public policy knowledge-based economies: Foundations and frameworks.* Waynes Parsons.

Versailles, D.W. (ed) (2005). , Knowledge networks, Defense Networks. Thematic issue of the *Revue d'économie industrielle*, 3em Trimestre, december.

# SECTION II

## GROUPWARE AND WEB INTERFACES

Management of Technology: New Directions in Technology Management
M. Hashem Sherif and T.M. Khalil (Editors)



# 11

# USABILITY: PROVIDING BETTER INFORMATION SYSTEM INTERACTION

*Simone Bacellar Leal Ferreira, Faculdades IBMEC*
*Marie Agnes Chauvel, IAG PUC Rio*
*Marcos Gurgel do Amaral Leal Ferreira. Holden Comunicação*

## INTRODUCTION

Information is essential to any organization's success and efficacy. Given that all organizations involve people working and cooperating together, it is important that the information flows properly through all parts of the organization. The importance of information and the globalization process are the key factors for the growth of the information technology market; information technology can be decisive to the success or failure of a company, allowing an organization to be agile, flexible and strong (Albertin, 2000). As both a cause and consequence of this fact, the Internet is changing the way in which companies function and people work. Because of this crucial role of information, organizations spend a large part of their budget with information systems, and they need quality information.

Organizations have found in web-based systems a reliable means of improving the quality and flow of information. These systems, as well as playing an important role in the treatment, processing and distribution of information, are becoming increasingly needful, not only because they permit a new modality of business, but also because they constitute an important marketing channel (Ferreira, 2001) & (Ferreira, 2004).

Since the dialogue between man and machine is established by means of the user interface, the visible part of the system, the interface becomes an important part of information systems (Tognazzini, 1995), (Shneiderman, 1997) & (Cogburn, 2003). A powerful and easy to use interface can only be developed if there is a way of guaranteeing that the NFR (non functional requirements) usability is taken into consideration at the system definition (Bias, 1994).

Usability is defined as the degree to which a product is easy and fast to learn, efficient to use, easy to remember, causing no operating errors, offering a high degree of satisfaction to the user, and solving the task it is designed for.

Failure to take NFRs into consideration has been reported in literature (Breitman et al, 1999) (Davis, 1993), (Cysneiros and Leite, 1999). This article defines the non-functional usability requirements as well as it proposes a usability taxonomy that was put together using as source the general literature on design and usability and the authors' practical experience with the topic.

## USABILITY

Only recently the matter of usability has been perceived as important to information systems professionals. Driven by the market, organizations are going online in order to position themselves on a new way of performing business. Since the technology infrastructure used to construct web sites can deal with images, sounds and text composition, it became more evident that the output of information should be treated with care (Ferreira, 2003).

Information system must be designed with the purpose of establishing a productive interaction between the system and their users in order to increase people's productivity while performing their tasks. They must satisfy the expectations and needs of their users. To achieve this end, the NFR (non functional requirement) usability must be present in any method for systems construction.

The communication between users and an Information System (IS) is established by means of the IS interface. A good IS design must guarantee a transparent communication, that is, it must assure that when a user accesses the IS to perform any task, he or she needs only to focus their energy on the intended task (Norman, 1986), (Norman, 1999) & (Jokela , 2004), (Seffah, 2004).

To have users focusing their attention mainly on their tasks, the process of software development must be "user centered", that is, its interface must be designed with the objective of satisfying the expectations and needs of users. The design of an interface that considers user characteristics and the NFR usability is a difficult process for many reasons, but most of this difficulty can be traced to the lack of attention on NFRs during the system definition process. Building systems that take in consideration NFRs, require the availability of a corpus of knowledge to help the engineer in the task of defining the system to comply with those requirements.

## USABILITY TAXONOMY

Figure 1 presents the usability taxonomy that was put together using as source the general literature on design and usability and the authors' practical experience with the topic. The usability taxonomy is organized around two main categories (Pressman, 2004): presentation and data entry.

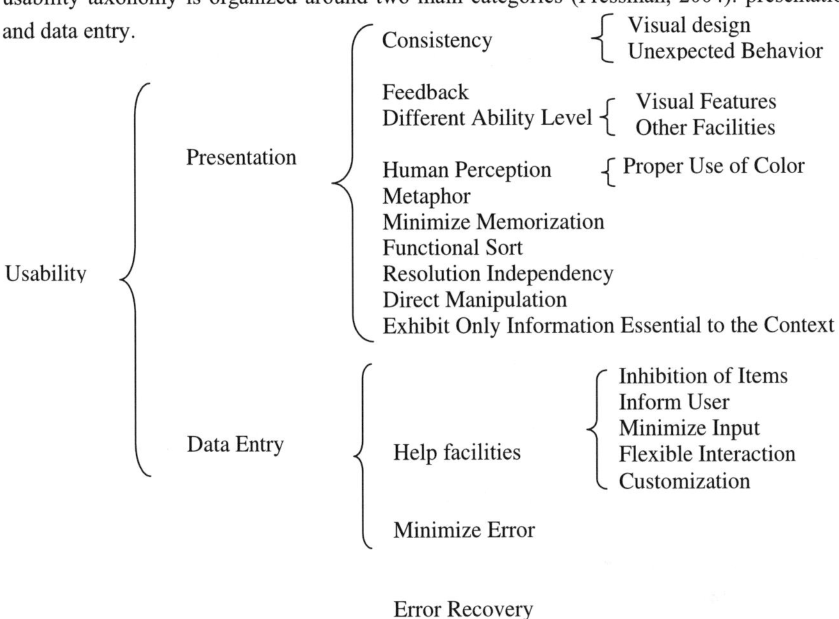


**Figure 1. Usability Taxonomy**

## PRESENTATION CATEGORY

*Consistency.* Consistency is one of the main features for the usability of an interface. It helps avoiding the frustration induced when a system does not behave in an understandable and logical way. Moreover, it allows a person to generalize the knowledge about one aspect of the system to other aspects (Foley, 1997). To be consistent, menus, commands, information exhibitions, and all the functions of an interface must have the same visual presentation (Nielsen, 2000).

*Visual Design.* Naturally all users expect to see the same layout, no matter in which part of the site they are. Menus, icons, options, figures must all be at the same position among all site's pages. Sites that change layouts between sections may frustrate users, as they expect to find the same features throughout the whole navigation process (Nielsen, 2000) & (Ferreira, 2003).

*Unexpected Behaviors.* Another serious problem often found in sites is the unexpected behavior caused by bad design. As an example, a "help" link should not take the user to a "FAQ" page, and vice-versa. (Ferreira, 2003).

*Feedback.* In any kind of communication, feedback is very important. When two people talk, they are constantly giving each other feedback through gestures, expressions and various other signs. In order to obtain a good interaction between humans and computer, reliable feedback must be supplied, however, this must be planned and programmed (Foley, 1997), (Nielsen, 2000) & (Nielsen, 2002).

A classical type of feedback presented in many information systems is the use of an hour-glass to indicate the machine is busy and that the user must wait (Ferreira, 2003). In many sites, this feedback is improved by replacing the hour-glass by an horizontal scroll bar that shows the percentage of work already performed. This is a better because it allows the user to do other things while the computer is busy.

One very good feedback often found in many e-commerce sites is the indication of the number of products already added by the user to the shopping cart and the total amount he will have to pay (Ferreira, 2003).

In well-designed sites, proper feedbacks orient the user when navigating through their pages. An example of a good feedback is when the site highlights the link that the user is about to choose. Once the user follows this link, his new location must be informed in some way. This can be accomplished by using the same name for the link and the page to which it leads (Ferreira, 2003). Another proper feedback related to links and navigation is when the site changes the appearance of visited links.

Messages must be very well selected. They cannot confuse or lead the user to hesitation. They must also take in account the security of the site. Some sites show messages when the user makes a mistake while logging on to the site; although these messages consist of helpful feedbacks, they also represent a security issue. The error messages cannot specify which mistake was made, that is, they cannot specify whether the user typed the wrong login or the wrong password. A generic "access denied" error is more appropriate in such situations.

Websites must also always exhibit messages indicating to the user what he has done, where he is, if an option is not available, if a particular page is written in another language. Good sites also must take in account the task of filling out forms and therefore must assist users in doing so. When a user needs to fill out a form, he must input data in several fields. It must be shown to the user which fields are mandatory; this could be done by putting a red asterisks beside each mandatory field. The site must also indicate what kind of data must be input (all numbers, no space etc.) (Ferreira, 2003)

*Different Ability's Level and Human Behavior.* Since an interface must be designed in such a way that it can be used by experienced users and by beginners, it must meet some requirements (Nielsen, 2000).

*Use of Visual Features.* Visual features, such as pictures and icons, are excellent tools for beginners; they help them to better visualize they actions. Another visual feature that should be used is the icon; an icon is a pictorial representation of a function, an object, an action, a property or any other concept (Foley, 1997).
Well designed icons can be recognized faster than words; if well chosen, they become independent of language, making the use of the interface possible to users who speak different languages. Well-designed icons should have the following properties:

Easy Recognition: how long it takes a user to find out their meaning.

Easy to remember: how long it takes a user to recall its meaning.

Easy to discriminate: how easy is it to a user to recognize the icon among other icons.

Proper use of icons: "different icons for the same action" or use of "one same icon for different functions"

Another serious problem is the use of different icons for the same action or the use of the same icon for different functions. Many sites use very similar icons among their pages (these icons only differ from each other by means of the text above them) for different actions; sometimes these icons are so similar that it would be more effective to use a second different icon for one of the actions. This would avoid user's doubts and facilitate navigation through the site.

*Use of Other Features.* Some features like menus, forms and prompts are great aid to the beginners and are present along the entire site. Since many times advanced users consider these features an obstacle, well designed interfaces must also allow the use of accelerators such as function keys and textual commands, in order to make the interaction faster (Foley,1997).

*Human Perception.* The perception of each person depends on her abilities to perceive and to treat information. Variations of physical abilities, behavior and personality influence the success of a system. Each user possesses a cognitive style that determines how he perceives the information. To create an interface that in fact can be used by different people, it must be possible to display its content in different forms in order to accommodate the different perceptions (Pressman, 2004). Despite the trend of using graphical elements in the web sites design, much information continue to be given in the literal form. Reading constitutes an essential activity in many systems. The text size, the font source, upper/lower case, the location and color are factors that directly affect the easiness with which the information is perceived, that is, its usability.

*Proper Use of Color.* The color, basic element in any communication's process, may interfere with emotions and cognition process of a person (Marcus, 1987) & (Marcus, 1998); it can deliberately be used to reach specific objectives. The combination of colors must be carefully chosen (Jackson, 1994), (Marcus, 1987), (Marcus, 1998) and (Ferreira, 2003). The appropriate use of colors may help to produce a quick and correct assimilation of the information. Its inappropriate use may turn the information incomplete, ambiguous or unintelligible for the user. Its impact in the effectiveness of the interface depends on the relevance of its use for the performance on a task and on the situation and environment where the task takes place (Smith, 1987). People associate colors to diverse situations of their lives. These associations depend on diverse aspects: geographic, cultural, age. Based on this property, colors can be used to help users to navigate among a site.

The interface designer of the site must be careful while choosing the colors. Color must be used with the purpose of improving communication. The use of color must be well planned in order to help people to do associations with some situations of their lives. Different colors must used to help users to identify different items (each page related to a specific topic (section ) of a site must be designed with different colors) (Marcus, 1997) & (Ferreira, 2003).

*Metaphors.* The designer must take advantage of people's knowledge of the world around them by using metaphors to convey concepts and features of the site; the use of metaphors that involve familiar concepts turns the interaction less hostile and easier (Apple, 1992) & (Marcus, 1998).

*Minimize Memorization.* A good interface invokes the user's recognition rather than recall memory whenever possible. Mnemonic names and well-designed icons must be used. Since the signs (icons, command's names etc.) are the essential elements of a screen, they must be well produced. During development process, the designer must pay attention to the choice and design of the signs so that they do not induce doubts (Pressman, 2004).

*Functional Command's Sort.* The menu's bars offer many options for the users; they consist in a good way to access functions not constantly requested. It reduces the memory load for the users and its content depends on the site, but, generally, the several pages of a site have similar bars, with its items arranged horizontal or vertically. When people need to deal with amount of items, it is known that they feel more comfortable if the number of items is not greater than seven more or less two (Millers' law) (Ferreira, 2003), thus, a menu must respect these limits.

Besides being presented according to Millers' law, the items listed in the menu must be properly classified; different types of options must be placed in distinct parts of the menu. This can be properly done if the designer considers that the word menu is a metaphor with the restaurants' menu. Normally, in a restaurant's menu, the options are grouped together according to the kind of food (sea food, meat, pasta ... etc.). In the same way, in an interface's menu, the options must be grouped following some functional similarity criteria established by the designer (Ferreira, 2003).

When an interface has more than seven more or less two, sub-menus (pull-down menu or hierarchical menus) must be used. One of the advantages of a pull-down menu is that it is called only when it is necessary, thus saving screen space, without polluting the screen and without offering a series of options that can confuse the user (Foley, 1997) & (Shneiderman, 1997).

*Direct Manipulation.* Direct manipulation makes people believe that they control the objects represented by the computer; an object on the screen must remain visible while the user is performing any action on the object; in this way, the impact of the operation on the object may be immediately perceived by the user. In the same way, when the mouse passes over any object that may be manipulated, this must be highlighted (Foley, 1997).

*Exhibit only the information that is essential to the context.* In order to be better assimilated, only the information relevant to the current context or mode must be shown; the user must not have to be looking for many different data to find out what he needs to execute his/her task. To improve the information quality, when possible, distinct windows must be used to show information of different types and at least one part of each window must be visible (Pressman, 2004).

*Resolution-Independent Design.* Another issue that must be considered when designing usability-oriented sites is the resolution-independent design. In traditional interfaces, the designer knows for which environment he is designing; he has total control on each pixel of the screen that appears for the user, and he can be sure how each element will be seen in the screens, independent of the resolution of its monitor.

In Web, the designer has no control on the layout of the interfaces. Once the user can access the Internet in many ways, design for web must adequately be planned. One of the basic principles of constructing resolution-independent sites is to, instead of using fixed sizes to design elements of the interface, specify layouts as percentages of the available space (Nielsen, 2000) & (Nielsen, 2002). This really must be considered once many people and organizations still have low-resolution's monitors.

*Data Entry.* Users spend a lot of time choosing commands, typing data and others inputs. A good interface must minimize the time that the user spends with these tasks. The following guidelines improves the interface's usability when dealing data entry (Pressman, 2004):

*Help Facilities.* Help must be supplied for every input action. A Customer service page must be provided with the contacts of the staff and with the indication of where the users can find detailed information about the sites. Many facilities must be implemented: when a user passes the mouse over some screen's elements, tips sometimes maybe useful if they are shown over these elements; these facilities allow the user to find out the utility of many items without going to the customer service (Foley, 1997).

*Minimize Error Possibilities.* One of the objectives of a good interface is to prevent that its users commit errors. Well-designed interfaces must provide error prevention mechanisms that guide the users within any context and make it difficult for the user to do things that are not allowed in that context. Therefore, the user will not choose an invalid option and afterwards receive an error message (Foley, 1997).

*Inhibition of Items not Valid.* Items not valid in the current context should be inhibited or disabled by changing the icon's appearance (for instance, changing its color).

*Inform How the User Must Input Data Correctly.* The user must be informed of how he must fill in any field. The sites must guide the user in this task: whenever there is minimum or maximum limit of characters, this should be indicated either by the length of the field or a real-time character counter. This information must be given to the user before he fills the field and sites must indicate mandatory fields.

*Minimize the amount of input.* A good interface minimizes the number of actions necessary for any input, reducing the task of typing. For instance, when the user is registering into a site, his or her street address may be discovered by having them type the zip code first, then having the website do a look-up and automatically fill out the address field for the user.

*List Boxes and Radio Buttons should be used to restrict user answers and, at the same time, to save the users time.* The site must not inquire the user to input data when it is not necessary. If the user informs his birthday, he must no be asked to fill his age (Ferreira, 2003)

*Flexible Interaction.* A well-designed interface must allow the users to control their interaction; they must be able to skip unnecessary actions, to modify the order of the actions and recover from errors without leaving the site or losing data that has already been entered (Foley, 1997).

*Customization.* A good interface must allow the user to customize its commands, colors, and messages (Foley, 1997).

*Provide Error Recovery.* Experimental evidences show that people are more productive if their mistakes can be readily corrected (Foley, 1997). So a well-designed site must provide a good error recovery (undo, cancel, correct...). By providing this error recovery, the user feels more comfortable to explore unlearned facilities without fear of failure. This encourages exploratory learning. Basically there are two types of errors: functional and syntactic.

Syntactic errors occur when commands are typed with wrong parameters or names; in this case, the site must provide a clear message. This can be provided by, showing error messages to the user immediately after makes a mistake without allowing the user to finish the whole only then to be informed of a mistake. In such cases, a user would be forced to review his information and submit the form (sometimes more than once) until the system considers his form acceptable. Modern techniques in web applications allow for a user to be informed as soon as he makes a mistake, instead of only after the form has been submitted.

Functional errors are the most serious; they occur when the user executes a command he didn't mean to, leading to unexpected results. Sites must present error recovery features. As an example, any action or dialog should have a cancel button (Ferreira, 2003).

## CONCLUSIONS

In this paper the authors have argued about the importance of the NFR usability in the overall quality of information systems and developed a taxonomy that may help many web designers in their task of developing usability oriented web systems. So, these NFR issues, present in the taxonomy, must be dealt with during the definition phase of the information system and not afterwards.

Applying the process presented in this article, which re-uses well established heuristics from the HCI literature, early on should lead to higher quality information systems. In a competitive market, the NFR usability for e-commerce applications will be of fundamental importance to the success of an enterprise.

This paper contributes as stressing the importance of the NFR usability as well as providing a list of characteristics that should be presented or avoided when building interaction in e-commerce applications. We also believe that our work is on the direction of building a corpus of knowledge about NFR and to represent that knowledge using the NFR framework (Chung et al, 2000). Once this knowledge is represented as NFR graphs we plan to pursue a conflict analysis of on the usability NFR graph.

## REFERENCES

Albertin, A.L. (2000) "O Comércio Eletrônico Evolui e Consolida-seno Mercado Brasileiro". São Paulo: Published in Revista de Administração de Empresas, v.40, n. 4, p. 42-50, Out./Dez

Albertin, A.L (2001). "Valor Estratégico dos Projetos de Tecnologia de Informação". São Paulo: Published in Revista de Administração de Empresas, v.41, n. 3, p. 42-50, Jul./set.

Apple Computer (1992): Macintosh Human Interface Guidelines-Addison-Weslwy Company

Breitman,K. K., Leite J.C.S.P. (1999 ). The World's Stage: A Survey on Requirements Engineering Using a Real-Life Case- Study. Journal of the Brazilian Computer Society No 1 Vol. 6 Jul. pp:13:37.

Bias, R.G. and Mayhew, D.G. (1994.) "Cost-justifying usability".- Academic Press.

Chung, L., Nixon, B., Yu, E. and Mylopoulos,J (2000). "Non-Functional Requirements in Software Engineering" Kluwer Academic Publishers.

Cogburn, D.L (2003). "HCI in the so-called developing world:what's in it for everyone" - Interactions Volume 10 , Winds of change Special Issue: HCI in the developing world Pages: 80 - 87 2003 ISSN:1072-5520 March /April

Cysneiros, L.M. and Leite, J.C.S.P (1999). "Integrating Non-Functional Requirements into data model" 4th International Symposium on Requirements Engineering – Ireland June.

Davis, A. (1993) "Software Requirements: Objects Functions and States" - Prentice Hall.

Ferreira, S.B.L and Leite, J.C.S.P.( 2004) "Sistemas de Informação Globalizados: Desafios Culturais" – Proceedings of the XXVIII ENAMPAD,. Curitiba, Paraná.

Ferreira, S.B.L and Leite, J.C.S.P (2003 ) "Avaliação da usabilidade em sistemas de informação: o caso do sistema submarino". Proceedings published in the journal Revista de Administração Contemporânea-RAC. Publicação quadrimestral da ANPAD – Associação dos Programas de Pós Graduação em Adminstração, v. 7, n. 2, p. 115 até 137. Abril/Junho ISSN: 1415-6555

Foley, J. D., Dam, A. V., Feiner, S. K. & Hughes, J. F. (1997) Computer Graphics - Principles and Practice - Addison - Wesley Publishing Company – Second Edition.

Jackson, R., MacDonald L. e Freeman K.( 1994) "Computer Generated Color:A Practical Guide to Presentation and Display"-John Wiley & Sons.

Jokela, T.( 2004) "When good things happen to bad products:where are the benefits of usability in the consumer appliance market?" interactions Volume 11 , Issue 6- Pages: 28 – 35 ISSN:1072-5520 – November/ December

Leite, J. C. S. P. (2004) "Engenharia de Requisitos" – Class Notes "Engenharia de Requisitos" - Depto. de Informática da Pontifícia Universidade Católica do Rio de Janeiro

Marcus, A.( 1987) "Color: A Tool for Computer graphics Communication"-Color in Computer Graphics no 24- SIGGRAPH

Marcus, A.( 1998) "Metaphor design in user interfaces" - ACM SIGDOC Asterisk Journal of Computer Documentation Volume 22 Número 2 Pgs: 43 – 57 – ISSN:0731-1001 Maio

Nielsen,J and Tahir,(2002) "Homepage:Usabilidade–50 Websites desconstruídos" RJ Editora Campus

Nielsen, J.( 2000) Designing Web Usability. Indianopolis: News Riders Publishing.

Norman, D.A. (1999.) "The Invisible Computer:why good products can fall, the personal computer is so complex, and information appliances are the solution". Massachusets–MIT Press.

Norman, D.A.( 1986) "User Centered Systems Design" - Lawrance Earlbaum Associates .

Seffah, A. and Metzker, E.(2004) "The obstacles and myths of usability and software engineering" - Communications of the ACM -Volume 47 , Issue 12 The Blogosphere - Pages: 71 - 76 - December

Shneiderman, B. (1997). "Designing the User Interface – Strategies for Effcetive Human-Computer Interaction". Massachusetts -Addison_wesley

Pressman, R.S.( 2004)Software Engineering-A Practioner's Approach–6th ed., McGraw-Hill,Inc.

Smith, W.( 1987) "Computer Color: Psychophysics, Task Application and Asthetics" - Color in Computer Graphics no. 24- SIGGRAPH.

Tognazzini, B. (1995). "Tog on Software Design" Massachusetts -Addison_wesley

(http_1)-Usability-10/9/2004 http://www.oslo.sintef.no/avd/32/3270/brosjyrer/engelsk/index.html

Management of Technology: New Directions in Technology Management
M. Hashem Sherif and T.M. Khalil (Editors)



# 12

# VISUALISED INDICATORS OF LINKS IN THE WORLD WIDE WEB: BIOTHECHNOLOGY AND INFORMATION SCIENCE

*Marianne Hörlesberger, Edgar Schiebel, ARC systems research GmbH, Technology Management, Vienna, Austria*

## INTRODUTION

The measure of visibility on the Web is the number of links. To analyse the linkage behaviour is a question of structure. Network Analysis methods have been developed for investigating structures in social co-operation networks and in many other networks, like the networks in cells or networks in food chains. Such methods are used and adapted for analysing networks in the World Wide Web. In this contribution we focus on the analysis of linkages in the fields of biotechnology and information science in the World Wide Web and on the visualisation of their Web-networks with the BibTechMon$^{TM}$ (**Bib**liometric **Tech**nology **Mon**itoring), a tool developed at ARC systems research. The data is provided by the institute CINDOC (Madrid) as part of the "European Indicators, Cyberspace and the Science-Technology- Economy System" (EICSTES) European research project in the Fifth Framework Programme (www.eicstes.org).

We derive indicators for analysis and visual display and apply time study the patterns of co-linking in the fields of biotechnology and information among European universities and research institutes in the years 2001.Further analysis of the available dataset of the URLs of the European universities and research institutes and their linkage behaviour is represented in the EU project EICSTES. (www.eicstes.org).

## BACKGROUND

We have to distinguish between Internet and World Wide Web. The World Wide Web is a network of Web pages containing information, linked by hyperlinks from one page to another. The Internet is a physical network of computers linked by optical fibre and other data connections (M. E. J. Newman; 2003). Google™ and AltaVista™ have developed special algorithms to find the most relevant documents in the Word Wide Web quickly and rank them according to the number of links. In this study, we are focusing on the linkage behaviour to discover the current authorities and hubs in biotechnology and information science of universities and research institutes of the European member states.

BibTechMon is a software tool for structuring, visualising and analysing data (Kopcsa, A., Schiebel, E., 1998). The method of this tool is based on the calculation of co-occurrences of objects. After normalizing the co-occurrences to values between 0 and 1 (There are different indices which can be used), the objects are brought to visualisation via the spring model (a method used in mechanics). The output of BibTechMon is a network where a node is an object. An object can be a key-term in a document, an author, a patent, a Webpage, an URL and so on – in our case an URL. A node finds its position in the network because of its relationship to all other nodes. A node closer to in the middle of a network has a quite homogeneous relationship to all nodes in the network. The edges represent the relationship between the objects. Two objects are connected, have an edge together, if they occur together in documents, in patents, or they have a link to the same URL, and so on. The get an idea of the different possibilities of BibTechMon for further analysis see also www.arcs.ac.at/S/ST/BibTechMon. This contribution focuses only on a special feature of web analysis.

## DEFINITIONS

The determination of "authorities" and "hubs" is important for a search engine to find relevant documents in the World Wide Web. Computer scientists have developed different methods, measurements and indicators to structure, to analyse or to describe the huge amount of information in the World Wide Web (Barabási, A. L. 2002, Faloutsos, M., Faloutsos, P. and Faloutsos, Ch. 1999, Kleinberg J.1998). In this paper we consider URLs and links of their

Web pages to other URLs. Therefore we are interested in "in-degree", "out-degree", "authorities", "hubs" as well as network indicators like "density" and "centrality". We show how to visualize this data in a way that can help making sense of the data.

The *in-degree* of a Web page is defined as the number of links pointing to a page. A Web page with many incoming links is an *authority*. The *Out-degree* is the number of outgoing links from a page. A page with a large out-degree is a *hub*. (Note: The definitions of "authorities" and "hubs" depend on the theory and algorithm in the widespread field of cyber-metric.)

The rank of a Web page that links to many hubs is higher than a Web page with the same number of links to ordinary pages. Similarly, the number of incoming links from hubs is used to rank authorities.. Therefore a *highly rated authority* is an URL with many incoming hub links and a *good hub* is an URL with a outgoing links to authorities.

*Actor degree centrality.* The degree of a node is the number of adjacent nodes. It is used to estimate the actor degree centrality $C_D(n_i)$ as defined by (see Wasserman and Faust 1994, p. 178)

$$C_D(n_i) = \frac{d(n_i)}{g-1}$$

where $d(n_i)$ is the degree of node $n_i$ and g is the total number of nodes n. The degree of a node is the number of edges connected to the node. This index is independent of g and can therefore be compared across networks of different sizes. The index takes on values from 0, if $n_i$ has no adjacent nodes, to 1, if all remaining nodes in the network are directly adjacent to node n. The centrality shows how often a node is located on geodesics in a network. Nodes with a high centrality play a central role in the network

*Density.* The density of a network is defined as the numbers of lines paths in a network, expressed as a proportion of the maximum possible number of lines paths. The formula for the density is

$$\frac{l}{n(n-1)/2}$$

where l is the number of edges present and n is the total number of nodes. It can take on values from 0, if nodes are totally unconnected, to 1, if all nodes are connected (Wasserman and Faust 1994, p. 101). The density is a measure the speediness of information exchange in a network. Furthermore the indicator "density" gives us the possibilities to compare different networks.

We have to distinguish between in-degree and out-degree. "Despite the billion documents on the Web, nineteen degrees of separations suggest that the Web is easily navigable. To be sure, if there is a path between two documents, the path is typically short. [...]. The Web is directed." as different computer scientist have proofed and Barabasi explains in [Albert-Laszlo Barabsi, 2002]. We use this direction (incoming and outgoing links respectively) for structuring and getting indicators or the Web.

## INPUT DATA

The Web sites of the fifteen European research institutes of the years 2001 and 2002 with their URLs and their outgoing links are the basis of our dataset. The input data of the Web come from "crawls" of the network, in which a Web page is found only if another page points to it. A crawl covers only a part of the Web (as all crawls do at present) pages. A Web page is more likely to be found the more other pages point to it. This suggests for instance that our measurement of fraction of pages with low in-degree might be underestimated. This behaviour contrasts with that of a citation network. A paper can appear in the citation indices even if it has never been cited. Each Web site can be allocated to a code which gives information about the content of the Web site. Isidro F. Aguillo, CINDOC-CSIC, Madrid used the so called UNESCO codes to identify the content of the Web sites. We extracted the URLs allocated to topics of biotechnology as given in table 1.

**Table 1. UNESCO codes for biotechnology web sites**

| | |
|---|---|
| 2302 | biochemistry |
| 2403 | biochemistry |
| 2409 | genetics |
| 2414 | microbiology |
| 2415 | molecular biology |
| 3101 | agricultural chemistry |
| 3202 | biochemical technology |
| 3309 | food technology |

**Table 2. UNESCO codes for information science web sites**

| | |
|---|---|
| 1203 | computer science |
| 1207 | operations research |
| 2203 | electronics |
| 3304 | computer technology |
| 3307 | electronic technology |

## GENERAL STATISTICS OF THE DATA

Before we go into detail we will describe the huge amount of records with some general statistics. The emphasis is on the links, especially on the outgoing links. Figure 1 and figure 2 represent the number of outgoing links in the two considered fields of the years 2001 and 2002. We see that in almost each country there are at least four times as many outgoing links in information science than in biotechnology. The gap between the two years is not so big (the runaways in Finland in information science, in the United Kingdom and Sweden in biotechnology are not considered in detail). cTLD stands for **C**ountry **T**op-Level **D**omain.

**Figure 1. Number of outgoing links (in thousand) in information science**

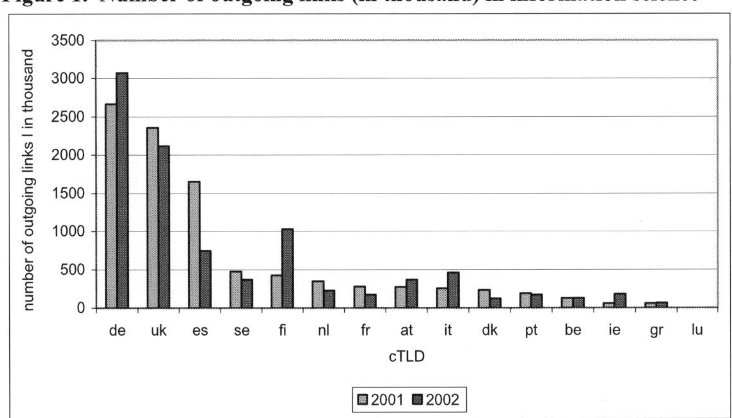


at: Austria, be: Belgium, de: Germany, dk: Denmark, es: Spain, fi: Finland, fr: France, gr: Greece, ie: Ireland, it: Italy, lu: Luxembourg, nl: Netherlands, pt: Portugal, se: Sweden uk: United Kingdom

**Figure 2. Number of outgoing links (in thousand) in biotechnology**

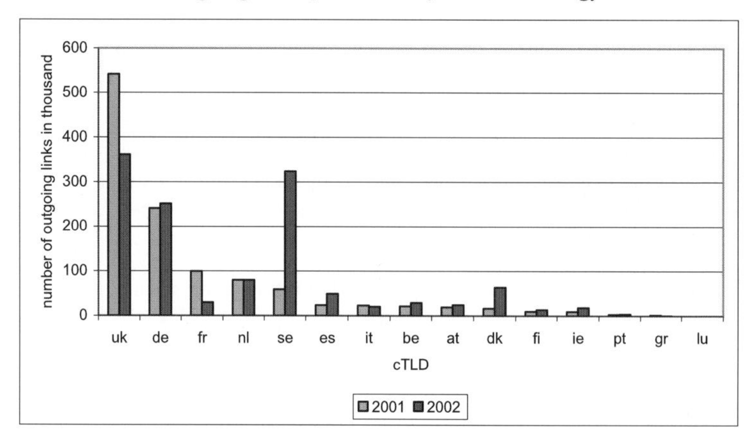


at: Austria, be: Belgium, de: Germany, dk: Denmark, es: Spain, fi: Finland, fr: France, gr: Greece, ie: Ireland, it: Italy, lu: Luxembourg, nl: Netherlands, pt: Portugal, se: Sweden uk: United Kingdom

Figure 3 represents the number of outgoing links per Web site. As we expected it shows that information science is more connected, e.g. it has a network with a higher density in the World Wide Web than biotechnology. Although biotechnology is a modern science, and was established in the time where Internet "grew", biotechnology does not use the World Wide Web in the same intensity as information science does. Are the presence and the density of a science community in the World Wide Web a question of knowledge and capability of handling Internet technologies? Although the results from this investigation cannot be generalized, it is reasonable to assume that the use of the Internet is a question of access to Internet and knowledge of this technology. Furthermore we learn from figure 3 that northern European Countries (especially Finland, Sweden, Denmark, and Germany) are better represented or connected in the World Wide Web in both fields than the southern part of Europe. It is a fact of the access to Internet and to latest technology and also a fact of culture, as different studies have shown.

**Figure 3. Number of outgoing links per Web page in different European countries**

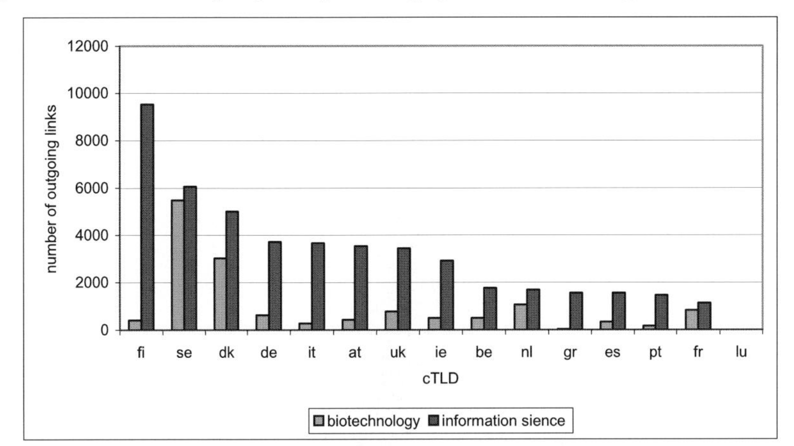


at: Austria, be: Belgium, de: Germany, dk: Denmark, es: Spain, fi: Finland, fr: France, gr: Greece, ie: Ireland, it: Italy, lu: Luxembourg, nl: Netherlands, pt: Portugal, se: Sweden uk: United Kingdom

## VISUALIZATION WITH BIBTECHMON

The input is data like Web sites with their out-going respectively incoming links in our case. The output of BibTechMon is a network where a node is an object, in our case an URL as already mentioned above.

The World Wide Web delivers a very huge amount of records for analysis, e.g. there were about 1.6 billions outgoing links of university and research websites with the cTLD "de" in 2002. An excellently working computer could probably calculate a network of all connections of the World Wide Web. But would it be possible for us to recognise any structure in this calculated network on a computer monitor afterwards? We focused on the visualisation of data of different countries in the two named fields. According to an OECD report the Netherlands are the most active country in the field of information technology while Belgium is very busy in biotechnology (OECD Observer, 1999). BibTechMon delivers the visualised networks.

## RESULTS FOR INFORMATION SCIENCE-WEB-SITES

**Figure 4. Diagram for information science websites in the Netherlands (2002), outgoing links.**

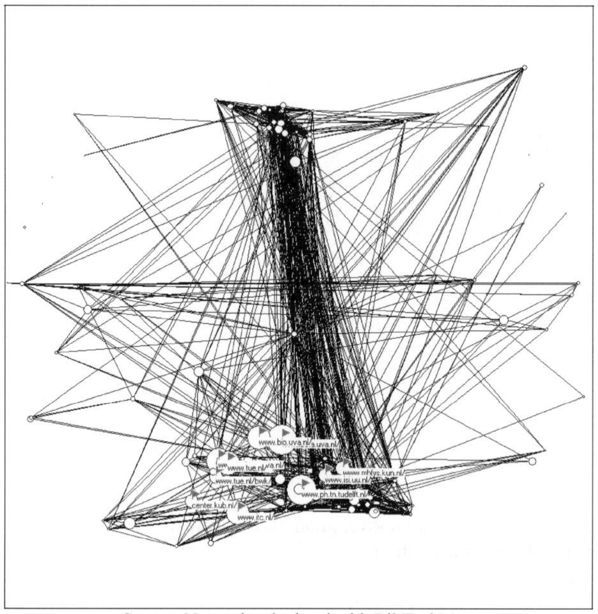


Source: Network calculated with BibTechMon

**Table 3. The 10 URLs with the highest out-degree of the network in figure 4.**

| URL | Out-degree (Frequency) | Authority Rank | Centrality |
|---|---|---|---|
| www.beta.uva.nl | 5014 | 1 | 0.0839891 |
| www.ph.tn.tudelft.nl | 4995 | 7 | 0.0278647 |
| www.swi.psy.uva.nl | 3599 | 6 | 0.0212022 |
| www.itc.nl | 3111 | 15 | 0.0116334 |
| www.tue.nl | 3054 | 75 | 0.0385492 |
| www.bio.uva.nl | 2908 | 9 | 0.0141328 |
| www.mbfys.kun.nl | 1091 | 8 | 0.0219521 |
| www.isi.uu.nl | 1033 | 5 | 0.0302007 |
| www.tue.nl/bwk | 1017 | 3 | 0.0061191 |
| center.kub.nl | 937 | 12 | 0.0013670 |

The network in figure 4 has 102 nodes (different URLs) and 1,857 edges, but only 900 of them are shown in the network, because of a better overview. The out-degree is exactly the "frequency" in BibTechMon terminology. In this figure the size of a node represents the out-degree. Nodes with a large out-degree are called hubs.

The 10 nodes with the largest out-degree are selected in the network (marked and with their names in figure 4). These nodes are the URLs listed in table 3. The entries in column "Authorities" (in table 3) are the in-degrees of the considered URLs. The highest in-degree of 75 is associated with the URL *www.tue.nl* followed by *www.itc.nl* with an in-degree of 15 of the selected URLs in the network. The third rank goes to *cente.kub.nl* with an in-degree 12. Therefore we conclude that the "best" hubs of the network in figure 4 are *www.tue.nl, www.itc.nl, center.kub.nl,* because as mentioned above, good hubs are created by authorities. Table 3 in column "Authority's Rank" shows this).

The values of actor degree centrality are listed in the column "Centrality" (table 3). *www.beta.uva.nl* has the highest actor degree centrality followed by *www.sens.el.utwente.nl* and *www.tue.nl/bwk.* This indicator represents another quality of a network. The density of this network is 0.3605125. It is not even 50% but this network has the highest density in our considered networks here. This means that information passing this network goes relatively quickly through the network.

The incoming links for "networks of URLs based on their incoming links" are only from the Netherlands. The study of authorities is limited to the incoming links of the Netherlands. We cannot compare the networks in figure 4 and figure 5 directly, because figure 4 does not contain only cTLD of the Netherlands.

**Figure 5. Diagram for information science websites in the Netherlands (2002), incoming links**

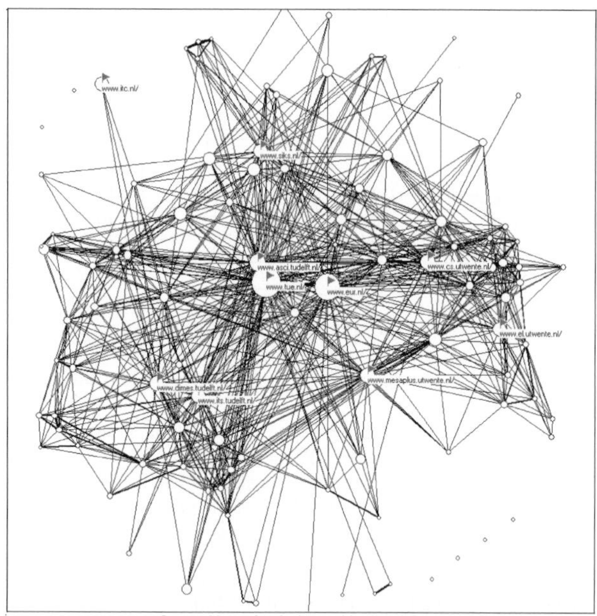


Source: Network calculated with BibTechMon

**Table 4. The 10 URLs with the highest in-degree of the network in figure 5.**

| URL | In-degree (Frequency) | Hub Rank | Centrality |
|---|---|---|---|
| www.tue.nl | 75 | 3054 | 0.1325022 |
| www.eur.nl | 58 | No hub | 0.1148556 |
| www.asci.tudelft.nl | 24 | 174 | 0.1371627 |
| www.cs.utwente.nl | 19 | 162 | 0.0314476 |
| www.mesaplus.utwente.nl | 19 | 188 | 0.0611665 |
| www.dimes.tudelft.nl | 18 | 154 | 0.0168684 |
| www.siks.nl | 16 | 358 | 0.0293806 |
| www.its.tudelft.nl | 16 | 50 | 0.0414918 |
| www.el.utwente.nl | 15 | 619 | 0.0133879 |
| www.itc.nl | 15 | 3111 | 0.0001267 |

There are 102 nodes (URLs) in this network with 783 edges. The first impression of the network in figure 5 is that the nodes with the highest frequency are quite in the middle. This is because the connections of the nodes with the highest frequency are connected similarly to all other nodes. There is a more a balanced connection in the network. As described in figure 4 a node is an URL. In this case two nodes are connected if they have they same incoming link. So the in-degree is given by the "Frequency" (table 4). URLs with the best in-degree are authorities. The ten URLs with the best in-degree are shown in table 4. Good authorities are "created" by good hubs. The values in column "Hubs" in table 4 represent the quality of the authority (the nodes marked and with their URL names in the network, figure 5). When we consider the selected URLs (marked nodes in the network, marked with the URL names in figure 5) *www.tue.nl* is the best authority because it is a link of many hubs. On rank two there is *www.itc.nl* then *www.el.utwente.nl* follows.

It seems that *www.tue.nl* was one of the most important Web sites of information science of the Netherlands in 2002. *www.eur.nl* is not created by a hub, but it has a high in-degree of ordinary pages and a high centrality. The actor degree centrality is listed in the column "Centrality" (table 4). The five URLs with the highest values are *www.asci.tudelft.nl, www.tue.nl, www.eur.nl, www.mesaplus.utwente.nl, www.its.tudelft.nl. www.tue.nl* is among the best ones too. The density of this network is 0.1520093. This density value is low, about 15%. The information going through this network needs more time to reach each node than the network in figure 4.

## RESULTS FOR BIOTECHNOLOGY-WEB-SITES

The field of biotechnology is represented completely differently in the World Wide Web. The results of the general statistics are supported by visualisation. When one considers the network you could get the impression of looseness. We show it with the sample of Belgium.

**Figure 6. Connectivity network for biotechnology websites in Belgium (2002), outgoing links.**

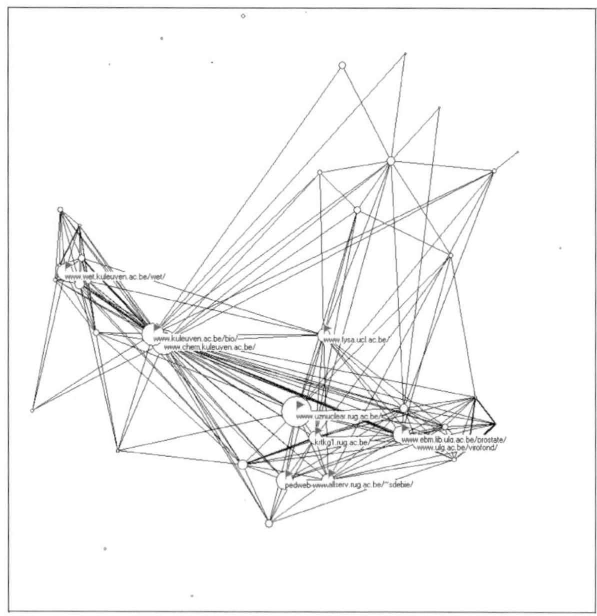


Source: Network calculated with BibTechMon

**Table 5. The 10 URLs with the highest out-degree of the network in figure 6.**

| URL | Out-degree (Frequency) | Authority Rank | Centrality |
|---|---|---|---|
| www.uznuclear.rug.ac.be | 1154 | 3 | 0.0328883 |
| www.chem.kuleuven.ac.be | 765 | No authority | 0.0988105 |
| www.kuleuven.ac.be/bio | 640 | 4 | 0.2042612 |
| pedweb-www.uia.ac.be/pedweb | 377 | 1 | 0.0035672 |
| www.ebm.lib.ulg.ac.be/prostate | 370 | | 0.0115545 |
| www.wet.kuleuven.ac.be/wet | 349 | 23 | 0.0024560 |
| allserv.rug.ac.be ~sdebie | 221 | | 0.0079762 |
| www.fysa.ucl.ac.be | 211 | 3 | 0.0141519 |
| krtkg1.rug.ac.be | 199 | 3 | 0.0113534 |
| www.ulg.ac.be/virofond | 135 | 1 | 0.0048122 |

We have 45 different URLs of universities or research institutes as nodes in the network with 201 edges. There are two nodes in the south west of the network which are strongly connected to most of the other nodes. Two nodes are connected in this network if they link to the same URL. The hubs in this case are shown in table 5. The best hubs are URLs which link to good authorities. The best ones here are *www.wet.kuleuven.ac.be/wet* and *www.kuleuven.ac.be/bio* as column in table 5 for the "Authority Rank" shows. *www.chem.kuleuven.ac.be* is not created by an authority, but it has a high out-degree and a high centrality value.

The values with the highest actor degree centrality are allocated to *www.kuleuven.ac.be/bio, www.chem.kuleuven.ac.be, imol.vub.ac.be, www.ulg.ac.b/cwbi, www.md.ucl.ac.be/pharma facm.* The density of the network is 0.2030303. This density value is lower than that in figure 4. The network in figure 6 – this here - and the network in figure 4 are networks of outgoing links. The network of outgoing links of information science has density more than 15% higher than the network of outgoing links of biotechnology. That means that information is running faster in information science.

At last we represent the network URLs based on their incoming links (the incoming links are only with a country top level domain of Belgium).

**Figure 7. Connectivity network for biotechnology websites in Belgium (2002), incoming links.**

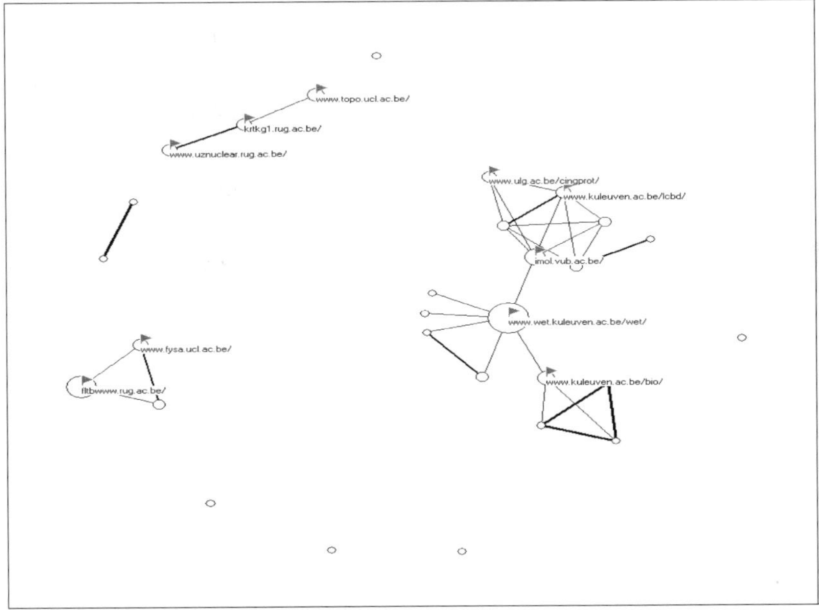


Source: Network calculated with BibTechMon

**Table 6. The 10 URLs with the highest in-degree of the network in figure 7.**

| URL | In-degree (Frequency) | Hub Rank | Centrality |
|---|---|---|---|
| www.wet.kuleuven.ac.be/wet | 23 | 349 | 0.2037037 |
| fltbwww.rug.ac.be | 12 | No hub | 0.0000000 |
| imol.vub.ac.be | 6 | 23 | 0.1455026 |
| www.kuleuven.ac.be/bio | 4 | 640 | 0.0952381 |
| www.topo.ucl.ac.be | 4 | 62 | 0.0000000 |
| krtkg1.rug.ac.be | 3 | 199 | 0.0026455 |
| www.fysa.ucl.ac.be | 3 | 211 | 0.0000000 |
| www.kuleuven.ac.be/lcbd | 3 | 37 | 0.0026455 |
| www.uznuclear.rug.ac.be | 3 | 1154 | 0.0000000 |
| www.ulg.ac.be/cingprot | 3 | 4 | 0.0000000 |

The network in figure 7 seems very loose. But we should take into account that for networks based on incoming links we can only use the incoming links of Belgium in this case. The network in figure 7 has 29 nodes with 33 connections. The ten URLs with the highest in-degree are in table 6. Which of these authorities are the best ones? The column "Hubs" represents this: *www.uznuclear.rug.ac.be, www.kuleuven.ac.be/bio* and *www.wet.kuleuven.ac.be/wet. fltbwww.rug.ac.be* is not created by a hub, but has a high in-degree, means is linked by ordinary pages. The actor degree centrality is listed in the column "Centrality". The five URLs with the highest values are *www.wet.kuleuven.ac.be/we, imol.vub.ac.be, www.kuleuven.ac.be/bio, mda04.fmv.ulg.ac.be, www.kuleuven.ac.be/lcbd.* The density of the network is given with 0.0812808. This density value is low. The information in this network needs a long time to reach each node.

When we consider both networks of Belgium we see that *www.kuleuven.ac.be/bio* and *www.wet.kuleuven.ac.be/wet* were the most important URLs of biotechnology in Belgium of 2002.

## CONCLUSIONS

We have shown that BibTechMon tool can be used to derive indicators for structuring Web data and visualises them. Furthermore it supports indicators for centrality and density in the sense that they are also visible in the generated networks. This contribution shows that there are differences in the representation of different research fields and there is a geographical difference. Those fields which have had a "natural" access to the technology Internet like mathematics, physics, electronic technology etc. are represented very well in the World Wide Web. The universities of the northern European countries are represented better in the World Wide Web than the southern part. We assume that it is a question of access to technology. The next steps to improve our method are to implement further adequate indicators from the available sample of network indicators taking advantage of the various methods being currently developed to map the World Wide Web to find structures and to discover laws in this virtual world. There is a lot ahead of us, and the human being probably will not be able to see the whole complex and huge World Wide Web.

## REFERENCES

Aguillo, I. F. (2002). Cybermetrics, Definitions and Methods for an Emerging Discipline. Séminaires de l'ADEST, Paris, 14 February 2002. www.upmf-grenoble.fr adest seminaires ISIDRO Cybermetrics.ppt.

Barabási, A. L. (2002). Linked. How Everything Is Connected to Everything Else and What It Means for Business, Science, and Everyday Life. *A Plume Book.*

Brandes, U.; Erlebach Th. (2005). Network Analysis, Methodological Foundations. *Springer Verlag Berlin Heidelberg.*

Faloutsos, M ; Faloutsos, P and Faloutsos, Ch. (1999). On Power-Law Relationships of the Internet Topology *Computer Communication Review,* **29**, 251

Faust, Katherine - Wassermann, Stanley (1994): Social Network Analysis: Methods and Applications. *Cambridge University Press.*

Kleinberg, J.,(1998). Authoritative Sources in a Hyperlinked Environment, *Proceedings of the ACM-SIAM Symposium on Discrete Algorithms.*

Kopcsa, A., Schiebel, E. (1998). Science and Technology Mapping. A New Iteration Model for Representing Multidimensional Relationsships. *Journal of the American Society for Information Science (JASIS)*, **49**, 1, 7-17.

Newman, M. E. J. (2003). The Structure and Function of Complex Networks, *lanl.arXiv.org e-Print archive mirror*, March 2003

OECD Observer, 1999.

*Classification of the technology.* In order to categorize the WHIP Web-groupware, the features of the technology were compared to the three models selected for classification: Wenger's Typical Groupware Facilities (2001), Johansen's Time/Space Matrix (1988) and Dennis and Valacich's Theory of Media Synchronicity (1999). First, the WHIP Web-groupware conforms to all twelve of Wenger's (2001) criteria (or facilities) therefore allowing decent support to communities of practices (see table 1).

**Table 1. Typical Web-groupware facilities useful to a community of practice**

| **Virtual Space:** |
|---|
| 1- A home page to assert the community's existence and describe its domain of activities |
| 2- A conversation space for on-line discussion |
| 3- A facility for floating questions to the community or a subset of the community |
| 4- A directory of members with some information about their areas of expertise in the domain |
| 5- A shared workspace for synchronous electronic collaboration, discussions or meetings |
| 6- A document repository for the community's knowledge base |
| 7- A search engine good enough to retrieve information members need from their knowledge base |
| 8- A set of community management tools (mostly for the platform's coordinator) |
| 9- The ability to spawn sub-communities, subgroups and project teams |
| **Technological platform:** |
| 1- Easy to learn and use |
| 2- Easily integrated with the other software regularly used by members of the community |
| 3- Not too expensive. Large investments may impede the adoption of the platform |

(Adapted from Wenger, 2001)

Using Johansen's (1988) Time/Space Matrix, the WHIP technology tools and services are classified as an asynchronous collaboration system fit to support the work of geographically distributed virtual teams. The application is well adapted for work activities that can be sequenced and achieved in parallel. The WHIP groupware features are similar to those of the lower-right quadrant of Figure 1 (below). Since the WHIP technology is composed of asynchronous tools and services, according to Dennis and Valacich's Theory of Media Synchronicity (1999), the technology's media capacity is best suited for the process of conveyance, information sharing and exchange. This process does not need a high level of synchronicity since members of the team do not have to consult the information simultaneously.

**Figure 1. Time /Space Matrix**

| | **Same space** | **Different space** |
|---|---|---|
| **Same time Synchronous** | Face-to-face meeting, Brainstorming, Vote, PC and projector, Electronic white board, GDSS, Chat | Chat, Tele-conference, **Video-conference,** Liaison satellite, Audio-conference, Shared white board, Shared application |
| **Different time Asynchronous** | Team room, Document management system, Discussion forum, E-mail, Workflow, Project management | **E-mail, Workflow, Document repository, Discussion forum, Group agenda, Cooperative hypertext and organizational memory, Version control, Meeting scheduler** |

(Adapted from Johansen, 1988)

*Comparison of the stakeholders' perceptions.* The results of the interviews and questionnaires with three different types of stakeholders (manager, IT analyst and team member) were compared. Since each type of stakeholder carried out different tasks and activities on WHIP, it seemed interesting to compare the perceived impact of the use of technology on i) the overall organization, ii) the virtual working groups and iii) individual members. Table 2 summarizes the results and shows divergences and similarities.

In table 2, we see that respondents belonging to all selected virtual groups expressed different needs and expressed a variety of opinions on the impact and usefulness of the technology. Most of them appreciate services such as the file download center and the discussion forum and found the technology easy to learn and easy to use. Overall, there are not many perceived disadvantages. Stakeholders show a tendency to mirror their own concerns and answer accordingly. Managers are mostly preoccupied with organizational efficiency and low costs; virtual working groups, for their part, are concerned with team processes and their outcomes, while individuals generally emphasize personal matters.

As for the organization itself, the development and use of the technology to support virtual teams brought about an increase in efficiency for two main reasons. First, the increase in efficiency is primarily attributable to the significant decrease in distribution cost since the organization produces a large number of documents related to valuable knowledge regarding major topics of relevance to industry partners. Members of teams and communities can access information and documents faster through the Web-groupware. The decreased cost of coordination is a benefit for the organization when virtual teams are supported by the technology. Second, part of the efficiency improvement is also due to the low total cost of ownership (TCO) of the technology, such as set-up, development, training and maintenance costs. For future development, IT analysts and managers are preoccupied with the open network and client standards of the underlying Web-groupware technologies. These observations are similar to Wheeler *et al.*'s (1999) findings, which indicated that a low TCO and the development of open standards were the major determinants in organizations' adoption of a Web-groupware technology.

**Table 2. Stakeholders' perceptions of the impact of the WHIP technology**

| | **Stakeholders** | | |
|---|---|---|---|
| | **Manager** | **T Analyst** | **Individuals in team/group or community** |
| **On the organization** | | | |
| **Perceived advantages (ex post)** | - Visibility<br>- Increased access to information<br>- Wider distribution of information<br>Efficiency<br>- Cost reduction:<br>Fast response time<br>Resources<br>TCO<br>- No effect on travel frequency<br>- Faster response to members<br>- Increase in service quality<br>- Standard applications: easier and less costly to manage | - Increased access to information,<br>-Wider distribution of information<br>Efficiency<br>- Cost reduction:<br>Fast response time<br>Resources<br>TCO<br>- Video-conference | - Increased access to valuable information<br>-Access to group work history<br>- Improved resource utilization<br>- Improved work processes<br>- Does not seem to affect travel frequency<br>- Video-conferences very rarely or never used<br>- Increased customer satisfaction |
| **Advantage (measured)** | - Decrease in distribution cost | - Decrease in distribution cost | |
| **On the virtual working groups** | | | |
| **Perceived advantages (ex post)** | | - Fast response time | - Accelerates information exchanges and allows easier communication<br>- Better understanding of what others are doing<br>- Decreased feeling of isolation<br>- Recognition of personnel efforts<br>- Knowledge and skill development |
| **Perceived disadvantages (ex post)** | None | - Automatic delivery of forgotten password<br>- Lack of standardization | - Slow response time<br>- Limited number of tools |

The interview results also brought an interesting observation to light: although all teams within the organization worked virtually, WHIP was not perceived in the same way by members of different task forces. This incited us to divide the respondents to the questionnaire into two distinct task-oriented categories in order to identify relevant differences. Three respondents had positions in the marketing department while the other five worked in the operations department. In order to gain a better understanding of WHIP, the operations-oriented category had to be split into two subclasses: teams (team_OP) and communities of practice (community_OP). The first subclass is composed of teams and groups while the latter is exclusively composed of communities of practice. The marketing-oriented category is composed of teams from the Marketing division.

The results presented in table 3 indicate that all respondents were unanimous in saying that the use of the WHIP Web-groupware technology improves the accessibility of valuable information and provides critical data about the team's history. These clear results confirm the claims of several authors such as Wenger and Snyder (2000) who present groupware as a technology that enhances the collaboration and communication processes necessary to support virtual team activities

**Table 3. Results from virtual teams, virtual groups and virtual communities**

| | **Operation-oriented** | | **Marketing -oriented** |
|---|---|---|---|
| | **Community_ OP (3)** | **Team_OP (2)** | **Team _MK (3)** |
| **Technology and the organization** | | | |
| 1- Your organization has created a vision for the company and has shared clear goals | + | | - |
| 2- The management approach in your organization promotes initiative among team members | ++ | | - |
| 3- Your organization encourages the use of electronic communication and information systems | ++ | | ++ |
| Would you say that the use of WHIP … | | | |
| 4- Helps reach business objectives | ++ | | ++ |
| 5- Enables a better use of resources | ++ | | + |
| 6- Improves work processes | ++ | | + |
| 7- Increases customer satisfaction | ++ | | |
| 8- Increases the visibility of the organization | + | | + |
| **Technology and the task outcome**<br>When your team uses WHIP, would you say that the technology … | | | |
| 9- Provides adequate tools to perform team tasks | + | ++ | |
| 10- Increases the quality of the team task outcome | | | |
| 11- Allows the work to be more task-oriented | | | - |

| | **Operation-oriented** | | **Marketing -oriented** |
|---|---|---|---|
| | **Community_ OP (3)** | **Team_OP (2)** | **Team _MK (3)** |
| 12- Decreases the delivery time of the project | | | |
| 13- Decreases development costs | | ++ | |
| 14- Enables the work to be completed within budget | | | |
| 15- Decreases the number of face-to-face meetings | | | -- |
| 16- Decreases time spent on travel | | | -- |
| 17- Decreases time spent on telephone conversations | ++ | | -- |
| 18- Is a determinant in achieving goals | ++ | ++ | |
| **Technology and the team outcome** When your team uses WHIP, would you say that the technology … | | | |
| 19- Supports communication among members | ++ | | |
| 20- Supports collaboration among members | ++ | | |
| 21- Increases the level of trust among members | | | |
| 22- Increases the cohesion of the team | | | |
| 23- Helps to provide a social context for the team | | -- | |
| 24- Improves access to valuable information | ++ | ++ | ++ |
| 25- Provides critical information about the team's history | ++ | ++ | ++ |
| 26- Increases access to valuable people (expertise) | | | |
| 27- Increases the quality of decision-making | | | |
| 28- Increases the quality of problem-solving | | | |
| 29- Helps to address disagreements promptly | | -- | |
| 30- Increases the team's productivity | + | | |
| 31- Provides adequate electronic methods of communicating effectively with team members | + | ++ | |
| 32- Meets the overall needs of the team's work | + | | |
| **Technology and personal satisfaction as a member of the team** When your team uses WHIP, would you say that the technology … | | | |
| 33- Helps you better understand what others are doing | ++ | | - |
| 34- Eliminates isolation | ++ | -- | - |
| 35- Enables you to have greater control over your work | + | -- | - |
| 36- Improves your reputation | + | | + |
| 37- Incites you to work with the team again | + | | - |
| 38- Creates some changes in your workload | | | + |
| 39- Clarifies your responsibility level | + | | |

| | Operation-oriented | | Marketing -oriented |
|---|---|---|---|
| | Community_ OP (3) | Team_OP (2) | Team _MK (3) |
| 40- Helps recognize personal work efforts | ++ | | |
| 41- Creates the opportunity to develop your knowledge and skills | ++ | | |

The groupware-related literature mentions organizational benefits such as effectiveness, quality and productivity but very few of them were identified in this study, as shown in table 3 (questions 4, 6, 10, 28, 29 and 31). Surprisingly, these benefits were not mentioned by any of the respondents (community or team). As shown in table 2, managers did not mention and could not name any organizational disadvantage brought about by the use of the technology since it supports the needs of most virtual groups at a low cost.

*Effects of the technology on virtual team members.* Members of communities of practices (community_OP) are the most satisfied users of the technology as they appreciate its support for communication and collaboration with members of the community. Our results in table 3 show that the individuals belonging to virtual communities of practice are the only ones (among all virtual team types) to acknowledge personal benefits. They also feel that the technology i) helps them better understand the tasks of the other members of the team, ii) eliminates the feeling of isolation and iii) helps recognize personal efforts and enables the development of knowledge and skills. These findings confirm some of the results obtained by other authors studying communities of practice (Millen et al., 2002). These communities are created when a large group of people gather together around a common interest during the exploration stage of their work to basically share ideas and information. The Web-groupware is the tool used to convey the information (Dennis and Valacich, 1999).

The results in table 3 also show that operation-oriented virtual team members (team_OP) are less satisfied with the technology, although they indicate that it provides adequate tools to perform team tasks and achieve their goals. Members of virtual teams need to agree on terms more frequently than other groups such as communities of practice. Tools are required to support key decision activities (for example conflict solving or decision-making). These virtual team members require synchronous tools such as voting, chat and shared workspace and require Web-groupware to provide task-oriented functionalities (Rico and Cohen, 2005).

Several teams in the marketing division (team_MK) seamed to use the Web-groupware technology differently. They have adapted the use of the technology to their needs; for example, some teams simply use the Web-groupware as a file transfer application (FTP) to share project and work-in-process documents with their clients worldwide. This confirms the general principles of Adaptive Structuration Theory (AST) whereby the technology transforms the way people work in the same way that people adapt the technology to their needs (Manevski and Chudoba, 2000). The results in table 3 show that marketing-oriented team members tend to be unsatisfied with the technology. The marketing team members believed that the tools could help them perform better but felt that the support from management was inadequate and lacked clarity (see questions 1 to 8 in table 3).

According to these results, the Web-groupware has some weaknesses. Its capabilities for social protocols, presence and transition tasks as well as automated administrative tasks are deficient. Since its standardization some time ago, the technology has not evolved and is not regularly maintained by the company. The application is sometimes unreliable and slow, but still manages to work well enough to provide the typical facilities to support most needs of virtual communities of practice. In order to support large communities of practice, it is more important to provide a simple and available technology than to provide a complex and evolving technology (Wenger, 2001).

## CONCLUSION

The objective of this study was to analyze the organizational impact of a Web-groupware application on a firm's activities and to observe how the technology supports virtual teams. Our results and analysis show that the major benefits for an organization are information visibility, efficiency (in terms of human resources and distribution costs), responsiveness and low total cost of ownership (TCO). For all virtual teams and communities of practice, the use of the Web-groupware technology makes valuable information accessible and allows for consultation of the team's history. Members of communities of practice are the most satisfied with the Web-groupware technology and are the only ones to acknowledge individual benefits.

Some of our findings are consistent with previous research in the field such as Wheeler *et al.* (1999). However, this research focuses on one technology in a specific setting and may not be generalizable to other settings. Some of our results indicate that virtual team types and team tasks play an important role in the selection and performance of a Web-groupware technology to support virtual teams. One interesting research avenue would be to study the relevance of virtual team members' media preferences for communication (Im *et al.*,

2005) as another factor to take into account when selecting or developing a Web-groupware technology. Many avenues are still open for further research as empirical studies pertaining to global virtual teams are just beginning (Manevski and Chudoba, 2000). Consequently, more empirical research should be undertaken to obtain more information about organizational requirements governing the development of an evolving groupware technology that could be tailored to the growing needs of virtual teams' activities. Some of the findings may be helpful for companies considering the use of Web-groupware. It is important to observe the different virtual team types carrying out activities in the organization and to identify their key characteristics in order to select appropriate Web-groupware services and functionalities to support their work (Im *et al.*, 2005; Rico and Cohen, 2005).

## REFERENCES

Büchel, B. and S. Raub (2002). Building Knowledge-Creating Value Networks. *European Management Journal,* 20(6), 587-596.

DeMarie, S. D. (2000). Using Virtual Teams to Manage Complex Projects: A Case Study of a Radioactive Waste Management Project. *The PricewaterhouseCoopers Endowment for the Business of Government, Grant Report* 19; http://www.businessofgovernment.org/pdfs/DeMarieReport.pdf

Dennis, A. and J. S. Valacich (1999). Rethinking Media Richness: Towards a Theory of Media Synchronicity. *Proceedings of the 32nd Hawaii International Conference on System Science.*

Ferran-Urdaneta, C. (1999). Teams or Communities? Organizational Structures for Knowledge Management. *SIGCPR'99, ACM,* 128-134.

Im, H-G., J., Yates. and W. Orlikowski (2005). Temporal Coordination through Communication: Using Genres in a Virtual Start-Up Organization. *Information Technology and People*, 18(2), 89-119.

Jarvenpaa, S. L., T. R. Shaw and D. S. Staples (2004). Towards Contextualized Theories of Trust: The Role of Trust in Global Virtual Teams. *Information Systems Research*, 15(3), 250-267.

Johansen, R. (1988). *Groupware: Computer Support for Business Teams*. New York: The Free Press.

Kierzkowski, Z. (2005). Towards Virtual Enterprises. *Human Factors and Ergonomics in Manufacturing,* 15(1), 49-69.

Lurey, J. S. and M. S. Raisinghani (2001). An Empirical Study of Best Practices in Virtual Teams. *Information Management,* 38, 523-544.

Manevski, M. and K. M. Chudoba (2000). Bridging Space over Time: Global Virtual Team Dynamics and Effectiveness, *Organization Science*. 11(5), 473-492.

Massey, A. P., Y. T. Caisy, Y. T. Hung, M. M. Montoya-Weiss and V. Ramesh (2001). When Culture and Style Aren't About Clothes: Perceptions of Task-Technology Fit in Global Virtual Team. *Group'01, ACM*, 207-213.

McGrath, J. E. (1984). *Groups: Interaction and Performance*. Englewood Cliffs, NJ: Prentice Hall.

Millen, D., M. A. Fontaine and M. J. Muller (2002). Understanding the Benefits and Costs of Communities of Practice. *Communications of the ACM*, 45(4), 69-73.

Mills, K. L. (2003). Computer-Supported Cooperative Work Challenges. In: *Encyclopedia of Library and Information Science* (2nd Edition), (M. Dekker, ed.), pp. 678-684. New York: Publisher?.

Pinelle, D. and C. Gutwin (2000) A Review of Groupware Evaluations. *Proceedings 9th IEEE International Workshops on Enabling Technologies: Infrastructure for Collaborative Enterprises (WET ICE'00)*, Gaithersburg, MD, June 2000, IEEE Press, 86-91.

Rico, R. and S. G. Cohen (2005). Effects of Task Interdependence and Type of Communication on Performance in Virtual Teams. *Journal of Managerial Psychology*, 20, 261-274.

Saadoun, M. (1996) *Le projet groupware: Des techniques de management au choix du logiciel groupware*. Paris: Eyrolles.

Townsend, A.M., S. M. DeMarie and A. R. Hendrickson (1998). Virtual Teams: Technology and the Workplace of the Future. *The Academy of Management Executive*, 12(3), 1-17.

Wenger, E. C. (2001) Supporting Communities of Practice, a Survey of Community-Oriented Technologies, Version 1.3, 65; http://www.ewenger.com.

Wenger, E. C., and W. M. Snyder (2000). Communities of Practice: The Organizational Frontier. *Harvard Business Review*, 78, January-February, 138-145.

Wheeler, B. C., A. R. Dennis and L. I. Press (1999). Groupware Comes to the Internet: Charting a New World. *The DATA BASE for Advances in Information Systems*, 30(3-4), 8-21.

Management of Technology: New Directions in Technology Management
M. Hashem Sherif and T.M. Khalil (Editors)



# 14

# THE EXTERNAL LINKAGES OF COMMUNITY OF PRACTICE: INTEGRATING COMMUNITIES USING INTERNET TECHNOLOGY FORUMS

*Dimitris Assimakopoulos and Jie Yan, Grenoble Ecole de Management, France*

## INTRODUCTION

The notion of Community of Practice (CoP) has attracted considerable interest throughout the 1990s and early 2000s as the locus of intensive knowledge creation and sharing. In particular, CoP is where tacit, rather than codified, knowledge is created, applied, shared and made sense of (Brown and Duguid 2001, 1998, Wenger 1998). However, the majority of the literature focuses on how communities of practice emerge and operate as relatively closed entities within organizational boundaries. Community members are co-located and share tacit knowledge mainly through face to face interaction. Few empirical studies have been carried out so far to explore knowledge sharing activities beyond the boundary of organization and specific CoPs (Kimble et al 2001). This research aims to shed light in the latter by studying the external advice seeking linkages of software engineers during their product development process in an engineering CoP within a leading Chinese start up company. Our case study of Advanced Systems Development Corporation (ASDC) is a small software engineering CoP in Beijing where software engineers make use of various social resources outside the company to seek advice in order to solve the technical problems arising in their everyday development work.

More specifically, this paper focuses on the role of a specialized Internet software technology forum: China Software Developer Net (CSDN), increasing our understanding of how Internet technology forums promote knowledge sharing across organizational boundaries, connect distributed software engineering communities across the rails of common practice, and integrate real world communities with virtual ones fostering the technological practice at a national scale (Assimakopoulos 2006). The paper is organized in four additional sections. The main concepts are highlighted in section 2. The research methodology and case study setting are presented in section 3. The main empirical findings are discussed in section 4. Finally the evaluation and conclusions are drawn in section 5.

## COMMUNITY OF PRACTICE AND VIRTUAL COMMUNITY

On the basis of increasing recognition of the value of tacit and context-specific nature of knowledge for innovation and competitive advantage, recent research (see, for example, Nonaka and Konno 1998, Brown and Duguid 1998, Teece 2001) tends to recognize that sharing of context-specific knowledge is an iterative, dynamic and interactive process associated with work and life practices embodied in informal CoPs, rather than formal organizational functions, departments and the like. According to Wenger (1998), a CoP refers to a group of people informally and contextually bound in a work situation who collectively applies a common competence in the pursuit of a common enterprise. Through a common practice, such a group of people develops a shared mental model, a common language, and common behaviors with respect to a specific practice. CoPs are likely to engage in innovative activities because of their constant adaptation to changing membership and changing circumstances. CoPs interact with each other and are influenced by one another through their members who often maintain multiple memberships and belong to different CoPs at the same time. Such informal structures facilitate learning, cross-fertilization and continuous innovation unparalleled within formal organizational hierarchies.

In Wenger's (1998) framework, however, CoP is a fairly closed, inward looking and self-evolving informal entity. Members are closely connected with each other and don't seem to maintain many external linkages beyond the organizational boundary. The knowledge sharing process is organized mainly through daily interactions. This is probably true for CoPs that operate in relatively low-tech environments and with a simple social configuration such as claim processors (Wenger 1998), copier salespeople (Østerlund 1996), photo-copier repairmen (Orr 1996), midwifes, butchers, tailors, and others (Lave and Wenger 1991). In these social and organizational settings, the knowledge base of respective CoPs is relatively simple and stable. The situation however is rather different in some knowledge intensive and high-tech industries, such as information technology (IT) industry. Technological innovation in IT is very fast. The underlying knowledge base is under rapid update and integrated through complex organizational arrangements such as joint ventures, alliances and outsourcing contracts for shortening lead development times.

Informal personal linkages often serve as the channels for rapid exchange of information and knowledge of great value for innovation (Assimakopoulos and Macdonald 2003a and 2003b, Powell 1998, Johannisson 1998, Saxenian 1994). More than two decades ago, Rogers (1982) pointed out that much information for innovation in high technology flows by informal means, in personal networks, by means of information exchange among individuals. Personal networks seem to empower high-tech firms to be more innovative and flexible, thus generating competitive advantage (Cohen and Fields 1999). In current business settings characterized by fast technological and organizational changes, people increasingly rely on their own personal networks, rather than formal organizational arrangements to get information and knowledge for solving everyday job related problems (Nardi et al 2001).

The widespread adoption of Internet in the last decade also fuelled a new form of informal inter-personal support structure, the virtual community. People congregate in virtual venues on the Internet to share information, knowledge, personal feeling, and other valuable resources. Rheingold (1993 p.5) termed this phenomenon as virtual community and defined it as ‘social aggregations that emerge from the Net when enough people carry on those public discussions long enough, with sufficient human feeling, to form webs of personal relationships in cyberspace’. Internet forums are often interest-based and operate like personal communities without propinquity in which people provide support and sharing valuable information and knowledge with regard to a common interest with other fellow members over great geographical distances.

## METHODOLOGY

This research adopted a qualitative strategy based on ethnography (Bryman 2004) and case study (Yin 1994) appropriate for exploring emerging phenomena, such as the role of Internet technology forums in software development. Ethnography provides an opportunity to study in depth the everyday life of an organization or community in its natural setting. The research paid particular attention to the advice seeking linkages of the software engineers, based on the assumption that tacit knowledge sharing takes place through inter-personal interaction and problem solving processes. By tracing the advice seeking linkages during the engineers' everyday work over a considerable period of time, the researchers managed to gain a more detailed understanding of the knowledge sharing process within and across the local CoP.

The CoP under study is located within a small innovative software company, Advanced System Development Corporation (ASDC), in Beijing, China. ASDC is a joint venture between IBM and the computer science department of Tsinghua University. It is located in Shangdi high-tech Industrial Park, in which hundreds of IT firms cluster, including China's largest computer manufacturer Legend Group, the top two Chinese software companies UFSOFT and Kingsoft, and many foreign IT companies. ASDC employed 24 software engineers at the time of the fieldwork.

Participant observation in ASDC took place for three and a half months in 2002. One of the authors joined the company and stayed in the development room all working hours. The researcher had his own cubicle at the central part of the development room, and therefore could hear and see what the engineers were talking and doing without being noticed. The researcher built good personal relationships with the engineers and frequently talked with them about research related topics over lunch and other informal occasions. Data from observation and informal discussions were recorded in the form of detailed notes taken during or after discussions and events happening. Towards the end of the field study, 15 formal interviews were carried out with key informants. Moreover a questionnaire survey was conducted covering all the engineers in ASDC.

During the participant observation, one of the researchers also registered as a member in a specialized Internet technology forum: China Software Developer Net (CSDN) in order to observe how the online advice seeking takes place, how the Internet forum is organized, and how the virtual community is interplaying with the real world community. Hundreds of discussion posts were downloaded and recorded. An online survey was also carried out in

CSDN to collect data about the motivation of the software engineers' participation in the online technical discussion.

## EMPIRICAL FINDINGS

*Advice Seeking from Personal Linkages.* During their everyday work practice, the software engineers frequently talk with colleagues about their development work. They need to share information, knowledge and techniques in order to work efficiently, and they seem very happy to do so. The engineers' shared professional experience makes them feel close to each other, and they have developed some common sense of how to deal with their everyday work. According to Wenger (1998) this group of engineers can easily be characterized as a CoP. The software engineers depend on various resources to solve the technical problems arising in their everyday development work. For them, seeking advice from somebody who has experience and knowledge is the most dynamic and efficient way, especially for some complex and difficult-to-define technical problems.

According to our findings most of the advice seeking happens among the members of the local CoP within the firm (Yan and Assimakopoulos 2003, Assimakopoulos and Yan 2006). When internal advice seeking cannot solve problems, engineers often seek advice from external resources, mainly from Chinese language Internet technology forums and to a much lesser extent from their personal networks. Seeking advice from personal networks for solving technical problems is not the first choice for ASDC software engineers. The engineers would rather prefer to discuss with colleagues, check user guides, or inquire in Internet technology forums, rather than to contact their personal linkages. Based on our questionnaire survey, 13 engineers (54.2%) state that they prefer to discuss with colleagues first, and only when failing, they turn to contact personal linkages; the other 11 engineers (45.8%) never contact their personal linkages for software development related problems; none of the engineers prefer to seek advice from personal linkages first.

These figures are supported by the participant observation. During the three and half month participant observation in ASDC, the researcher only recorded very a few cases when engineers contacted their friends out of the company seeking advice for software development related problems. It is difficult to estimate precisely the percentage of advice seeking from personal networks, but the frequency it happens in ASDC is less than once every two weeks in the whole community. Comparing to the internal advice seeking from colleagues, which takes place about twice or three times per engineer everyday, the frequency of external advice seeking from personal network is rather insignificant.

*Advice Seeking from Internet Technology Forums.* On the other hand, ASDC engineers frequently seek advice and discuss their technical problems in Chinese language Internet technology forums. A quarter of ASDC engineers makes online enquiries more than once everyday; a third of engineers make it twice or three times every week, and about 40 percent enquire once every week or less. Overall 13 percent of engineers support the statement that their development work is heavily relying on Internet technology forums and that, without them, they cannot effectively solve the everyday problems in their work. About half suggest that the Internet forums are important to their work, though, they could get similar help and support from other resources. And a bit more than a third thinks the Internet forum is not important as they can get the same help and support from other sources. It is worth also pointing out that no ASDC engineers choose the statement that Internet forums are not important at all and they do not use Internet forums in their daily work.

Seeking advice from Internet forums is like a conversation based on message exchanges. The engineer describes the problem in brief words, posts it in the forum, and then waits for replies. In some popular forums replies usually come back within a few hours, if not minutes. A reply often points out what is wrong and gives possible solutions. The senders are often software professionals having experience and knowledge about similar problems. Most of the replies are less than 5 lines in length, but few words seem enough to help solve specific problems. Some posts which include original code may be longer up to several pages. In some long posts, the contents are obviously copied from electronic documents. The senders advise to refer to the documentation for finding information about solving the problem. The vast majority of messages are written in mixed Chinese and English language, i.e. the code of software program in English, and the diagnosis of the problem and suggestions for possible solutions in Chinese.

In some cases when the problem is rather complex, the questioning-and-replying often evolves into an interactive discussion among many interested participants. The final solutions are often collaborative group results. It is common after several suggestions are provided by different respondents, the engineer who initially asked the question tests all the suggestions and reports back to the forum the results including input and output, error messages, compiler feedback, and other related information. In this way, more and more contextual information is provided and the online discussion goes deeper and deeper. Although most of the discussions complete within 10 exchanges, some enquiries get back 30 or more replies. Sometimes this interactive discussion would last a few hours, even one or two days.

*China Software Developer Net.* Based on our questionnaire survey, all the ASDC engineers listed up to two Internet technology forums from which they often seek advice. A total of 14 forums were suggested, including China Software Developer Net (http://www.CSDN.net), China Java Sun forum (http://www.java.sun.com.cn), Tsinghua University BBS (http://bbs.tsinghua.edu.cn), and several others. Among them, CSDN is the most popular one, listed by 9 out of the 24 software engineers in ASDC. CSDN is one of the biggest Chinese language Internet software technology forums, with over 200,000 software professionals in IT firms all over China registered as members. CSDN has 30 sub-forums covering almost all the software technical areas. Everyday about 80,000 people visit the forum with unique IP address, and deliver more than 1,500,000 page views. There are always 2,000 to 3,000 members keeping online in the forum during working hours.

CSDN forum has put together a set of accounts or indicators for fostering online discussion among software engineers, including expert point account, reputation account, and membership grade system. The expert account reflects how expert the member is and how much contribution s/he has made to public discussions. Upon registration, each member is given an expert account with 200 points, which increases by 10 points every day. Posting a message adds 5 points to the account. When making an enquiry, the member must promise a number of expert points to the potential repliers, say 30, 50, or more, depending on how difficult the question is and how urgently the reply is needed. The promise has to be sufficiently attractive that other members will answer the question. In order to have enough points to ask questions, CSDN members must keep answering questions. Members with high expert points are well respected in the forum as they are considered highly qualified experts, have solved many technical problems, and have continuously helped other people in the forum.

The reputation account is an indicator of how well a member complies with the rules of the forum. Every member gets 100 reputation points at registration. Bad behavior causes deduction of the points, for example: breaking the promise to transfer expert points after a problem is solved, using impolite phrases, posting meaningless messages, and the like. In other cases, reputation points increase. The sub-forum coordinator determines whether to add or subtract points to members' accounts. When a member has few reputation points, no one cares to answer his/her questions, and the right to post messages is lost when reputation points run out. Last but not least the membership grade system, similarly to the military rank, classifies the members into 10 grades from first to fifth level and then from one to five stars on the basis of expert points. Different memberships have different ranges of right in the forum. The technical advice from high grade members often gets more attention, and the members themselves are highly admired and respected in the forum.

Every day hundreds, if not thousands, of questions are discussed in CSDN. The titles of the posts are in various styles. Some are straightforward like 'How to transfer MS Access file to XML page?', 'A question about C++ pointer'; some emphasize the urgency of the problem, for example, 'Online waiting for VB expert!'; some try to attract attention by promise of expert points such as '100 points for suggestion about a JSP design', etc. Most of the problems can be resolved within few exchanges, while a very small number of problems cannot find satisfactory solutions even after many rounds of discussion. However, an enquiry getting no reply is a very rare phenomenon in CSDN. When the problems are solved, the posts are moved to a 'resolved-postings' board, some frequently asked questions are moved to FAQ board, and some with excellent technical solutions are moved to 'elite-postings' board. Members who do not wish to make an enquiry can search in these boards and get similar technical supports.

*The Sense of Community on the Internet.* One project team leader in ASDC is an uncompromising member of CSDN. He always keeps the CSDN window open in the background of his computer when he works and refreshes it from time to time. Sometimes after lunch when other engineers are chatting and relaxing, he is busy answering questions in CSDN. When he was asked why he likes answering questions in the forum, he said:

> *"When developing software, it is impossible that you know everything. Some problems seem too difficult, but in the eyes of the people who know, they are very easy. One or two words can save one or two hours of work. The situation is like when you are in a foreign place and ask direction from a local man in the street. It is very easy for him to tell you which way to go. Why not to tell you?"*

Based on the online survey in CSDN inquiring why members answer questions posted by unknown net "friends", several reasons were suggested. Many CSDN members think people ought to and should help each other; they also benefit from the advice provided by other people and they want to pay back in the same way; they also treat the ongoing online

Brown, J.S. and P. Duguid (1998). Organizing Knowledge. *California Management Review*, 40 (3), 90-112.

Bryman, A. (2004) *Social Research Methods* (2nd edition). Oxford University Press, Oxford.

Cohen, S. and G. Fields (1999). Social capital and capital gains in Silicon Valley. *California Management Review*, 41, 2, 108-130.

Gabrenya, W.K. and K.K. Hwang (1996). Chinese social interaction: Harmony and hierarchy on the good Earth. In: *Handbook of Chinese Psychology* (M.H. Bond ed.), Oxford University Press, Hong Kong.

Granovetter, M.S. (1973). The Strength of Weak Ties. *American Journal of Sociology*, 78, 1360-1380.

Haines, V.A and J.S. Hurlbert (1992). Network Range and Health. *Journal of Health and Social Behavior*, 33, 254-266.

Johannisson, B. (1998) Personal networks in emerging knowledge-based firms: spatial and functional patterns. *Entrepreneurship and Regional Development*, 10 (4), 297-315.

Kimble, C., P. Hildreth, and P. Wright (2001) Communities of Practice: Going Virtual, In *Knowledge Management and Business Model Innovation* (Y. Malhotra ed), 220-234. London: Idea Group.

Lave, J. and E. Wenger (1991). *Situated Learning: Legitimate Peripheral Participation.* Cambridge University Press, Cambridge.

Nardi, B.A., S. Whittaker, and H. Schwarz (2001). It's not what you know, it's who you know. [online] http://www.firstmonday.org/issues/issue5_5/nardi/index.html

Nonaka, I. and N. Konno (1998). The concept of 'Ba': Building a Foundation for Knowledge Creation. *California Management Review*, 40 (3), 40-54.

Oliver, P., G. Marwell, and R. Teixeira (1985). *A theory of critical mass: I. interdependence, group heterogeneity, and the production of collective action.* American Journal of Sociology, 91 (3), 522-556.

Orr, J.E. (1996). *Talking About Machines: An Ethnography of a Modern Job.* Cornell University Press, Ithaca.

Østerlund, C. (1996). Learning Across Contexts: A Field Study of Salespeople's Learning at Work. Skriftserie for Psykologisk Institute, 21 (1).

Powell, W. (1998) Learning from collaboration: knowledge and networks in the biotechnology and pharmaceutical industries. *California Management Review*, 40 (3), 228-240.

Rheingold, H. (1993). *The Virtual Community: Homesteading on the Electronic Frontier*. MIT Press, Cambridge, MA.

Rogers, E. (1982). *Information exchange and technological innovation: the transfer and utilization of technical knowledge*. Lexington Books, Lexington MA.

Saxenian, A. (1994). *Regional advantage*, Harvard University Press, Cambridge, MA.

Sproull, L and S. Faraj (1995). Atheism, Sex and Databases: The Net as Social Technology. In *Public Access to the Internet* (Kahin, B. and J. Keller eds.), 62-81. MIT Press, Cambridge, MA.

Teece, D.J. (2001). Strategies for Managing Knowledge Assets: the Role of Firm Structure and Industrial Context. In: *Managing Industrial Knowledge* (Nonaka, I. and D.J. Teece eds.). Sage Publication, London.

Wenger, E. (1998). *Communities of Practice: Learning, Meaning, and Identity*. Cambridge University Press, Cambridge.

Yan, J. and D. Assimakopoulos (2003) Knowledge Sharing and Advice Seeking in a Software Engineering Community. In: *Processes and Foundations for Virtual Organizations* (L.M. Camarinha-Matos and H. Afsarmanesh eds.), 341-350. Kluwer Academic, Dordrecht.

Yin, R. (1994). *Case Study Research*. Sage Publication, Thousand Oaks, CA.

# SECTION III

## TECHNOLOGY TRANSFER AND TECHNOLOGY DIFFUSION

Management of Technology: New Directions in Technology Management
M. Hashem Sherif and T.M. Khalil (Editors)



# 15

# TECNOLOGY-BASED INVESTMENT OF GERMAN FIRMS IN CHINA – MOTIVES AND NATURE

*XiangDong Chen, The School of Economics & Management, Beijing University of Aeronautics & Astronautics*
*Guido Reger, Department of Economics and Social Sciences, University of Potsdam*

## INTRODUCTION

China, as being the largest foreign direct investment (FDI) host country in the world, has been increasingly attracting international attention from companies and policy makers. As more and more German firms enter the Chinese market, the investment is becoming larger in size and of higher quality. Therefore, issues of the motives and nature of German FDI in China and related technological activities have become a more important topic for both Chinese and overseas researchers

FDI has been discussed widely in the scientific community of international business and management. Special concern has been focused on foreign companies' entry modes and their investment strategies in a certain country or region, particularly in cases where market potential or cultural differences between home and host country are high. China, being the largest FDI host country in the world since 2002, and as a fast growing developing nation, has typical characters in both economic and technological development, and has been increasingly attracting international attention. Number of international studies regarding the case of China has been increasing especially in recent years, among which studies by Western scholars are in the majority. On the other hand, multinational enterprises (MNEs) from different countries have been analysed in FDI related studies, of which German companies are reported as one of the most active FDI driving forces in the world, with particular strength in the manufacturing area in developing countries.

This research aims at analysing FDI movement of German companies in China and the technological activities related to this. The study and the survey should provide up to date insights and lessons for both academic researchers and business practitioners in the field of innovation with an international business context. From a methodological viewpoint our study includes:

- a review of empirical and theoretical studies,
- an analysis of German companies investing in China based on the database of the Delegation of the German Industry and Commerce (GIC) in Shanghai,
- a mail survey among German companies active in China.

The paper is structured as follows: first, a summarized literature review on foreign direct investment and technological activities. Then, main results of our database analysis and mail survey among German firms investing in China. Conclusions are drawn in the final section.

*Foreign direct investment and technological activities – a literature review.* Foreign direct investment (FDI) has been one of the most striking issues currently discussed in the scientific journals on innovation as well as international business. FDI is defined as "investment that brings (foreign) investors effective control and is accompanied with managerial participation" (Robock and Simmonds 1983, 6) and is mainly conducted by MNEs. Special concern has been focused on foreign companies' entry modes and their investment strategies in countries or regions where market potential or cultural differences between home and host country are high. China is one of the countries of this kind. Ever since 2002, China became the largest host country in the world in terms of attracting international investment, particularly from MNEs in more industrialized countries. On the other hand, multinational enterprises (MNEs) from different countries have been analysed in FDI related studies (e.g. Xu 2000, Bu 2001, Buckley, Casson 1998, Dunning 1998, Sanyalla, Guvenli 2000), of which German companies are reported as one of the most active FDI driving forces in the world, with particular strength in manufacturing in developing countries.

The development of German FDI into China in the last decade is closely linked with trade relations between the two countries. Based on trade related statistical data, in recent years, China has become one of the important trade partners of German companies with a positive increase of 67% and 88% in terms of export and import value respectively between 1996 and 2001. Among overall FDI inflows into China from different countries and districts,

German investment increased significantly in recent years, particularly between 1996 and 1998. Figure 1 compares the German FDI inflows (see real FDI at the right vertical axis) with overall FDI inflows (see real FDI at the left vertical axis).

**Figure 1. FDI inflows into China between 1990 and 2001 (total investment vs. investment from Germany)**

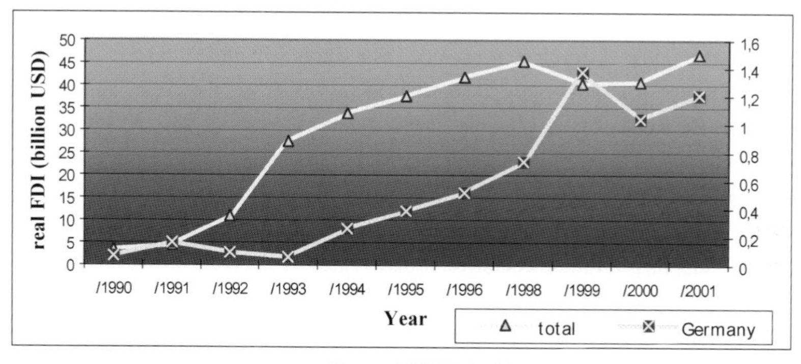


Source: MOFTEC, China.

Along with increasing demand for lowering down trade and production costs, FDI is becoming more and more a vitally important tool or operating channel for international companies to transfer and to leverage various resources, which has been emphasized in recent years not only by companies in capital host countries but also by ones in capital exporting countries. Thus in some developing countries such as in China, competitive advantage, right location, as well as so called created asset synergy are frequently discussed as necessities in attracting FDI. For example, from a capital supplier's point of view, it is generally acknowledged that there are four main motives for foreign direct investment: (1) to seek natural resources, (2) to seek new markets, (3) to restructure existing production through rationalization and (4) to seek strategically related created assets (see Narula and Dunning 2000). These motives can be broadly divided into two types. The first three ones represent motives which are primarily asset-exploiting in nature: the investing company's primary aim is to generate economic rent through the use of its existing firm-specific assets in the home country. On the other hand, the fourth motive is an asset-augmenting activity, whereby the investing firm wishes to enrich its existing assets by investing its capital into foreign locations and tap into the host country's knowledge sources. Apparently, the fourth motive and related entry mode can create wealthier technology and knowledge, but at the same time, the nature of the investment is decisive. Although there is an increase in asset-seeking FDI in some developing countries during the last decade this still seems to be the exception rather than the rule (see Narula and Dunning 2000). Main reasons can be listed as lower average educational level of working forces, less technological capabilities and organizational skills – all in all a less developed national and regional innovation system - in developing countries.

On the other hand, FDI in developing countries as a whole still proves to be most challenging and sometimes highly unsatisfactory. Beamish (1985, 1987, 1988) did exclusive work on joint ventures of multinationals in developing countries and his research showed that developing countries had a higher level of instability. A report from UNCTAD (1998) also indicates the increasing reliance of less developed countries on FDI as a source of capital, technology and knowledge. Although inward FDI does not represent the only option available to the economic development of these countries' it may represent the most efficient option. Narula and Dunning (2000) give four reasons. Firstly, the acquiring technological know-how through entering foreign markets is an expensive undertaking, and given the shortage of domestic capital this option is not open to many developing countries. Secondly, liberalized market means that overseas firms are likely to be more eager to maintain controls of their competitive advantages, either through establishment of wholly owned subsidiaries or through joint ventures. There are exceptions, though generally this happens only where strong strategic reasons or structural distortions exist, for instance where the host country has a strong bargaining position, or where the technology has reached the status of a commodity. Thirdly, infant industry protection is supporting creation of a domestic sector, however, protected markets are a limited option within the framework of the World Trade Organization (WTO). Fourthly, the complementary resources necessary to establish a viable and strong domestic sector are usually very capital and knowledge-intensive.

In host countries, particularly in developing countries, competition is also keen for the 'right' investment to be attracted for the country or region. Hence, so called specialized FDI or sequential investment, or even the phenomena of investment in clusters, becomes vitally important for developing countries, because they offer the opportunity of receiving production knowledge, technology and innovation. Studies show that attracting specialized FDI to a particular sector can alter the sequence of industrial upgrading (see Williamson and Hu 1994) because specialized FDI may help to improve the created assets associated within certain sectors. Moreover, created assets in any one sector may have significant knowledge flow externalities into another one, which, in turn, may represent significant input to another sector. But this presumes the presence of a virtuous circle and the development of appropriate clusters. On the other hand, sequential investment in higher valued sectors is important. Blomstrom (1989) in his study revealed that this kind of activity provided the most significant potential spillovers, although generally the opportunities for sequential investments are limited.

*Empirical Results: Motives and Nature of German FDI in China - Research approach.* Our empirical results are based on two elements: (1) an analysis of the database of the Delegation of the German Industry and Commerce (GIC) in Shanghai (in the following GIC database) and (2) a mail survey among German companies with FDI in China. The first source for our empirical investigation was the database of Shanghai'sI, which we cleared up for our scientific purposes. The GIC database contains in total 1515 records of German firms investing in China until January 2001, however, only 415 at the time of survey provided more detailed information on their investment nature and were included in our FDI analysis.

The written survey is the second source and was conducted in the end of 2001 among 164 companies with their headquarters in Germany and those sample companies had foreign direct investment in China. The original data stems from the cleared up GIC database. We included in our sample all German companies that had production facilities in China and exclude those firms that only had administrative offices. The questionnaire was written in English. The hypotheses and the questionnaire were built on the analysis of international and Chinese empirical studies on FDI in China, including studies specifically on German companies and their investment in China. The mail survey was accompanied by telephone and personal interviews. 33 responses were received and 21 questionnaires were filled in completely and could be included in our analysis (which represents response rate of 12.8%).

*Distribution of German FDI according to regions, branches and entering time.* The analysis of the cleared up GIC database shows that the investment of German companies in China are concentrated in certain areas and highly geographically differentiated, such as in Shanghai City area (39%), Beijing City area (26.5%), Eastern China (13.5%, of which Jiang-su Province accounts for 77.6%), and southern China (8.2%, of which Guangdong Province accounts for 77.0%) (see Table 1). The German firms in these four major cities and provinces represent 87.15% of all China-based German companies' investment. Unlike investment distribution from Hong Kong and other Asian countries and districts, German investment is not very much condensed in deep southern China, but heavily concentrated upon Shanghai City area, and some eastern part of China where large local manufacturing companies are located. The reason why Beijing area accounts for a large ratio can be attributed to the large numbers of representative offices or holding companies of German firms which may also reflect that larger MNEs are the dominating parts of German investment in China. The detailed rank of Chinese cities and provinces attracting German companies are shown in Table 1, whereby data from two sources - the GIC database and our mail survey – are compared.

**Table 1. Geographical distribution and ranking of the investment of German firms in China**

| Typical district in China | GIC database | Own mail survey |
|---|---|---|
| Beijing City | 26.47% (2) | 11% (4) |
| Shanghai City (coast city) | 39.00% (1) | 31% (1) |
| Jiangsu Prov. (eastern coast province), | 7.70% (3) | 19% (2) |
| Shandong Prov. (eastern coast province), | 3.58% (5) | |
| Zhejiang Prov. (eastern coast province) | 2.23% (7) | |
| Guangdong Prov. (southern coast province) | 6.55% (4) | 11.4% (3) |
| Fujian Prov. (southern coast province) | 1.62% (8) | |
| Liaoning Prov. (north eastern coast province), | 3.17% (6) | 7.7% (5) |
| Jilin Prov. (north eastern, inner land) | 1.28% (10) | |
| Tianjin City (coast city) | 3.17% (6) | 0.0% |
| Sichuan Prov. (Southern west China, inner land) | 1.35% (9) | 7.7% (5) |
| Hubei Prov. (central China, inner land ) | 1.28% (10) | 3.9% (6) |
| Hebei Prov. (central north China, inner land) | 0.81% (11) | |
| Anhui Prov. (central China, inner land) | 0.68% (12) | |
| Sum | 98.92% | 99.0% |

Source: GIC database and own mail survey

*Note: those samples with shares less than 0.50% are excluded, which means that the rest 1.08% of investment in terms of company numbers are scattered in other 11 provinces and cities, and there are still other 7 provinces with no German's investment at all.*

Generally speaking, the geographic distributions in the two data sets are rather similar. Eastern coast cities and districts (including Shanghai city) are heavily concentrated by German investment. One of the key reasons explained by a large German MNE is the closer distance from the manufacturing base to the company's major customers. As most important joint ventures and local enterprises, including state-owned, collective owned, and town and township enterprises are heavily located in these regions, this geographical distribution pattern of German investment reasonably reflects the manufacturing nature of the investment, and also applies to some business research in papers published in Chinese. Location factors for attracting western investment in China are usually ranked as (according to the importance of factors): infrastructure and suitable business facilities, convenient international trade and communication conditions with overseas buyers or suppliers, stability of local government policies and social life, highly qualified working staff, closeness to major customers, well established legislative system and business law, modernized managerial system, and convenience of local transportation. Apparently, these factors also imply important supporting conditions for longer term and market oriented investment.

Based on the GIC database, German companies invest in China in both manufacturing and services sector. If measured in numbers of firms invested, then manufacturing firms account for 74.7% while firms in service sector only account for 25.3%. Within the manufacturing sector, the most significant fields being invested are chemicals (21.75%) and mechanical sector (74.7%). Within the services sector, the investment is distributed by rank in trade and finance (35.6%), transportation and warehousing (28.5%), accounting and consultancy (15.7%), education and training (10.7%), design, installation, and repair (4.2%), computer software (2.9%), and law (2.4%).

According to Bu's (2001) recent survey on German companies in China, 86.3% of the investigated 199 firms established their business in China during 1994 –1996. The maximum lifetime of those firms is 13 years and the minimum is only 7 months, with an average duration of 3.5 years.

**Figure 2. German investment in China: entering time distribution by numbers of firms**

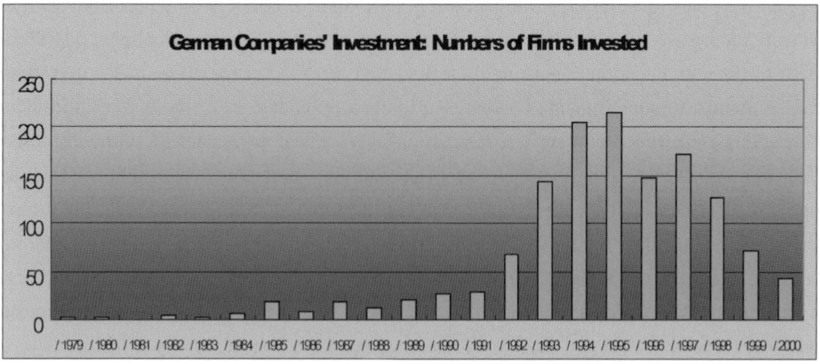

Source: calculated on the basis of the GIC database

Our analysis of the GIC database covering 415 German firms provides a more complete distribution pattern. Figure 2 shows the entering time of German firms into China from 1979 till 2000. They invested in China mainly between 1993 and 1997. Most sample companies (73.4%) entered China after 1992, while most large German MNEs (50%) began their R&D investment also after 1992. Apparently, many German companies began their China operation based on a long-term vision, particularly after 1992. However, a larger drop in the number of investing firms occurred after 1998, which can be interpreted as the negative influence of the Asian financial crisis. However, large-scale investment, which is normally conducted by larger MNEs, continued. Especially in recent years, German MNEs have shown their sequential investment with larger volume.

*Foreign direct investment and technology transfer.* As far as technology transfer issues are concerned, 76.9% of the German companies investigated in our mail survey responded that they had transferred technology into China through their subsidiary, 7.7% of the investigated firms expressed their intention to transfer technology in the future, and 15.4% of our sample neither transfer technology nor have such intentions. The technology transfer involved is mainly characterized by production equipment. Only 18.8% of our sample companies mentioned that their products were adapted to local needs through R&D activities, and 12.5%

provided new product designs. On the other hand, 50% of the sample firms renovated their products only through marketing terms (package, etc.), 6.5% might do so in the future, and another 12.5% companies mentioned that they directly transferred original designs into China.

Further, if we consider a more detailed nature of the technology being transferred, Table 2 provides more information based on our survey. Three modes are classified and defined here, namely, hardware transfer (to indicate production routine with international standards), on-site software transfer (to indicate the transfer of more practical production-oriented technology, or operating know-how), and idea transfer (to indicate transfer of more design-type of technology, or know-why type knowledge). The first mode of technology transfer provides means of international production routine, normally with enlarged production capacity, while transfer of on-site software can promote local learning of practical techniques and operation knowledge in a wider sense. The third mode of transferring technology is the most advanced in the sense of gaining knowledge and may provide key opportunities for the recipient to catch up with the rapid change of the market, though this type of technology transfer is still very much limited.

**Table 2. Three categories of technology transfer of German firms investing in China**

| Classification | Items | Ratio | Nature |
|---|---|---|---|
| Hardware transfer | Complete set of technical equipment | 6.2% | Learning of production routine<br>Sub total: 20.0% |
| | Key technical equipment transfer | 13.8% | |
| On-site software transfer | Technical document & on-site problem solving | 18.5% | Learning of Know-how<br>Sub total: 70.7% |
| | Technical consultancy for production problems | 12.3% | |
| | Technical personnel & technical training | 26.1% | |
| | Management & quality control skills | 13.8% | |
| Idea transfer | Product prototype | 4.6% | know-why- type Learning<br>Sub total: 9.2% |
| | Patent license | 4.6% | |

*Position in supply chain.* Our sample companies' operation in terms of supply chain in China is significantly positioned at mid and upper stream markets for China's domestic industrial buyers. Table 3 reveals that German firms' investment in China clearly focuses on industrial buyers (83.5%), primarily buyers in Chinese market (75.1%). Another important nature of investigated companies is reflected to be upstream buyers oriented (70.9%). On the other hand, our data also indicate that most (75.3%) of the investigated companies purchase semi-manufactured products for their own production from Chinese domestic market.

These facts imply that German FDI in China is heavily localized in terms of both product output and materials input, with strong support from their steady supply chain cooperation (which can be revealed from the larger share of purchasing on special purpose parts as these special purpose product supplies generally require longer term inter-firm relations). Therefore, it can be concluded that the German subsidiaries are well positioned in the Chinese market for longer-term operations and are focussed on local industrial suppliers.

**Table 3. Investigated German firms in China – supplying and purchasing nature**

<table>
<tr><td></td><td colspan="4">(Industrial market)<br>Outside of China market</td><td colspan="4">(Industrial market)<br>China domestic market</td><td rowspan="3">Consumer goods market (Chinese & overseas market)</td></tr>
<tr><td rowspan="4">Supplying nature</td><td colspan="2" rowspan="2">Upstream sectors</td><td colspan="2" rowspan="2">Down stream sectors</td><td colspan="2">Upstream sectors</td><td colspan="2">Down stream sectors</td></tr>
<tr><td>Joint ventures</td><td>Locally owned</td><td>Joint ventures</td><td>Locally owned</td></tr>
<tr><td colspan="2">4.2%</td><td colspan="2">4.2%</td><td>37.5%</td><td>29.2%</td><td>4.2%</td><td>4.2%</td><td rowspan="2">16.6%</td></tr>
<tr><td colspan="4">Sub total: 8.4%</td><td colspan="4">Sub total: 75.1%</td></tr>
<tr><td rowspan="5">Purchasing nature</td><td rowspan="2">Natural resource</td><td colspan="2" rowspan="2">General purpose parts</td><td rowspan="2">Special purpose parts</td><td colspan="2">General purpose parts</td><td colspan="2">Special purpose parts</td><td rowspan="5">N/A</td></tr>
<tr><td>Joint ventures</td><td>Locally owned</td><td>Joint ventures</td><td>Locally owned</td></tr>
<tr><td>2.0%</td><td colspan="2">10.3%</td><td>7.7%</td><td>12.8%</td><td>20.5%</td><td>21.0%</td><td>21.0%</td></tr>
<tr><td></td><td colspan="3">Sub total: 18%</td><td colspan="2">Sub total: 33.3%</td><td colspan="2">Sub total: 42.0%</td></tr>
<tr><td colspan="4">Sub Total: 20%</td><td colspan="4">Sub Total: 75.3% excluding natural resource</td></tr>
</table>

*Motives, success factors, difficulties, and future plans.* An important part of our questionnaire was designed to ask the German companies for their perceptions on different aspects of their investment projects in China (refer to Table 4). 52 questions in total in this part are distributed into 7 groups. Questions in Group 1 are directly related to investment motives in general, while questions in Group 2, 3, 4 concern investment motives reflected from management routine transfer, competition strength, and technical innovation. Group 5 and 6 concern successful and difficult factors during their investment operations in China, and finally, questions in Group 7 ask the companies about their investment plans in China in the near future. The response in the questionnaire is measured through Likert Scale between 1 (neglectable) and 5 (extremely important), and 0 (not sure, which indicates that the respondent is not sure about the answer). Kreutzberger (2000) and Liu (2000) also conducted surveys on German companies' investment projects in China and their research results can be compared to our results.

**Table 4. Major perceptions of German companies on their investment in China**

| | Rank | Mean | Std. Deviation |
|---|---|---|---|
| **Perception Group 1: Major motives of German companies for their investment in China:** | | | |
| Entering into the Chinese market | 1 | 4.8571 | .5345 |
| Increasing market share in China | 2 | 4.2000 | .8619 |
| Effectively using local natural & manpower resource | 3 | 3.3571 | 1.4991 |
| Establishing a strong production base for sales in the Asian region | 4 | 2.9333 | 1.3345 |
| Being part of supply chain to satisfy demand from other European firms in China | 5 | 2.7692 | 1.4233 |
| **Perception Group 2: Important strengths in production system of subsidiary in China** | | | |
| Well accumulated business information facilities | 1 | 3.7692 | 1.8328 |
| Innovation & change | 2 | 3.6364 | 1.5015 |
| Management qualification | 3 | 3.0833 | 1.6214 |
| Technical equipment qualifications | 4 | 2.4167 | 1.8320 |
| **Perception Group 3: Important strength of subsidiary in competing with other firms in China** | | | |
| Advanced production technology for world quality standard | 1 | 3.8667 | 1.4075 |
| Strong distribution network in the world | 2 | 3.0714 | 1.6392 |
| Professional technology & expertise in niche market | 3 | 3.0000 | 1.4606 |
| Strong marketing team and expertise | 4 | 2.8571 | 1.8752 |
| Differentiation capability in providing versatile products | 5 | 2.5714 | 1.6968 |
| Successful member of supply chain worldwide | 6 | 1.9333 | 1.5337 |
| **Perception Group 4: Major contribution factors to increase innovation at the subsidiary** | | | |
| Active technology transfer between German parent and subsidiary | 1 | 4.3333 | .8876 |
| Technical training for local employees | 2 | 3.9167 | 1.1645 |
| Appropriate human resource management to attract skilled workers | 3 | 3.5833 | 1.3114 |
| The advanced product/ service brought to China | 4 | 2.9167 | 1.0836 |

| | Rank | Mean | Std. Deviation |
|---|---|---|---|
| Significantly updating local quality guarantee system | 5 | 2.9167 | 1.6765 |
| Significantly updating local production equipment | 6 | 2.6667 | 1.4975 |
| Successful networking with European firms in China | 7 | 2.4615 | .9674 |
| Well established technical equipment/technicians from Chinese partners | 8 | 2.4167 | 1.3114 |
| Strong local R&D capability within subsidiary in China | 9 | 2.0000 | 1.4142 |
| **Perception Group 5: Major factors which enable successful operations in China** | | | |
| Right product/ service choice | 1 | 3.6250 | 1.7842 |
| Good relationship between German and Chinese technical personnel | 1 | 3.6250 | 1.6279 |
| Important support from local government in China | 2 | 3.5714 | 1.4525 |
| Right choice of geographical region in China | 3 | 3.2857 | 1.3260 |
| Partners' interests are well protected and properly managed | 4 | 3.2000 | 1.7403 |
| Right partner choice | 5 | 3.0000 | 2.0702 |
| **Perceptions Group 6: Major problems in investment projects in China** | | | |
| Practically confusing on Chinese business law system | 1 | 3.1538 | 1.4632 |
| Lower quality of locally produced raw materials in China | 2 | 3.0000 | 1.4676 |
| Ambiguity of responsibility in Chinese management system | 3 | 2.9231 | 1.2558 |
| Lack of mutual trust between German & Chinese management | 4 | 2.8667 | 1.5523 |
| Market information in China is not precise | 5 | 2.8462 | 1.2810 |
| Lack of intellectual property right protection on company's operation | 6 | 2.7857 | 2.0069 |
| Higher change & mobility of employees in the joint venture | 7 | 2.7692 | 1.1658 |
| Negotiation process is complex and time-consuming | 8 | 2.6923 | 1.8432 |
| Foreign exchange balance problem due to larger import | 9 | 2.5714 | 1.5549 |
| Strong and negative local government intervention | 10 | 2.2857 | 1.2666 |
| Different local technical standard | 11 | 2.2143 | .8926 |
| Loosely controlled quality guarantee system in China | 12 | 2.1429 | 1.3506 |
| Lack of stable and economic local distribution channel | 13 | 2.0714 | 1.4392 |
| Lack of market demand for the products of the subsidiary in China | 14 | 1.7143 | 1.0690 |
| **Perceptions Group 7: German companies' further investment into China for the future** | | | |
| Introducing more advanced products into China-based joint venture | 1 | 3.5000 | 1.4544 |
| Enlarging investment scale on the same product | 2 | 3.0000 | 1.2536 |
| Building up internal R&D activities in the China-based subsidiary | 3 | 2.6429 | 1.5495 |
| Deepening production co-operation (e.g. production resource) | 4 | 2.4615 | 1.3301 |
| Retraction from placing our production in the Chinese market | 5 | 2.0000 | 1.1767 |
| Retraction from manufacturing in China | 6 | 1.5714 | .8516 |
| Retraction internal R&D activities in the China-based company | 7 | 1.3636 | .6742 |

Perception Group 1 describes the major motives of German firms. Entering into the Chinese market and increasing the market share play dominant role. In contrast, being part of the industrial supply chain to satisfy demand from other European companies in China plays the least important role. Market dominance of the motives is similar to other surveys. In Kreutzberger's work (2000), market development, expansion and market share were the top choices of his sample companies whereas low labour cost appeared to be the least important, which is similar to our survey. Liu (2000) also indicated that the most important motives of German companies' investment in China was still the entering into local market, while lowering production cost and reducing import barriers were mentioned as less important.

The questions in perception group 3 describe important strengths of the German subsidiary and joint ventures for their successful competition in China. Top ranking items in this group by the sample companies are an advanced production technology to meet world quality standard, a strong distribution network, and a strong professional technology and expertise in a niche market. A strong marketing team and expertise, the capability for product differentiation and being members of the world-wide supply chain do not play a prominent role.

Major contributing factors to increase the level of innovation at the subsidiary in China were part of our questionnaire in perception group 4. The most important choice seems to be an active technology transfer between parent firms in Germany and subsidiaries in China, followed by an intensive training of local technical employees, an appropriate human resource management which attracts highly skilled workers. Factors of average importance are advancement of initial product / service brought to China, and significance of updating local quality guarantee system.

Considering perception of Group 5, we intended to answer what were the major factors to support successful operation of the German subsidiaries in China. Key factor, according to our survey, was the choice of right product or service, a good relationship between the German and Chinese technical personnel and workers, and support from local government in China. This is in contrast to Kreutzberger's survey (2000) and Liu's research (2000) in which effective marketing and effective distribution channels were mentioned as key factors to companies' success. However, in this part of our survey differences in the ranking of the answers are not very high.

We asked the firms also what the major problems were with their investment in China (refer to perception Group 6, Table 4). The eight top-ranked difficulties are, respectively related to, a practical confusion with the Chinese law system, a lower quality of locally produced raw materials, ambiguity of the responsibility in the Chinese management system, lack of mutual trust between the German and Chinese management teams, an un-precise market information in China or a too fast change in the market, a lack of intellectual property right protection, a higher change and mobility of employees in the subsidiary, and a complex and time-consuming negotiation process. A strong and negative intervention of local government and a lack of market demand seem to play a minor role. If the most important problems are grouped together, one can say that the main difficulties of the German subsidiaries are in the legal frame conditions, a less sufficient quality and cultural differences. Insufficient legal frame conditions and especially the poor protection of intellectual property rights are mentioned as one of the most undesirable factors in other studies as well (see Bennet et al 2000, Jin, von Zedtwitz 2003).

The answers related to those sample companies' further plans of their investment in China point into the direction of differentiation and market enlargement (see perception Group 7, Table 4). Introducing more advanced products through Chinese subsidiary and enlarging the investment scale on the same product are of major importance. On the other hand, retraction from Chinese market hardly plays any role in the plans of the investigated German firms. Obviously, the companies have been and will be able to deal with those difficulties and regard their engagement into China's market as a long-term plan and a strategic move. Meanwhile, positive confirmation on importance of introducing more advanced products and even building up of internal R&D in the German subsidiary in China may also imply that in the future – at least partially - the Chinese market and customers may be considered as much more advanced and sophisticated ones.

## Summary and Conclusions

It can be concluded that the preferred geographic locations of German companies in China are well established in those typical industrial regions, where a good business infrastructure is much more improved. Further, the market focus of the sample German firms is clearly on the Chinese domestic market and industrial buyers. The production system and purchasing behaviour are therefore strongly localised. Technology transfer from German parent to its subsidiary in China focuses mainly on production technology. Technological activities – if performed in China – include only a minor number of cases where idea generation, design activities, or product development can be found. Product development activities are therefore primarily related to adapting original product to local needs.

The motives of the German companies' investment are clearly dominated by market-oriented strategies. Most of the German firms have a long-term vision related with their FDI in China. Clearly, the establishment of a production base and the transfer of production technology are all necessary to serve Chinese market-oriented investment. It is no wonder that an advanced production technology is regarded as the most important strength for successfully competing in China.. Technology transfer therefore is very active and a localized production and management system have been well organized. From point of view of the German firms in this survey, most companies consider their strategic achievements in China to be successful.

Main difficulties with the investment of the German firms caused problems around three large issues, namely, legal frame conditions, product quality, and intercultural differences. However, the problems mentioned do not seem to be so high that they can not be overcome: a retraction from production in China is still a neglectable part of the future plans of the investigated companies. In contrast, introduction of advanced products in China is rather one of those positive choices for the planned investment.

According to Narula and Dunning (2000) there are four main motives for FDI: (1) to seek natural resources, (2) to seek new markets, (3) to restructure existing production through rationalization and (4) to seek strategically related created assets. Various indicators of our empirical research clearly show that the FDI of the German firms are market-oriented. This may be in contrast to results of other studies. For instance, recent research (see Edler, Meyer-Krahmer, Reger 2002, Reger 2002) has analysed the R&D internationalisation of 209 North American, Japanese and western European (including German firms) technology-intensive firms and concluded that the western European firms gave more room to build up centres of excellence and own competences in R&D units abroad. Von Zedtwitz (2003) showed in his study on green-field R&D labs of twelve multinationals in China that their missions were development focussed and oriented to local businesses and customers. Further, several of these labs have worldwide mandates for certain products and technologies. Both studies would have suggested that - at least - some of our German firms investigated perform R&D in China to develop new products for Chinese market and follow the fourth FDI mode, which is dedicated to seeking strategically related created assets. Although differences in the results can be explained by different objects under investigations (i.e. von Zedtwitz analysed explicitly green-field R&D whereas we looked at foreign direct investment as a whole), another explanation may lie in different development stage of China itself. At present, the FDI mode represents average development stage of this huge country in which establishment of qualified production foundations is the key for the country's economic and market growth. With a greater differentiation and sophistication of the Chinese innovation system it can become more attractive for asset-seeking investment, which may in turn enrich the national innovation system again.

Finally, it should be noted that our sample of German companies investing in China was not large enough to be representative. Therefore, the results of our survey should be taken with care and have an exploratory character. The sample of other studies is small either and obviously further empirical research is needed.

## ACKNOWLEDGEMENT

This research was kindly sponsored by the German Academic Exchange Service (Deutscher Akademischer Austauschdienst - DAAD) and through a project supported from the Natural Science Foundation of China (NSFC, project no. 70273004). It would not have been possible without these supports. The authors wish to express their grateful acknowledgement to the DAAD and NSFC, and also to the editors of this book.

## REFERENCES

Beamish, P.W. (1985). The characteristics of joint ventures in developed and developing countries. *Columbia Journal of World Business*, 20, 13–19.

Beamish, P.W. (1987). Joint venture in LDCs: partners election and performance. *Management International Review*, 27, 23–37.

Beamish, P.W. (1988). *Multinational joint ventures in developing countries*. Routledge, New York.

Bennett, D., Liu, X., Parker, D., Steward, F., Vaidya, K. (2000). *Technology transfer to China: a study of strategy in 20 EU industrial countries.* Aston Business School Press, Birmingham.

Blomstrom, M. (1989). *Foreign Investment and Spill-over: A Study of Technology Transfer to Mexico.* Routledge, London.

Bu (2001). German companies' investment in China and their promoting systems. *Shanghai Economic Research* (in Chinese).

Buckley, P., Casson, M. (1998). Models of the multinational enterprise. *Journal of International Business Studies*, 29, 21-44.

Dunning, J.H. (1998). Transnational corporations: an overview of relations with national governments. *New Political Economy*, 3, 280-284.

Edler, J., Meyer-Krahmer, F., Reger, G. (2002). Changes in the Strategic Management of Technology - Results of a Global Benchmarking Study. *R&D Management*, 32, 149-164.

Jin, J., von Zedtwitz, M. (2003). Technology transfer in China – the recipient's perspective. Paper accepted at the R&D Management Conference 2003, Manchester, 7 – 9 July 2003.

Kreutzberger, P. (2000). An OECD member country perspective: experience of German investment promotion in China. OECD-China Conference on Foreign Direct Investment, Xiamen, 11 - 12 September 2000.

Liu, Yongjin (1997). German's investment analysis. *World Economy and Politics* (in Chinese).

Narula, R., Dunning, J.H. (2000). Industrial development, globalization and multinational enterprises: new realities for developing countries. *Oxford Development Studies*, 28, 141-164.

Sanyalla, R. N., Guvenli, T. (2000). Relations between multinational firms and host governments: the experience of American-owned firms in China. *International Business Review*, 9, 119–134.

Reger, G. (2002). Internationalisation of research and development in western European, Japanese and North American multinationals. *International Journal of Entrepreneurship and Innovation Management- Special Issue on Entrepreneurship, Innovation and Globalisation,* 2, 164-185.

Robock, S. H., Simmonds, K. (1983). *International Business and Multinational Enterprises, (3rd ed.).* Richard D. Irwin, Homewood (IL).

UNCTAD (1998). *World Investment Report 1998: Trends and Determinants.* United Nations, Geneva, New York.

Von Zedtwitz, M. (2003). Foreign R&D laboratories in China. Paper accepted at the R&D Management Conference 2003, Manchester, 7 – 9 July 2003.

Williamson, P., Hu, Q. (1994). *Managing the Global Frontier.* Pitman Publishing, London.

Xu, Bin (2000). Multinational enterprises, technology diffusion, and host country productivity growth. *Journal of Development Economics*, 62, 477 – 493.

Management of Technology: New Directions in Technology Management
M. Hashem Sherif and T.M. Khalil (Editors)



# 16

# INDUSTRIAL DEVELOPMENT: DOES TECHNOLOGY TRANSFER WORK IN THE AIRCRAFT INDUSTRY?

*Harm-Jan Steenhuis, Eastern Washington University, Spokane, USA*
*Erik J. de Bruijn, University of Twente, Enschede, The Netherlands*

## INTRODUCTION

Boskin and Lau (1992: 50) found that "technical progress is by far the most important source of economic growth of the industrialized countries". Due to the importance of technology and technological progress, it is therefore not surprising that industrially developing countries have explicit strategies for technological development. For example the Indonesian government formed BPIS, Badan Pengelola Industri Strategis or the Agency for Strategic Industries which explicitly focuses technological development on several strategic industries including steel, aircraft, shipbuilding, and telecommunications. It has been assigned a mission to implement integrated management, technical guidance and control on state-owned enterprises operating in this field. It was meant to accelerate the industrial development of Indonesia, technologically as well commercially. (Raillon, 1990). One of the technological development strategies used is technology transfer from industrialized countries (Sharif, 1988). In this regard, a broad range of literature has developed around technology transfer, see for example (Madu, 1989; Reddy and Zhao, 1990; Cusumano and Elenkov, 1994; Sharif, 1994; Al-Ghailani and Moor, 1995; Bruun and Mefford, 1996; Marcelle, 2003). However, despite the efforts of industrially developing countries and despite the range of literature, the successes of reaching industrialization and economic growth are still limited. In this chapter, an in-depth analysis of technology transfer strategies in one industry will be provided to develop knowledge about why some countries have been more successful than others and how heir approaches were different.

To illustrate this the focus is on the commercial aircraft industry. The aircraft industry is targeted by a number of industrially developing countries, e.g. Brazil, China and Indonesia, as a strategic industry. Furthermore, it has been stated that "few other industries combine in as large a measure a crucial role in national security, a major contribution to national economic health and foreign trade, and a flagship role in the global posture of technological leadership" (U.S. Committee on Technology and International Economic and Trade Issues, 1985, p. 18). We will examine the technology transfer approaches followed by Brazil, China, Indonesia and Romania and will evaluate at how successful the approaches have been.

## COMPETING IN THE COMMERCIAL AIRCRAFT MANUFACTURING INDUSTRY

Because this study is focused on the commercial aircraft industry, it is essential to gain a basic understanding of what it takes to compete in this industry because new competitors will be faced with existing competitors. Also, one should keep in mind that this may be a rather 'tough' industry since long standing companies such as Lockheed, Saab, Fokker, McDonnell-Douglas and British Aerospace have all ceased to compete in this industry.

A range of aircraft industry studies was analyzed to get insight into the characteristics of the aircraft manufacturing industry these included for example (Phillips, 1971; U.S. Committee on Technology and International Economic and Trade Issues, 1985; Hayward, 1986; Todd and Simpson, 1986; U.S. Department of Commerce, 1986; Yoshino, 1986; Mowery, 1987; Newhouse, 1988; U.S. International Trade Commission, 1993; Eriksson, 1995; Bilstein, 1996; Lynn, 1998; U.S. International Trade Commission, 1998). Furthermore, industry publications such as Aviation Week & Space Technology, Flight International and Interavia were also analyzed over an extended period. This literature reveals a combination of characteristics that distinguishes commercial aircraft manufacturing from many other industries.

1. Design; technology has been a key determinant in the industry, therefore companies competing in this industry will have to be able to develop state-of-the-art new aircraft, typically requiring large and long-term R&D investments.
2. Production; the production of aircraft requires skilled labor. It is further characterized by low production volumes and long production lead-times. Due to the high value, much financial resources are tied up in production.

3. Marketing and sales; (1) selling aircraft requires a global sales and after sales network, financial packages for customers, and it requires dealing with a highly politicized process. (2) Demand for commercial aircraft is cyclical. The cyclical effect for regional aircraft is less prominent than in large aircraft because the market is less mature. Cyclical demand places a burden on companies because they need to have sufficient money to survive the cyclical downturn. (3) Aircraft have high value (sales prices), are sold infrequently, and in relatively large amounts. Aircraft are also often ordered in 'large' quantities. (4) There is reasonable doubt about the profitability of aircraft production. Average return on investment for the industry is low and many companies have been forced to leave the market. In the large commercial aircraft industry both Airbus and Boeing, the only two companies in that market segment, are known to have incurred heavy losses in the mid-1990s. Many authors benchmark the sales of 600 aircraft as a signal that the product has been successful. Since 1952 there have been only 11 commercial jet aircraft types of which more than 600 units were sold.

All in all, this means that having the capability to produce an aircraft is not nearly enough to survive. In addition, companies need to be able to design aircraft, establish a global support presence, and they need substantial financial resources to survive long time periods during industry down-turns. Due to space limitations, the analyses in this chapter are limited to the technological aspects. The analyses of the importance of financial resources and the linkage with the military sector, although not denied, are restricted.

## TECHNOLOGY TRANSFER AND KNOWLEDGE

When a technology is transferred, a lot of this process involves technological knowledge. Wallender (1979: 26) even states that "Technology, defined most simply, is knowledge." Some insightful studies on knowledge and knowledge management are (Argote, Beckman and Epple, 1990, Bohn, 1994; Hedlund, 1994). A particular focus on tacit elements can be found in Tsang (1994), Katz et al. (1996), Grant and Gregory (1997), Marcotte and Niosi (2000), Chai et al. (2003) and Steenhuis and de Bruijn (2004). Transferring tacit knowledge is hard because this knowledge is not codified and takes a long time to be absorbed.

In this chapter, a distinction will be used that was made by Teece (1976) Teece (1976: 35) distinguishes three types of knowledge:

- system-specific knowledge

- firm-specific knowledge
- industry-specific knowledge

Wallender (1979: 26) and Mansfield et al. (1982: 28) distinguish similar categories. This distinction of knowledge types was developed because of the relationships between types of knowledge and the channel for and cost of technology transfer. Also, the distinction will be used to look at whether these types of knowledge are effectively transferred. In addition, due to the importance of R&D and marketing, a distinction will also be made between production related knowledge versus R&D and marketing related knowledge. Industry specific knowledge refers to technical knowledge that is common to an industry and possessed by all firms within it. This knowledge is required for producing a general industry product or managing a general industry process. System specific knowledge refers to that knowledge and know-how necessary for the production of a specific product. This is acquired through engaging in certain tasks or projects which are linked with the production of a specific item. Other firms producing a similar good would, in the course of actual operation, probably obtain a similar type of knowledge. Firm specific knowledge refers to production or process knowledge or know-how unique to an specific firm. Such knowledge is not necessarily linked to the production of any given product and may derive from activities peculiar to a single firm. It may include technical knowledge that would go beyond what another firm producing similar products may acquire. Conceptually, these knowledge types make sense although in practice, there may be some overlap. For the aircraft industry, industry specific knowledge is for example the rules and regulations about certification and quality requirements. It also includes general production processes such as riveting or metal cutting. System specific knowledge is the design of a particular product as well as product specific processes, i.e. process planning sheets and knowing how to perform these processes. Firm specific knowledge relates to for example production processes that are firm specific. These can overlap with industry specific knowledge. For example a company can have established procedures for chemical treatments but because of the traditionally national orientation of the industry, these chemical treatments may differ by company, e.g. at different temperatures or with different compositions.

## CASES

Four companies/countries were selected: Romaero from Romania, IAe from Indonesia, AVIC from China and Embraer from Brazil. These were selected because they are prime examples of industrially developing countries that have made the aircraft industry a strategic industry. These companies are analysed to determine what technology transfer strategies they followed with a focus on the type of knowledge involved. The analysis is conducted against the background of competition 'rules' in the commercial aircraft industry1.

*Romaero (Romania) - Technology transfer strategy.* In 1968, the Romanian government targeted the aircraft industry as high-priority economic activity and established the Centrul National al Industriei Aeronautice Romane (CNIAR) as an umbrella organization under the auspices of the Ministry of Machine Building Industry. Technology was transferred to Romaero (initially called IAvB (Intreprinderea de Avioane Bucuresti) during two projects:
Starting in 1968; the licensed manufacturing of the Britten-Norman Islander (8-passenger propeller-aircraft) as part of an offset agreement with the UK. Romaero served as a supplier to Britten-Norman.

Starting in 1978; the licensed manufacturing of the BAC 1-11 (a 90 to 110 passenger jet-aircraft) as part of a counter trade agreement with the UK. The goal was for Romaero to learn to independently produce the BAC 1-11 through 8 phases, containing a total of 22 aircraft, with increasing domestic content. The license agreement was for a total production of 82 BAC 1-11 aircraft until 1996.

*Implementation.* The licensed manufacturing of the Islander was successful and Romaero currently still produces the Islander. For the mostly inexperienced Romanian company this technology transfer related to learning to produce a particular aircraft (system-specific). Romaero was only responsible for production, it did not have responsibility for marketing or design (R&D) activities. Furthermore, Britten-Norman 'controlled' the production and had continuously people stationed at the Romaero.

The BAC 1-11 technology transfer program was less successful. By 1992 the technology transfer program was terminated. At that time only 9 aircraft were completed and these contained many parts manufactured by BAe. Although the aircraft received the equivalent of the UK's aviation certification (CAA) and were therefore viable for export, they were all sold to customers in Romania.

1 The cases have been developed based on numerous sources in particular industry publications. Due to space limitations references for the cases are not listed but they can be provided upon request. Please direct your request to hsteenhuis@mail.ewu.edu or by mail to Dr. Steenhuis, College of Business and Public Administration, Eastern Washington University, 668 N. Riverpoint Blvd., Suite A, Spokane, WA 99202, USA.

With regard to production knowledge, Romaero learned, although not completely, how to produce the BAC 1-11 (system specific knowledge). Some of the methods used were specific for BAe and were different than for the Islander (firm specific knowledge). It also had to learn more about industry wide certification procedures (industry specific knowledge). R&D and marketing knowledge were not part of the licensing agreement and although the intention of the license agreement was to sell 42 of the 82 aircraft outside of Romania (the domestic market was too small), it is questionable whether this would have been successful since the aircraft was at the end of its life cycle (a reason for BAe to sell the license).

Ultimately Romaero has failed to become an independent aircraft manufacturing company. It has not designed and developed medium/large aircraft on its own and in 1994 Romaero changed its strategy towards manufacturing parts and assemblies.

*IAe (Indonesia) - Technology transfer strategy.* IAe (Indonesian Aerospace; before August 2000 known as IPTN) was formed in 1976 by the Indonesian government to provide a vehicle towards Indonesia's industrial transformation. IPTN developed a four phase long-term plan. The four phases were:

- Technology transfer through licensed production, i.e. the use of existing production and management technologies to produce goods already on the market. This was implemented, starting in 1976, through the licensed production of the C-212 (24 passenger turboprop).
- Technology integration, i.e. the use of existing technologies in the design and production of completely new products. This was implemented, starting in 1979, through the joint-development with CASA of the CN-235 (44 passenger turboprop).
- Technology development, i.e. the further development of existing technologies and investment in new technologies. This was implemented, starting in 1989, through the indigenous development of the N-250 (68 passenger turboprop).
- Large-scale basic research to support the first three phases and to defend the technological superiority already attained. This was initiated in 1995 by the indigenous development of the N-2130 (80-130 passenger jet).

*Implementation.* In 1976 a license agreement to produce the C-212 (24 passenger turboprop), with increasing Indonesian content, was reached with CASA from Spain. Around 1987 IAe was able to completely manufacture the C-212 by itself. That is, it learned how to produce this aircraft, i.e. system-specific knowledge was transferred. They were primarily sold to Indonesian customers because IAe was not able to receive certification from Western aviation authorities. For comparison: by the end of 2002 IAe sold approximately 94 whereas CASA sold more than 460 of the C-212 in 42 countries. IAe was moderately successful with this technology transfer. The technology transfer included mainly system specific knowledge and design and marketing knowledge was not transferred. Although marketing knowledge was not included in the transfer, IAe had the advantage of a large domestic market in combination with government control (less need for marketing).

In 1979 IAe and CASA started with the joint development of the CN-235 (44 passenger turboprop), i.e. emphasizing R&D knowledge and improving production knowledge. Duplicate production lines were setup in Spain and Indonesia but IAe again had certification problems (industry specific knowledge). By 1996 the Indonesian built CN-235 still had not gained FAA/JAA certification although the Spanish CN-235 (with more than 50% Indonesian content) were certified. By December 2002 about 47 CN-235 had been produced and delivered by IPTN compared to about 250 by CASA. Although some Indonesian CN-235s were sold to foreign military forces, no aircraft were exported on purely commercial grounds.

With substantial Western assistance, the 'indigenous' development of the N-250 (68 passenger turboprop) was initiated in 1989, i.e. the indigenous expansion of R&D knowledge. The first aircraft was rolled out in November 1994, about a year behind original plans. In an attempt to cut cost, get access to finances and international markets, and to ease the certification process, plans were made to open an assembly line in the US. However, this did not materialize and FAA certification was again not achieved. IAe then enlisted a team of European aerospace consultants to try to help achieve JAA certification and in 1997 a marketing and technical joint-venture agreement with a German group to market and assemble the N250 was made but partly due to financial troubles this was again not implemented. No N-250 aircraft has yet been sold.

With help from Western companies IAe started the $2 billion indigenous development program of the N2130 (80-130 passenger jet) in 1995. Similar to the N-250 program, the N2130 used Western experts and dealt with design knowledge, marketing knowledge and industry specific production knowledge. It is not possible to judge whether IAe had acquired the required knowledge since the financial constraints became overwhelming and IAe had to quit the program in its early stage.

Overall, IAe has only marginally succeeded in becoming an independent aircraft manufacturer. Aside from certification issues (industry specific knowledge), IAe has yet to demonstrate that it developed sufficient indigenous R&D and marketing capabilities since so far it has relied on foreign expertise. Furthermore, although IAe has some system-specific production knowledge, it is questionable whether it has built up enough general production expertise (industry specific and firm specific). IAe's financial difficulties and the claim of an Indonesian airline official that he could lease Boeing 737s for the same price as the CN-235 indicates that IAe's production cost are too high.

*AVIC (China)-Technology transfer strategy.* China has been involved in the production and development of commercial aircraft since the 1950s. Between 1950 and 1977, China was highly dependent on Russia. It license produced (1956) the Y-5 (19 passenger An-2 piston aircraft). Then moved on to improving, by reverse engineering, Russian aircraft in the late 1950s and early 1960s. Examples are the Y-7 (50 passenger An-24 turboprop) and Y-8 (14 passenger An-12). After this, an attempt was made for developing aircraft independent of Russia. In the 1970s China developed and produced the Y-11 (9-10 passenger turboprop) and the Y-12 (17 passenger turboprop, derivative of the Y-11). By 1973 the development of the Y-10 (a 150 passenger jet) was initiated. Two prototypes were built but after that the program was terminated. From a Western perspective it was viewed as a clumsy attempt to reverse-engineer the Boeing 707-300. The experiences with these aircraft in many instances were faced with certification difficulties. In the late 1980s and early 1990s, a co-production agreement was reached with MDD for the assembly of 25 MD-82 kits (a 170 passenger jet). The program was later expanded to 35 aircraft. 15-20% of the airframe content was provided by Chinese industry.

In 1993 Aviation Industries of China (AVIC) was founded which mapped out guidelines for the development of commercial aircraft. This involved domestic production, cooperation, and achievement of goals in three phases.

- The co-production of the MD-90 with MDD to improve manufacturing capabilities.
- The development of a 100-passenger aircraft by cooperating with another international company.
- The domestic development and manufacturing of a 180-passenger aircraft.

*Implementation.* From the mid-1950s until the 1980s China license produced small aircraft, i.e. system specific knowledge was transferred. From there, it handled small design changes (design knowledge) and it was able to develop small turboprop aircraft on its own. However, the design of a large jet aircraft failed. In the late 1980s and early 1990s China focused again on producing existing aircraft, i.e. system specific knowledge was transferred for the MD-82.

Since 1993 the plan to produce the MD-90 has failed. No MD-90 was completed although parts were made in China. Part of the reason for this was the expected high cost of Chinese production. The second phase, the joint development of a 100 passenger aircraft also failed. In 1994 contacts were made with South Korea to develop a civil aircraft but it did not materialize. In 1996 AIR and AVIC talked about the development of the AE-100, a completely new aircraft. After it was concluded that this was not feasible, the development of a derivative of an Airbus, the AE31X was discussed with Airbus but this also fell through. Other unsuccessful attempts were made with Fokker and Boeing.

China then deviated from its strategy and went back to licensed production. In 1997, production of ATR-72 parts was initiated with the intention of having a licensed production line in China. The latter never happened. In 1999 AVIC was divided into AVIC I and AVIC II. AVIC I's focus is on large- and medium-sized aircraft while AVIC II gives priority to feeder aircraft and helicopters.

In 2001 AVIC I and Fairchild Dornier entered talks to examine the feasibility of producing the proposed 528JET in China but, partly due to the demise of Fairchild, the 528JET was never produced. In 2003 the Chinese conglomerate D'Long bought the 728 program but production has yet to start. In 2002 AVIC I and Bombardier signed a tentative agreement to co-produce the CRJ-700/900 in Shanghai. By May 2003, the talks stalled.

AVIC II in the mean time talked with a group of Dutch investors in 2002 and signed an agreement to revive Fokker 70/100 production by the end of 2003. So far no production has taken place. Also in 2002 AVIC II signed a joint venture agreement with Embraer for the production of the ERJ-145 aircraft. In December 2003, the first Chinese-built ERJ-145 was completed.

In 2002 AVIC I set up a dedicated company to manage development of a Chinese 79 to 99 seat regional jet aircraft, the ARJ21. By 2004 work on the ARJ21 is progressing and AVIC I claims that it has sealed launch orders from three customers for 35 ARJ21 regional jets.

*Embraer (Brazil)-Technology transfer strategy.* The strategy of Brazil can be described in three phases. The first phase, from 1950 until the 1970s was focused on developing knowledge in the areas of design, production and marketing. The second phase, throughout the 1980s and 1990s focused on developing more expertise in these three areas by making incremental changes. The third phase, since 1999 is focused on increased indigenous design.

*Implementation.* Embraer was created in 1969 with the express purpose of promoting the development of the local aircraft industry. After six years of operation, it had three lines of aircraft including the commercial aircraft EMB-110. This was a derivative of the French Nord 262 and developed under French guidance, i.e. it included transfer of design knowledge as well as system specific production knowledge.

In 1974, Brazil represented the largest single export market, outranking both Canada and Germany, for U.S. light aircraft (general aviation) manufacturers. U.S. manufacturers delivered 726 aircraft to Brazil in that year at a cost of $600 million. Severely pressed by this time with foreign exchange constraints and confident of its technical capabilities and sufficient internal market demand, Brazilian development authorities felt it was an appropriate moment for Embraer to begin a manufacturing program of light aircraft in close cooperation with a foreign aircraft manufacturer. Brazil sent a mission to the three major U.S. small aircraft producers, Piper, Beech and Cessna to solicit proposals. Each was told that Embraer desired to develop their own technical, managerial, manufacturing and marketing capabilities in small aircraft production and to reserve exclusively the domestic market thereafter for Brazilian produced aircraft. That is, the transfer included all types of knowledge. As a result of negotiations, Piper was selected.

By 1985 Embraer had indigenously developed the EMB-120, a 30-seat turboprop aircraft which was derived from the EMB-110. Embraer thus extended its design and production knowledge incrementally. It received FAA (1985) and European certification (1986). The EMB-120 was quite successful and captured a third of the total market for 30-40 seat commuters providing Embraer with international marketing experience. In 1989 Embraer decided to venture into what was then a niche market for regional jets by indigenously developing the ERJ-145, a 50-passenger jet-aircraft. The ERJ-145 was not a completely new design but rather it used for example the fuselage of the EMB-120.

In the 1994 Embraer was privatized. During the search for new owners, the ERJ-145 project was stopped but after the privatization it accelerated. The ERJ-145 development effort came at the right time. The market for regional jets was growing rapidly, e.g. by more than 50% between 1998 and 1999. In 1996 the ERJ-145 was introduced and in the same year it received FAA certification JAA followed in 1997. It was a successful product and as a result, Embraer returned to profitability in 1998 after 11 consecutive years in the red.

In 1997 Embraer announced a smaller derivative of the ERJ-145, the ERJ-135, a 37-passenger jet. This was another indigenous incremental extension of design, production and marketing knowledge. In 1999 Embraer announced that it would develop a new 70-108 seat jet-aircraft family; the ERJ170/190 program. This represents the first indigenous commercial aircraft design for Embraer although even this program is not completely indigenous since it uses foreign partners. Embraer budgeted $600 million to develop the ERJ170 and $150 million more for the ERJ190. At later points, the development costs for the ERJ170/190 were revised to an estimated $850. In 2000 another derivative of the ERJ-145, the ERJ-140, a 44-passenger jet was announced. Yet another opportunity to improve, incrementally, their design, production and marketing knowledge.

Since 1998 Embraer has been profitable each year although since 2001 profit has been declining. Also, in 1999 Brazil was told by the WTO that it had to stop providing illegal export subsidies in support of regional jet sales. Brazil's PROEX program was providing up to a 3.5% reduction in interest rates on loans to purchasers of exported Brazilian aircraft.

## CONCLUSION

Considering the 'rules' for competition in the commercial aircraft industry it can be assessed that production capabilities alone are insufficient. Companies are also required to possess R&D and marketing capabilities. It is therefore surprising that Embraer is the only company that explicitly focussed on transferring production as well as design and marketing knowledge. It is less surprising to note that Embraer is the only company so far that has had success in establishing itself. However, it should be noted that with the initial transfer of design knowledge for the EMB-110 around 1965 and the design, production and marketing knowledge from Piper around 1974, it took until 1999 before Embraer developed a new aircraft the EMB-170/190 and even in that instance it used foreign partners. The other aircraft that were developed in the intermittent 30 years used many common elements. This shows that if a focus on all types of knowledge (design, marketing and the three types of production knowledge) is maintained and if given enough time (facilitated by a large domestic market and government financial support) it is possible to develop into a global competitor.

Romaero is the only company that has officially abandoned its goal of becoming an aircraft manufacturer and remains a parts manufacturer. Romaero is also the only company that tried to build up its industry by purely focussing on technology transfer through licensing agreements. The lesson to be learned from this is that licensing agreements are oriented on system specific production knowledge. A sustainable position requires R&D and marketing knowledge and this is therefore not likely to occur. Furthermore, the Romaero experience shows that system specific knowledge is limited in its applicability. There was little synergy between the Islander and the BAC 1-11 production. Industry specific knowledge still had to be built up (indicating that system specific knowledge is narrower and not sufficient to understand the industry) and some of the system specific knowledge is actually firm specific knowledge (indicating again that there is limited potential for 'transferring' this knowledge to the production of other aircraft). These are indications that there are tacit elements that are not transferred.

China and Indonesia followed similar strategies. Both initially license produced aircraft but both experienced, in follow-up projects, that this system specific knowledge has limited general applicability. Furthermore, the difficulties of both countries show that design knowledge does not get implicitly transferred with production knowledge (although Embraer's experience seems to indicate that there seems to be some synergy between transferring design knowledge and subsequently production). Similar to Romaero's production knowledge transfer experiences, it also illustrates that design knowledge has system specific elements and more general industry elements since both companies had difficulty applying their design experiences from one project in another project. Here also, the commonality of different types and sizes of aircraft seems to be very limited. IAe has given up on most of its ambitions, China is still working on developing its industry, albeit by using many foreign experts. Given enough time it may succeed although it is questionable whether its leap-frog approach to design will be successful especially seen in the light of the incremental and long-term approach that Embraer followed.

Overall, the conclusion is that regardless of management issues in technology transfer and appropriate technology (does it fit with the environment) a key aspect in the failure of technology transfer to contribute to industrial development is that they are often too narrowly defined. That is, these transfers generate skills in a narrow production area instead of on knowledge that creates a sustainable competitive industry position. It should be noted here that the conclusion is not that the case companies do not have sufficient manufacturing skills for the products that were transferred. The conclusion is that although the required skills could be transferred, these newly acquired skills were too specific to be useful for the production of other aircraft.

## REFERENCES

Al-Ghailani, H. H. and W.C. Moor (1995), 'Technology transfer to developing countries', *International Journal of Technology Management,* Vol. 10, No. 7/8, pp. 687-703.

Argote, L., S.L. Beckman and D. Epple (1990), 'The persistence and transfer of learning in industrial settings', *Management Science,* Vol. 36, No. 2, pp. 140-154.

Bilstein (1996), *The American aerospace industry, From workshop to global enterprise,* Prentice Hall International, London.

Bohn, R.E. (1994), 'Measuring and managing technological knowledge', *Sloan Management Review,* Fall, pp. 61-73.

Boskin, M.J. and Lau, L.J. (1992). In: *Technology and the wealth of nations* (N. Rosenberg, R. Landau and D.C. Mowery, eds.), Chap. 2, pp. 17-55. Stanford University Press, Stanford.

Bruun, P. and R.N. Mefford (1996), 'A framework for selecting and introducing appropriate production technology in developing countries', *International Journal of Production Economics,* Vol. 46/47, pp. 197-209.

Chai, K.H., M. Gregory and Y. Shi (2003), 'Bridging islands of knowledge: a framework of knowledge sharing mechanisms', *International Journal of Technology Management,* Vol. 25, No. 8, pp. 703-727.

Cusumano, M.A. and D. Elenkov (1994). 'Linking international technology transfer with strategy and management: a literature commentary', *Research Policy,* Vol. 23, pp. 195-215.

Eriksson, S. (1995), *Global shift in the aircraft industry: a study of airframe manufacturing with special reference to the Asian NIEs,* Ph.D. dissertation, School of Economics and Commercial Law, University of Gothenburg, Sweden.

Grant, E.B. and M.J. Gregory (1997), 'Tacit knowledge, the life cycle and international manufacturing transfer', *Technology Analysis & Strategic Management,* Vol. 9, pp. 149-161.

Hayward, K. (1986), *International collaboration in civil aerospace,* Frances Pinter, London.

Hedlund, G. (1994), 'A model of knowledge management and the N-form corporation', *Strategic Management Journal,* Vol. 15, pp. 73-90.

Katz, R., E.S. Rebentisch and T.J. Allen (1996), 'A study of technology transfer in a multinational cooperative joint venture', *IEEE Transactions of Engineering Management,* Vol. 43, pp. 97-105.

Lynn, M. (1998), *Birds of prey, Boeing vs. Airbus: a battle for the skies,* Four Walls Eight Windows, New York.

Madu, C.N. (1989), 'Transferring technology to developing countries – critical factors for success', *Long Range Planning,* Vol. 22, No. 4, pp. 115-124.

Mansfield E., A. Romeo, M. Schwartz, D. Teece, S. Wagner and P. Brach (1982). *Technology transfer, productivity, and economic policy.* W.W. Norton & Company, New York.

Marcelle, G.M. (2003), 'Reconsidering technology transfer', *International Journal of Technology Transfer and Commercialization,* Vol. 2, No. 3, pp. 227-248.

Marcotte, C. and J. Niosi (2000), 'Technology transfer to China. The issues of knowledge and learning', *Journal of Technology Transfer,* Vol. 25, pp. 43-57.

Mowery, D.C. (1987), *Alliance politics and economics, Multinational joint ventures in commercial aircraft,* Ballinger Publishing Company, Cambridge.

Newhouse, J. (1988), *The sporty game,* Alfred A. Knopf, New York.

Phillips, A. (1971), *Technology and market structure, A study of the aircraft industry,* Heath Lexington Books, Lexington.

Raillon, F. (1990), *Indonesia 2000, The industrial and technological challenge,* CNPF-ETP & Cipta Kreatif, Paris & Jakarta.

Reddy, N.M. and L. Zhao (1990), 'International technology transfer: a review', *Research Policy,* Vol. 19, pp. 285-307.

Sharif, M.N. (1988), 'S&T policy, Problems, issues and strategies for S&T policy analysis', *Science and Public Policy,* Vol. 15, No. 4, pp. 195-216.

Sharif, N. (1994), 'Integrating business and technology strategies in developing countries', *Technological Forecasting and Social Change,* Vol. 45, pp. 151-167.

Steenhuis, H.J and E.J. de Bruijn (2004), 'Exploring knowledge transfer within manufacturing networks and codified information characteristics: the hidden dangers of inaccurate information', *International Journal of Technology Transfer and Commercialization,* Vol. 3, No. 4, pp. 433-453.

Todd, D. and Simpson, J. (1986), *The world aircraft industry,* Croom Helm, London.

Tsang, E.W.K. (1994), 'Strategies for transferring technology to China', *Long Range Planning,* Vol. 27, pp. 98-107.

U.S. Committee on Technology and International Economic and Trade Issues (1985), *The competitive status of the U.S. civil aviation manufacturing industry,* National Academy Press, Washington D.C.

U.S. Department of Commerce (1986), *A competitive assessment of the U.S. civil aircraft industry*, Westview Press, Boulder and London.

U.S. International Trade Commission (1993), *Global competitiveness of U.S. advanced-technology manufacturing industries: large civil aircraft,* U.S. International Trade Commission, Washington D.C.

U.S. International Trade Commission (1998), *The changing structure of the global large civil aircraft industry and market: implications for the competitiveness of the U.S. industry,* U.S. International Trade Commission, Washington D.C.

Wallender III, H.W. (1979), *Technology transfer and management in the developing countries: company cases and policy analyses in Brazil, Kenya, Korea, Peru and Tanzania,* Ballinger Publishing Company, Cambridge.

Yoshino, M.Y. (1986), 'Global competition in a salient industry: the case of civil aircraft' in: Porter, M.E. (ed.) (1986), *Competition in global industries,* Harvard Business School Press, Boston.

Management of Technology: New Directions in Technology Management
M. Hashem Sherif and T.M. Khalil (Editors)



# 17

# TECHNOLOGICAL CAPABILITIES OF HIGH TECHNOLOGY FIRMS IN CROSS BORDER ALLIANCES

*Zandra Balbinot, HEC - Montreal, Canada*
*Luiz Paulo Bignetti, Unisinos, Brazil*

## INTRODUCTION

The literature on innovation has consistently discussed the role of strategic alliances in developing new technologies and new markets. In fact, strategic alliances are responsible for a significant part of all new cross-border ventures started in the last ten years. High technology firms established in developed countries tend to prefer cooperation agreements with local firms instead of the riskier installation investments required to enter new markets. Local firms, when unable to develop advanced technologies, envision alliances as a means of increasing their competitive capacity by capturing new knowledge and by upgrading internal capabilities.

When strategic alliances are developed, asymmetric knowledge levels between contracting firms represent, ironically, both a justification and an inhibitor for technology transfer. On one hand, the difference in knowledge may be the motivation to promote the flow of technology from the emitter to the receptor. On the other hand, if the receptor is not able to absorb technology - that is, if the technological levels of the two firms are very far apart - knowledge transfer could become difficult to promote.

These asymmetries are even larger when the joint agreement is established between newly industrialized countries' companies (NICCs) and firms from developed countries. In order to study how alliances perform under such asymmetries, this article focuses on the efforts made by five Brazilian firms in absorbing technology from more developed firms through technological transfer agreements. Two concepts are at the core of the study: technological capability and absorptive capacity. These concepts together were used to define what is termed as the learning potential of the firm.

## TECHNOLOGICAL CAPABILITY

Technological capability of a firm is the ability to make effective use of technological knowledge in efforts to assimilate, use, adapt, and change existing technologies. It enables the firm to create new technologies and develop new products and processes in response to a changing economic environment (Kim, 1997, p. 4). It is considered as the local capability, that helps in the absorption, adaptation, modification and innovation of the imported technology involving, technological change (Kharbanda & Jain, 1997). These attributes are very important to make NICCs' more competitive in the international market.

Technological capability of firms is an attribute concerned especially with the improvement of products and processes and with the development of new technologies. There are four possible types of technological capability development (Leonard-Barton, 1995; Fransman and King, 1984):

- acquisitive – the ability to search and acquire new technology
- operative – the ability to master technology through use
- adaptive – the ability to adapt technology
- innovative – the ability to create technology independently.

These types of technological capabilities indicate a crescent complexity in the management of innovation. In a joint venture, technological capability is an attribute of both partners – even though that of the originator of the technology – the emitter – is larger than that of the receptor. The technological capability is the ability to conduct innovations in the firm's area of expertise.

For the effect of this research we consider the following factors as those that affect the firm's technological capability: 1) the existence of an R&D department or a similar organizational structure; 2) the percentage of total revenues invested in R&D; 3) the qualification of personnel involved in R&D and in product development; 4) the kind of local 'departmental culture' which facilitates the flow of information inside the firm and enhances the internal interest for knowledge diffusion; 5) how close this department is of being a transferor, as Leonard-Barton said, a *theoretical continuum of transfer situations stretches from the simple sale of equipment by source to receiver to the final absorption of so much knowledge that the receiver becomes technology source, capable of reversing the flow of knowledge* (1995, p. 220). We believe that by considering these factors, we are able to identify the technological capability level of each of the organizations that we analyzed.

Furthermore, for an effective transfer of technology, the receptor needs to have the ability to assimilate the incoming technology, i. e., to have an absorptive capacity. This is not an occasional ability: it is acquired throughout the entire organization's existence. It is a holistic attribute that characterizes the organizational capabilities in not only R&D, but also in areas such as marketing, production, finance and human resources. It is evident from this definition that the ability to exploit external knowledge is a critical component in the innovative capabilities and is directly related to the firm's stock of knowledge – that is, to the firm's prior knowledge related to the technology to be transferred (Cohen & Levinthal, 1990). Therefore, a firm that has accumulated more prior knowledge will require less learning to attain a given level of performance in the alliance and, consequently will not be as dependent on its partner as a firm with less prior knowledge. Therefore, it is conceived in this study that past experience with alliances should be taken into account when evaluating the absorptive capacity of a firm.

Although being different concepts, technological capability and absorptive capacity are both dependent upon the organizational structure adopted by the recipient firm. Knowledge transfer and adoption will generally be facilitated in a more *organistic*, horizontal, structure, with fewer levels of authority, stronger channels of communication between levels and higher degrees of freedom and autonomy for people. This type of arrangement facilitates informal exchanges and enhances the transfer of tacit knowledge.

It is important to stress that environmental forces play important role in the development of both technological capability and absorptive capacity. For example, in the context of this research, the Brazilian government followed a strict policy of protectionism, prohibiting the entrance of products that could menace the existing internal market. The intention was also to permit Brazilian firms to gain expertise. With such impossibility of making agreements with high technology firms abroad, many Brazilian companies were obliged to develop their own technological capabilities and, also, their absorptive capacity.

Comparing absorptive capacity and technological capability, we can state that the former requires a substantial investment in intangibles, such as external sources of technology, training, managerial skills, and R&D. In this sense, absorptive capacity takes much more time to develop than technological capability. It refers to more organizational characteristics, related to organizational change and learning, processes that are developed throughout the firm's history.

Furthermore, there can only be one organizational absorptive capacity that grows throughout the firm's life. Yet, a firm may have many technological capabilities that, at the end, represent the innovative driving force within it. As a result, absorptive capacity becomes a *sine qua non* condition to understanding the partner's language even though it does not generate an explicit advantage to the firm as technological capability does. If a firm develops several technological capabilities, the overall absorptive capacity will increase. In addition, initial absorptive capacity would seem to be an important pre-requisite in the selection of a partner to improve the firm's technological capability.

Therefore, technological capability and absorptive capacity differ in terms of specificity, range, location, development time, roles and connections. Table 1 presents some of these differences between the two concepts.

**Table 1. Absorptive capacity versus technological capability**

| **Elements** | **Absorptive capacity** | **Technological capability** |
|---|---|---|
| Specificity | One for each organization | Several |
| Location | All functional areas | R&D |
| Development time | Long (more than 3 years) | Short to medium (a few days to 3 years) |
| Advantage generation | Potential | Effective |
| Innovative role | Passive – Support | Active – Innovation |
| Connected to | Prior related knowledge (experience in all functional areas) | New knowledge in new product development |
| Location of improvements | All organizational areas such as training and managerial skills | Technological areas such as R&D and equipment acquisition |

Source: Balbinot, 2001

A third concept is used in this work to connect technological capability and absorptive capacity: the learning potential. What we are calling the learning potential level is the capacity of a certain firm of acquiring and putting into use a particular technology. This learning potential is composed by the firm's organizational capacities and the firm's technological capability. In other words, it is considered that the learning potential level of a certain firm will be the sum of its absorptive capacity and technological capability associated to the non-technological variables that can interfere in the whole process. As already pointed out, the absorptive capacity favours a firm's ability to recognize, find and understand technology. The

technology to a partner. This implies assimilating and applying the information. However, we do not believe that Polonia is ready to recognize the value of this information because it has a low absorptive capacity. Its joint venture experience reinforces this observation. The lack of experience of its managers was a factor that conducted to a less-than-desirable outcome: the loss of decision-making control. We can say that Polonia is technologically ready for the transfer but managerially immature with regard to its alliance strategy.

Stemac and Inepar recognize the importance of information exchange for their firms. They identify its value and, sometimes, even convince their partners that a certain agreement can be of great value to them both.

Aeroeletrônica and Info possess an important learning potential. Like Polonia, they both are ready to receive technology because they have a highly developed technological capability. However, they differ from Polonia's because both are ready to embrace a cooperative strategy. They have the required absorptive capacity to recognize new information and apply it in order to achieve their goals. They are also in high technology demanding industries that lead them to continuously develop technology.

Certainly, this does not imply that these firms will have the same learning potential forever. As was stated earlier, learning potential changes on a situation-to-situation or technology-to-technology basis. As Polonia acquires experience and a higher absorptive capacity, its learning potential will rise. An important change in technology can also diminish Stemac and Inepar's learning level. As a result, firms need to work hard in order to continuously maintain and improve their levels.

The crossing of data obtained about the alliances indicates how Brazilian firms improved their technological capability through alliances. Table 5 summarizes the information concerning the improvement on technological capabilities obtained from the partnerships. The following elements we taken into account:

- The final result of the alliance or the achievement of the goal, which was to get the technology transferred. As already mentioned, the learning potential is a *sine qua non* condition to achieve firms' objectives
- Technological capability. According to our study, the higher the technological capability, the easier it will be for a firm to understand a certain technology from its partner
- The absorptive capacity. This establishes if a firm possesses a basic condition to choose a cooperative strategy as the means to improve its technological level.

As seen from the table, except for Polonia, all partnerships achieved the proposed goals and even exceeded them.

**Table 5. Technological Capability Improvement through Alliances**

| | Inepar | Aeroeletrônica | Info | Stemac | Polonia |
|---|---|---|---|---|---|
| **Goal achievement** | Yes | Yes and more | Yes and more | Yes and more | No, but it anticipated some technological developments |
| **Technological capability** | Medium-to-high | High | High | Low-to-medium | High |
| **Absorptive capacity** | High | Medium-to-high | High | Medium-to-high | Low |

Source: Balbinot 2001

## CONCLUSION

This study investigated the effects generated by alliances in the improvement of Brazilian companies' technological capability. We believe some of the findings open the door to other researches on this subject. As we already mentioned earlier in our research, we are neither trying to prove that alliances are the predominant means by which newly industrialized countries' firms improve their technology nor that it is the predominant means by which developed countries' firms enter new industrialized economies. We simply intended to understand this particular phenomenon and observe more closely this important method of leveraging new industrialized countries' firms' technological capability.

There are some interesting findings that emerged from this study. First, the cooperative strategy in the form of technological alliances is not possible for every firm. There are some prerequisites that must be fulfilled before this option can be chosen. The technological capability level plays a major role in this choice. Since to be successful alliances demand interaction, firms must be *able* to interact. Much more than simply being unified, interaction denotes being able to understand one another. This is only possible if partners speak the same language. Here, we are referring to both the idiom and the technological language. Furthermore, to use the technological language firms' personnel must have achieved a certain technological degree of understanding. As a result, Killing's idea (1980) regarding partner's dependence is also relevant in this context: where technology is more advanced, the necessity of interaction will be higher as will the partners' dependence if technologically inferior.

A second consideration is that, according to the technological capability level and the type of technology firms are interested in, interaction can be avoided. For example, a mature technology represents a low-embedded element that can be easily found or replaced by other information from a firm's technological database. This is possible because possessing a higher technological capability level, this personnel has a high capacity for problem resolution and already has a problem routine. With this much richer knowledge database, people are therefore capable of combining different information until they find an appropriate solution to new problems. This happened with Polonia that, even with a very low interaction, succeeded in transferring the technologies it needed.

A third observation is that technological alliances involve many more elements than just technology. Managerial experience is vital to its success. Polonia showed that the lack of experience in the field might cause serious damage to the company. However, the vast experience of Inepar's CEO also facilitated the abrupt end to its joint venture. Even if it was unexpected, Inepar got what it wanted. Beyond management experience, contract negotiations can also be a very tricky aspect of any alliance. Like managerial experience, it is also something that can change the entire relationship if it is not well executed. For example, Polonia and Aeroeletrônica had problems due to poor contract negotiation, for example. Additionally, the five companies' managers showed a high awareness on the fact that knowledge must be spread through the entire organization. They also shared the recognition to the fact that trust, either between partners or among collaborators inside the firm, is a vital factor for the success of the alliance.

This study shows that, in an unstable conjuncture, developed countries' firms choose to form alliances with local companies to enter a new market. Using this strategy they reduce their risk of failure since they use partner's knowledge of the local environment. More than that, developed countries' firms search for solid, established partners in order to associate their name to a local partner with a prestigious reputation. This was certainly the case for Stemac and Inepar. As a matter of fact, Stemac's partner not only had its name associated to a prestigious company, but it also secured access to a huge developed distribution structure. As a result, the chosen Brazilian companies normally counted on important complementary assets to convince their partners to form an alliance. Polonia and Info showed an impressive technological capability level, for example.

Finally, according to some of the managers, the alliance strategy generates undeniable advantages to a country. It brings financial advantages to the hosting country in at least two ways: (1) by avoiding equipment imports and (2) by creating an important source for exports.

As a qualitative study, this analysis has some limitations. The findings cannot be generalized since it is a study of five cases. However, it must be said that some of the companies discussed are leaders in their markets. This is the case of Inepar and Stemac. Info, on the other hand, shares the entire Brazilian market with just another company. Since the market opening in Brazil, Aeroeletrônica remains the only Brazilian company in this industry that has survived. As a result, we believe that the cases nonetheless are a good representative sample of different types of situations that may be analogous to other firms' circumstances. More research, involving other sectors, would be an interesting corollary to these early findings.

## REFERENCES

Arvanitis, R. and N. Vonortas (2000). Technological Transfer and Learning Through Strategic Alliances – International experiences: introduction to the symposium. *Journal of Technology Transfer,* 25, 9-12.

Balbinot, Z. (2005). *Building Technological Capability in Brazilian Firms Through Alliances.* Thesis. HEC, Montreal.

Balbinot, Z. (2001). *Building Technological Capability in Developing Countries' Firms Through Alliances.* Thesis Proposal. HEC, Montreal.

Bell, M. (1984). Learning and the Accumulation of Industrial Technological Capability in NIC. In: *Technology Capability in the Third World* (Fransman, Martin and K. King eds.), pp.187-209. Macmillan, London.

Cohen, W. and D. Levinthal (1990). Absorptive capacity: a new perspective on learning and innovation. *Administrative Science Quarterly*, 35, 128-152.

Fransman, M. and K. King, 1984. *Technology Capability in the Third World.* Macmillan, London.

Furtado, A. T. and A. Gomes de Freitas (2000). Technological Transfer and Learning Through Strategic Alliances – International experiences: introduction to the symposium. *Journal of Technology Transfer*, 25, 23-36.

Gilbert, M. and M. Cordey-Hayes (1996). Understanding the Process of Knowledge Transfer to Achieve Successful Technological Innovation. *Technovation*, 16, 301-312.

Inkpen, A. (1996). Creating Knowledge Through Collaboration. *California Management Review*, 39, 123-140.

The Economist Intelligence Unit (1999). *Investing, Licensing & Trading in Brazil.* The Economist Intelligence Unit, New York.

Kharbanda, V.P. and A. Jain (1997). Indigenization and Technological Change at the Firm Level – the case of the black and white TV picture. *Technovation*, 17, 439-456.

Killing, P. (1980). Technology Acquisition: license agreement or joint venture. *Columbia Journal of World Business*, Fall, 38-46.

Kim, L. (1997). *Imitation to Innovation: the dynamics of Korea's technological learning.* Harvard Business School Press, Boston.

Leonard Barton, D. (1995). *Wellsprings of Knowledge: building and sustaining the sources of innovation.* Harvard Business School Press, Boston.

Nonaka, I. and H. Takeuchi (1996). A Theory of Organizational Knowledge Creation. *International Journal of Technology Management*, 11, 833-845.

Polanyi, M. (1966). The Logic of Tacit Inference. *Philosophy*, 41, 1-18.

Management of Technology: New Directions in Technology Management
M. Hashem Sherif and T.M. Khalil (Editors)



# 18

# COMPARITIVE EUROPEAN PERSPECTIVES ON THE DIFFUSION AND ADOPTION OF TELEWORK AMONGSTS SMEs

*Keith Dickson and Fintan Clear*
*Brunel Business School, Brunel University, Uxbridge, England*

## INTRODUCTION

According to a prediction made by AT&T in 1971, 50% of all Americans would be working from home by 1990 (Sturesson, 1998). While this prediction appears wildly optimistic with the benefit of hindsight, telework (as a form of home-working) has long been seen by its proponents as a panacea to many of society's ills. The 1973 oil crisis, for example, prompted Nilles *et al.*(1976) to advance 'telecommuting' in response to this crisis at a time when technology was still relatively expensive. Often underlying much popularist thinking and writing on telework is a technological determinist assumption that given the right technology, it is inevitable that teleworking will 'take off'. Such a position, this paper will argue, is untenable given the complexities associated with implementation of new technologies. Even today when the appropriate technology is relatively cheap and far more advanced, telework still does not enjoy anything like the take-up predicted. This suggests that non-technical complexities related to the adoption and management of telework may not have been fully understood nor adequately addressed.

The eGap research project (eGap, 2004), whose qualitative findings are summarised in this paper, was designed to investigate these complexities in small and medium-sized enterprises (SMEs) from a pan-European perspective. Sponsored by the European Commission's IST Programme, eGap findings contribute to a literature that includes other cross-national IST studies including ECaTT (2000), EMERGENCE (2003) and SUSTEL (2004). For example, the ECaTT survey not only identified positive and negative responses to new organisational forms associated with telework, but also underlined the differences between various European countries regarding telework implementation and usage (ECaTT, 2000). Other European comparative studies include those by Peters and Den Dulk (2003), which reports on differences in managers' views in northern and southern European countries, and Raghuram *et al.* (2001), which examines variances in flexible employment practices across Europe.

However, before we can advance, the term 'telework' itself needs to be defined as its usage is problematic. There are a wide variety of terms that describe telework in some aspect or other. Qvortrup examines terminology surrounding telework, and provides a long list of terms including, "teleworkers, telecommuters, flexiworkers, distance workers, electronic homeworkers, teleguerillas, home-based nomads, electronic moonlighters, satellite office workers, mobile teleworkers, full- and part-time homeworkers, telecottage workers" (Qvotrup, 1998, p. 23). These are not all synonymous with 'telework', he notes, and are based in any event on different criteria related to various technical, geographical, organisational and legal aspects. After reviewing various definitions by other commentators, the eGap project adopted the following definition of telework in order to capture as broad a picture of practice as possible - "working offsite (eg at home, at a customer site, on the move) whilst linked all day or for some period in the day to a firm's computer systems" (eGap, 2004, p.1) eGap examined the adoption and practice of telework under a number of themes (flexible working, work-life balance, work measurement/control, corporate social responsibility, and business performance) by questioning stakeholders including actual 'teleworkers' themselves, their managers, trades unions, technology providers, business support agencies, and national/regional policy-makers. Stakeholder responses are then examined from differing units of analysis, including the micro or individual view, the meso or firm-level view, and/or the macro or societal view. Before looking at these qualitative findings, a brief introduction to some key issues for the eGap project is set out below.

*Telework and the Rights of the Individual Teleworker.* Telework raises a number of issues with regard to human factors, especially in terms of flexible working and/or home-working arrangements. If telework for the most part is *home working*, then family environs and dynamics are pertinent to the debate. While the main carers for children – mothers – have always had to juggle working and care responsibilities, the adoption of telework for many fathers opens up opportunities for new domestic arrangements. But Casimir (1998) notes that such new vistas do not necessarily translate into more egalitarian sharing of domestic roles unless the woman also has a full-time job. If the woman does not work or has a part-time job, then Casimir finds that the man takes little additional responsibility for domestic and familial tasks. Other researchers examine the general impact of telework on the lives of 'virtual workers'. One analysis, performed at an IBM site, revealed perceptions of greater productivity, increased flexibility and longer work hours due to telework, as well as an equivocal influence on work/life balance and a negative influence on teamwork (Hill *et al.*, 1998).

In the UK, flexible working has been the subject of recent legislation such that since April 2003, permanent employees with a child under six or a disabled child under 18 have become eligible to approach their employer – in formal legal terms - to discuss their care needs, and by implication, to ask for flexible working. In research pre-dating this, Perin (1998) observes that flexible schedules and work locations are only truly flexible for those on the top management rungs. It will be interesting to see whether the new legislation benefits non-management cadres therefore. Another legal development concerns health and safety issues and 'Employer's Liability Insurance' in regard to home working. Somewhat paradoxically, failure to enforce such legal strictures could be seen as a facilitator to telework, as there would be an avoidance of certain costs for the employer or employee. However, if a teleworker had an accident whilst working at home, then home insurance cover might be invalidated.

According to Bibby (1996), trades unions across Europe have identified a number of issues in terms of the rights of home-based teleworkers. These include, the preservation of employment status, voluntary participation, the right to continuation of some degree of workplace working, remuneration of home expenses incurred, the right to privacy, measures to combat isolation and to promote career development, safe working conditions, and adequate alternative childcare facilities. Furthermore, trades union fears in the UK were raised by a national report that noted that teleworking could lead to the development of a two-tier employment structure, with full-time, permanent home-based workers at the periphery (TUC, 1998). To some, the success of teleworking is bound up in the nature of formal telework agreements; thus the same report identifies 'consultation', the 'voluntary nature of the agreement (to telework)' and 'timescale' as three factors that must be considered. The issue of formal agreements is further explored, for example, by Stradwick and Ellis (1998) who look at telework practice at Mobil Oil and the Co-op Bank.

*Telework, Management Control and Trust.* From a managerialist perspective, any shift towards more distributed forms of working begs questions for firms in terms of the control, empowerment, supervision and performance evaluation of teleworkers. In this vein, Johnson (1998) highlights the potential for 'discretionary service behaviour' whereby remote workers may exhibit positive or negative behaviour depending on whether they perceive that the 'psychological contract' with their employer to be 'intact' or 'breached'. If the latter is the case, then there may be instances of 'tele-shirking' (ie avoidance of work tasks in some measure) and 'imbalanced relationships' (where a teleworker aligns their loyalties to a firm's customers and/or suppliers rather than to the firm itself). One inhibiting influence to the adoption of telework therefore has been the fear that workers, as reported by Olson (1988), shirk their work tasks if left without physical management oversight.

This raises the core issue of employer/employee trust, a topic explored by many writers on telework including Handy (1995) and Huws *et al.*(1990). In essence, the key question whether individuals working remotely can be trusted to be conscientious in regard to their work tasks. In a study looking at on-line trust in financial services, Knights *et al.*(2001) explore how problems of trust and especially control are managed. They observe how, "a long tradition of management thought conceptualises trust and control as opposing alternatives" (p. 3), but argue that this dichotomy is false. For them, trust and control are not necessarily polar opposites - rather, they may be complementary and may be combined to varying degrees in everyday working life whether for professionals (who are ascribed as having high levels of trust and requiring low levels of control) or for 'workers' (with low levels of trust and high levels of control). Trust, however, is a two-way attribute in that workers also place trust in their employer that, for example, their wages will be paid and the terms of their working contracts will be honoured.

## Project Description and Methodology

eGap was a European Commission-funded project that analysed the reasons why, within specific professional working environments, telework in SMEs faces difficulties or success in implementation. The overall objective of the project was to highlight 'best practice' for implementing appropriate and sustainable telework activities within SMEs whilst building on previous European research noted earlier.

The eGap study focused on SMEs with between 1 to 249 employees, in accordance with normal EU firm size classifications, in five member countries. For comparative purposes, well-defined and economically significant regions in each country were selected, from which the sample of SMEs were drawn. The regions were:- Rhone-Alpes in France; Emilia Romagna in Italy; Central Transdanubia in Hungary; Tampere in Finland; and 'Greater West London Wedge' (six London boroughs) in the UK.

The project used both quantitative and qualitative methodologies in evaluating telework experiences within the SMEs and analysed relevant data and insights given by the various stakeholders. Cross-regional analysis aided in highlighting 'best practice' for a given environment. The project combined three types of investigation:

- Analysis of the different political, legal, financial and technological environments that influenced telework implementation, which together highlight the specific national/regional conditions for telework's progress or delay. A trans-national analysis is reported in Mako *et al.*(2002).
- Quantitative surveys of at least 300 SMEs within each region of the 5 European partner countries in various sectors of manufacturing and services. The surveys were undertaken via telephone interviews between November 2002 and January 2003 and a comparative analysis was produced by De Nicola *et al.*(2003).
- Sixty qualitative, face-to-face interviews carried out in each region with selected individuals both within the sample of SMEs (e.g., owners, managers, teleworkers) and with other relevant stakeholders such as regional policy makers and trade union representatives. Thus 300 actors across Europe were interviewed, using a semi-structured questionnaire, on their telework attitudes and experiences. The interviews took place in the summer of 2003 and a trans-national comparative summary was written by Dickson and Clear (2003).

## Survey Findings

The qualitative findings discussed below are taken from the eGap trans-national report (Dickson and Clear, 2003) that synthesised individual partner findings from the interviews and so is cited extensively below. There are a large number of factors that were found to affect the diffusion and adoption of telework, a selection of which have been grouped for the purposes of this paper, under the themes of 'trust and work autonomy', 'change management' and 'regional infrastructure support'.

*Trust and Work Autonomy.* A common thread running through all the national findings was the view that for firms and their employees to practise telework successfully, then certain pre-conditions must exist in terms of general management culture. Fundamental to such a culture is trust in employee motivation, and faith in an individual teleworker's professionalism and self-discipline. The Italian partners see such an approach as based on a 'logic of collaboration', which they argue is uncommon in small businesses in Emilia Romagna (ibid, p18). All the research partners argue that in the absence of this management approach telework is unlikely to be anything other than a marginal activity in SMEs. In any event, the eGap partners observe that managers enjoy autonomy and the trust of their employer as part of their role. For other employees, the level of trust afforded teleworkers may be based on measurement of output rather than measurement of input (such as hours worked). Therefore, for sales personnel, for example, the UK partners observe how, "success or failure with meeting sales targets will define a set level of trust for the firm towards their employee" (ibid , p. 40).

A management culture in which trust of employees is lacking and dominated by physical oversight of employees (and what the Italian partners term as the 'logic of subordination') will militate against successful teleworking. Once 'out of sight', sceptics argue that employees would be out of control and as a result would fail to exhibit a sense of responsibility towards their employer, leading inevitably to a decline in productivity. Additionally, the UK partners observe that in a home environment where individuals are used to relaxing, it may be more difficult for workers (including managers) to motivate themselves to work. In the same vein, the Italian partners observe that, "once distanced from the rhythm of the working environment, workers become less productive" (ibid, p. 41).

Notions of trust also impinge on wider commercial interests such as transaction security and intellectual property. The Hungarian and UK partners note, for example, the need for firms to protect sensitive and confidential information, especially in relation to financial dealings, and some interviewees emphasize that security of transactions is more difficult to manage at a distance. The UK partners raise an issue relating to intellectual property (IP), such that if valuable industrial knowledge were accessible from home, then the illegal extraction of such commercially sensitive information and intellectual property is easier. (ibid, p. 31). Despatch of valuable data is but a few keystrokes away. Even though the data in question was held centrally, it nevertheless highlights the potential dangers that IP holders face through extending a firm's ICT network into the home. The UK authors conclude that managerial concerns over IP protection may well slow telework diffusion as a result.

*Change Management.* Trust or lack thereof is also linked by the eGap partners to organisational structure. The Italian partners note that in those firms where telework was not practised, there was evidence of deeply rooted antipathy by entrepreneurs to new methods of work that might take office-based staff off-site. They are critical of the inability of SMEs in Emilia Romagna to change traditional management practices, and feel that, "a general problem of mentality and backwardness was identified in which the culture of visual controls prevails" (ibid, p. 33). The issue of 'visual controls' or 'physical oversight' is noted, to varying degrees, by all partners, and is linked by them to firms with hierarchical reporting structures.

As the French partners observe, "work organisation still appears to be deeply influenced by practices of the industrial era (e.g. direct supervision, wages connected to presence, etc.) and by cultural specificities (i.e., the weight of hierarchy in the sector)" (ibid, p 33). This goes some way to explain a common cry that, "old hierarchical rigidities (need) to be broken down in order to allow telework to thrive and for its benefits to be enjoyed" (ibid, p. 33). The French authors add that, "a traditional company must reconsider its whole structure and organisation in order to successfully implement telework" (ibid, p. 33-34).

Traditional structures and demarcation are bound up with the current technologies in use, as is most clearly seen in Hungarian SMEs, which militate against the diffusion of telework. Additionally, due to limited financial resources, SMEs in Hungary appear more interested in adopting telework on an opportunistic basis. For example, subsidies to SMEs during cycles of central government initiatives appear to directly influence the level of adoption. In these cases, when such funds become available, telework jobs are created, but when funding ceases, so too do the jobs. French researchers find that management issues related to remote working, "are not yet tackled, because generally most teleworkers are top managers, sales staff and/or training instructors working off-site. These workers are generally able to be self-managed at a distance and self-organised off-site" (ibid, p. 42). This highlights the challenge to SMEs wishing to extend teleworking to non-management ranks.

Moving from a paradigm where traditional onsite working predominates to one where distributed forms of working was a norm was judged to be problematic by many respondents. Risks to a firm's overall business performance were noted, for example, by Finnish and UK researchers who put forward arguments that the dispersal of employees would, over time, lead to degradations in internal service delivery and organisational learning. The Finns note that, "the flow of information inside the company and the transferring of tacit knowledge, in particular, constitute the most challenging areas to be developed in the future" (ibid, p.41). Thus the Finn, together with the French and Italian partners emphasize that there is no real substitute for face-to-face communications.

There are problems raised by telework for work measurement. The French partners point to the difficulty of measuring productivity for remote workers in small firms. Increased overheads also can be an issue; as the Italian partners observe, "To be able to carry out part of one's work from a distance, a huge amount of organisational work is needed for the planning and codification of tasks" (p. 42). Additionally firms appreciate that telework does not suit all workers as the Finnish partners noted: "teleworkers (are) expected to be independent and to have self-discipline as well as an entrepreneurial attitude towards their work" (p. 42). So while some workers enjoy the autonomy that telework can bring, others do not.

*Regional Infrastructural Support and Policies.* The eGap project was also concerned with the regional environment and infrastructure within which teleworking activities were taking place in order to highlight particularly significant initiatives or influences. Regional policy initiatives in telework occur within all the five partner regions, though each has unique features and effects (ibid, p38). In Finland and Hungary, such initiatives are clearly rooted in the national framework, whilst in France, Italy and the UK, regional initiatives appear more likely to come from non-governmental regional agencies such as business consortia (eg, Chambers of Commerce in France), multi-party regional agreements as in Italy, or from combined business/local government fora as in the UK. Their importance cannot be underestimated because their position and therefore influence is often due to their direct contact with the more important protagonists such as the SMEs or trade unions.

The existence of a plethora of regional agencies in West London, all with varied responsibilities loosely connected to economic development issues would suggest that there are many apparent supporting institutions in the area to assist in adoption and diffusion of ICTs and telework (ibid, p.37). However, few of these agencies have much specific interest in telework *per se*, and even when they do address it, there is no coherent or co-ordinated agreed framework between the various agencies, from which interested SMEs might draw some real guidance or support. This finding finds resonance in other regions too, where little regional infrastructural support for telework can be identified unless it is part of a stronger national programme. This is the case in Hungary, but even there the regional commitment appears to dissolve once the national programme ends. There were some French suggestions that telework activity contributes to regional land planning in France and that regional communications infrastructure has fostered SME development, but other French respondents, greater in number, were more sceptical on this latter issue, noting the region did not exhibit high awareness of ICT issues relating to SMEs (ibid, p. 37).

In France, regional government is not directly involved in telework development among SMEs, though it might be involved in indirect financial support. More significant are the Chambers of Commerce and Industry (CCI), with strong business memberships, which are largely financed by taxes levied by local authorities on local firms. A CCI makes up a 'general-purpose, regional economic community' with a strong interest in local development programmes so that, for example, they encourage local actors to adopt and use ICTs more efficiently. SMEs are privileged targets as they play a leading role in the local economy.

In the Tampere region of Finland the advantages of telework have been long recognised. The city of Tampere enjoys high economic growth rates, and acts as a magnet to people in surrounding towns searching for better opportunities. Telework is seen therefore as one way of warding off this net migration. Paradoxically, another problem in Tampere is the recruitment and retention of skilled employees as the number of those who leave the labour market each year is larger than the number of those who start work (ibid, p. 36).

In Emilia Romagna, appreciation of relevant infrastructural developments in that region was more positive. Everyone recognized recent efforts made in the region to encourage the development of ICTs and many are convinced that they live in the most technologically advanced region in the country. One interesting Italian development is the establishment of 'telecentres' where independent teleworkers can work or interact. Interviewees maintain that they are useful for training purposes and exposing young people to using ICTs, while noting that a well-frequented telecentre can resolve the problems of the unsociable nature of telework (ibid, p.37).

A similar 'drop-in' centre, initially established with local government funds but now run privately, exists in West London where firms' executive staff are encouraged to join for advanced ICT training and to discuss 'state-of-the-art' ICT developments for their organisations. It was argued that such positive 'hands on' experiences for the executives has beneficial effects on the diffusion of telework in much the same sort of way that demonstrations of the latest technology by ICT manufacturers have on sales.

Perhaps the most interesting regional initiative exists in Italy, with two specific regional agreements being recently signed by representatives of SMEs and trade unions, though it appears too early to tell whether these agreements will be widely embraced. These collective agreements reflect the level of attention being given by all parties to the practice of telework and its future potential. Both agreements, based respectively in Bologna and Modena, recognise telework as a positive instrument for the individuals, in terms of personal choices and family requirements, and for collective benefits such as transportation, work viability, privacy, healthcare and quality of life (ibid, p. 51).

## CONCLUSIONS

If the five eGap regions are taken together, it is clear that the principal inhibiting influences for the adoption and diffusion of telework are related to human and organisational factors rather than technological ones. Thus this paper highlights the importance of trust and work autonomy, change management and regional infrastructural support on telework adoption and practice.

In terms of trust and work autonomy, for the majority of a firm's personnel, there are still tendencies – to a greater or lesser extent depending on the region – on the part of many firms to prefer 'physical oversight' as the dominant form of management control. This appears to be the major inhibiting influence on the diffusion and adoption of telework across the five regions. The fear of what individuals might do or not do when 'out of sight' underlines a basic lack of trust in employees, and without trust telework is unlikely to be successful. As the Italian partners stress, management thinking based on the 'logic of collaboration' needs to replace thinking based on the 'logic of subordination'. Thus hierarchical models of control need to be reconfigured to allow greater autonomy and worker discretion. However, such autonomy may not suit all individuals.

In terms of change management, one key to such a shift in approach may be the measurement of output from individuals as opposed to measurement of input. The eGap partners found that those teleworking in SMEs were mainly from management grades, individuals who already have a great deal of autonomy to organise their own work, and who tend to be measured by performance. In these terms, telework is still in its infancy as many of the issues concerning remote working for SME staff are still waiting to be tackled, including work measurement.

In terms of regional infrastructural support, each of the five partners note many unique regional features and policies with regard to telework, and this makes it difficult to generalise across the five regions. However in Finland and Hungary, regional initiatives appear to be rooted in national strategies, while in France, Italy and the UK, regional initiatives appear dependent to some extent on non-governmental consortia or agencies. Nevertheless all partners voice criticisms about a lack of overall coherence at the regional level towards telework.

Other than for reasons of retention of valued staff members and the extension of the geographical scope of sales regions, the challenge for telework is that it is not market driven in the same way that developments in, say, mobile phones are. So proponents of telework might talk of the efficiencies that telework can bring to bear on a small firm's operations, but these are not readily apparent to the owners of firms (ie those with the greatest power to influence telework adoption) who may view any such proposition with fear. So governments, whether national, regional or local, try pushing from the top. The subsequent problem is that bureaucratic policies and directives, however well-intentioned, do not appear to meet the needs of SMEs wishing to adopt telework. Certainly there is much SME apathy noted in the national reports towards poorly co-ordinated, fragmentary regional/national telework policies. This may well corroborate the introductory perception that diffusion of telework will be slower than proponents might wish. It may take a new generation of entrepreneurs who are better-versed in ICT exploitation before telework takes off in SMEs.

## ACKNOWLEDGEMENTS

The authors gratefully acknowledge the financial support of the European Commission for the funding of this research. They also acknowledge the contributions of the researchers in the other four partner countries (Italy, France, Hungary, Finland) to this research and the edited use of material from their national studies.

## REFERENCES

Bibby, A. (1996), *Trade Unions and Telework*, International Trade Secretariat FIET, Available from: <http://www.andrewbibby.com/fietrpt.html> [accessed 07-09-05]

Casimir, G. (1998), Notions from the home: changes in household activities due to telecommuting, in R. Suomi, P. Jackson, L. Hollmen and M. Aspnas (Eds), Teleworking *Environments. Proceedings of the Third International Workshop on Telework*, Turku Centre for Computer Science, Turku, Finland.

Dickson K and F Clear (2003), *Transnational Report of the Qualitative Research Phase: A Comparative Analysis of Regional Findings*, eGap Project, European Commission. Available from: <http://www.egap-eu.com> [accessed 15-09-05]

Di Nicola P., E. Como and F. Della Ratta Rinaldi (2003), *Transnational Report on the Surveys*, eGap Project, European Commission. Available from: <http://www.egap- eu.com> [accessed 15-09-05]

ECaTT (2000), *Benchmarking Progress on Electronic Commerce and New Methods of Work*, IST Programme, European Commission. Available from: <http://www.ecatt.com> [accessed 01-09-05]

eGap (2004), *E-Society Gap Assessment Project*, IST Programme, European Commission <http://www.egap-eu.com> [accessed 10-09-05]

EMERGENCE (2003), *Estimation and Mapping of Employment Relocation in a Global Economy in the New Communications Environment*, IST Programme, European Commission. Available from: <http://www.emergence.nu/erdb> [accessed 17-09-05]

Handy C. (1995), Trust and the Virtual Organisation, *Harvard Business Review,* May-June, pp.40-50

Hill J., B. Miller, S. Weiner and J. Colihan (1998), Influences of the virtual office on aspects of work and work life balance, *Personnel Psychology*, 51, 667-683

Huws U., W. Korte, and S. Robinson (1990), *Telework: Towards the Elusive Office*, John Wiley, Chichester

Johnson, S. (1998), Teleworking Service Management. Issues for an integrated framework in Jackson, P and J. Van Der Wielen, *Teleworking: International Perspectives*, Routledge, London

Knights D., F. Noble, T. Vurdubakis and H. Willmott (2001), Chasing Shadows: Control, Virtuality and the Production of Trust, *Organization Studies*, 22, 311-366

Mako, C., M. Illéssy, and P. Tamási, (2002), *Transnational Report on the Local Environments*, eGap Project, European Commission. Available from: <http://www.egap-eu.com> [accessed 12-09-05]

Nilles, J., R. Carlson, P. Gray and G. Hanneman (1976), *The Telecomunications-*

*Transportation Trade-off,* Wiley, New York.

Perin C. (1998), Work, space and time on the threshold of a new century in P. Jackson and J. Van Der Wielen (1998), *Teleworking: International Perspectives*, Routledge, London

Peters P and L. Den Dulk (2003) Cross Cultural Differences in Managers' Support for Home-Based Teleworking, *Int'l J. of Cross Cultural Mgt*, 3, 329-346.

Olson M. (1988), Organisational Barriers to Telework in W. Korte, W. Steinle and S. Robinson (Eds), *Telework: Present Situation & Further Development of a New Form of Work,* North-Holland, Amsterdam

Qvortrup, L (1998), From teleworking to networking: definitions and trends in P. Jackson and J. Van Der Wielen, J, *Teleworking: International Perspectives*, Routledge, London

Raghuram S, M. London and H. Larsen (2001), Flexible employment practices in Europe: country versus culture, *Int'l J. of Hum. Resources Mgt*, 12, 738-753

Stredwick, J. and S. Ellis (1998), *Flexible Working Practices*, Institute of Personnel and Development, London.

Sturesson, L (1998), The Mis-Match Between Suppliers and Users in Telework, in P. Jackson and J. Van Der Wielen, J, *Teleworking: International Perspectives,* Routledge, London.

SUSTEL (2004), *Sustainable Teleworking: Understanding and managing its Economic, Environmental and Social Impacts*, IST Project, European Commission. Available from: <http://www.sustel.org> [accessed 30-09-05]

TUC (1998), *New Information and Communications Technologies at Work,* Trades Union Congress, London.

Management of Technology: New Directions in Technology Management
M. Hashem Sherif and T.M. Khalil (Editors)



# 19

# TECHNOLOGY READINESS: THE ADOPTION OF THE WIRELESS COMMUNICATION TECHNOLOGY IN FINNISH ICT AND FOREST COMPANIES

*Jukka-Pekka Bergman, TBRC, Lappeenranta University of Technology, Finland*
*Jarno Käppi, TBRC, Lappeenranta University of Technology, Finland*[**]
*Sanna Sintonen (Taalikka), TBRC, Lappeenranta University of Technology, Finland*[***]
*Petteri Laaksonen, TBRC, Lappeenranta University of Technology, Finland*[****]

## INTRODUCTION

The challenge of assessing future technologies and markets is determining the need for new products and services and their users that do not yet exist (Day, 2000). In the present market turbulence, the introductions of new product and service innovations have increased enormously. They can be *incremental* (continuous) refinements and enhancements of existing products and services, or production and delivery systems, *radical* (discontinuous) totally new

* Technology Business Research Center, Lappeenranta University of Technology, P.O.Box 20, FI-53851 Lappeenranta, Finland. E-mail: bergman@lut.fi
** Technology Business Research Center, Lappeenranta University of Technology, P.O.Box 20, FI-53851 Lappeenranta, Finland. E-mail: jarno.kappi@lut.fi
*** Technology Business Research Center, Lappeenranta University of Technology, P.O.Box 20, FI-53851 Lappeenranta, Finland. E-mail: sanna.sintonen@lut.fi
**** Technology Business Research Center, Lappeenranta University of Technology, P.O.Box 20, FI-53851 Lappeenranta, Finland. E-mail: petteri.laaksonen@teliasonera.com

product and service categories, or production and delivery systems, or *architectural* reconfigurations of the system of components that constitutes the product (Burgelman *et al.*, 1996; Miller & Morris, 1999). In aggregate, innovation means a new way of serving new needs of new or existing customer segments to sustain the competitive advantage of the customer and the innovator, e.g. an organization (see e.g. Burgelman *et al.*, 1996; Markides, 1997). Despite the differences in innovations, proactive innovation management needs to have specific information about the progress of technology diffusion in organizations.

However, it should be noticed that not all the innovations that enter the market are diffused at the same speed. Sometimes it seems to take an amazingly long time for new technologies and innovations to be adopted by those who seem most likely to benefit from them. According to Martinez et al. (1998), the speed of the diffusion of innovation does not depend only on the characteristics of the product itself, but also on the predispositions of the target adopters. Van de Ven (1986) states that innovative ideas do not penetrate the larger social systems without a champion. Innovation is not an enterprise of a single innovator; it is a network building effort (Rogers, 1995; Nonaka & Toyama, 2003). Therefore, it is important to find common factors that affect the adoption of innovations in organizations. Categorizing potential adopters is one possible way to search for target markets for new products, develop strategies in order to penetrate the different adopter categories, and to predict the obsolescence or emergence of a product through time (Martinez *et al.* 1998).

The present paper discusses the innovation adoption process and evaluates the state of implementation of the wireless technology in two different industries: the ICT industry, which is the main producer of wireless solutions, and the Forest industry, which is the major user of these solutions. In this paper, a quantitative method, the factor analysis has been used as the assessing tool of technology readiness when utilizing new technology on the organizational level. The purpose of the paper is to categorize adopters (organizations) according to their capabilities to make the decision about the adoption on the basis of knowledge embedded in their organization about the innovation. This organizational knowledge includes the determinants of the innovation adoption, which are located in different processes of the organization. The assumptions of this study concerning the technology readiness of the wireless communication technology are based on the results of a survey carried out in Finnish ICT and forest companies during a three-year research project. The project was conducted at Lappeenranta University of Technology and funded by the Technology Agency of Finland and the participating companies.

## THE ADOPTION OF INNOVATIONS IN ORGANIZATIONS

New product and service innovations take time to diffuse across markets. The speed of the diffusion of an innovation depends on different factors that facilitate the diffusion process. According to Rogers (1995), diffusion is a learning process where an innovation is communicated via certain channels, through time, between the individuals of a social system. Van de Ven (1986) supports the idea that the innovation adoption is a networking process among people, who become committed to the innovation through transactions. Due to that, organizations adopt innovations only through individuals acting as organizational agents producing behavior that leads to learning (Senge, 1990; Argyris, 1999; Storey & Kelly, 2002). The process presumes that individuals recognize useful data and information, and are then able to transform it, through some process, into knowledge that brings future value for the organization (Inkpen, 1996; Nonaka & Toyama, 2003; von Krogh *et al.* 2001). In other words, the diffusion occurs on the macro level, but it would not be possible without the adoption of the innovation in micro level, i.e. in individual level. The adoption is viewed as a process in which an organization analyzes the positive and negative aspects of an innovation on the basis of knowledge embedded in its members. The actual adoption of an innovation takes place when the end result of these analyses is a positive one.

*The organizational adoption process of innovations.* All types of organizations adopt innovations to respond to changes in their external and internal environments. Innovations come into organizations in two ways: they can be generated in an organization or they can be adopted from another organization (Damanpour and Gopalakrishnan 1998). According to Damanpour and Gopalakrishnan (1998), the adoption of an innovation entails improved effectiveness or performance from the adopting organization, and the environment has a great influence on the decision-making process concerning the adoption of an innovation. Ozanne and Churchill (1971) argue that the organizational adoption process is a decision process that eventually leads through the purchase to the implementation of an innovation. The adoption process is always based on the decision of an individual or on a consensus of a decision-making unit (van de Ven 1986, Khalfan *et al.* 2001). For the adopting organization, the innovation adoption process (Fig. 1) includes awareness of the innovation, attitude formation, evaluation, decision to adopt, trial implementation, and sustained implementation (e.g. Rogers 1995, Frambach *et al.* 1998).

Thus, the initiation stage in the adoption process begins with the awareness of the innovation's existence. After this begins the formation of attitudes toward the innovation and the evaluation of it with the help of the information received from the market. On the basis of the received information, the potential adopter forms favorable and/or unfavorable attitudes toward the innovation, and assesses it through the perceived innovation characteristics (Rogers 1995). After the initiation, the organization either adopts or rejects the innovation. The decision to adopt is a decision to make full use of the innovation as the best course of action available (Rogers 1995). Thereafter, the innovation is first implemented on a trial basis, and if this is successful, the implementation of the innovation will continue, and the innovation becomes systematically used (Zaltman *et al.* 1984).

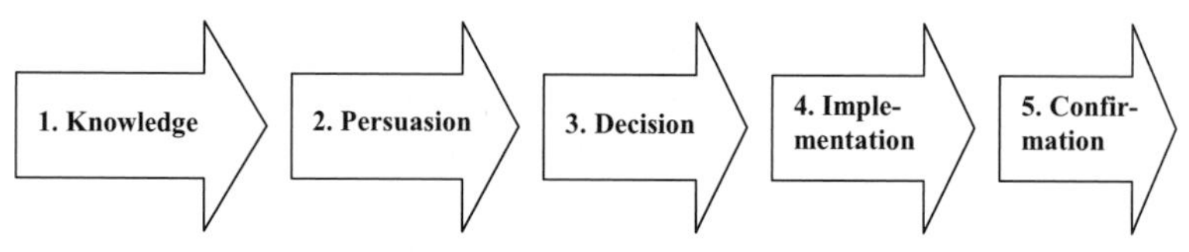


**Figure 1. The model of the stages in the innovation-decision process (Rogers 1995).**

*The determinants of the organizational adoption of innovations.* The organizational adoption process is influenced by several factors of the innovation. According to Frambach and Schillewaert (2002), the perceived characteristics of an innovation drive the decisions of the members of an organization. Rogers (1995) has proposed a list of five characteristics perceived by individuals that affect the adoption of innovation, the facilitators of which are relative advantage, observability, compatibility and trialability. The biggest inhibitor of the adoption is the perceived complexity. However, it has to be noticed that the perceived characteristics are part of the attitude formation toward the innovation, and are based on the adopter's own perceptions. Moreover, the environment in which the adopter operates has its own factors that affect the adoption process, for instance, competition (e.g., Mansfield 1961, Robertson and Gatignon 1986) and other environmental characteristics like heterogeneity and dynamism (e.g., Miller and Friesen 1982). Research in the field of innovation adoption in organizations has mainly focused on the effect of organizational characteristics on the adoption process. Several researchers (e.g., Aiken and Hage 1971, Dewar and Dutton 1986, Damanpour 1992) suggest that organizational size is a major determinant in the adoption of innovation for several reasons. Other organizational characteristics, like centralization, formalization and specialization, have also been found to affect innovation adoption in organizations (e.g., Moch and Morse 1977, Hull and Hage 1982, Grover *et al.* 1995, Subramanian and Nilakanta 1996). As a whole, adoption process is influenced by the several factors, and by examining them the organizational innovativeness can be evaluated and determined.

## ORGANIZATIONAL INNOVATIVENESS AND ADOPTER CATEGORIES

*Innovativeness.* Martinez et al. (1998) argue that the adoption of an innovation depends on the innovativeness of the adopters. Rogers (1995) defines innovativeness as a degree to which an individual is quicker in adopting an innovation than other members of the same system. Damanpour and Gopalakrishnan (1998) state that organizational adoption can be conceptualized by the speed and rate of the adoption. The speed of adoption is related to the timing of the innovation and reflects the organization's responsiveness and its ability to adopt the innovation quickly. The rate of adoption relates to the extent of innovativeness in the organization. According to Miller and Friesen (1982), the organizational capability to adopt innovations also depends on strategic intentions. An entrepreneurially oriented organization is more prepared of adopting innovations compared with a conservatively oriented organization which is more or less slower to adopt innovations.

*Categories of adopters.* According to Rogers (1995), the classification of a system's members into adopter categories is based upon the relative time at which an innovation is adopted. Martinez et al. (1998) also argue that the adopters can be classified if the speed of adoption is known and if the adopter can be identified. In other words, adopters can be classified according to the moment in time when they adopt and the degree of innovative behavior they present (Miller and Friesen 1982). Rogers (1995) has proposed the most widely used and accepted classification of adopters based on the timing of adoption. According to Rogers (1995), the adopters of innovations can be classified into five categories: (Fig. 2)

*(1)* *Innovators (pioneers)* have several common characteristics. They can be said to be venturesome. They are interested in new ideas and have an ability to understand and apply complex technological knowledge. They bring new innovations into the social

systems (Rogers 1995). Miller and Friesen (1982) state that entrepreneurial firms can be seen to fulfill these premises.

*(2)* *Early adopters* have the greatest opinion leadership in most systems. They are part of the social system and serve as role models for many other members of the social system. Early adopters decrease the uncertainty about a new idea by a communication process. (Rogers 1995)

*(3)* *Early majority* wants some proof that the innovation is feasible before adopting it, but they still do not want to be the last ones. Their innovation decision takes relatively longer than that of the former groups'. (Rogers 1995)

*(4)* *Late majority* adopts new ideas just after the average member of a system. Adoption for them is an economic necessity brought about by the increasing network pressure. They also have relatively scarce resources, which means that uncertainties related to the innovation must be considered carefully before the adoption. (Rogers 1995)

*(5)* *Laggards* are the last ones to adopt an innovation. Laggards make their decision according to past experiences. Laggards need to have a stable environment and they are not familiar with uncertainties. Their decisions are entirely rational, and they are extremely traditional (Rogers 1995). According to Miller and Friesen (1982), organizations that belong to this category have a very conservative attitude toward new innovations.

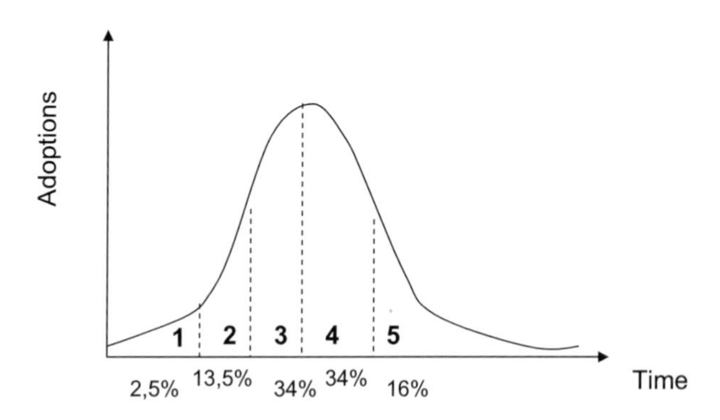


**Figure 2. Innovation adopter categories (Martinez et al. 1998; Rogers 1995).**

According to Miller and Friesen (1982), organizations are systems of individuals, and therefore their position in the innovation adoption process can be determined. The adoption of a new innovation that emerges in an organization or is adopted outside the organization, is always strategy driven. An entrepreneurial (innovator) organization that actively seeks new innovations is taking a risk, and is capable of adopting innovations at a high speed and rate. In the other extreme, a conservative (laggard) organization avoids risks and the time-frame of the adoption process is long. Adoption of an innovation is always a path-dependent learning process which varies according to the organizations (Zollo & Winter, 2002).

## TECHNOLOGY READINESS

Organization's capabilities are developed through learning processes and the integration of routines (Zollo & Winter, 2002; Argyris, 1999), which denotes its ability to build, reconfigure and renew resources, capabilities and routines in a changing business environment (Eisenhardt and Martin, 2000; Teece *et al.*, 1997). Capability building involves testing and selecting new knowledge combinations and modifying knowledge systems, skills, procedures and routines (Nonaka *et al.*, 2000; Zollo & Winter, 2002). Technological capabilities may offer sustainable competitive advantage to an organization in rapidly changing markets only if it is able to recognize changes and reconfigure its asset base and routines continuously to disseminate new innovations into its own processes. According to Hartman et al. (2000) and Jutla et al. (2002), readiness is a measure of a company's preparedness to exploit the opportunities in a certain field of business and technology. As a construct technology readiness refers to people's capabilities to embrace and use new technologies for accomplishing set goals (Parasuraman, 2000). As a whole, the technology readiness of an organization can be characterized as the level of fit between technological innovation and organizational capabilities.

The level of innovation adoption can be determined through assessing the state of readiness in organizations (Parasuraman 2000, Khalfan *et al.* 2001, Snyder-Halpern 2001). Miller and Friesen (1982) claim that the innovation adoption capabilities of companies are different. According to them, some companies are more ready to take risks and adopt a new technology or enter into new markets. Nowadays, the number of new technologies and innovations is increasing every moment at a much faster pace than ever before, and thus the adoption speed for them has also increased. The flip side of this, even though the penetration of new innovations has increased enormously, is the growth of observable fatigue and exhaustion among consumers against new technologies (Alsop 1999, Mossberg 1999). A plausible explanation for the inverse relationship between penetration and use rates is that more recent adopters of new technologies may not be technologically as savvy as early adopters, and may therefore not be avid users: another plausible explanation is product complexity coupled with the lack of user-friendly instructions and support device.

The situation described above demands immediate attention in the form of clarifying the state of technology readiness and categorizing possible customers depending on their adoption level of new technologies in order to approach them and market new services and products efficiently. The reason for this is aiming one's marketing efforts directly to right customers when it is known which readiness level and adopter categories one's customers belong to. Innovation adoption depends on the readiness of an organization to make the decision to adopt. Decisions in organizations are always related to individuals and their capabilities to make decisions which differ between the individuals (Rogers 1995). If we are able to recognize the diffusion of new products, services or ideas, it will help us to understand better the behavior of the members in a certain system (Martinez *et al.* 1998). For example, from the vendor's point of view, it is important to know the state of adoption in the target industry and companies. This makes it possible to create effective strategic plans and marketing strategies (Miller and Friesen 1982).

## METHODOLOGY

*Data collection.* The present paper applies the data collected in a wide web-based survey that was conducted among Finnish ICT and forest companies in the autumn of 2002. The purpose was to define the state of the adoption of the wireless communication technology in the companies' business use. The questionnaire was divided into five sectors: the management, business processes, and know-how of the company, resources, and legal factors to make it easier for the respondents to understand the questions and their context and after that to respond to them. The companies were at first contacted by telephone in order to reach the correct respondent and verify their willingness to participate in the survey. If the respondent agreed to participate, a link to the survey was sent to him/her by e-mail. The potential respondents were at first contacted on e-mail. The selected respondents of the survey were IS managers or similar persons in the ICT or forest cluster who were familiar with or were responsible for the implementation plans and resources of their companies to use and invest in wireless solutions. In total, 143 companies of the selected 222 companies responded, and the response rate of 64% was considered to be high enough for the study.

*Measurement.* In order to test the relation between technology readiness and the adoption of innovation, it was necessary to create measure scales for these two issues. The statements in the survey described technology readiness as well as the state of the adoption of the wireless technology. The measurement properties of all the questions had been shown to be reliable in the studies from which they were adopted. The questions were measured on a five-point Likert scale. An exploratory factor analysis was conducted in order to find out the dimensions of technology readiness and the state of the adoption process, i.e. innovativeness. The factor analysis provided three applicable factors. The results of the factor analysis are briefly presented in Table 1.

**Table 1. Results of the factor analysis.**

| Statements in the questionnaire | Factor1 | Factor2 | Factor3 |
|---|---|---|---|
| Knowhow1 | .828 | | |
| Knowhow2 | .815 | | |
| Knowhow3 | .794 | | |
| Knowhow4 | .786 | | |
| Knowhow5 | .758 | | |
| Knowhow6 | .688 | | |
| Knowhow7 | .635 | | |
| Knowhow8 | .615 | | |
| Learning1 | | .771 | |
| Learning2 | | .729 | |
| Learning3 | | .644 | |
| Innovativeness1 | | | .751 |
| Innovativeness2 | | | .605 |
| Innovativeness3 | | | .596 |
| Initial eigenvalues | 8.849 | 2.329 | 1.793 |
| % of variance explained | 32.773 | 8.626 | 6.643 |
| Cronbach's $\alpha$ | .9166 | .6989 | .7396 |

Of the three factors extracted, the first two were considered to indicate different dimensions of technology readiness. The first dimension for readiness discusses the ability of an organization to evaluate the present processes with the innovation and the importance of the innovation to the organization's survival or success. This dimension was renamed as *know-how* presenting a first stage in the learning process (Argyris 1999). The second dimension of readiness captures the capabilities to learn from past experiences and then transfer this *learning* for future use, which refers to the second stage in the learning process (Argyris 1999). The third factor represents the state of the adoption process, namely, innovativeness. This measure captures the state at which the organization is in implementing the wireless technology. The reliabilities of the constructs were assessed by Cronbach's alpha. Based on the analysis it can be said that the measurement constructs were appropriately formed, reaching the suggested level of $\alpha$>.70 (Hair *et al.* 1998).

## ANALYSIS AND RESULTS

In order to find out the relationship between readiness and innovation adoption, the companies were at first clustered on the basis of the two readiness dimensions, *know-how* and *learning*. A k-means cluster analysis was conducted and three clusters were requested. Because time has passed since the wireless technology was introduced, it is appropriate to suggest that the diffusion of the wireless technology is still in a growing state, and only three adopter categories can be recognized. The cluster analysis provided three clusters that were appropriate for the purposes of the paper. The final cluster centers are presented in Table 2. At this point, it is suggested that innovators have the highest readiness related to the wireless technology, and the latest adopters have the smallest readiness. Thus, the clusters were renamed on the basis of the readiness values.

**Table 2. Final cluster centers.**

| | Innovators | Early adopters | Early majority |
|---|---|---|---|
| No. of companies | 47 | 64 | 36 |
| Know-how | 3.915 | 2.165 | 2.044 |
| Learning | 3.884 | 3.897 | 2.491 |

After this the task was to test whether the innovativeness is different among these clusters. This was done with the help of one-way analysis of variance. The ANOVA analysis (Table 3) showed that there is a significant difference between the clusters based on their innovativeness.

**Table 3. Mean comparison of innovativeness between the clusters.**

| | No. | Mean | Std. Deviation |
|---|---|---|---|
| Innovators | 47 | 3.692 | .6376 |
| Early adopters | 64 | 3.258 | .9257 |
| Early majority | 36 | 2.653 | .7348 |
| F-value 17.315 | | Sig. .000 | |

The *innovators* were clearly the most innovative, i.e., their state of adoption has reached the highest level and they are the ones having the highest readiness. In the case of the two remaining clusters, the results of the ANOVA also support the positive relationship between readiness and innovation adoption. *Early adopters* are less innovative than *innovators*, but more innovative than the *early majority*. Correspondingly, the *early majority* is the least innovative with the smallest readiness.

## CONCLUSIONS AND LIMITATIONS

In this paper, the stage of the adoption of the wireless communication technology in organizations was analyzed and viewed as organizational innovativeness. The paper also proposes measures that determine the organizations' state of technology readiness and puts companies into categories according to their technological capabilities. With the help of the survey, the readiness of the Finnish ICT and Forest industry companies concerning the wireless technology was defined.

According to the results, the state of readiness might be evidence of the fact that the wireless technology itself is still emerging and only the most advanced firms are implementing it in their processes. Therefore, it was impossible to identify clear groups of *late majority* or *laggards*. One of the important results of the paper was the identification of three reliable measurement constructs (know-how, learning and innovativeness), that were formed when applying the factor analysis. Additionally, a cluster analysis was conducted using the readiness level (based on know-how and learning factors) and three adopter categories were found (i.e., *innovators*, *early adopters*, *early majority*). Thus, we were able to recognize the existence of a relationship between technology readiness and the stage of the adoption process. Those companies that are already implementing the technology have higher readiness related to know-how and learning. Thus, these companies have all the necessary knowledge to apply the wireless technology to their business processes. Those companies that are in the beginning of the adoption process have less knowledge concerning the wireless technology and its solutions. Marketers can, in their own way, facilitate the adoption of the later adopters by offering information and thus complementing their knowledge base; i.e., more focus is needed concerning the later and non-adopters.

In the following some aspects of limitations and further research are discussed. One limitation of the present study was the time lag that exists between the earliest adopter and the later ones. At the time of the survey, the innovators had already adopted the wireless technology, and their answers had a different knowledge background as they were more experienced users of the technology. However, the results still indicate that the further the adoption process, the higher the readiness; thus, the later or non-adopters do not have that kind of readiness yet. The results also showed that organizations can be categorized on the basis of their readiness for wireless technology, but the identification of the categories was not discussed in this paper. Research paths further on could be in the identification of the companies, and this way more applicable information would be provided, for instance, for innovation marketers. These kinds of results will be available in the future.

However, this research gives a link between the adoption of innovation and technology readiness, i.e. the higher the technology readiness, the more innovative the organization is in adopting the new technologies.

## REFERENCES

Alsop, S. (1999). Have I Told You Lately That I Hate Windows? *Fortune*, **140**, 177-178.

Aiken, M. and J. Hage (1971). The Organic Organization and Innovation. *Sociology*, **5**, 63-82.

Argyris, C. (1999): *On Organizational Learning*, 2nd ed., Blackwell, Oxford.

Burgelman, R. A., M. A. Maidique, and S. C. Wheelwright (1996), *Strategic management of technology and innovation*. 2nd ed., Irwin, Chicago, USA.

Damanpour, F. (1992). Organizational Size and Innovation. *Organization Studies*, **13**, 375-402.

Damanpour, F. and S. Gopalakrishnan (1998). Theories of Organizational Structure and Innovation Adoption: The Role of Environmental Change. *Journal of Engineering and Technology Management*, **15**, 1-24.

Day, G. S. (2000). Assessing Future Markets for New Technologies. In: *Wharton on Managing emerging technologies* (G. S. Day, J. H. Schoemaker and R. E. Gunther eds). John Wiley & Sons, New York.

Dewar, R. D. and J. E. Dutton (1986). The Adoption of Radical and Incremental Innovations: An Empirical Analysis. *Management Science*, **32**, 1422-1433.

Eisenhardt, K. and J. Martin (2000). Dynamic capabilities: What are they?. *Strategic Management Journal*. **21,** 10-11, 1105-1121.

Frambach, R. T., H. G. Barkema, B. Nooteboom and M. Wedel (1998). Adoption of a Service Innovation in the Business Market: An Empirical Test of Supply-Side Variables. *Journal of Business Research*, **41**, 161-174.

Frambach, R. T. and N. Schillewaert (2002). Organizational Innovation Adoption: A Multilevel Framework of Determinants and Opportunities for Future Research. *Journal of Business Research*, **55**, 163-176.

Grover, V., M. Goslar and A. Segars (1995). Adopters of Telecommunications Initiatives: A Profile of Progressive US Corporations. *International Journal of Information Management*, **15**, 33-46.

Hair, J. F., R. E. Anderson, R. L. Tatham and W. C. Black (1998). *Multivariate Data Analysis*. Prentice Hall, New Jersey.

Hartman, A., J. Sifonis and J. Kador (2000). *Net Ready - Strategies for Success in the E-economy*. McGraw-Hill, New York.

Hull, F. and J. Hage (1982). Organizing for Innovation: Beyond Burns and Stalker's Organic Type. *Sociology*, **16**, 564-577.

Inkpen, A. C. (1996) Creating knowledge through collaboration, *California Management Review*, **39**, 1, 123-140.

Jutla, D., P. Bodorik, and J. Dhaliwa. (2002). Supporting the e-business readiness of small and medium-sized enterprises: approach and metrics. *Internet Research: Electronic Networking Applications and Policy*, **12**, 2, 139-164.

Khalfan, M. M. A., C. J. Anumba, C. E. Siemieniuch and M. A. Sinclair (2001). Readiness Assessment of the Construction Supply Chain for Concurrent Engineering. *European Journal of Purchasing & Supply Management*, **7**, 141-153.

Mansfield, E. (1961). Technical Change and the Rate of Imitation. *Econometrica*, **29**, 741-766.

Markides, C. (1997). Strategic Innovation, *Sloan Management Review,* **Fall/Spring**, 9-23.

Martinez, E., Y. Polo and C. Flavián (1998). The Acceptance and Diffusion of New Consumer Durables: Differences between First and Last Adopters. *Journal of Consumer Marketing*, **15**, 323-342.

Miller, D. and P. H. Friesen (1982). Innovation in Conservative and Entrepreneurial Firms: Two Models of Strategic Momentum. *Strategic Management Journal*, **3**, 1-25.

Miller, W. L. and Morris, L. (1999), *4th generation R&D - Managing Knowledge, Technology, and Innovation,* 2nd ed, John Wiley & Sons, Inc., New York, USA.

Moch, M. K. and E. V. Morse (1977). Size, Centralization and Organizational Adoption of Innovations. *American Sociological Review*, **42**, 716-725.

Mossberg, W. S. (1999). AT&T´s One-Rate Plan Falls Short of Promise for Broad, Easy Use. *Wall Street Journa*l, **234**, B1.

Nonaka, I. and R. Toyama (2003). The knowledge created theory revisited: knowledge creation as a synthesizing process, *Knowledge Management Research & Practice*, **1**, 1, 2-10.

Nonaka, I., R. Toyama, and N. Konno (2000). SECI, Ba and leadership: a unified model of dynamic knowledge creation. *Long Range Planning*, **33**, 5-34.

Ozanne, U. B. and G. A. Churchill (1971). Five Dimensions of the Industrial Adoption Process. Journal of Marketing Research, **8**, 322-328.

Parasuraman, A. (2000). Technology Readiness Index (TRI): A Multiple-Item Scale to Measure Readiness to Embrace New Technologies. *Journal of Service Research*, **2**, 307-320.

Robertson, T. S. and H. Gatignon (1986). Competitive Effects on Technology Diffusion. *Journal of Marketing*, **50**, 1-12.

Rogers, E. M. (1995). *Diffusion of Innovations*. The Free Press, New York.

Senge, P. (1990). *The fifth discipline: the art and practice of the learning organization*. Doupleday, New York, USA.

Storey, C. and D. Kelly (2002) Innovation in services: The need for knowledge management, *Australian Marketing Journal*, **10**, 1, 59-70.

Subramanian, A. and S. Nilakanta (1996). Organizational Innovativeness: Exploring the Relationship Between Organizational Determinants of Innovation, Types of Innovations, and Measures of Organizational Performance. *Omega*, **24**, 631-647.

Teece, D. J., G. P. Pisano, and A. Shuen (1997). Capabilities and strategic management, *Strategic Management Journal*, **18**, 7, 509-533.

van de Ven, A. H. (1986). Central Problems in the Management of Innovation. *Management Science*, **32**, 590-607.

von Krogh, G., I. Nonaka, and M. Aben (2001). Making the most of your company's knowledge: a strategic framework. *Long Range Planning*, **34**, 421-439.

Zaltman, G., R. Duncan and J. Holbeck (1984). *Innovations & Organizations*. Malabar, FL.

Zollo, M. and S. G. Winter (2002). Deliberate learning and the evolution of dynamic capabilities, *Organization Science*. **13**, 3, 339-351.

# SECTION IV

# BUSINESS DEVELOPMENT

M. Hashem Sherif and T.M. Khalil (Editors)


# 20

# STRATEGY FORMATION IN PHARMACEUTICAL DRUG DISCOVERY

*Christos Tsinopoulos, Durham Business School, Durham, UK*

## INTRODUCTION

*"During the next century we shall surely obtain a full understanding of the body (through the human genome project), and then discover how to cure the disease and save the patient" (Mann, 1999, p. 197).*

For pharmaceutical organisations such challenges motivate their business strategy and shape their competitive landscape in terms of profits, costs, and ethics. With significant technological advances in the drug discovery process and the development of the biotechnology industry, pharmaceutical organisations are facing increased pressure to produce more and better drugs, at a faster rate and with greater economic benefits to the business. As with other industrial sectors, the pharmaceutical sector is a highly competitive and global industry. Yet, unlike most other sectors the pharmaceutical industry focuses on and allocates the majority of its resources to the process of drug discovery, whilst processes such as manufacturing, marketing, and logistics are very much secondary (Halliday et al., 1997). Today, the success of the drug discovery process relies heavily on the successful application of scientific knowledge and technology, yet, back in the early 1900s there was a limited understanding of human biology and chemistry.

Accompanying this progress in drug discovery has been an increasing popularity of research into the formation and change of organisational strategy (Mintzberg, 1996,

Whittington 1993, Quinn, 1989), which has led to the identification, and classification of various strategy types along the continuum of *entirely deliberate* to *entirely emergent* (Mintzberg 1994a, Mintzberg 1994b). Despite the popularity of this research, there is limited application of the principles of strategic management to drug discovery. Existing studies of drug discovery focus on the optimisation of the drug discovery process mainly through the use of new knowledge and technology (e.g. FitzGerald, 2000, Harvey, 1995, Jensen and Sandstad, 1998, Krantz, 1998, Merritt, 1998, Bernhardt and McCulley, 2000, Danheiser, 1997, Schneider, 2000, Spence, 1999), the effect of organisational networks on the process of drug discovery (e.g. Gambardella, 1992, Arora and Gambardella, 1990, Oliver, 2001, Deeds and Hill, 1996, Tapon et al., 2001), the absorptive capacity (e.g. Lane and Lubatkin, 1998, Cockburn and Henderson, 1998), the effect of mergers and acquisitions (e.g. Halliday et al., 1997, Graves and Langowitz, 1993, Henderson, 2000, Henderson and Cockburn, 1996), and the evolution of integrative competence as a factor in productive research (e.g. Henderson, 1994, Henderson and Cockburn, 1994, Cockburn et al., 2000).

Although these studies provide valuable theoretical and empirical research about the drug discovery business, and its effectiveness, there is almost no information about the defining strategies and the strategic management process that accompanies and influences such practice. There is no existing introductory account to and definition of drug discovery strategy. This paper aims at filling this gap by building a theoretical framework for understanding pharmaceutical drug discovery from a strategic management perspective. It seeks to examine drug discovery strategies, while understanding the factors that influence and shape them. Addressing these issues requires a comprehensive and robust link between the discipline of strategic management and the process of drug discovery. Such a link could provide the platform for further empirical research and the development and validation of theories related to drug discovery strategies.

## METHODOLOGY

To meet its aim this paper employs a business history methodology (Hendry, 1992). This methodology determines the role that history can play in social science theory building. The methodological strength of the business history approach lies in its ability to apply the longitudinal approach to research with the contextual sensitivity and richness of the case study approach, and its replicability (Hendry, 1992) and is thus, in accord with and complementary to the aim of this paper.

In the research presented in this paper historical data was collected and analysed in two stages. During the first stage data was collected from several publicly available sources that report the history of the pharmaceutical industry and individual organisations (e.g. Kepos, 1995, Davenport-Hines and Slinn 1992, Jones 2001, Mann, 1999, Weatherall, 1990, etc.). As will be explained in the following section, four factors that influence the formation of drug discovery were developed, knowledge, technology, organisation's routines and processes, and environment. Accordingly the data was coded and classified under these four headings.

The second stage used current theory of the development and formation of these factors to develop a theoretical framework for understanding pharmaceutical drug discovery from a strategic management perspective. This analysis proceeded in a process of iterating between the historical data and the theory on the formation and development of the four factors knowledge, technology, organisation and environment. Similar methodological approaches to the analysis of data may be found in Lovas and Ghoshal (2000), and Moenaert, (2000).

## ELEMENTS THAT INFLUENCE THE CHANGE OF BUSINESS STRATEGIES

A common proposition in strategic management literature is the desire to align an organisation's strategy with its environment (Venkatraman and Prescott, 1990). Central to this alignment are three organisational elements; (i) environment, (ii) organisation's routines and processes, and (iii) resources (as will be argued in the next section of the paper the key resources affecting drug discovery strategies are knowledge and technology). A change in these factors leads to a change in the resulting strategy. Depending on the strategic stance that is adopted the change could be seen as the result of either careful design or reaction to the new environmental status.

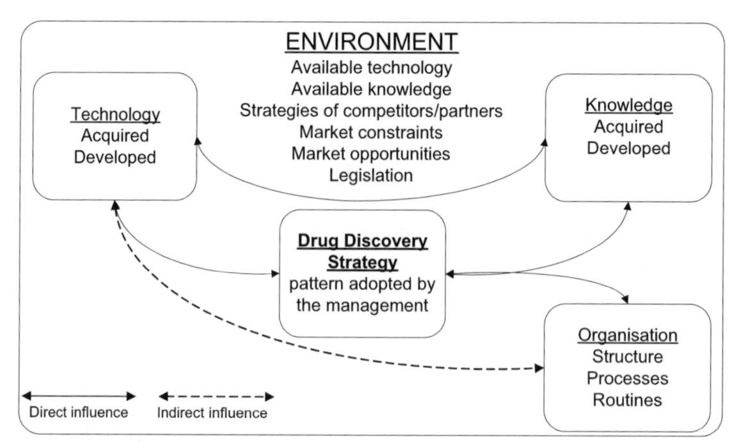


**Figure 1. Factors influencing the drug discovery strategy**

The paper uses data and literature to build a link between these strategic factors and drug discovery. The proposed theoretical framework is depicted in Figure 1 and each element is discussed in greater detail in the following sections.

*Resources.* The first factor, resources, includes the internal means and developments that can be drawn upon to accomplish the firm's goals, and especially those unique features called distinctive competencies (Selznick, 1957). Resources are converted into final products or services by using a wide range of other organisation assets and bonding mechanisms such as management information systems, trust between management and labour etc. (Amit and Schoemaker, 1998). Barney (1986) argues that for organisational resources to hold the potential of sustained competitive advantage they must be valuable, rare, and imperfectly imitable. Such organisational resources may include accumulated knowledge (Helfat, 1997, Drew, 1999, Krogh et al., 2001), technology (Dougherty et al., 1998, Arthur, 1989), and physical assets (Amit and Schoemaker, 1998). As identified through the analysis of the data the key resources that have shaped the drug discovery strategies are knowledge and technology. Hence, these are discussed in greater length.

*"Knowledge. Knowledge has emerged as the most strategically significant resource of the firm"* (Grant, 1996, Janszen, 2000). Scientific knowledge is generated by the social practice of exploring, mapping and mathematically codifying patterns in the behaviour of nature. During the age of botanicals (pre 1800s (Somberg, 1996)), scientific knowledge was limited. The discovery of new drugs was based not on scientific exploration, but on a mixture of empiricism and prayer (Lesney, 2000). As civilisation progressed, the information that was available on how the human body functioned and its reaction to various chemical entities generated the foundations of this scientific knowledge.

An organisation's knowledge capital is accumulated through interrelated and independent functions such as R&D, technology acquisition, experiential learning, organisational learning, and network knowledge. Drug discovery requires that once new knowledge is obtained becomes available for decision-making (Koretz and Lee, 1998). However, the exponential growth of scientific knowledge and skills makes the issue of availability of knowledge complex (Liyanage et al. 1999). Therefore, techniques aimed at improving the coordination of research methods, knowledge utilisation and assimilation processes are continuously being developed (e.g. bioinformatics).

An illustration of the use of knowledge as a core competency in pharmaceutical organisations is the recovery of the European pharmaceutical industry after the Second World War. The war had destructive effects on the capital stock and physical asset investment in European pharmaceutical organisations. However, shortly after the War various new products quickly emerged helping to revitalise the industry (Bogner and Thomas, 1996). The ability of this industry to quickly recover technological and business momentum suggests that the core competencies of the firms were not in their physical plant and technology, but in the collective knowledge they possessed about organic chemistry and the associated techniques of their research laboratories' personnel (Bogner and Thomas, 1996).

To enhance the development of new knowledge pharmaceutical organisations establish external strategic links and networks with other organisations and institutions to gain access to a specific set of tangible and/or intangible resources necessary for the development of innovations (Estades and Ramani, 1998).

Yli-Renko et al. (2001) have found a positive relationship between social interaction and network ties and knowledge acquisition. To be part of such a network and to be able to effectively exploit the information that circulates in the network has become '*even more valuable than being able to generate new knowledge autonomously*' (Gambardella, 1992). The effectiveness of such networks depends on the organisations' location (Deeds et al., 1999), the number of strategic alliances (Deeds and Hill, 1996), and the organisations' experience in selecting network partners (Graves and Langowitz, 1993).

The ability to value assimilate, and apply new external knowledge to commercial ends is a critical success factor (Jensen and Sandstad, 1998) and has been called *absorptive capacity* (Lane and Lubatkin, 1998, Cohen and Levinthal, 1989, Cockburn and Henderson. 1998). The absorptive capacity depends on various factors including an organisation's level of prior related knowledge (Cohen and Levinthal, 1990), the common basic knowledge shared between the two organisations that exchange knowledge (Simonin, 1999), the similarity of the two organisations compensation practices (Lane and Lubatkin, 1998), and the organisational structure (Lane and Lubatkin, 1998, Stork, 1998).

In summary, the scientific knowledge acquired by an organisation, is a resource critical to the success of the discovery of new drugs. Such knowledge is generated tacitly, but is then codified and combined with other existing knowledge. The resulting knowledge is then communicated both within an organisation and with other organisations and institutions. The absorptive capacity of an organisation is also critical in the formation of the drug discovery strategy as it reflects the ability of an organisation to use the external knowledge and convert it into new drugs.

*Technology*. The second factor that influences and shapes drug discovery strategy is *technology*. The rate of technological change particularly in the pharmaceutical industry is high and is constantly accelerating. The introduction of computational power in the streamline pharmaceutical research during the 1970s further accelerated this trend. The more a technology is adopted the more experience is gained by it and the more it is improved (Arthur, 1989). Technological innovation processes are important because they introduce dynamics into economic growth and impact the wider society (McKelvey, 1996). Also, technical change may require organisational rearrangements, which renders changes in structures and routines (Thomke, et al., 1998).

Technology represents the systematic utilisation of knowledge; it is the application of scientific information (Roman, 1968). Knowledge of the structure of DNA in the 1960s led to the technology necessary for the development of biotechnology (Frey and Lesney, 2000).

Therefore, there is a strong link between knowledge and technology. In fact the role of knowledge in technical change has been the subject of increasing attention in the 1990s (Nightingale, 2000). Recent studies have documented that the most frequent motivation for alliance formation is the development of new technologies (Deeds and Hill, 1996).
New technology has facilitated the development of new drugs through the development of sophisticated instrumentation. Since the WWII the rate of technological advancement in pharmaceutical R&D has been dramatically accelerated. The development of computers and their use into mainstream research has also increased the momentum of technical change. Nowadays, technologies allow pharmaceutical products to be designed by identifying potential drugs at the level of the human genome. In addition, advancements in IT have led to the development of super-efficient tools for the collection, assimilation and analysis of large amounts of data.

Advancements such as genomics, proteomics, rational drug design, combinatorial chemistry, high throughput screening, and pharmacogenomics are considered to be the key technologies of the pharmaceutical industry in the last two decades (Ratti and Trist, 2001, Bellott et al., 1997), These technologies are now used by most pharmaceutical companies (Ratti and Trist, 2001).

The development of scientific knowledge over the last century has resulted partly in the development of new technology. New technology in turn has altered the pattern by which new drugs are discovered. This alteration has influenced both the success rates of drug discovery and the structure of pharmaceutical organisations since new capabilities are now required. Consequently, technology is similar to scientific knowledge in that it constitutes an important asset of a pharmaceutical organisation, and is critical to any drug discovery strategy.

*Organisation's routines and processes.* The importance of this factor became apparent after the 1930s when scientists from different disciplines had to work together to develop new instruments and new drugs. The scientific knowledge required to discover new drugs can be divided into subject areas, which can be composed in a modular fashion to define larger pieces of knowledge. This culture of rationalisation encourages division of labour (firstly introduced in the 1930s when physical chemists and physicists collaborated with biochemists and biologists to invent instruments such as the electron microscope (1931), the ultracentrifuge (1924), and the pH meter with a glass electrode (1921) (Pizzi, 2000)) amongst individuals into specialised segments of the drug discovery process (Valle and Gambardella, 1993). The scientific disciplines that underpin drug discovery include molecular biology, physiology, biochemistry, analytic and medicinal chemistry, crystallography, and pharmacology (Cockburn and Henderson, 1998, Stork, 1998). Having large number of individuals from these disciplines (Gittins, 1997) working together to ensure that resources from different functions are present is considered one of the most important factors in achieving fast development (Dorabjee et al., 1998, Bernhardt and McCulley, 2000, Jensen and Sandstad, 1998)).

The increasing need for various disciplines resulted in greater systematisation of research. This systematisation however, has been criticised for stifling creativity and hence the level of success usually measured as the number of new chemical entities. During the 1960s and 1970s when new compounds were the result of long screening procedures, the volume of experimentation determined the level of success. Nowadays however the design of theoretical compounds is possible and creativity is no longer linked with the economies of scale of laboratories (Arrow, 1983). Therefore, to achieve greater levels of success individuals should be given autonomy to organise their own activities, whilst following their choice of research along the strategic objectives set by the managers (Valle and Gambardella, 1993). Hence, the management challenge of pharmaceutical organisations is to exercise appropriate control on a research team without influencing its creativity. Omta et al. (1994) have suggested that the arguably greater success of the Anglo-American organisations in comparison to continental European firms is partly due to the greater emphasis on human resources management.

In addition, the trend for mergers, acquisitions and alliances in the pharmaceutical industry, popularised in the 1980s, has made the issue of managing the individuals even more critical. Organisations with different histories, symbols, ideologies, ways of doing things, and

ways of thinking about things have been joined together. These differences often make working together a difficult task to manage (Stork, 1998). This difficulty has led to the development of techniques for managing innovation such as project management. The aim of project management is to develop a sound overall plan that includes contingency plans, rapid identification of bottlenecks, and vigorous resolution of each bottleneck when it appears. This in turn could create an efficient development process (Anderson, 1996).

To summarise, the growth of the body of scientific knowledge and technology in the pharmaceutical sector, have created the need for specialisation. This specialisation in turn has created the need for communication interfaces between these individuals and the teams they are part of. The management techniques, which have emerged to address these issues, face the challenge of exercising control without influencing creativity. Over the last century, these techniques together with scientific knowledge and technology have played an important role in the formation of drug discovery strategies.

*Environment.* Environmental aspects, which have influenced the drug discovery process over the period data was collected, include technology and knowledge of other organisations, the legislation and political situation that directly influence the drug discovery process, and the diseases that are targeted. Knowledge and technology and their effect on strategy making were addressed in the previous sections. Legislation and political policies affect drug discovery strategy by imposing a set of rules and routines that have to be followed to ensure that the drug is safe and efficient (Drews, 1998). Finally, diseases constitute the most critical part of the environment since the discovery of a successful cure for a disease can provide an organisation with a competitive advantage. The number of diseases that are still uncured and could therefore provide potential targets for research of the pharmaceutical organisations is still high. History has indicated that as one disease is eliminated or controlled another takes its place. AIDS is a recent example of a disease that has emerged, whereas obesity has made the progression from a cosmetic preoccupation to a topic of major concern (Williams and Mallick, 1987). In addition, the increase in the geriatric population will result in an increase of the occurrence of diseases like arthritis, senile dementia, and Alzheimer's (Williams and Mallick, 1987).

## CONCLUSION

This paper has implemented a business history methodology to collect data on the formation and implementation of drug discovery strategy to build a theoretical framework for understanding pharmaceutical drug discovery from a strategic management perspective.
A key element of the resulting framework, and also a stance of this paper, is that strategy making in the drug discovery context is seen as a process of leaping from one state to another. Therefore, drug discovery strategies are patterns of management behaviour that emerge due to changes of external factors such as diseases, technology, political, and social circumstances. In particular, advances in scientific knowledge and technology have driven organisations to transform their strategic configurations to a more *rational* approach. Also viewing drug discovery strategy as a pattern of management behaviour allows for serendipity, a crucial factor in any research activity and particularly in the discovery of new drugs.

The formation of a drug discovery strategy is achieved using the strategic factors: knowledge, technology, and organisation's routines and processes. The environment within which the drug discovery strategies are formed and executed consists of the corporate strategy, the strategies of the competitors, the available knowledge and technology and finally legislation. Knowledge, technology, and organisation's routines and processes are used to create and protect an organisations' competitive advantage and consequently to meet the goals set by the corporate strategy.

The theoretical framework developed and analysed in this paper provides a rigorous link between strategic management and pharmaceutical drug discovery. Such a link provides the platform for further empirical research and the development and validation of theories related to drug discovery strategies.

## REFERENCES

Allen, T.J. (1997). Managing Organisational interfaces, *Food and Drug Law Journal*, **52**, 176-177.

Amit, R. Schoemaker, P. (1998). Strategic Assets and Organizational Rent, The *Strategy Reader*, Susan Segal-Horn (Ed), 200-219, Blackwell Business, UK.

Anderson, R.J. (1996). Managing the Overall Portfolio for Successful Discovery and Development, Welling, P.G., Lasagna, L., Banaker, UV, (Eds) 79-115, *The Drug Development Process. Increasing Efficiency and Cost-Effectiveness*, Marcel Dekker, New York.

Andrews, K.R. (1971). The *Concept of Corporate Strategy*, Dow Jones Irwin, Illinois.

Arora, A. Gambardella, A. (1990). Complementary and External Linkages: the Strategies of the Large Firms in Biotechnology, The *Journal of industrial Economics*, **38**, 4, 361-379.

Arrow, K. (1983). Innovation in Large and Small Firms, *Entrepreneurship*, Ronen, J., (Ed), Lexington, Chapter 1.

Arthur, W.B. (1989). Competing Technologies, Increasing Returns, and Lock in By Historical Events, The *Economic Journal*, March, 116-131.

Baden-Fuller, C. Stopford, J. (1998). Maturity Is a State of Mind, The *Strategy Reader*, Susan Segal-Horn (Ed), 125-140, Balckwell Business, UK.

Barney, J.B. (1986) Strategic Factor Markets: Expectations, Luck, and Business Strategy, *Management Science*, **32**, 1231-1241.

Bellott, E.M. Bondaryk, R. Luther, A.L. (1997). Combinatorial Chemistry in the Drug Discovery Process, *Clinical Research and Regulatory Affairs*, **14**, Nos. 3&4, 231-241.

Bernhardt, S.A. Mcculley, G.A. (2000). Knowledge Management and Pharmaceutical Development Teams: Using Writing to Guide Science, *Technical Communication*, February/March, 22-34.

Bogner, W. Thomas, H. (1996). Drugs To Market: Creating Value and Advantage in the Pharmaceutical industry, Pergamon, New York.

Cockburn, I.M. Henderson, R.M. (1998). Absorptive Capacity, Coauthoring Behavior, and the Organization of Research in Drug Discovery, *The Journal of industrial Economics*, **XLVI**, 157-182.

Cockburn, I.M. Henderson, R.M. Stern, S. (2000). Untangling the Origins of Competitive Advantage, *Strategic Management Journal*, **21**, 1123-1145.

Cohen, W.M. Levinthal, D.A. (1989), Innovation and Learning: two Faces of R&D, *Economic Journal*, **99**, 569-596.

Danheiser, S. (1997). Laboratory Automation and Robotics To Play A Major Role in the Drug Discovery Process, *Genetic Engineering News*, **10**, 9-10.

Davenport-Hines, R.P.T. Slinn, J. (1992). *Glaxo: A History To 1962*, Cambridge University Press, Cambridge.

Deeds, D.L. Cecarolis, D. Coombs, J. (1999). Dynamic Capabilities and New Product Development in High Technology Ventures: An Empirical Analysis of New Biotechnology Firms, *Journal of Business Venturing*, **15**, 211-229.

Deeds, D.L., Hill, C.W.L. (1996). Strategic Alliances and the Rate of New Product Development: an Empirical Study of Entrepreneurial Biotechnology Firms, *Journal of Business Venturing*, **11**, 41-55.

Dorabjee, S. Lumley, C.E. Cartwright, S. (1998). Culture, Innovation and Successful Development of New Medicines – An Exploratory Study of the Pharmaceutical Industry, *Leadership and Organization Development Journal*, **19**, 4, 199-210.

Dougherty, D. Borrelli, L. Munir, K. O'Sullivan, A. (1998). The Interpretive Flexibility of an Organization's Technology as a Dynamic Capability, *Advances in Strategic Management*, **15**, 169-204.

Drews, J. (1988,). *In Quest of Tomorrow's Medicines*, Birhasuer Verlag, Switzerland.

Estades, J. Ramani, S. (1998). Technological Competence and the influence of Networks: A Comparative Analysis of New Biotechnology Firms in France and Britain, *Technology Analysis & Strategic Management*, **10**, No 4., 483-495.

Farjoun, M. (2002). Towards an Organic Perspective on Strategy, *Strategic Management Journal*, **23**, 561-594.

Fitzgerald, K., (2000). In Vitro Display Technologies – New Tools for Drug Discovery, *Drug Discovery Technologies*, **5**, 6, 253-258.

Frey, R. Lesney, M.S. (2000). Anodynes and Estrogens: the Pharmaceutical Decade, The Pharmaceutical Century: Ten Decades of Drug Discovery Supplement To American Chemical Society, 92-109.

Gambardella, A. (1995). Science and innovation the US Pharmaceutical industry During the 1980s, Cambridge University Press, Great Britain.

Gambardella, A. (1992). Competitive Advantages From in House Scientific Research: the US Pharmaceutical industry in the 1980s, *Research Policy*, **21**, 391-407.

Gittins, J. (1997). Why crash pharmaceutical research, *R&D Management*, **27**, 1, pp 79-85.

Grant, R.M. (1996). Prospering in Dynamically Competitive Environments: Organizational Capability As Knowledge integration, *Organization Science*, **7**, 4, 375-387.

Graves, S.B. Langowitz, N.S. (1993). Innovative Productivity and Returns to Scale in the Pharmaceutical Industry, *Strategic Management Journal*, **14**, 593-605.

Halliday, R.G. Drasdo, A.L. Lumley, C.E. Walker, S.R. (1997). The allocation of resources for R&D in the world's leading pharmaceutical companies, *R&D Management*, **27**, 1, 63-77.

Hannan, M.T. Freeman, J. (1989). *Organizational Ecology*, Harvard University Press, Cambridge MA.

Harvey, A.L. (1995). interdisciplinary Approaches To Drug Discovery: An Academic Approach, *interdisciplinary Science Reviews,* Vo. **20**, 2.

Helfat, C.E. (1997). Know-How and Asset Complementarity and Dynamic Capability Accumulation: the Case of R&D, *Strategic Management Journal*, **18**, 5, 339-360.

Helfat, C.E. Raubitschek, R.S. (2000). Product Sequencing: Co-Evolution of Knowledge, Capabilities and Products, *Strategic Management Journal*, **21**, 961-979.

Henderson, R. (1994). The Evolution of integrative Capability: innovation in Cardiovascular Drug Discovery, *Industrial and Corporate Change*, **3**, 3 607-630.

Henderson, R. (2000). Drug Industry Mergers Won't Necessarily Benefit R&D, *Research and Technology Management*, July-August, 10-11.

Henderson, R.. Cockburn, I. (1994). Measuring Competence? Exploring Firm Effects in Pharmaceutical Research, *Strategic Management Journal*, **15**, 63-84.

Henderson, R. Cockburn, I. (1996). Scale, Scope and Spillovers: the Determinants of Research Productivity in Drug Discovery, *Rand Journal of Economics*, **27**, 1, Spring, 32-59.

Henderson, R. Orsenigo, L. Pisano, G.P. (1999). The Pharmaceutical Industry and the Revolution in Molecular Biology: Interactions among Scientific Institutional and Organizational Change, *The Sources of industrial Leadership*, Mowery, D., Nelson, R., (Eds), Chapter 7, 267-311, Cambridge University Press, New York.

Hendry, J. (1992). Business Strategy and Business History: A Framework for Development, *Advances in Strategic Management*, **8**, 207-225 Horn (Ed), Chapter 12, 239-265, Blackwell Business, Oxford.

Janszen, F. (2000). The *Age of innovation*, FT Prentice Hall, Great Britain.

Jensen, I. Sandstad, O.R. (1998). The Learning Project Organisation, *Drug Development Research*, **43**, 134-142.

Jones, E. (2001). The Business of Medicine: The Extraordinary History of Glaxo, A Baby Food Producer That Became One of the World's Most Successful Pharmaceutical Companies, Profile Books, London.

Kepos, P. (Ed), (1995). *International Directory of Company Histories*, St James Press, Detroit.

Koretz, S. Lee, G. (1998). Knowledge Management, *Journal of Knowledge Management*, **2**, 2, 53-58.

Krantz, A. (1998). Diversification of the Drug Discovery Process, *Nature Biotechnology*, **6**, December, P. 1294.

Krogh, G. Nonaka, I. Aben, M. (2001). Making the Most of your Company's Knowledge, *Long Rang Planning*, **34**, 421-439.

Lane, P.J. Lubatkin, M. (1998). *Strategic Management Journal*, **19**, 461-477.

Lesney, M. (2000). Patents and Potions: Entering the Pharmaceutical Century, The Pharmaceutical Century: *Ten Decades of Drug Discovery*, Supplement To American Chemical Society, 18-31.

Liyanage, S. Greenfield, P.F. Don, R. (1999). Towards a Fourth Generation R&D Management Model-Research Networks in Knowledge Management, *International Journal of Technology Management*, **18**, Nos ¾, 372-393.

Lovas, B. Ghoshal, S. (2000). Strategy as Guided Evolution, *Strategic Management Journal*, **21**, 875-896.

Mann, J., (1999). *The Elusive Magic Bullet: the Search for the Perfect Drug*, Oxford University Press, Oxford.

Mckelvey, M.D. (1996). *Evolutionary innovations: the Business of Biotechnology*, Oxford University Press, New York.

Merritt, A.T. (1998). Uptake of New Technology in Lead Optimisation for Drug Discovery, *Drug Discovery Technology*, **11**, 11.

Mintzberg, H. (1994a) Rethinking Strategic Planning, Part I: Pitfalls and Fallacies, *Long Range Planning*, **27**, 3, 12-21.

Mintzberg, H. (1994b). Rethinking Strategic Planning, Part II: New Roles for Planners, *Long Range Planning*, **27**, 3, 22-30.

Mintzberg, H., (1996). Ten Ideas Designed To Rile Everyone Who Cares About Management: Musings On Management, *Harvard Business Review*, July-August, 61-67.

Moenaert, R.K. Caeldries, F. Lievens, A. Wauters, E. (2000). Communication flows in international product innovation teams, *Journal of Product Innovation Management*, **17**, 360-377.

Oliver, A.L. (2001). Strategic Alliances and the Learning Life-Cycle of Biotechnology Firms, *Organization Studies*, **22**, 3, 466-489.

Omta, S.W.F. Bouter, L.M. Van Engelen, J.M.L. (1994). Managing Industrial Pharmaceutical R&D: A Comparative Study of Management Control and innovative Effectiveness in European and Anglo-American Companies, *R&D Management*, **24**, 4, 303-315.

Pizzi, R. (2000). Salving With Science: the Roaring Twenties and the Great Depression, *The Pharmaceutical Century: Ten Decades of Drug Discovery Supplement To American Chemical Society*, 34-51.

Quinn, J.B. (1989). Strategic Change: Logic Incrementalism, *Sloan Management Review*, Summer, 45-60.

Ratti, E. Trist, D. (2001). The Continuing Evolution of the Drug Discovery Process in the Pharmaceutical industry, *Il Farmaco*, **56**, 13-19.

Roman, D.D. (1968). Research and Development Management: the Economics and Administration of Technology, Appleton-Cntury-Croft, New York.

Schneider, I., 2000, Robotics Drives the Drug Discovery Process, *Genetic Engineering News*, **20**, 2, 20 and 36-37.

Selznick, P. (1957). *Leadership in Administrative Frame-Work*, Harper & Row, New York.

Simonin, B.L. (1999). Ambiguity and the Process of Knowledge Transfer in Strategic Alliances, *Strategic Management Journal*, **20**, 595-623.

Somberg, J. C. (1996). The Evolving Drug Discovery Process, *The Drug Discovery Process: increasing Efficiency and Cost Effectiveness*, Welling, P. G., Lasagna, L., Banakar, U.V. (Eds), Marcel Dekker, New York.

Spence, P. (1999). From Genome To Drug – Optimising the Drug Discovery Process, *Progress in Drug Research*, **53**, 157-191.

Stinchcombe, A.L. (1965). Social Structure and Organisations, *Handbook of Organisations*, March, J.G, March (Ed), 142-193, Rand Mcnally and Co, Chicago.

Stork, D. (1998). Not All Differences Are Created Equal: Not All Should Be Managed the Same: the Diversity Challenge in Pharmaceutical R&D, *Drug Development Research*, **43**, 174-181.

Tapon, F. Thong, M. Bartell, M. (2001). Drug discovery and development in four Canadian biotech companies, *R&D management*, **31**, 1, 77-90.

Thomke, S. Von Hippel, E. Franke, R. (1998). Modes of Experimentation: An innovation Process-and Competitive-Variable, *Research Policy*, **27**, 315-332.

Valle, F.D. Gambardella, A. (1993). Biological Revolution and Strategies for innovation in Pharmaceutical Companies, *R&D Management Journal,* **23**, No4, 287-302.

Venkatraman, N. Presott, J.E. (1990). Environment-strategy coalignment: An empirical test of its performance implications, *Strategic management journal*, **11**, 1-23.

Weatherall, M. (1990). *In Search of A Cure: A History of Pharmaceutical Discovery*, Oxford University Press, New York.

Whittington, R. (1993). *What Is Strategy and Does It Matter*, Routledge, London.

Williams, M. Malick, J.B. (1987). Drug Discovery and Development: Reflections and Projections, *Drug Discovery and Development*, Williams, M., Malick, J.B., (Eds), 3-32.

Wilson, I. (1992). Realizing the Power of Strategic Vision, *Long Range Planning*, Vol **25**, 5, 18-28.

Yli-Renko, H. Autio, E. Sapienza, H.J. (2001). Social Capital, Knowledge Acquisition, and Knowledge Exploitation in Young Technology-Based Firms, *Strategic Management Journal*, **22**, 587-613.

Management of Technology: New Directions in Technology Management
M. Hashem Sherif and T.M. Khalil (Editors)



# 21

# PROCESS OF TECHNOLOGICAL CAPABILITY DEVELOPMENT: CASES FROM CHINA'S MOBILE PHONE INDUSTRY

*Maximilian von Zedtwitz*[1] *and Jun Jin*[2]

*1 Research Center for Technological Innovation, School of Economics and Management, Tsinghua University, Beijing, P. R. China,*

*2 Asia Research Centre, University of St.Gallen, St.Gallen, Switzerland*

## INTRODUCTION

Technological capability (TC) plays a strategic role in the competitive advantage of a firm, an industry, and even a country (Lall 1990). This is why it has become a focus of attention not only among academics, but also among business managers and government officials, particularly in developing economies (Lall 1990, Miyazaki 1995, Kim 1997). There is extensive research on the TC development in newly industrialized economies (NIEs) and emerging NIEs (e.g., Malaysia and Thailand) (e.g. Lall 1990, Kim 1997), most of which focusing on heavy and chemical technology (HCT) industries or labor-intensive industries (see e.g. Lee *et al.* 1988, Kumar *et al.* 1999, Lee 2001). Very little research has been on information and communication technologies (ICT), even though they are playing a key role in the development of companies and national economies.

However, ICT have not just been 'imported' in their mature stage without adaptation or modification. This import does not seem to follow Kim's (1980) model whereby it is supposed to progress from the acquisition, and assimilation of mature technologies before moving to the, improvement of growing or emerging technologies. Furthermore, Kim's model stipulates separate stages and a linear transition through these stages.

Recently, Gao (2003) found that 1) TC development in telecommunication equipment manufacturing firms in China did not follow Kim's model, and that 2) these firms did research to improve mature technologies. Gao's study suggests that some firms that deviate from the assumed way of TC development, i.e., those firms that start to develop their own proprietary technology early, improve their TC more effectively than firms that follow the traditional paradigm (Kim's model). Chen and Qu's study (2003) also suggests that Kim's theory may not meet development needs of China. Therefore, it is essential to examine Kim's three-stage model in an emerging industry in China.

Based on these observations, we decided to pursue the following research question: Can we modify Kim's TC model to fit TC development in fast emerging economies? Since our observations were rather conceptual and unstructured, we decided to elaborate this question first with in-depth cases studies to develop a sharper understanding of the potential divergence of empirical practice from Kim's model. The goal of our paper is thus to develop a working hypothesis for further research on the basis of well-founded observations.

## LITERATURE REVIEW

*Technological capability.* The definition of technological capability varies in perspective, depending on the aims of researchers. Lall (1990: 17) defines TC in a narrow sense as the capability to execute all technical functions entailed in operating, improving and modernizing firm's productive facilities. Kim (1997: 4) points out that in developing countries 'technological capability' could be used interchangeably with 'absorptive capacity' (Cohen and Levinthal, 1990), i.e., that of absorbing existing knowledge, assimilating it, and in turn generating new knowledge.

In this paper, we define technological capability as the capability to make effective use of the technical knowledge and skills, not only in an effort to improve and develop products and processes, but also to improve the existing technology and to generate new knowledge and skills in response to the competitive business environment.

*The development process of technological capability.* The study of TC development is extensive and empirically oriented. Most research focuses on the TC development process in NIEs. A wide range of research (e.g. Westphal et al. 1985, Lee et al. 1988, Lall 1990, 1993, OECD 1994, Kim 1980, 1999, Kumar et al. 1999, Kim and Nelson 2000) argues that the TC development process in NIEs follows three steps:

1. Domestic firms transfer mature technology from multinational companies (MNCs);
2. Then they absorb the transferred technology and diffuse the technology within the firm and in the industry, even in the whole economy;
3. Eventually, these firms then innovate and develop their own, new technologies.

Kim (1980) developed a three-stage model of acquisition, assimilation and improvement of technology, which extends Utterback's model in advanced countries (1985) to describe the TC development process in developing countries. To summarize, Kim's theory of the TC development process is as follows:

- In developing countries, the state of technological capability develops from mature technology to growing technology and to emerging technology.

- Most firms in these countries are at the stage of mature technology, few reach the emerging technology stage.
- There are clear and discernible boundaries between the different three stages.
- The technological capability must develop from one stage to the next, step by step.
- The main R&D activities of firms in developing countries are acquisition and assimilation of mature technologies, not development.

More research in developing countries supports Kim's idea that firms make efforts to master transferred mature technologies and practice them efficiently, but firms make no or only little technology improvement (Dahlman *et al.* 1987, Lall 1987, 1990). Moreover, the TC development of firms generally follows the three-stage model, moving from acquisition to assimilation and finally to improvement (or innovation). Other researchers examined firms in Korea, such as Samsung, to provide further evidences for this TC development process (e.g. Kim 1997, 1999, Lee 2001).

*Mobile phone industry in China.* In less than two decades, China's mobile phone industry has undergone four generations of mobile phone technologies[1], from analog to digital mobile phone technology. Attracted by the high profit and low competition in the Chinese mobile phone industry in 1990s, many Chinese domestic firms were drawn into producing GSM mobile phones at the end of 1990s. Mobile phone manufacturers in China grew from 5 firms in 1997 to 37 firms and over 200 manufacturing sites in 2004. In addition, China's domestic mobile phone manufacturers are growing fast, holding over 40% of the Chinese market in 2004, up from 0% before 1999.

---

[1] The 1st generation (1G) mobile phone technology, TACS (Total Access Communication System), is an analog technology. The other three generations mobile phone technologies are digital technologies. Their main difference is in the bandwidth used and the coding technique. The bandwidth of 2nd generation (2G), such as GSM (Global System for Mobile Communication) is the narrowest. The bandwidth of the 2.5th generation (2.5G), such as CDMA (Code Division Multiple Access) and GPRS (General Packet Radio Service) is wider than that of 2G, but narrower than that of the 3rd generation (3G). 3G systems include CDMA2000, WCDMA (Wideband Code Division Multiple Access), and TD-SCDMA (Time Division-Synchronous Code Division Multiple Access).

China produced TACS mobile phones from the early 1990s. However, TACS usage declined soon and all TACS systems were closed down in 1997. TACS existed in China for a few years only. Chinese firms started to produce GSM mobile phones in 1996. China produced all mobile phones under foreign brands before 1999. With the intensive efforts and TC development based on assembling imported parts, Chinese local firms have produced mobile phones with indigenous intellectual property rights (IPRs) technologies[2] (their own developed

and designed parts and software) since 1999. In 2001, China opened the 2.5G mobile phone market (CDMA and GPRS). 2.5G mobile phone technology and products are an investment focus of Chinese firms. All Chinese domestic firms produce GPRS or CDMA mobile phones. In order to narrow the technology gap with the advanced countries and improve the competitive competence of China in the future, the Chinese government encourages the investment in 3G technology, an emerging technology in the world. With the support from Chinese government and the technology alliance with Siemens, DTT Corporation proposed its TD-SCDMA standard, which became one of the three 3G standards in the world. China has not decided which standard(s) would be adopted though the Chinese 3G mobile phone market will be open soon. Chinese firms collaborate with local and foreign firms for all standards of 3G mobile phone technologies and products.

In short, Chinese firms not only produce GSM, CDMA, and GPRS mobile phones but also invest in R&D in these mobile phone technologies and products as well as 3G mobile phone technologies and products.

---

[2] IPRs of Chinese firms are mainly focusing on the applied-level of chip technologies, such as the software design and new function development. Though they reinvest in R&D on key chip technologies, it is hard for Chinese firms to master and develop the core technology of mobile phone chip, which is monopolised by less than 5 MNCs in the world.

## RESEARCH METHODOLOGY

Since we were driven by a theoretical research question based on some unstructured empirical observations, we decided to develop our ideas first by means of an in-depth investigation of a multi-case study. The case research was designed to avail us with a critical review of Kim's model, and to develop hypotheses that could be used for subsequent empirical quantitative research. We focus on the TC development process of four Chinese mobile phone manufacturers that were able to develop their TC rapidly and progress from 1G to 3G mobile phone technologies.

The four companies will be designed as A–D. These are the leading Chinese mobile phone manufacturers and fall into two categories: the first consist of as telecommunication systems and equipment manufacturers (Companies A, B and D) and the second those that have extensive experience in commercial products marketing (Company C).

Before conducting the interviews, we collected secondary data from books, newspapers, websites, and so on, to familiarize ourselves with firms and the industry. Interview is the dominant method. We conducted 25 long interviews face-to-face or over the phone. The interviewees included senior managers, middle managers and senior engineers. Each interview lasted between 90 minutes and 150 minutes. We continued to collect secondary data, e.g. information published on related websites and interviews with external academic experts, to maximize the validity and reliability of case studies according to the theory stipulated by Yin (1989).

In this research, technological capability is evaluated by (1) the market scale to present the change of production capability; (2) the change of R&D fields, such as developing from assimilation mature technology to investment in emerging technology; and (3) the usage level of indigenous IPRs in a product. Patents and publications were not used as a measurement because Chinese firms rarely apply for patents and are restricted in their publications.

## TC DEVELOPMENT OF FOUR FIRMS

The history of 1G mobile technology in China is very short and lasts only from 1990 to 1997. In the four firms, only Company A produced 1G mobile phones. Company A imported 1G mobile phone production lines at the beginning of 1990s, assembled imported parts and sold foreign brand 1G mobile phones. Their development of 1G mobile phone failed because of the organization reform of cooperative institute and shortages of independent development capabilities.

The development of GSM mobile phones in China started in 1996. In the mid-1990s, Company A imported a turn-key plant to assemble foreign brand 2G mobile phones. Its joint venture (JV) with a USA MNCs produced same brand but relative latest styles of 2G mobile phones[3] too. Through sending employees to study in foreign countries and intensive internal regular on-site training, Company A assimilated the transferred 2G technology. Thanks to its R&D center in the USA, it produced its first set of 2G mobile phones with 50% of indigenous IPRs in 1998. Later, Company A produced its own brand 2G mobile phones.

In contrast, Companies B and C lacked basic mobile phone production capabilities when they decided manufacture them. They imported production lines and assemble imported parts even though they sold 2G mobile phones under their own brands. With its extensive R&D experience and strong telecommunication R&D capability generated from its production and development of telecommunication switch equipment, Company B organized its R&D team

---

[3] At first, the JV was set up to produce CDMA equipment. But the government did not open the CDMA market at that time. The JV had to produce 2G mobile phones much later than Company A. Now, the joint venture only produces foreign brand of 2.5G mobile phones and 2.5G mobile equipment. The competition between Company A and its JV did not block their development because of the low competition and high profit in China's market and their different target customers.

to develop 2G mobile phone technologies and products while they assimilated the transferred technology to improve their production capability. Company C gradually improved its development capability and production capability through internal learning system, cooperating with the foreign partner (e.g. sending employees to do train in the foreign company), and recruiting engineers as well as acquiring a Chinese telecommunication institute to build up its R&D group.

Company D had a JV with a foreign manufacturer when it entered the mobile phone industry. However, because this JV operated independently, it could not take advantage of the knowledge gained in the JV to improve its indigenous production capability. Therefore, Company D had to build an R&D center in the USA and to import a production line to produce its own brand 2G mobile phones.

A common feature of all four firms is that while producing 2G mobile phones, they all have invested in the development of 2.5G mobile phone technologies. They built 2.5G R&D centers, recruited professional expertise and started to cooperate with other organizations in anticipation of the 2.5G market to prepare for their production of 2.5G mobile phones in 2000.

Company B, in particular, conducted its R&D in 2.5G technology, particularly the 2.5G switch equipment, in 1995, even before it produced 2G mobile phones. Furthermore, since 2002, Chinese firms have invested in the R&D for 3G mobile phones and joined the 3G Forum to participate in the development of the nascent market, where standards are being developed. In particular, the contributions of the four firms in the 3G Forum is around TD-SCDMA products because China has not decided which standard to be adopted. Table 1 summarizes the technological activities of the various firms under study.

It should be also noted that the four firms produce a small part of 2G and 2.5G mobile phones through OBM[4] in an effort to catch up the fast changing of this market.

---

[4] OEM: original equipment manufacture; OBM: own brand manufacture; ODM: own design manufacture.

**Table 1. Technological Activities of the Firms under Study in Different Generations of Technologies**

| Technology | Company A | Company B | Company C | Company D |
|---|---|---|---|---|
| 1G | Turnkey-plant imported (OEM), and assimilate* | — | — | — |
| 2G | OEM and JV to acquire, assimilate to be OBM, and R&D to be ODM | Turnkey-plant imported (OBM), assimilate and do R&D at the same time | Turnkey-plant imported (OBM), assimilate, late R&D | JV to acquire, assimilate to be OBM, then R&D to be ODM |
| 2.5G | Cooperate to do R&D, with acquisition and assimilation at the same time | | | |
| 3G | Cooperate with others to do R&D | | | |

In sum, when the four firms moved into mobile phone manufacturing, they lacked the necessary production technology. So they acquired the production technology from MNCs through importing production lines or setting up JVs. Then they assimilated and improved the transferred technology, and developed new products and technologies with their intensive internal efforts and cooperation with others. Firms advanced from being an OEM or an OBM (assembling imported parts and selling under own brands) to an ODM. While Company A, B, C and D are producing 2G (mature technology), 2.5G (growing technology) mobile phones, they put heavy investment in R&D in 2G, 2.5G, and 3G concurrently. 2G, 2.5G and 3G mobile technologies exist concurrently in China.

## DISCUSSION

The development of 1G and 2G technologies, in the case of Company A, followed the technology trajectory of acquisition, assimilation and development. However, the fact that

Company A attempted to invest in the R&D of TACS mobile phones contradicts Kim's theories (1980) and Lall's studies (1990) that firms in developing countries do not need to research and develop the mature technology. This supports Gao's study (2003) in that firms in developing countries that invest in mature technology improve the effectiveness of their TC.

Company B acquired, assimilated and developed the 2G mobile phone technology all at the same rather than consecutively. This may be because Company B had strong telecommunication R&D capability to help them to assimilate the transferred 2G production technology and develop new 2G products in a short time though the firm lacked the 2G production technology. In addition, China's mobile phone manufacturers conducted R&D and production concurrently on mature (2G), growing (2.5G), and emerging (3G) technologies. For instance, the four firms started to put heavy investment to develop some 2.5G technology locally while they were producing 2G mobile phones. Obviously, these results contradict Kim's theory regarding the sequence of development of technological capability. We hypothesize that this concurrent pursuit of different technologies is a consequence of the speed of development of the Chinese market (with GDP growth rates of 8-10% annual for more than twenty years) as well as of the competitive nature of the mobile phone industry itself.

With respect to 2G technologies, all four firms acquired them from MNCs through the importation of production line or through JVs, then assimilated and developed their own GSM technologies. Concurrently and independently, they developed new 2G mobile phones with indigenous IPRs or through OBM. Therefore, even the development of 2G technologies followed Kim's technology trajectory, all stages were taking place at the same time. This result again challenges Kim's theory of distinct stages, but here we hypothesize that this behavior is a result of the successive generations that are occurring in parallel within the worldwide mobile phone industry. This parallel development has forced firms to acquire and assimilate the transferred technology and, at the same time, invest in the development of new technology.

Interviews with managers reveal that two factors encouraged firms to invest in a mature technology: a desire to improve their existing TC by expanding the application of the mature technology and because they thought the transferred mature technology as an advanced technology to adopt.

*Four stage of technological capability process.* Given the observations in our case studies, we believe that Kim's three-stage model should be refined. Based on our notion of receding technologies and using product life cycle theory as a reference, we propose a fourth stage to complement the three stages identified by Kim (1980). We define the recessive stage as the stage of technology obsolescence in advanced countries.

In Figure 1, T1, T2, T3, T4 mean different generations of technologies, developing from the 1st generation to the 4th generation. In the cases, 1G is represented by T1, 2G by T2, 2.5G by T3, and 3G by T4. Every generation technology in advanced countries undergoes four stages: developing from emerging to growing, mature and recessive. There is a concurrent area in the model, where we find different generations of technologies at different stages at the same time (e.g. the grey area in Figure 1).

Figure 1 illustrates that in advanced countries, technology life cycles are long and relatively distinct (upper part of the figure). Firms in developing countries acquire, and then assimilate, foreign technologies in order of maturity: first, technologies that are already in a recessive phase; then mature technologies and finally growing technologies. In the fourth stage, domestic firms themselves develop their own indigenous technologies after they have reached the international level of technological capabilities. Since technologies are changing fast, different stages of technologies coincide, such as the grey part in Figure 1. As firms may not have undertaken much R&D to create those technologies, they concurrently import and assimilate them; therefore the boundaries among the various stages of technology acquisition collapse and the stages become interlaced.

Firms in developing countries that acquire and assimilate a technology in the recessive stage could invest to improve the acquired technology. However, because the recessive technology will be phased out soon, most firms in developing countries do not take that route Take TACS mobile phone technology as an example. When China imported TACS technology, it was a recessive technology in the mobile phone industry[5] in advanced countries. In the four firms, only Company A produced TACS mobile phones. Though it was a recessive technology in advanced countries, Company A attempted to develop indigenous TACS products. After the failure of Company A in its TACS development program, GSM become the focus of Chinese mobile phone industry and the whole TACS market, including TACS service was terminated in China in 1997.

---

[5] According to the characteristics of technology in the mobile phone industry, the emerging stage is defined as the period in which a technology is new and there is (are) no one/several standard(s) accepted by all countries. In addition, the emerging technology is only adopted in several countries and at the early stage of commercialization. The commercial result is uncertain. The growing stage is the period when a technology is diffusing, there is (are) technology standard(s) and the commercialization proceeds smoothly, but the dominant technology is not public. The mature stage is the period that the commercialization of a technology succeeds and most technology is public.

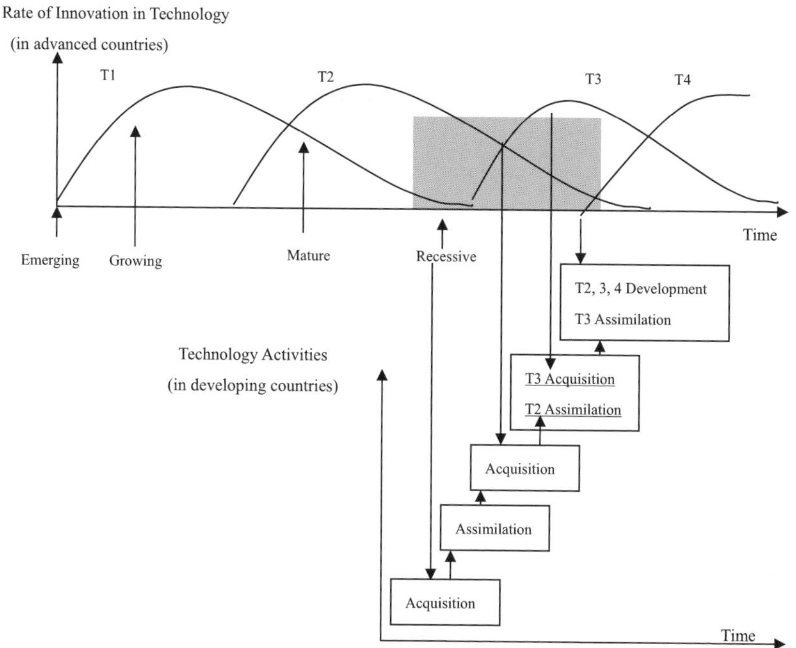


**Figure 1. Four Stages of TC Development**

Note: T1: 1st generation technology; T2: 2nd generation technology; T3: 3rd generation technology; and T4: 4th generation of technology

## CONCLUSIONS

With the diffusion of ICT, the life cycle of technology is getting shorter. It is necessary and possible for firms in developing countries to acquire the growing technology, even to develop growing and emerging technologies when they assimilate and develop a mature technology.

This research examined the TC development process in China's mobile phone industry. Based on research results, we extended Kim's three-stage TC development model to four stages, adding a complementary stage of recessive technology. Based on the four-stage model, we observed that:

1. The boundaries among the different stages are fuzzier than predicted by Kim: firms in developing countries undertake concurrent activities (acquisition, assimilation, and development) in mature, growing and emerging technologies at the same time.
2. Firms in developing countries may concurrently invest in the R&D of mature, growing and emerging technology.

This four-stage model provides new insights in technology management in China in particular, in developing countries in general. It suggests that technology managers should employ different methods to manage different phases of technologies. In addition, managers in developed countries and developing countries alike need to balance the effort in investment and IPRs management in different phases of technologies, particularly technologies belonging to distinct phases but developing concurrently. Furthermore, MNCs need to consider cooperation with firms in developing countries to develop emerging technologies. Moreover, the four-stage model indicates that firms in developing countries have more opportunities in growing and emerging technologies to develop TC and compete with MNCs.

As this paper is based on four cases, the generalization of research results is limited. Thus, further research and investigation (with more cases or quantitative research) is necessary to validate the findings in this paper. In addition, the research results need to be examined in other developing countries to formulate generalized propositions.

## REFERENCES

Chen, J. and W. G. Qu (2003). A new technological learning in China. *Technovation*, **23**, 861-867.

Cohen, W. M. and Levinthal, D. A. (1990). Absorptive capacity: a new perspective on learning and innovation. *Administrative Science Quarterly*, **35**, 128-152.

Dahlman, C. J., B. Ross-Larson and L. E. Westphal (1987). Managing technological development: lessons from newly industrializing countries. *World Development*, **15**, 6, 759–775.

Gao, X. (2003). *Technological Capability Catching Up: Follow The Normal Way or Deviate*. PhD Thesis: MIT Sloan School of Management.

Kim, L. (1980). Stages of development of industrial technology in a developing country: a model. *Research Policy*, **9**, 254–277.

Kim, L. (1997). *Imitation to Innovation: the Dynamics of Korea's Technological Learning*. Harvard Business School Press, Boston.

Kim, L. (1999). Building technological capability for industrialization: analytical frameworks and Korea's experience. *Industrial and Corporate Change*, **8**, 1, 111–136.

Kim, L. and R. R. Nelson (eds.) (2000). *Technology, Learning, and Innovation: Experiences of Newly Industrializing Economies*. Cambridge University Press, Cambridge.

Kumar, V., U. Kumar and A. Persaud (1999). Building technological capability through importing technology: the case of Indonesian manufacturing industry. *The Journal of Technology Transfer*, **24**, 81–96.

Lall, S. (1987). *Learning to Industrialize: The Acquisition of Technological Capabilities in India.* Macmillan, London.

Lall, S. (1990). *Building Industrial Competitiveness in Developing Countries*. OECD, Paris.

Lall, S. (1993). Promoting technology development: the role of technology transfer and indigenous effort. *Third World Quarterly*, **14**, 1, 95 –108.

Lee, J., Z. Bae, and D. Choi (1988). Technology development processes: a model for a developing country with a global perspective. *R&D Management*, **18**, 3, 235–250.

Lee, Y. S. (2001). *Technology Transfer and the Role of Information in Korea*. Research Proposal for ADBI: http://myhome.hanafos.com/~youngsae/tech_trans20011019.htm.

Miyazaki, K. (1995). *Building Competences in the Firm: Lessons from Japanese and European Optoelectronics.* St. Martin's Press, New York.

OECD (1994). *Effective Technology Transfert, Co-operation and Capacity Building for Sustainable Development: Common Reference Paper*. OECD, Paris.

Utterback, J. M. and W. J. Abernathy (1975). A dynamic model of process and product innovation. *Omega*, **3**, 639 –656.

Utterback, J. M. (1994). *Mastering the Dynamics of Innovation*. Harvard Business School Press, Boston.

Westphal, L. E., L. Kim and C. J. Dahlman (1985). Reflections on the Republic of Korea's acquisition of technological capability. In: *International Technology Transfer: Concepts, Measures and Comparisons* (N. Rosenberg and C. Frischtak, eds.), pp.167–221. Praeger, New York.

Yin, R. K. (1989). *Case study research: Design and methods*. Sage, Newbury Park.

Furthermore, the end user is no longer the only consideration in defining the objectives of an innovative product design. This is because it is necessary to distinguish between a user and a customer so that the expectations of each can be taken into account. For example, the owner of a fleet of vehicles (i.e., the customer) will have a different set of expectations in terms of profitability and durability form the driver (i.e., the user) who would be mostly concern with the functions that are related to ease of use. There are also the shareholders who expect simply from the innovation that it contribute to increased profitability. As a result, a horizontal cooperation has also to improve the industrial performance through an optimal use of the available means in respond to the demands of the market (customers or users) as well as of the shareholders in terms of reducing the cost of production.

Finally, we want to note that in a horizontal cooperation, each partner is dependent on the performance of the other partner (or others partners). As a result, the performance of the project depends on the quality of the process for information sharing to ensure an optimal use of resources and to acquire a competitive edge over other competitors.

*Factor Four : Integration of social criteria in a learning organisation.* Within an organization, innovation involves a learning process after the introduction of new techniques and tools. (Hage 1999) considers that the process of innovation is a complex division of labor that challenges the intellectual or problem solving or learning capacities of that organization. Thus, technological innovations depend on a combination of the skills and will of the workers and of management. When workers are involved, they contribute to sustainable organizational performance, because each individual feels fee to choose how to exert his potential towards the firm'ss desired goals.

We can also see the importance of this factor from the angle of competences. All firms employ three ingredients in their production: labor, capital and knowledge. Furthermore, in a highly competitive situation, all firms must have an ability to innovate (Khalil 2000). Yet innovation depends on the capability to manage change and to develop competencies to create more knowledge. This is why competences are the value adding combinations of capabilities and resources (Gorman and Thomas 1997). So, in order to make profits, all firms must control their human capital to increase productivity, not only as a form of labor, but also as a strategic resource for knowledge to have a sustained competitive force. Technological innovation generates new ways of conduct and requires new competencies, new capabilities and so a new organization. So, all firms must be able to introduce a technology culture that influences employees behavior. The industrial plants of the automobile industry are so sophisticated that firms must encourage a work force with high levels of training in order to maintain competitive advantage. The impact of production workers on productivity and in particular on technological innovation is examined in the economics literature. In many cases, innovation for productivity improvement involves some resistance to technological change in firms or organizations. Conversely, production workers are always affected by the manner in which a technology is introduced into the organization. So, the introduction of technological innovation must logically integrate social criteria.

Economic considerations alone would lead us to view the production workers as a key central element in the automobile industry. However, technological innovation is accompanied by an intensive global competition, which creates significant difficulties in structuring and managing organization in industry. And the main difficulty lies in the fact that it is always a confrontation between capital and labor (by competing visions on the way capitalist development involved).

To overcome these problems, it is necessary to develop adequate perspectives as to the factors underlying such worker's opposition and to develop social strategies for dealing with it constructively. For example, Utterback (1979) clearly states that the capacity for improvement is dependent on an organizational structure that guarantees the optimum dissemination of all acquired knowledge. In other words, a firm's capacity to innovate depends on its social capabilities. If generally, in the European car industry, the structures are able to maintain basic competencies and their capitalization, the specialized competencies required by a project of horizontal cooperation demand a strong and attractive social capacity. For salaries, it must be a real chance of careers and it must constitute an economic and social recognition too. So, both social and economics decisions must be "based on a stable internal compromise between the main institutional actors of the enterprise (stakeholders, management, workers, union)" (Tommaso 2004) to ensure the most innovative and flexible organization. Firms must so develop structural organisational autonomy that is to say an organisation opens to its environments with a just in time capacity of reaction (Jary and Jary 1991).

## Preliminary Results from the PSA-Ford Horizontal Cooperation : the PSA Point of View

The PSA Peugeot Citroën Group is the second largest European automobile manufacturer, with two general name brands (Peugeot and Citroën), and enjoys financial, industrial and technological synergies. The growth strategy for the group is to place "attractive, differentiated and competitive" vehicles on the market at a high rhythm (that is, with increasingly shorter development cycles). To achieve these objectives, the group has significantly increased its investment in R&D since 1998 in order to explore emerging technologies to gain a substantive competitive advantage (product, process or materials).

To achieve its growth target and control costs, the PSA Peugeo-Citroën Group has adopted a strategic cooperation strategy. These cooperation projects relate to sharing, from time to time, with other manufacturers the development and production of components or vehicle structures for which the large scale factor bears a meaning. The group thereby broadens its product offering and renews its motors while benefiting from technical and cultural enrichment.

In 1998, J-M Folz, the President of PSA Peugeot-Citroën and J. Nasser, the then President of Ford Motors Company, announced a joint development of a new family of diesel motors with the objective of completing this development in two and a half years (shared study costs). They decided to use for this project a PSA plant located in Tremery, north-east of France. In 1999, the two signed an agreement in order to expand the cooperation to the field of diesel motorization, leading to the study of various scientific projects following a logic focusing on savings and efficiency, which, in our minds, is similar to the creative destruction described by (Schumpeter 1934). As a result, the first results of the horizontal cooperation can be see both as a technological innovation booster (operationalization of factors one and three of the critical success factors) and also a social and organisational improvement (operationalization of factors two and four).

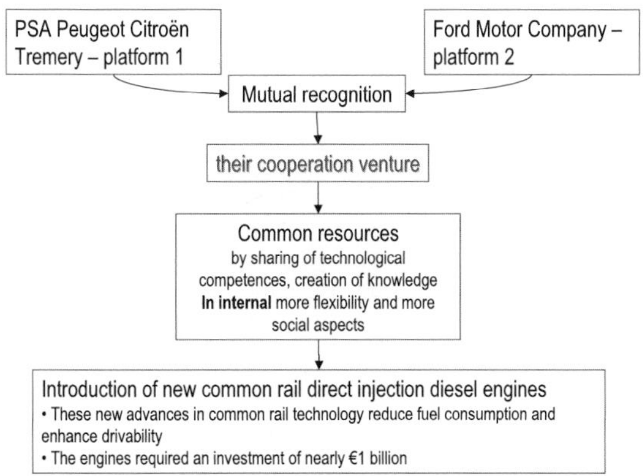


**Figure 1. The PSA-FORD horizontal cooperation**

*A technological innovation booster.* PSA Peugeot Citroën and the Ford Motor Company are introducing new 1.4, 1.6 liter, 2 liter, 2.7 liter V6 and a new family of engines for light commercial vehicles. New common rail direct injection diesels fuel allow for consumer economy, clean combustion, outstanding performance and low running noise. The High Diesel Injection (Hdi) system coupled with the particulate filter (FAP) is one of the cleanest engines in the world. The use of particle filters makes this engine clean as a petrol engine, a weighty argument for customers that are very sensitive to problems of environment.
By 2005, they have jointly manufactured more then 9000 engines a day, for a total development and production investment of 1.22 billion euros. The engine is installed on more than 37 different vehicle models of both partners.

For PSA and Ford, the competitive advantage expected by this project is quite clear. This is the first engine of this type to be developed by European car manufacturers, a high quality diesel engine that is environmentally clean and with low fuel consumption but, with significant enhancements to driving features compared with previous generations.

Figure 2 shows the direct impact of the cooperation on the type and number of cars manufactured by PSA. We can note a stabilisation of the gasoline type and a drastic increase in diesel type. This tendency is confirmed for 2005. So, as the sale of the diesel engines increases, this project is become a real opportunity for PSA for internal growth through a modification of its traditional product line.

To sum up, the main objective of the cooperation is to bring up to the partners a new range of products, more innovative and varied.

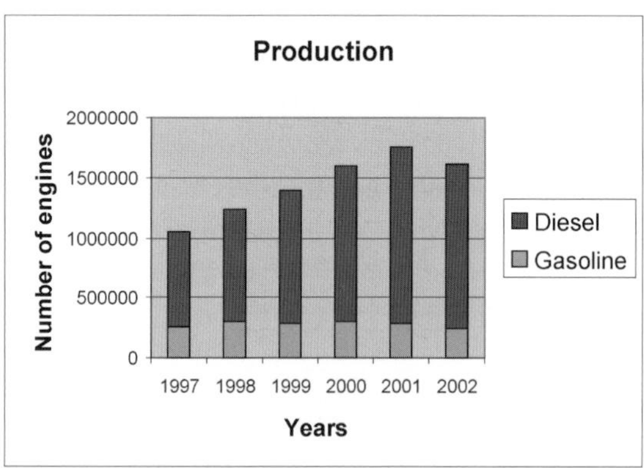


**Figure 2. Type and number of cars manufactured by PSA**

*A specific project organisation with a positive skills impact.* Tremery is a current PSA Peugeot Citroën plant, where both the basic engines and the Hdi diesel engine are manufactured. The plant has 4100 employees. The industrialisation of the diesel engine required a consistent program of technological investments with the creation of 3 assembly lines and 10 manufacturing workshops (which represent for example 3000 programable automats , 625 specific assembly machines, 700 numeric command and robots and also a real investment in quality and environmental norms (the plant is now certified for ISO 9002, EAQF (Evaluation of Supplier Quality Capability) and ISO 14001.

Furthermore, the plant is organised in modular units, each unit being dedicated to a specific point of the manufacturing process. As a result, it is easy to stop one unit without stopping the entire production to adapt the fabrication to the requirements of the just in time process. The key words of that kind of organisation are: flexibility, reactivity to the demand and ergonomics.

From an employee's point of view, the choice of modular manufacturing line induced a reorganisation of the global plant to ensure an optimal mix of old employees and the new ones, employed in order to assume the increase of engines production due to the cooperation. The aim is to favour cross-learning to globally increase the knowledge and know-how within the plant. As a result, the Tremery plant has become a high technology site with skilled workers. This induced a permanent process of training and learning in order to maintain the knowledge.

In this way, in 2004, PSA had decided to increase its training percentage from 2% to 4 % of the salaries mass only for the employees of the Tremery plant The training regime aims to accompany workers throughout their career through two main axes: a better integration of youths and a constant training to technologies and job evolutions.

## Conclusion

A horizontal cooperation agreement is typically set to meets the specific requirements of various stakeholders. The main reason is that it is a voluntary and negotiated step. Through this kind of cooperation, two automotive groups aim at increasing their productivities and improve their industrial excellence.

The potential benefits of an horizontal cooperation dedicated to R&D activities are known: to extend the scope in Research and Development, economies of scale and access complementary technical and technological capabilities. These benefits are the results of generative process of cooperation based on four KFS: Resource Sharing, Partners' choice, Improvement of industrial performance through innovation boosting, Integration of social criteria in a learning organisation. Cooperation also requires the development of an innovative problem solving methodology to increase efficiency, to improve innovation capabilities and to develop a common industrial culture among all parties.

Finally, our preliminary results allow us to conclude that a well-managed horizontal cooperation can bring about the expected results in terms of a better capacity to launch innovative technologies on the market, faster than when each manufacturer act alone.

## REFERENCES

Aubert S., (2006) Déterminants et effets d'une stratégie de coopération horizontale au sein du secteur automobile, Thèse de Doctorat en Sciences de Gestion, Université de Metz. To be defend.

Dosi G., Teece D.J, Winter S., (1990). Les frontières des entreprises, *Revue d'économie industrielle*, Paris.

Faulkner D.O, (1995). International Strategic Alliances, Co-operating to compete, Maidenhaed/ McGraw-Hill, Oxford, UK.

Gorman P., Thomas H., (1997). The theory and practice of competence based competition. Long Range Planning, *International Journal of strategic Management*, V30, P615-620.

Hage J.T., (1999), Organizational innovation and organizational change, *Annual Review of Sociology*, V25, p597-622, Harvard Press.

Hagedoorn J., (1993),. Understanding the rationale of strategic technology partnering: interorganizational modes of cooperation and sectoral differences, in *Strategic Management Journal*, p.371-385.

Huber, G.P., (1991). Organizational learning: The contributing processes and the literatures. *Organization Science* **2**: (1) , 88-115.

Hymer S.H, (1972). The internationalisation of Capital. *The Journal of Economic Issues*, **6**,.91-105.

Jary D. and Jary J. (1991)., The Harper's Collins dictionary of Sociology, pp. 347-349, Harepre, New York.

Khalil T., (2000). Management of Technology, The Key to Competitiveness and Wealth Creation, Mc Graw Hill, Kidlington, Oxford, UK.

Nelson,S. and Winter, D (1982). An Evolutionary Theory of Economic Change, Harvard University Press, Cambridge.

Penrose E., (1959). The Theory of Growth of the Firm, John Wiley and sons, New Work Press.

Perrin J. and Soënen R. (2002), Enjeux d'une approche interdisciplinaire des mutations industrielles, Coopération et connaissances dans les systèmes industriels, Hermès Sciences, Paris.Pettigrew A.M., Massini S. and Numagami T. (2000), Innovative Forms of Organising in Europe and Japan, *European Management Journal*, vol.18, n.3, 259-273.Porter, M.E, (1980),. *Competitive Strategy*, The Free Press, New York.

Schumpeter A, (1934). The Theory of Economic Development, Harvard University Press, Cambridge.

Tommaso P. (2004). Where did it go wrong? Hybridisation and crisis of Toyota Motor Manufacturing UK, 1989-2001, The productive models in the automobile industry and in other industrial or service sectors, GERPISA, N°37.

Utterback J. M. and Hill C.T. (1979). The Dynamics of Product and Process Innovation in Industry, Pergamon Policy Studies, Oxford, UK.

Management of Technology: New Directions in Technology Management
M. Hashem Sherif and T.M. Khalil (Editors)



# 23

# ARE TECHNOLOGY AND COMPETITION POLICIES CONTRADICTORY?

*Kalevi Kyläheiko, Lappeenranta University of Technology, Finland* *
*Martti Virtanen, Finnish Competition Authority, Finland* **

## INTRODUCTION

*Posing the question.* Modern technology policy is designed to enhance the competitiveness of the business community by means of technological skills and capabilities. This goal is to be attained by spurring technological innovations. Technology policy is, in essence, becoming innovation policy both at national and regional levels. It is about building up an institutional environment conducive to innovation activities; it is about fostering collaboration and networking between economic actors to assemble their resources in order create innovations and follow-on innovations and to utilize these innovations effectively.

Furthermore, innovation activities no longer necessarily follow the linear model - from the research laboratories to the commercialization of new products and diffusion of new knowledge. On the contrary, innovations are governed by recursive feedback mechanisms among the various stages and actors in the innovative process. Innovations increasingly require resources and capabilities that a single company cannot any more create all alone or even control. Hence, promoting R&D-based networking amongst the firms is an essential part

* Department of Business Administration, Lappeenranta University of Technology, P.O. Box 20, FIN-53851 Lappeenranta. Email: Kalevi.kylaheiko@lut.fi
** Finnish Competition Authority, P.O. Box 332, FIN-00530 Helsinki

of modern technology policy. It is this collaboration and networking which often, from a regional perspective, is also called regionally organized clustering.

As innovations are of overriding importance for technology policy, it is of great importance to analyze the impact the other fields of public policy have on the incentives of creating innovations and of utilizing them effectively. Successful innovation policy nowadays necessarily requires effective coordination of public policy. Competition policy is one of the foremost branches of public policy to consider in this context. Unfortunately, there seems to be a potential trade-off between antitrust-based competition policy and innovation-promoting technology policy. The trade-off between static allocative efficiency (the implicit ideal of competition policy) and innovation based dynamic efficiency (the ideal of technology policy) has sharpened. In our view, it is necessary to admit that especially in the "new economy" sustainable competitive advantage has to be based on non-tradable routines and capabilities, which in turn make it possible to create market imperfections. Hence, one has to be ready to be more flexible when setting up the goals of modern competition policy. In some cases it is even advisable to fully reject the basic principles of traditional anti-trust competition policy and allow temporary monopolies. Before tackling this tension and the means to overcome it we will scrutinize the foundations and problems of modern technology policy.

## What are the Issues in Modern Technology Policy?

We start by introducing the logic of modern technology policy based on two basic knowledge-based concepts, namely *non-rivalness in use* and *non-excludability*. The concept "non-rivalness in use" means that many users can use a piece of knowledge without losing its use value (e.g. a software algorithm is open for everyone who has absorptive capacity to decode it). This is, of course, not true with commonplace private rival goods (e.g. a bottle of beer). From this perspective it is easy to understand why a piece of knowledge can be expanded infinitely. This again is an important constituent of the ability to generate useful innovative spin-offs or positive externalities as the economists call them.

The other concept of "non-excludability" means that the holder of a good cannot control who is using the good or its services, thus resulting in the danger of free riderism (e.g. the services of the lighthouses or military services can be used also by the people who have not paid for them). However, the fact that something is non-rival in use does not necessarily mean that its use cannot be controlled. To give an example, a piece of technological knowledge is clearly different from the service provided by the lighthouse. In many cases the holder really can control it simply by establishing intellectual property rights (e.g. by patents, copy rights, trade marks, trade secrets) or by controlling the access (e.g. the commercial cable or satellite TV's).

Next we'll categorize the commodity space in terms of (i) *rivalness vs. non-rivalness* and (ii) *excludability (appropriability) vs. non-excludability (non-proprietability).* Table 1a offers a typology of goods and services in terms of these two categories whereas Table 1b links them to the corresponding technology policy recommendations.

| **APPROPRIABILITY CONDITIONS** | | **DEGREE OF RIVALNESS** | |
|---|---|---|---|
| | | **Rival in Use Tangible goods or their services** | **Non-Rival in Use Intangible "discoveries" (infinite expansion)** |
| **Excludable** | *Based on strictly defined property rights or tacit knowledge embedded in the organizational structure* | (1) *Private goods*- e.g., piece of land, books, cars | (2) *Monopolized public goods* - e.g., commercial cable or satellite TV and ideas based on iron clad patents e.g. commercial cable or satellite TV |
| **Partially Excludable** | *Based on generic knowledge and/or partial property rights* | (3) *Semi-tradable private club goods -e.g., sailing or sports clubs* | (4) *Semi-tradable latent public goods* - e.g.. software, business models, databases, patentable scientific methods or findings, even human genome. |
| **Non-Excludable** | *Based on codified information and no property rights* | (5) *Non-tradable private goods* -fish in the lake -sterile insects used as pest control | *(6) Pure public goods* - e.g., pure science (mathematical algorithms or chemical equations) -non-patented scientific ideas -national defence, lighthouses |

**Table 1A. Typology of goods and services (Romer 1993; Kyläheiko 1995)**

| APPROPRIABILITY CONDITIONS | DEGREE OF RIVALNESS | |
|---|---|---|
| | **Rival in Use** | **Non-Rival in Use** |
| **Excludable** | Use open markets as a method to allocate! | Regulate monopoly distortions and facilitate diffusion, e.g., b means of compulsory licensing! |
| **Partially Excludable** | Use membership fees! | Strengthen property rights, subsidize, or give tax allowances (go to the direction of cell (2) or make it a part of public goods (cell 6) |
| **Non-Excludable** | Subsidize and control publicly! | Use public finance collected by taxes and produce publicly or privately (e.g. different types of universities)! |

**Table 1B. Technology policy recommendations suitable for different types of goods**

Table 2 introduces the main advantages and disadvantages of different types of goods and services and technology policies suitable for them.

| APPROPRIABILITY CONDITIONS | ADVANTAGES | DISADVANTAGES |
|---|---|---|
| **Excludable** | Clear property rights enable high-powered incentives to be used | The use of monopoly power results in welfare losses |
| **Partially Excludable** | Semi-powered incentives and some spillovers. | There are some free rider problems, since the property rights are not always clearly identified |
| **Non-Excludable** | Strong positive spillovers and rapid diffusion of new ideas. | Free riderism and low-powered incentives |

**Table 2. Advantages and disadvantages of different types of technology policies**

Now we relate the technological knowledge characteristics to the typologies of economic goods in Table 1a. They are based on the transformation of tacit technological knowledge into codified information, which gives knowledge most (but not all) of the following characteristics of a pure public good (David and Dasgupta 1994): (i): *high fixed costs and indivisibilities in the first time production (known as sunk "first copy" costs), (ii): low or zero marginal costs of reproduction and transfer*, and (iii): *non-excludability*. Traditional definition of technological knowledge assumes that it includes characteristics (i) - (ii) above but not necessarily (iii). Taken together, the first and second conditions imply non-rivalness (i.e. the second column in Table 1a), which has two important implications. First, from the production perspective, non-rivalness of technological information means that once generated a blueprint, chemical formula, software design, etc. can be (almost) freely expanded infinitely as an input in the replica process, which in turn implies falling average cost curves. Second, from the consumption perspective, non-rivalness implies that any consumer can use the same piece of information without diminishing its usefulness to anyone else or without loss of its intrinsic qualities. Exactly these positive spillovers of intangible "discoveries" are often regarded as main contributors to economic growth.

Another feature of non-rivalness is that it creates non-convexities in the production set (as the economists put it) that results in the problems of imperfect competition, since non-rivalness generates economies of scale both in the production and, more importantly, in the consumption sphere. These demand-related *network externalities* can easily be recognized in the field of telecommunications. The value of a telecommunication network for a single user is the higher, the more there are users. This means that an operator makes the more profit the more there are users in his network, since the willingness to pay of each customer is an increasing function of the amount of the users. This phenomenon comes close to the idea of the first mover's advantage or the idea that “the winner takes it all”, so typical for the information and telecommunications industry.

As emphasized by Romer (1993), this market imperfections generating part of the "public good" classification of technological knowledge was not clearly understood before the emergence of the new endogenous growth models in the mid 1980s. In his seminal article Arrow (1962) did recognize the problem but he combined it only with local non-convexities based on the indivisibilities within a firm's own production set. Global economies of scale related non-convexities that are much more important from the competition and innovation perspectives were not analyzed. However, just they generate the externalities, which depend upon co-evolutionary interplay between firms and their sub-contractors or customers through complementarities and interdependencies. These positive spillovers (cells 3-6) can be regarded both as the engine of modern capitalism and as a main source of hard to control market distortions called "natural monopolies". Here we have *an innovation fostering vs. competition destroying* tension in action.

Another remark relates to the third non-excludability condition (the third row in Table 1), which is not automatically fulfilled but depends upon institutional set-ups that regulate intellectual property rights (patents, copyrights, trademarks), which can be used for appropriating monopoly profits to innovators. Because of this reservation, one cannot generally regard technological information as a pure public good but rather as a *(semi)tradable latent public good* (sorry for this awkward concept). The non-excludability condition gives rise to the so-called Arrowian "appropriability framework".

## COPING WITH ARROW'S APPROPRIABILITY TRADE-OFF

Following the welfare economics of innovation tradition (that originated with Nelson 1959 and Arrow 1962) we focus upon the three knowledge categories for non-rival technological information in Table 1a. These are (i) *pure public* (cell 6), (ii) *semi-tradable public* (cell 4) and (iii) *monopolized* (cell 2) *codified information*. Interestingly, these three knowledge categories (gray zone in Tables 1a and 1b) cover the domain of standard national technology policy issues. (The case of *tacit knowledge* related to cell 2 is easier to cope with from the firm's perspective, since tacitness always makes it possible for a firm to generate monopoly power and hence profit from its innovation).

Arrow's seminal contribution dealt with extreme cases, i.e. cells (2) and (6) where a new piece of technological knowledge exhibits non-rival characteristics and generates positive spillover effects. Arrow managed to show that the invisible hand market mechanism cannot itself realize the first-best Pareto optimal solution (i.e. the most efficient static allocation of scarce resources) because of systematic built-in market failures. Without strong legal protection, private innovations are discouraged (cell 6) through free rider behavior, whereas strong legal appropriability (cell 2) encourages firms to innovate because of the lure of temporary monopoly profits. Unfortunately (from the competitive perspective) this in turn results in monopoly distortions and the socially undesirable slow diffusion of the new information. The tension between cases (2) and (6) is known as the Arrowian appropriability trade-off. Both behaviors (free rider behavior and monopoly) are partially present in the intermediate, semi-tradable latent public good case (the grey cell 4 in Table 1).

Next we offer some public economics-inspired remedies to overcome the Arrowian trade-off, thus resolving some aspects of the competition vs. innovation trade-off so relevant for modern national innovation systems. The first solution is the pure *public good solution* where the production and free diffusion of technological information are organized through the visible hand of national R&D laboratories and universities financed from tax revenue (of course, the universities can be private as well, if the basic research is mainly funded and controlled by national agencies). This institutional design solves the R&D cost-sharing problem that would otherwise result in underinvestment in the private sector. However, since publicly produced knowledge is uncertain, complex, asymmetrically distributed and based on team work, severe problems of monitoring emerge. They necessarily cause principal-agency problems and, consequently, lead to high transaction costs due to incomplete contracts and associated moral hazard and adverse selection problems.

The *semi-public solution* (cell 4 above) is nowadays the most common area where innovation vs. competition trade-off manifests itself. This solution is based upon encouraging private production and diffusion of technological information by granting, subsidizing and offering tax allowances for innovators who have to make their innovations public, for instance through compulsory or cross licensing systems (but not at a zero royalty rate) or lump sum rewards. In this case, the Arrowian trade-off can be overcome by subsidizing potential losses of non-existing temporary monopoly rents. However, initiatives are left to private innovators themselves. The idea is to promote technological diffusion by insuring private innovative firms against the free rider behavior and other risks of innovative endeavors.

The third route, which is becoming more and more popular especially in the United States is focused upon creating private markets for technological information by enforcing intellectual property rights using patents, copyrights, trademarks, etc. (a shift towards cell 2) or utilizing the tight appropriability obtained by means of tacitness. The idea is to break down the discouraging non-excludability condition and to provide high-powered incentives for taking part in "the winner takes it all" patent races. Now the biggest problem is market imperfections, which make it hard or even impossible to evaluate the optimal scope and length of a patent. There are also other obvious dangers, such as slow diffusion of technological information, duplication of R&D investments before patenting, potential lock-in into dysfunctional innovations due to too early patenting, and inefficient substitute technologies invented around the patented technology. Now we conclude the technological knowledge-related categories, which standard technology policy norms are based upon:

(1): Technology is basically treated as *non-rival* and *non-excludable* codified science-based information created by means of the innovative activities of scientists. The spill-overs diffuse rapidly through cultural evolution facilitated by compulsory licensing and an open source innovation model. Free rider problems discourage however private innovating. *Scientific competition based on reputation maximization rules over innovation profit-seeking!*

(2): Technology is basically treated as *non-rival* but *fully excludable* codified information or *tacit* knowledge, whose spillovers can be diffused only under the control of a mainly private innovator because of legally established property rights or tacitness. There are no free riders but there exist severe problems of imperfect competition and slow diffusion. P*rofit-seeking based on innovations rules over scientific competition!*

(3): Technology is treated as non-rival and partially excludable codified information or partially tacit knowledge whose spillovers can partially be diffused through cultural evolution. There are free riders, slow diffusion and imperfect competition problems. *Neither scientific competition nor profit-seeking alone rule but they co-exist!*

Table 3 below summarizes the pros and cons of two basic rival incentive-based solutions (1) and (2) from the *competition vs. innovation-promoting* trade-off perspective. The third solution above is intermediate as for advantages and disadvantages.

| | **PUBLIC GOOD BASED DIFFUSION ENHANCING SOLUTION** | **PRIVATE GOOD BASED MONOPOLY SOLUTION** |
|---|---|---|
| **ACTORS** | Universities as main drivers of new knowledge, firms as partners when providing knowledge as public goods. | Rent-seeking innovative firms as main drivers of innovations, universities as their partners when providing knowledge as "private" goods. |
| **MAIN INCENTIVE METHODS** | Scientists' reputation maximization._ Contract research with compulsory licensing or lump-sum rewards. | Expected profit maximization based on monopoly power. Market imperfections created by means of legal means or tacitness. |
| **MAIN ADVANTAGES** | Rapid diffusion of knowledge. Long term planning and goal set up possible. | High-powered entrepreneurial incentives. Lots of variations because on |

| | | |
|---|---|---|
| | Positive network and other externalities (=> spillovers). No underinvestment and no duplication of investment. | keen private competition. Private funding with own risk. Opportunity to share sunk first copy cost by networking. |
| **MAIN DISADVANTAGES** | Low-powered non-entrepreneurial incentives. The danger of free riderism. Asymmetric information, since the creators of new knowledge know more about its cost structure than the buyers => monitoring problems, principal-agency problems, moral hazards, adverse selection. Low variations of new ideas. Bureaucratic_because on public funding. | Monopoly distortions (dead weight losses). Slow diffusion of knowledge => fewer spillovers. Myopic goals Duplication of investment Lock-in into dysfunctional mode. Underinvestment |

**Table 3. Comparison of basic institutional designs for technology policy (cf. Kyläheiko 2005)**

## TOWARDS EVOLUTIONARILY INSPIRED TECHNOLOGY POLICY FRAMEWORK

The main advantage of using the public good classifications above is the opportunity to analyze the basic dimensions of national and regional technology policy by means of flexible welfare economics based tools. In this framework, R&D investments of firms are assumed to be subject to the same profit maximization calculations as other investments. It is also assumed that (i) there is a market for knowledge and (ii) profit opportunities are directly related to R&D investments through market conditions. As is well known future markets for contingent claims in an uncertain world are insufficient to support any efficient equilibriums. Furthermore, there are technology-related externalities and asymmetric distribution of technological information, which lead to inappropriate incentives, as shown already by Nelson (1959) and Arrow (1962). Consequently, it is natural to interpret most problems of technological change as market failures.

From this perspective we just have to balance two different kinds of market failures (the first one generated through the very nature of knowledge and the second one through market distortions) in terms of optimal technology and competition policy mix. Because of the strong market emphasis of the Paretian worldview, this policy mix is pro market biased as well, thus resulting in overemphasis of competition policy at the cost of innovation promoting technology policy. In our view, the world is not that simple, however, and the reasons for the emergence of innovation promoting vs. competition trade-off are deeper. We are tempted to think that they actually relate to such Hayekian issues like inherent uncertainty, dispersed knowledge, bounded rationality, and entrepreneurial alertness. Therefore, a more eclectic policy view is needed as well.

This brings us to the main disadvantage of the Paretian welfare-based approach, which treats the problems of technological change basically as market failures. The *main problem is that genuine technological progress organized by creative entrepreneurs is only possible in an inefficient world.* Welfare economics of innovation cannot take into account that technological change both emerges from uncertainty and informational asymmetries and generates new uncertainty, thus opening up new opportunities for alert entrepreneurs. As Schumpeter already pointed out, the equilibrium framework overstates (basically static) allocative functions of market for knowledge at the expense of dynamic innovative functions. Static efficiency is based on a given set of initial conditions, whereas dynamic efficiency implies the creation of new initial conditions through "creative destruction". *We are tempted to think that static allocative efficiency is overemphasized when compared to dynamic efficiency, which is harder to tackle by means of analytical weapons of welfare economics.*

The "market failure" interpretation also excludes tacit aspects of knowledge accumulation and, consequently, important parts of localized learning processes that can be understood only when one assumes that the agents operate under the constraints of complex, uncertain, dispersed, and imperfect knowledge. For these reasons, the obsession for viewing technological changes only from the "market failure" perspective is doomed to be one-sided. At the technology policy level, the emphasis on dynamic efficiency instead of allocative efficiency means that learning processes based on trial and error and absorptive capacities of the firms should be promoting, existing capabilities should be upgraded and more variety should be generated through deliberate policy measures (on evolutionary-inspired technology policy suggestions, cf. Metcalfe 1995).

## COMPETITION POLICY FROM INNOVATION PERSPECTIVE

Technology policy is nowadays primarily designed to enhance the competitiveness of the business community by means of technological skills and capabilities. This goal is to be attained by spurring technological innovations, and their spillovers both at the national, federal and firm levels. From this perspective, technology policy is, in essence, innovation promoting policy. Modern innovations require networking and other forms of collaboration because of dispersed knowledge pools, need for variation, and risk sharing due to large fixed sunk first copy costs.

As innovations are of overriding importance for technology policy, it is increasingly important to analyze the impact other fields of public policy have on the incentives of creating innovations and of utilizing them effectively, and coordinate these policies so that the overarching significance of innovations is taken into consideration in all branches of public policy. Competition policy no doubt is one of the foremost branches of public policy to consider on this score.

Modern competition policy and law has its origins in the emergence of electricity driven industrial mass production in the context of the Second Industrial Revolution in the beginning of the 20$^{th}$ century. Particularly the U.S. antitrust policy and law which has served as a model for modern European competition policy, had developed by World War II to an overall anti-monopoly policy that was designed to stifle market concentration, irrespective of whether it was attained by means of agreements, mergers or acquisitions, or through internal growth. The normative foundations of such a policy rested on the neoclassical perfect competition/monopoly dichotomy.

If we are tempted to think that this kind of competition policy should prevail, we would certainly have to conclude that technology and competition policies are indeed contradictory. Anything that technology policy does is designed to increase, from the static perspective, market power of the economic actors concerned. This is most obvious in the technology policy-inspired measures taken to strengthen immaterial property rights, but successful networks or clusters must dispose of substantial market power, too. Competitive advantage always amounts to a departure from the static perfect competition norm, as perfect competition is the only, naturally fictional economic state where no competitive advantages are present on the markets.

But the very goal of technology policy is not, to be sure, to create islands of long-lasting static monopoly power in the economy. The goal is rather to set in motion a dynamic economic process in which further development of the commodities and systems of commodities takes place through collaboration among economic actors. Under these circumstances, continued innovation is possible, which would safeguard sustainable competitive advantages for the economic actors, the whole economy or the particular region concerned. Thus, the inherent goal of technology policy is a steady stream of dynamic efficiency benefits that is certain to compensate any temporary losses from static market power. In order to realize this objective, forceful competitive pressure must be brought to bear in the relevant economic environment to encourage the economic actors to proceed on a dynamic path of further innovative development. If competition policy did lead into obstructing this kind of economic progress, the policy would certainly be flawed. But this would be bound to take place if the perfect competition norm would be uncompromisingly enforced. A purely static optimality-inspired competition policy would thus stand in stark contradiction with technology policy. But this a far cry from saying that all combinations of substantial static market power necessarily would result in fruitful dynamic efficiencies referred to above or that all such combinations of market power brought about by technology policy necessarily end up creating these dynamic efficiencies. Attempts to realize and utilize innovations through technology policy measures may merely lead to or be hampered by unilateral or contractual restrictive practices, or concentrations that indeed create substantial static inefficiency without producing essential dynamic efficiency in return. Competition policy must be geared to counteracting the latter manifestations of market power but let the successfully innovative arrangements with a further dynamic potential to carry forward.

In order to do so, competition policy requires an evolutionary intellectual foundation on competition that is based on a proper understanding of the competitive process, giving full credit to the role of firms and their quest for competitive advantages through superior knowledge and innovations. A proper understanding of technology policy and its results does inform competition policy-making in view of its intellectual foundations and challenges. But, as clearly suggested above, effective competition policy itself may actually be regarded as a prerequisite for a successful technology policy. Competition policy, too, can inform technology policy. Technology policy-makers should avoid arrangements that exclusively or preponderantly enable the economic actors concerned to monopolize or collude on the markets. It is obvious that the coordination of technology and competition policies is sine qua non for the success of the former policy.

A sensible technology policy may, on the other hand, lead to enhanced competition while failing to bring about unduly monopolistic or collusive market outcomes, which furthers the very goals of competition policy. It is from this angle that we can see the rationale for modern innovation promoting technology policy. A recent report by the Federal Trade

Commission (2003, recommendations in the executive summary) on the proper balance of competition and patent law and policy illustrates the growing need to coordinate the two policies. The report recommends a marked tightening of the patenting process so as to eliminate unjustified patenting and to increase the rights of third parties. The report maintains that as an extension of the scope of patentable subject matter is considered, careful attention should be given to consider possible harms to competition.

It is to be noted that competition policy, neither in the USA nor in Europe, has never fully lived up to the rigor of the active anti-concentration policies based on the ideal of the static competitive equilibrium typical for elementary microeconomics. Modern competition policy is, after all, viewed primarily as protecting the very competitive process. This policy should, in order to protect the market process, counteract competitors' agreements to put an end to mutual competition, and acts designed to exclude in an artificial manner at least equally efficient competitors from the markets. In certain, albeit few cases, competition policy must protect consumers from monopolistic excess prices. It must also be recalled that competition policy is not only about curbing monopolistic combinations; it is also about maintaining the very competitive order of the society. This suggests that the freedom of action of economic actors must not be compromised, should compelling efficiency reasons be wanting. It is not only static allocative efficiency that competition policy must strive for, but to achieve the optimal mix of *static allocative, productive* and *dynamic efficiencies*. The concept of *productive efficiency* refers to the ability to find out the most efficient production set ups whereas the concept of *dynamic efficiency* refers to the ability to generate innovations. The following Figure 1 illuminates the concerns of modern competition policy, which takes into account the needs for promoting productive and dynamic efficiencies as well. We will call the goal of such a policy mix as *workable competition*.

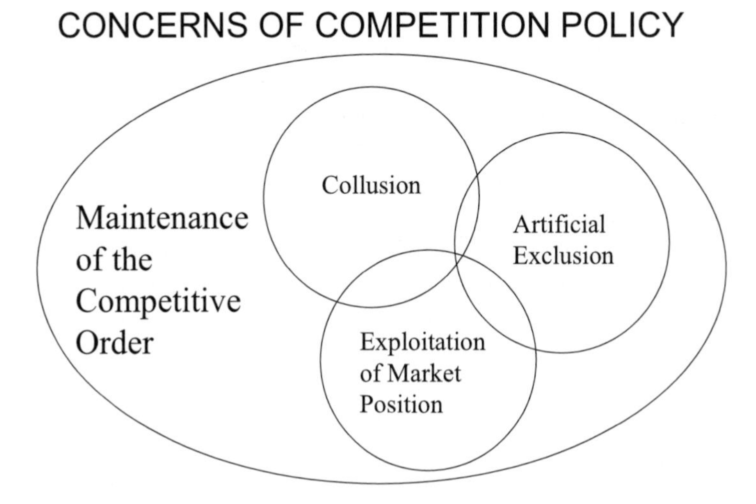


**Figure 1. Concerns of competition policy (Virtanen 1993)**

The core idea of *workable competition* already includes the assessment and comparison of opposite effects on static and dynamic efficiency. In our view, workable competition is the most appropriate description of the normative foundations of modern competition policy, both in the USA and in Europe (Purasjoki & Virtanen 1995).

It is thus arguable even on the basis of current competition policy that static market imperfections may be, at least in certain cases, necessary to increase dynamic efficiency. Therefore, there is indeed no inherent contradiction between technology policy and competition policy, as they currently exist. Technological advances that are in evidence - partly as a result of technology policy - will thus not impart any new perspective to current competition policy. From this perspective it should be clear that, to give just an example, a naked collusion on prices or markets is not going to be rendered more acceptable, nor outright artificially exclusionary behavior, just because this kind of conduct is somehow related to technology policy measures, however laudable goals these have (Määttä & Virtanen 2001).

We would, indeed, maintain that the real issue faced by modern competition policy when confronting the challenges set up by modern technology policy and the recent technological advances as well, is that it must be able to judge whether the (potential) far-reaching dynamic allocative efficiency gains compensate the static allocative efficiency losses due to less competition. This trade-off between dynamic efficiencies and static inefficiencies is also going to concern contractual cooperation directly involved in innovative activities (R & D cooperation agreements, specialization agreements, etc).

This challenge is particularly pronounced in what are known as *dynamically competitive industries or markets* (Evans - Schmalensee 2001; Lind - Muysert 2003). The new economy industries are the epitome of such industries, but the growing importance of knowledge-based innovations in the "old economy" clearly increase dynamism in the traditional old economy industries, too.

## TACKLING THE STATIC VS. DYNAMIC TRADE-OFF: ARE THERE EU AND US POLICY DIFFERENCES?

Under the current competitive law practice, it is internationally commonplace to require that there is clear and convincing evidence that efficiencies from restrictive practices or concentration will, to a reasonably degree, be passed to consumers at least in the long run. Should this evidence fail to be presented, the restrictive practice or concentration in question seriously risks to be banned under competition law. Dynamic, innovation-related efficiencies cannot possibly meet these evidential requirements. Likewise, particularly under the knowledge-based conditions of the new economy, the usual yardstick for assessing the passing-on of dynamic efficiency benefits to consumers, market concentration, is subject to a particularly high risk of error due to possibility of new innovators rapidly dethroning the dominant firms on the market (Plaetsikas & Teece 2001, Stenbacka 2002)). For example, in the EU competition policy, there are instances where competition authorities have reacted to these problems by prohibiting the restrictive practice or concentration in question mainly because of static inefficiencies they presumably generate. Particularly merger control seems to be the policy area where prohibitions of this kind have often been made (Monti 2001, Bishop and Caffarra 2001, Veljanovski 2001).

While it is one of the most topical issues for economic research to increase our ability to diagnose innovative processes and to anticipate their outcomes, we maintain that the most appropriate response to this challenge is to take conditional decisions that make it possible, within a reasonable range of time, to apply ex post remedies, that are typically structural in nature, to put an end to monopolistic practices or concentrations that are not intimately necessitated by any innovative outcomes (cf. Brodley 1996). Conditional decisions coupled with an authority to apply ex post remedies would also increase the timeliness of competition policy decision-making, which is important to the success innovative processes. Both in the USA and in Europe, cases directly concerning immaterial property rights have traditionally displayed the closest connection of competition policy and law with the aspirations of technology policy. Broadly speaking, there are two types of issues that have been dealt with:

- Artificial enlargement of the sphere of immaterial property rights out of their legal limits;
- Compulsory licensing as a remedy under competition law

The USA applied a strict antirust policy vis-à-vis immaterial property rights, patents in particular, from the late 1930s until the 1970s. Immaterial property rights were deemed to be inherently undesirable legal monopolies. Federal courts issued several decisions on compulsory licensing in the 1940s and 1950s. This is the period in which the U.S. federal antitrust policy most closely (if not fully) followed the static anti-concentration position. Since that time, federal antitrust policy has largely retreated from compulsory licensing. Currently, it is certainly an uphill task to persuade U.S. courts to order compulsory licensing save in strictly exceptional circumstances. (Muris 2001; Pitofsky 2001).

In the EU competition policy there have only been a few exceptional cases on compulsory licensing of immaterial property rights, the foremost of which is the Magill-TV Guide case (Jones & Sufrin 2001; Ritter & Braun & Rawlinson 2000). This case created what may be called a ”new product exception” for compulsory licensing. The relevance of this exception has been recently confirmed by the European Court of Justice (Judgment of the Court in Case C-418/01, IMS Health GmbH & Co. OHG and NDC Health GmbH & Co. KG). Latest developments suggest that this criterion might be even expanded in the future (Dolmans & Ilan 2003). In this respect, competition policies in Europe and in the USA seem to be taking opposite directions.

In the overzealously anti-concentration era of the US federal antitrust policy severe restrictions were imposed on the utilization of immaterial property rights in many other ways, too. There restrictions were known as the Nine No No’s. (Pate 2003). These were, in effect, nine per se prohibitions (e.g. patent pools were banned). Since the late 1970s rule of reason analysis has superseded per se prohibitions. As a rule, collaborative practices on innovations are allowed, if the concentration of the relevant market - which may be product, technology or innovation markets - does not exceed limit values and the practices contain no indications of naked restraints of competition (Antitrust Guidelines for Collaborations among Competitors 2000).

EU competition policy on the utilization of immaterial property rights is organized along the lines of group exemptions on various types of innovation-related agreements. The EU policy, too, is increasingly lenient, as one has turned away from detailed descriptions of accepted contract clauses and into explication of prohibited contract clauses. The group exemptions provide for market concentration limits below which the contracting companies are assured of taking advantage of the group exemption. Also comparable to current U.S. federal antitrust policy, account is taken for both product and technology markets.

The discussion above of U.S. and EU competition policies on the utilization of immaterial property rights and practices directly involved in innovations clearly shows that exclusive adherence to static optimality no longer governs competition policy. Nevertheless, policy seems to pay close attention, in addition to counteracting naked restraint of competition, to allowing only those practices, the market environment of which is only moderately concentrated. In other words, it is attempted to avoid making a trade-off between dynamic efficiency and severe allocative inefficiency. We maintain that both technology policy and the technological developments now in evidence will make it increasingly difficult to avoid such a trade-off imperative and distinguish efficiency-increasing practices from the efficiency-decreasing ones. We also argue that the very impact of technology policy and technological progress is to compel the competition authorities truly adopt the evolutionary economics-based workable competition norm, which, up till now, has been necessary only in a limited sense (cf. Jorde and Teece 1990). In addition, a more evolutionarily inclined interpretation of the nature of technological progress would make it easier to emphasize dynamic efficiencies instead of static efficiencies.

## CONCLUSIONS

In this article, we have discussed the relationship between technology and competition policies. We maintain that there is no inherent contradiction between the two policies. This is particularly so if the implications of the current *de facto* competition policy goal of maintaining a workable competitive process are duly considered. It is our position, however, that the increasing significance of innovations in business rivalry will increase the frequency of cases in which various kinds of restrictive practices that competition law deals with display both substantial static efficiency losses and the prospect of substantial dynamic efficiencies (i.e. innovations). Thereby, it will become increasingly difficult for competition policy makers to avoid the trade-off and approve only innovative practices or agreements that display little risk of substantial static efficiency losses, which up to now has been the policy pursued on both sides of the Atlantic Ocean. While we argue that diagnosing and predicting innovative activities constitute a major challenge for future research, we find the application of conditional decisions accompanied with an authority to apply any remedies to the practice in question in a predetermined future date a suitable way of handling the trade-off. This demeanor might in the long run render certain parts of ex ante control of competition, notably merger control, redundant.

## References

Antitrust Guidelines for Collaborations among Competitors (2000). Issued by the Federal Trade Commission and the U.S. Department of Justice.

Arrow, K.J. (1962). Economic Welfare and the Allocation of Resources for Inventions, in Nelson R.R. (ed.) The Rate and Direction of Inventive Activity: Economic and Social Factors, Princeton, Princeton University Press, 353-358.

Bishop, B. and Caffarra, C. (2001). Merger Control in "New Markets", *European Competition Law Review*, **22**, 31-33.

Brodley, J. F. (1996). Proof of Efficiencies in Mergers and Joint Ventures, *Antitrust Law Journal*, **64**, 575-612.

Dasgupta, P. and David, P. A (1994). Towards a New Economics of Science, *Research Policy*, **23**, 487-521.

Dolmans, M. and Ilan, D. (2003). Competition and IP. A health warning for IP owners: the Advocate General's opinion in IMS and its implications for compulsory licensing, *Competition Law Insight*, **Issue 11**, 12-16.

Evans, D. S. - Schmalensee, R. (2001). Some Economic Aspects of Antitrust Analysis in Dynamically Competitive Industries, NBER Working Paper 8268.

Jones, A. & Sufrin, B. (2001). EC Competition Law. Text, Cases, and Materials, Oxford University Press.

Jorde, T.M. - Teece, D.J. (1990): Innovation and Cooperation: Implications for Competition and Antitrust, *Journal of Economic Perspectives* **4,** 75-96.

Kyläheiko, K. Coping with Technology: A Study on Economic Methodology and Strategic Management of Technology, Lappeenranta University of Technology, Research Papers 48, Lappeenranta, Finland. 1995.

Kyläheiko, K. (2005): From Comedy of Commons to Tragedy of Anti-Commons, in Huber, G.,

Krämer, H. & Kurz, H.D. (Eds): Einkommensverteilung, technischer Fortschritt und struktureller Wandel, Metropolis Verlag, Marburg 2005, 191-207.

Lind, R. C. - Muysert, P. (2003). Innovation and Competition Policy: Challenges for the New Millennium, *European Competition Law Review*, **24**, 87-92.

Metcalfe, J.S. (1994). Evolutionary Economics and Technology Policy, *The Economic Journal*, **104**, 931-944.

Monti, M. (2001). Competition in the New Economy, Speech, 10th International Conference on Competition, May 21, Berlin.

Muris, Timothy J. (2001). Competition and Intellectual Property Policy: The Way Ahead, Prepared Remarks, American Bar Association Antitrust Section Fall Forum, Washington, DC, November 15, http://www.ftc.gov/speeches/muris/intellectual.htm.

Määttä, K. - Virtanen, M. (2001). Regulatory Principles in Modifying the Act on Competition Restrictions in a World Characterised by Network Externalities; University of Joensuu, Finland, Discussions Paper, Number 38.

R. Nelson. The Simple Economics of Basic Scientific Research, *Journal of Political Economy*, **66**, 1959.

Pate, R. H. (2003). Antitrust and Intellectual Property, Address before the American Intellectual Property Law Association, 2003 Mid-Winter Institute, Marco Island, Florida January 24, http://www.usdoj.gov/atr/public/speeches/200701.htm.

Pitofsky, Robert (2001). Challenges of the New Economy: Issues at the Intersection of Antitrust and Intellectual Property, *Antitrust Law Journal*, **68**, 913-924.

Pleatsikas, C. & Teece, D. (2001). The analysis of market definition and market power in the context of rapid innovation, *International Journal of Industrial Organization*, **80**, 665-693.

Purasjoki, M. - Virtanen, M. (1995). Is the Theory of Workable Competition Still Workable? In Marked, Konkurrance og politikk. Festskrift till Egil Bakke, Fagbokforlaget, Bergen, Norway, pp. 99-133.

Ritter, L. & Braun, W. D. & Rawlinson, F., (2000). European Competition Law: A Practitioner's Guide, Second Edition, Kluwer Law International.

Romer, P.M. (1993). Implementing a National Technology Strategy with Self-Organizing Industry Investment Boards, *Brookings Papers on Economic Activity*, 345-399.

Stenbacka, R. (2002). Microeconomic Policies in the New Economy, *Finnish Economic Papers*, **15**, 59-75.

Veljanovski, C. (2001). E.C. Antitrust in the New Economy: Is the European Commission's View of the Network Economy Right? *European Competition Law Review*, **22**, 115-121.

Virtanen, M. (1993). Market Dominance and Its Abuse in Competition Policy. An Economic Inquiry, Publications of European Institute, Turku, Finland. 5/93.

The user accesses the ATM through the magnetic band card issued by the financial entity (1). Once the card is validated by the ATM, the application requests the user's PIN and the type of transaction to be conducted. This information (2) is combined with control data (ATM number, date, time, transaction sequence, etc.) to create a requirements message to the authorizing system; this message, a Transaction Request, is sent (3) over a public or private data communications network.

The authorizing system (4) receives the Transaction Request and proceeds to decode and process the information as follows: card identification, PIN validation, financial transaction execution (or denial), application file updates, and reply preparation. The Transaction Reply is then sent (5) via the communications network to the ATM originating the transaction.

Upon Transaction Reply reception, the ATM decodes and processes the information and presents the transaction results to the user. If it is a cash request, the cash is presented (6); if it is an information request, it is shown on the screen or printed on a receipt. Finally, the ATM's application puts together and transmits (7) a Transaction Confirmation to the authorizing system including feedback on the success or failure of the transaction.

In general, a centralized system has the ability to connect with each and every ATM, and at the same time communicate with each and every centralized system that is required to complete a transaction.

## BIOMETRIC TECHNOLOGY

The term biometrics comes from the word bio (life) and metric (measurement). Biometric equipment has the capability to measure, codify, compare, store, transmit, and/or recognize a specific characteristic of a person with a high level of precision and trustworthiness. Biometric technology is based on the scientific fact that there are certain characteristics of living forms that are unique and not repetitive for each individual; these characteristics represent the only technically viable alternative to positively identify a person without the use of other forms of identification more susceptible to fraudulent behavior.

Biometric identification is utilized to verify a person's identity by measuring digitally certain human characteristics and comparing those measurements with those that have been stored in a template for that same person. Templates can be stored at the biometric device, the institution's database, a user's smart card, or a Trusted Third Party (TTP) Service Provider's database. Where database storage is more economic than plastic cards, the method tends to lack public acceptance; however, Polemi (1997) found that TTPs can provide the confidence that this method is missing by managing the templates in a trustful way.

There are two major categories of biometric techniques: *physiological* (fingerprint verification, iris analysis, hand geometry-vein patterns, ear recognition, odor detection, DNA pattern analysis and sweat pores analysis), and *behavioral* (handwritten signature verification, keystroke analysis and speech analysis). Deane *et al.* (1995) found that behavior based systems were perceived as less acceptable than those based on physiological characteristics. Of the physiological techniques, the most commonly utilized is that of fingerprint scanning.

Restricted in the past due to its high cost and lack of social acceptance, biometric identification is now experiencing a higher level of acceptance not only in high security applications such as banks and governmental facilities, but also in health clubs, sports events, office and industrial sites. Costs have been reduced to a reasonable level and functionality and reliability of the devices is today satisfactory. Biometrics is also increasingly included in a wide range of verification applications in e-commerce, financial electronic transactions, and health information systems patient data storage and dissemination.

*Components of a Biometric System.*

Figure 2 depicts the processes associated with a biometric methodology: enrollment, identification/verification, and learning.

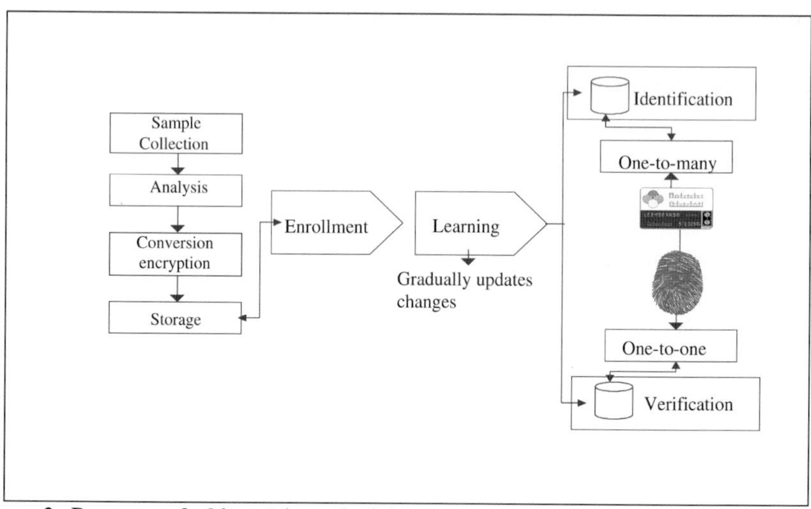


**Figure 2. Processes of a biometric methodology**

*Enrollment.* Prior to an individual being identified or verified by a biometric device, we must complete the enrollment process with the objective of creating a profile of the user. Enrollment is a relatively short process, taking only take a few minutes and consisting of the following steps:

1. Sample Capture: the user allows for a minimum of two or three biometric readings, for example: placing a finger in a fingerprint reader. The quality of the samples, together with the number of samples taken, will influence the level of accuracy at the time of validation. Not all samples are stored; the technology analyzes and measures various data points unique to each individual. The number of measured data points varies in accordance to the type of device.
2. Conversion and Encryption: the individual's measurements and data points are converted to a mathematical algorithm and encrypted. These algorithms are extremely complex and cannot be reversed engineered to obtain the original image. The algorithm may then be stored as a user's template in a number of places including servers, PCs, or portable devices such as PDAs or smart cards.

*Identification and Verification.* Once the individual has been enrolled in a system, he/she can start to use biometric technology to have access to networks, computer centers, buildings, personal accounts, and to authorize transactions. Biometric technology determines when a person could have access in one of the two forms be it identification or verification. Some devices have the ability to do both.

1. Identification: a one-to-many match. The user provides a biometric sample and the system looks at all user templates in the database. If there is a match, the user is granted access, otherwise, it is declined.
2. Verification: a one-to-one match requiring the user provides identification such as a PIN or a smart card in addition to the biometric sample. In other words, the user is establishing who he/she is and the system simply verifies if this is correct. The biometric sample with the provided identification is compared to the previously stored information in the data base. If there is a match, access is provided, otherwise, it is declined.

*Learning.* Each time the user utilizes the system the template is updated through learning processes taking into account gradual changes due to age and physical growth. These are later utilized by the system to determine whether to grant or deny access.

## INTEGRATED MODEL DEVELOPMENT

*Objective.* The primary objective is to develop a model to integrate biometric technology on ATMs while utilizing the existing infrastructure and, therefore, minimize the investment on technology upgrade. The model to be developed includes the integration of fingerprint biometric technology into the transaction authorization process in working ATMs. Many new ATM devices already include the ability to support these technologies; however, the capital investment in equipment replacement can be very large. Therefore, the main objective of this project is to develop a low cost and easy-to-implement solution.

*Methodology.* The following steps were taken in developing the model: (1) The process to be followed to identify an individual through a fingerprint biometric system was established and detailed; (2) The process followed in authorizing a transaction through an ATM system was identified; (3) The integration model was developed.

*Fingerprint Biometric System Transaction.* The biometric system differentiates between two principal elements: devices and users. The first element administers the existing devices; this sub-component is responsible for the activation and deactivation of the devices, recognition and storage of fingerprints and processing for subsequent comparison and validation. The second element is responsible for administering user information and the stored fingerprints for the purpose of authentication.

The two are interconnected, as we manage to decrease the number of persons wrongfully accepted, we will likely increase the number persons wrongfully rejected. Standards will need to be developed for worldwide application to ATM system hardware and software which guarantee acceptable performance levels.

2. *Scale of deployment.* Many systems do not live up to expectations because they prove unable to cope with the enormous variations among large populations or fail to take into account the needs of the people (Davies, 1994). Implementing biometrics on ATMs, impacts the entire banking user population; systems tested in controlled laboratory environments could provide results that differ greatly from the real world ATM users (Coventry, De Angeli and Johnson, 2003). A great deal of field trials, focus groups and surveys will have to be conducted before the technology is considered to be mature enough for the general public.

3. *Failure to enroll and failure to acquire.* The first one refers to users who do no possess the biometric or can not use the system (loss of fingers, accident/work activity induced fingerprint damage, etc.). The later, refers to situations where the interaction between the user and the system breaks down and the system fails to acquire adequate information. In the case of fingerprints, the potential impact of these two factors is thought to be as high as 10%. (Coventry, De Angeli and Johnson, 2003). Effective processes will have to be developed to manage these situations.

4. *Social issues.* There is great concern among the general public that widespread utilization of biometrics could lead to invasion of individual privacy and freedom. There are countries where the capture and storage of fingerprints by other than a government agency may be considered illegal; or where government may not want to outsource public functions to private industry. There is a segment of the population which fears computer or machine interface, and/or the natural resistance to change inherent to most humans. Successful deployment in a few countries will be necessary prior to widespread deployment.

5. *Security and identity theft.* This is perhaps the most difficult barrier to overcome; vulnerabilities include the use of "fake fingers" made out of gelatin (Leyden, 2002), and the reactivation of latent fingerprints left on the sensor's surface by applying pressure from a water filled bag (Thalheim,

Krissler and Ziegler, 2002). The security and storage issues associated with centralized databases containing the digital algorithms of fingerprints and related customer information, could be reduced by storing the template on a user smart card; however, the loss of the smart card to a criminal could lead to a permanent identity theft situation for which new procedures and technological solutions must be developed.

A number of means by which we may overcome some of these barriers were identified by Polemi in 1997, and are still very significant to the successful deployment of biometric-based applications:

1. Educate people on the technologies and the differences between this application and that of criminal databases.
2. Emphasize the advantages of biometric technologies, particularly the added security to transactions.
3. Provide awareness of when, how and where people are authenticated; they should know when and where they are identified and verified, and which technology is being used.
4. Continue the development and deployment of advanced encryption and other security techniques, not only at the system and application software level, but also for the network and hardware components.

## CONCLUSIONS

Automatic Teller Machines have become a mature technology which provides financial services to an increasing segment of the population in many countries. Biometrics, and in particular fingerprint scanning, continues to gain acceptance as a reliable form of securing access through identification and verification processes. This paper identifies a high-level model for the modification of existing ATM systems to economically incorporate fingerprint scanning; and, outlines the potential business and social advantages, as well as barriers, to using such system to disburse pension and welfare payments to an even larger segment of the world population.

A lot of progress has been made in this field; however, significant work remains to be done before the large scale deployment of trusted and secure biometric-based, standard ATM financial applications can be initiated.

## REFERENCES

Ashbourn, J. (2000). Biometrics. Advanced Identity Verification: The Complete Guide. *Springer Verlag, London*

Caelliet, W. (1994). Information Security Handbook. *England, Macmillan Press LTD.*

Clarke, R. (1994). Human Identification in Information Systems: Management Challenges and Public Policy Issues. *Information Technology and People.* **74**, 6-37.

Coventry, L., A. De Angeli, and G. Johnson (2003). Usability and Biometric Verification at the ATM Interface. *CHI Letters, **5**, 153-160.*

Davies, S.G. (1994). Touching Big Brother: How biometric technology will fuse flesh and machine. *Information Technology and People,* **7**, 4, 38-47.

Deane, F., K. Barrelle, R. Henderson, and D. Mahar (1995). Perceived acceptability of biometric security systems. *Computers & Security,* **14**, 3, 225-231.

General Accounting Office (1995). Electronic Benefits Transfer: Use of Biometrics to Determine Fraud in the Nationwide EBT program. *GAO/OSI-95-20.*

Kim, H.J. (1995). Biometrics, Is it a Viable Proposition for Identity Authentication Access Control? *Computers & Security.* **14**, 205-214.

Leyden, J. (2002). Gummi bears defeat fingerprint sensors. *The Register, Security, www.theregister.co.uk/2002/05/16/gummi_bears_defeat_fingerprint_sensors* .

Mehlman, B. (2002). Putting Biometrics to work for America. *Biometrics Consortium Conference,* Arlington Virginia.

Newham, E. (1995). The Biometric Report. *SJB Services.*

Polemi, D. (1997). Biometric Techniques: Review and evaluation of biometric techniques for identification and authentication, including an appraissal of the areas where they are most applicable. *Report for the INFOSEC Office of the European Commission DGIII.* Institute of Communications and Computer Systems, National Technical University of Athens.

Scholtz, J. and J. Johnson (2002). Interacting with identification technology: Can it make us more secure? *CHI2002 Extended Abstracts, ACM Press.*

Thalheim, L., J. Krissler and P. Ziegler (2002). Body Check: Biometric Access Protection Devices and their Programs Put to the Test. *Surveillance Technology: Biometricsgyre.org,www.gyre.org/news/related/Surveillance+Technology/Biometrics*

Zunkel, R. (1996). Biometrics and Border Control. *Security Technology & Design. **5**, 22-27.*

Management of Technology: New Directions in Technology Management
M. Hashem Sherif and T.M. Khalil (Editors)



# 25

# THE INFLUENCE OF EXTERNAL AND INTERNAL SOCIAL CAPITAL ON ORGANIZATIONAL GROWTH

*Aino Pöyhönen, Lappeenranta University of Technology, Finland*
*Jussi Waajakoski, Lappeenranta University of Technology, Finland*

## INTRODUCTION

With the dawn of the knowledge era, new determinants of organizational success have been proposed. The current literature on the intellectual resources of organizations emphasizes three main themes: intangible assets, the dynamic capabilities to create and modify these assets, and the social relationships in which the knowledge processes take place. Each of these approaches implies a different conception of knowledge in business contexts, and in order to fully understand value creation in the knowledge economy, it is ultimately necessary to generate knowledge on all three aspects.

This paper explores how social organization affects economic activity through examining social capital. Social capital is the sum of the actual and potential resources embedded within, available through, and derived from the network of relationships possessed by an individual or social unit (Nahapiet & Ghoshal, 1998). As the importance of collaboration across functions, competence areas and between organizations has grown, business sciences have become increasingly interested in studying issues which have traditionally belonged to the field of social sciences, such as relationships, social networks and interaction. Leveraging and creating the intellectual capital of the firm takes place through the interaction and communication within the organization and across its borders. Knowledge processes are essentially social by nature: knowledge is typically created, enriched, shared and leveraged in social interaction among several people. Most discussion and decision-making occurs in groups, and the social context influences the motivation and actions of individual organizational members to a significant degree. (E.g. Kogut & Zander, 1992; Brown & Duguid, 1991; Nonaka & Takeuchi, 1995.)

In fact, social capital is nowadays widely perceived as a necessary precondition of effective organizational behavior. Lesser (2000, 16), for example, argues, "Much as oil serves as the lubricant to ensure a vibrant and powerful engine, social capital acts as the fluid that enables the knowledge-intensive organization". Social capital has been related to such prominent drivers of competitive advantage as organizational knowledge (Lesser, 2000; Cohen & Prusak, 2001), intellectual capital (Nahapiet & Ghoshal, 1998; McElroy, 2002), communities of practice (Lesser & Prusak, 1999), effective inter-organizational collaboration (Walker et al., 1997; Yli-Renko et al., 2002), and development of virtual communities (Blanchard & Horan, 1998).

Even though it is widely agreed that knowledge is essentially social by nature and that social capital does matter to the corporate bottom line, there are relatively few previous studies that have empirically examined the impact of social capital on organizational growth. This paper looks at the social capital residing in both the intra-organizational and inter-organizational relationships of firms in a sample of 143 firms in the region of South Karelia, Finland. The relationship of internal and external social capital with organizational growth is examined quantitatively.

This paper addresses two gaps in the existing research. First, of the three approaches to corporate success in the knowledge economy, most prior empirical research has concentrated on the identification and measurement of intangible assets, and the description of competencies and capabilities in individual knowledge-intensive firms. Even though it is widely agreed that knowledge is essentially social by nature and that social capital matters to the corporate bottom line, there are relatively few prior studies that have empirically examined the impact of social capital on value creation. This paper addresses this question by examining the relationship of social capital and organizational growth in a sample of 143 firms in the region of Southern Karelia, Finland. In addition, this paper contributes to the existing literature by looking at both intra-organizational (internal) and inter-organizational (external) social capital. With the exception of Yli-Renko et al. (2002), previous studies have examined only one or the other analytical level. This enables the drawing of conclusions on the interplay and relative importance of these different forms of social capital.

## Social Capital – The Interplay of Social Relationships and Economic Activity

Social capital consists of the features of social structure that facilitate action (Coleman, 1988; Adler & Kwon, 2000, 90). It can be thought of as the wealth or benefit that exists because of an actor's (whether an individual person or an organization) social relationships (Lesser, 2000, 4). The positive consequences of social capital include improved information flows, as well as possibilities for influencing and controlling other actors within the social structure (e.g. Adler & Kwon, 2002, 28-33). Furthermore, social capital produces mutual support and increases trust, and thereby facilitates cooperation and coordination of collective action (Putnam, 1993). It is also said to provide justification and rationale for individual commitment, to enable flexible organization of work, and to facilitate the development of intellectual capital (Leana & Van Buren, 1999, 547-552; Nahapiet & Ghoshal, 1998).

Social capital as a resource bears both similarities and differences with other types of capital. First, like all other forms of capital, it is productive in that it facilitates achievement of certain goals (Coleman, 1988). Second, social capital is a resource that can be consciously built and invested in for the purpose of getting future returns (Adler & Kwon, 2000, 93). It is also appropriable, i.e. a social organization initiated for one purpose can also be used for other purposes, e. g. a network of friends can function as an efficient source of information about career opportunities (Coleman, 1988). In addition, social capital can function as a substitute or a complementary asset to other types of resources (Adler & Kwon, 2000, 94).

Social capital differs from financial capital in that it requires maintenance: interpersonal connections deteriorate unless they are revitalized once in a while. Furthermore, social capital does not depreciate with use, but is likely to be strengthened and developed when it is applied. (Adler & Kwon, 2000, 94.) Social capital exists in the relationships between people, and therefore it is a jointly owned resource, rather than controlled by any one individual or entity (Coleman, 1988). Finally, unlike any other form of capital, social capital can have negative consequences (Putnam, 2000).

The costs of social capital include the resources needed for maintaining relationships and norms. Another cost can be diminished creativity and innovation, as social capital rooted in highly cohesive relationships can lead to inertia, group think and dysfunctionally stable power structures (Uzzi, 1997; Leana & Van Buren, 1999, 547-552). Also corruption and in-group favoritism have been cited as possible negative consequences of social capital (Putnam, 2000).

## DIMENSIONS OF SOCIAL CAPITAL

Social capital of organizations has been studied both as an intra-organizational phenomenon and a quality of inter-organizational relationships. Intra-organizational social capital addresses the social structures within the organizational boundaries, whereas inter-organizational social capital addresses the relational qualities of collaborative arrangements among several organizations. The concept of social capital has been given multiple definitions and there are several views on its components. In this study, we base our discussion and empirical work on the definitions of Nahapiet and Ghoshal (1998) and Lesser (2000), since their definitions are explicitly aimed at social capital in organizations, and are well-suited for examining it both on the intra-organizational and the inter-organizational level. According to Nahapiet and Ghoshal (1998), social capital consists of structural, relational and cognitive dimensions. Similarly, Lesser (2000, 4-7) differentiates three primary dimensions of social capital: the structure of relationships, interpersonal dynamics, and common context and language. In the following section, we look at each of the components of social capital separately in more detail.

*Structural Dimension of Social Capital.* The structural dimension of social resides in social networks, i.e. clusters of relationships between people. Social networks have attracted more attention lately. The relational network of includes actors and the configuration of links among them. In this pattern of linkages, researchers are typically interested in e. g. the density and connectivity of the network and the frequency of interaction.

Ties between actors in the network can be classified as either strong, i.e. close and frequent, or weak, i.e. distant and infrequent. The classical work of Granovetter (1973; 1985) demonstrated that these two types of links produce different types of benefits. Strong ties tend to increase trust and diminish opportunism among actors and serve the satisfaction of expressive needs. Weak ties, on the other hand, produce information benefits, as most new knowledge is likely to come from actors who represent different social groupings from the actor's own immediate community.

The two types of social connections and their associated pros and cons can be related to two opposite views on how network structures create social capital. On the one hand, social capital can be seen as arising from the similarity, safety and predictability provided by a closely-knit community where all the members are linked by strong ties. On the other hand, weak ties and structural holes provide individual actors with flexibility (Gargiulo & Benassi, 2000), a wider array of information and control opportunities (Burt, 1992; Hansen, 1999), and thus produce relative advantage to these actors.

In the context of organizations, another important factor of structural social capital besides the number of links within a social network and the strength of these ties is the ability of the organizational members to locate relevant information sources. This includes finding explicit knowledge in e. g. databases, but more crucially, the ability to find and contact the persons with task-relevant tacit knowledge (Lesser, 2000). In inter-organizational relationships, another essential factor is the extent to which the relationship with the most important partner provides the organization with access to a wider network of business partners or customers (Uzzi, 1997; Yli-Renko et al., 2001).

*Relational Dimension of Social Capital.* The relational pattern alone does not suffice for painting an adequate picture of social capital, but it needs to be complemented by qualitative characteristics of interaction within these social structures. First, trust is an essential feature of relationships. Trust can be defined as the willingness to be vulnerable to another party based on the belief that the other is a) reliable, i.e. there is consistency between actions and words, b) open and honest, c) concerned about the well-being of the trusting subject, and d) competent (Mishra, 1996). The level of trust in a relationship has been shown to critically influence the outcomes of interpersonal, intra-organizational and inter-organizational level collaboration (e.g. Kramer & Tyler, 1997; Pöyhönen, 2002; Blomqvist, 2002), and it is often considered one of the primary features of social capital (e.g. Nahapiet & Ghoshal, 1998; Cohen & Prusak, 2001; Putnam, 2000).

Second, the content of values and norms within the social structure influence the interpersonal dynamics to a significant extent. For example, if there is a norm of amplified reciprocity within the social structure, the actors are more likely to behave altruistically, as their deed is likely to be reciprocated in the future (Coleman, 1988; Putnam, 2000). Third, the relational dimension of social capital also includes the closeness and personal nature of relationships. Relationships characterised by intimacy, personal quality, informality and mutual identification are likely to yield extensive support to the actors, and thereby facilitate action (e.g. Nahapiet & Ghoshal, 1998; Yli-Renko et al., 2001).

*Cognitive Dimension of Social Capital.* The third dimension of social capital consists of the shared mental models and narratives that enable effective collaboration (Nahapiet & Ghoshal, 1998; Cohen & Prusak, 2001). Obviously, interaction is easier to the extent that the parties understand each other and share a common context and language. Whereas the content of values and norms belongs to the relational dimension of social capital, the extent to which these are shared across the members of the organization, or the two collaborating organizations, is a feature of the cognitive dimension. In the context of organizations, the shared representations and interpretations should ideally form a strategic alignment throughout the organization, enabling the members to direct their efforts towards collective goals. According to Nahapiet and Ghoshal (1998, 244), this dimension of social capital has attracted the least research interest.

## SAMPLE, PROCEDURE AND MEASURES

The sample of this study was composed using statistical data provided by the regional council of South Karelia. The goal was to gather data from a representative sample of the largest firms in various industries within the region. The data was gathered with a semi-structured questionnaire sent by mail. The main question categories consisted of the company's history and development, the present state of the company, and its future prospects. Altogether the questionnaire was answered by a total of 143 companies. Table 1 shows how the companies were distributed among various industries.

*Organizational growth*, the dependent variable of the research, was measured by asking the respondent to assess the average increase of turnover per year in recent years. The average annual percentage of growth ranged from –20 to +50 (M = 8,76, SD = 10,57). There were some outliers with extremely large values in the data, and thus a logarithmic transformation was performed in order to contract the distances between large values. However, the variable was not normally distributed even after the transformation, and as a result, no parametric tests could be used to examine this variable.

**Table 1. Distribution of Sample by Industries**

| Industry | Number of Cases | % of Sample |
|---|---|---|
| Construction | 42 | 29,4 |
| Metal products and machinery | 36 | 25,2 |
| Logistics | 18 | 12,6 |
| Timber, paper and graphic | 15 | 10,5 |
| ICT | 11 | 7,7 |
| Tourism | 6 | 4,2 |
| Energy and environment | 4 | 2,8 |
| Chemistry and plastic | 4 | 2,8 |
| Food and drinks | 2 | 1,4 |
| Textiles and clothing | 1 | ,7 |
| Other activities | 4 | 2,8 |
| Total | 143 | 100,0 |

*External social capital* was measured with a composite of 7 questions depicting the amount of social capital in the relationship with the firm's most important business partner (an organization). The response format was a 5-point Likert scale. The scale included 2 items concerning structural social capital between these firms, 4 items concerning relational qualities of social capital, and 1 item addressing the cognitive dimension of social capital. The observed composite values ranged from 2,17 to 5 (M = 4,00, SD = 0,59). The coefficient alpha, which measures the internal consistency of a scale based on the average inter-item correlation, was .755, demonstrating sufficient internal reliability.

*Extensiveness of collaboration* between the focal firm and its most important partner was measured by asking the respondents about the types of inter-organizational cooperation taking place in this relationship. The questionnaire contained a multiple choice –type section with 11 types of collaboration, from which the respondent was asked to choose suitable options. Space was also provided for verbal responses in case a relevant type of collaboration was not mentioned in the list. The number of collaboration types ranged from 0 to 8, with an average of 1,62 and standard deviation of 1,34.

*Internal social capital* was assessed by a composite of 12 questions, containing 2 items on the structure of intra-firm networks, 8 items on the relational dimension, and 2 items on the cognitive dimension. All items were measured on a 5-point Likert-type scale. Composite values ranged from 2,42 to 4,67 (M = 3,69, SD = 0,50). Coefficient alpha for the composite was .783.

In the analyses performed, all of the independent measures were also used for classifying the data. In these cases, the data was split in half by using the median value as the classifying criterion. In addition, the data was classified based on whether the organization belonged to any regional inter-organizational networks. 123 companies did not belong to any such network while 20 firms did.

## ANALYSES AND RESULTS

Based on the literature, the hypothesis of the research was that both internal and external social capital are related to organizational growth. However, correlation analysis demonstrated no significant associations between either intra-organizational social capital and growth ($r = -0{,}19$, $p = 0{,}12$) or inter-organizational social capital and growth ($r = 0{,}11$, $p = 0{,}42$). Instead, internal and external social capital were strongly related with each other ($r = 0{,}23$, $p = 0{,}005$).

As the finding that social capital had no direct association with organizational growth was quite surprising considering the multiple theoretical claims to the contrary, the issue was further explored by taking other variables of the full questionnaire into account. In these analyses, two patterns of influence were found. In the first case, internal social capital was related with the extensiveness of inter-organizational collaboration, which in turn was related with growth. In the second case, an association of social capital and growth was found when the data was split into firms that belonged to a regional network and firms that did not.

### *CASE I: Extensive Collaboration*

When the data was split into groups according to the level of internal social capital, external social capital, and the extensiveness of collaboration with the focal company's most important partnering firm, correlations were as depicted in Figure 1 below.

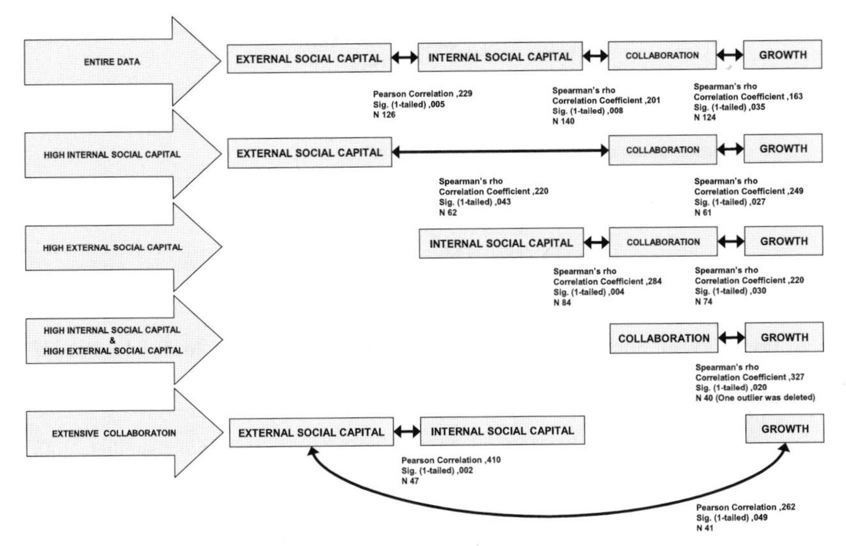


**Figure 1. Relations of Social Capital, Extensiveness of Collaboration and Organizational Growth in Split Data Analyses**

Based on the analyses, the amount of social capital seems to moderate the relationship of extensiveness of collaboration and growth. When only those firms were examined that had an extensive collaboration relationship with their most important business partner, the external social capital embedded in this relationship correlated significantly with the growth of the organization. As a result, the association of social capital with organizational growth can be depicted with Figure 2.

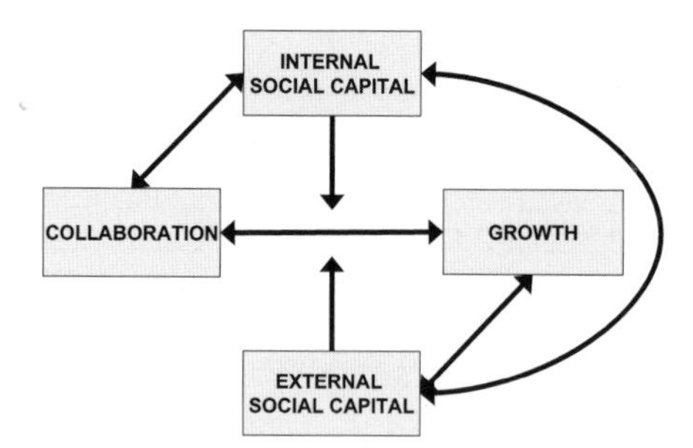


**Figure 2. Interplay of Social Capital and External Collaboration in Production of Organizational Growth**

As illustrated by Figure 2, internal and external social capital are related to one another. Both high internal and external social capital seem to be preconditions for the organization's ability to use external collaboration to power the growth of their turnover. Further, the level of internal social capital is related with the extensiveness of external collaboration. This can be interpreted to demonstrate that the higher the level of intra-firm social capital, the more likely the firm is to have many-sided cooperation with its most important partner company. It is also viable that many-sided cooperation with a business partner can improve internal social capital. However, it is more likely that a high level of intra-organizational social capital, i.e. extensive internal networks, high level of trust and communication, as well as shared mental models inside the company are prerequisites for developing a multi-faceted collaborative arrangement with another company.

Furthermore, if it is assumed that internal social capital precedes the formation of external social capital, then intra-firm social capital can be thought of as the very foundation of the whole model presented in Figure 2. In other words, the internal social capital of a company should reach a certain level before it can benefit from the external social capital embedded in its extensive partnerships. Thus, intra-organizational networks, communication, trust and understanding can be viewed as prerequisites for profiting from external social capital.

*Case II: Networking Company.* When only those firms that belong to some regional inter-organizational network are examined, the association of both internal and external social capital and organizational growth reaches a statistically significant level, as illustrated in Figure 3. In the studied region, there were two types of such inter-organizational networks:

subcontracting and maintenance networks of large-scale industries, and networks focusing on cooperation and shared marketing of a branch of an industry. Typically, a networked firm belonged to several networks. Both the internal and external social capital of these firms correlated directly with their growth.

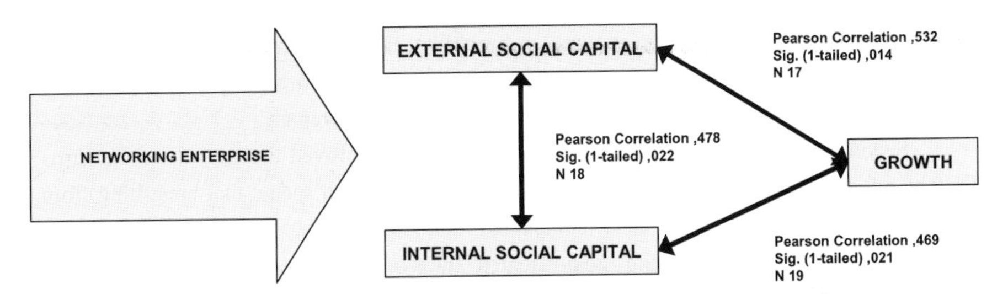


**Figure 3. Social Capital in Relation to Growth in Networking Enterprise**

As in the case with extensive collaboration with the most important business partner, it is possible that the causal direction goes from growth to social capital, so that the perceived benefits of belonging to an inter-organizational network induce the organization to develop its external and internal social capital. However, it seems more plausible to assume that the direction of influence goes from social capital to organizational growth.

## DISCUSSION

The aim of this research was to study the influence of internal and external social capital on organizational growth. However, in contrast to most of the existing literature, the results demonstrated that social capital is *not* directly related to organizational success in all cases. According to our results, social capital increases organizational growth of those firms that are engaged in extensive external collaboration, either with one main partner or through an inter-organizational network.

First, high external social capital had a direct positive impact on the growth of the organizations that were involved in an extensive, many-sided collaboration with another firm. This indicates that if a firm is closely collaborating with another company, it should invest in the development of social capital in this relationship. In other words, it is profitable to forge plenty of both formal and informal ties, developing trust, mutual values and commitment with this company. In addition, high internal social capital moderates the firm's ability to benefit from external relationships. This can be interpreted to indicate that in order for a company to be able to take advantage of external interaction, its own internal social capital should be on a certain level. This may indicate the necessity of a characteristic similar to absorptive capacity (Cohen & Levinthal, 1990; Zahra & George, 2002) the discussion on which suggests that the ability of a firm to benefit from external information flows is contingent on its internal knowledge resources. Similarly, perhaps well-functioning intra-firm interaction processes constitute a necessary basis for such processes also outside the company.

Secondly, both internal and external social capital improved the growth of the firms that belonged to a regional inter-organizational network. Thus, it seems that benefiting from social capital requires a systematic context of collaboration, e. g. in the form of a coordinated, relatively stable and goal-oriented inter-organizational network. If such a structure does not exist, then neither internal nor external social capital is transformed into financial value. Altogether the results demonstrated that there is a potential downside to social capital: if inter-organizational collaboration is conducted on a limited scope or in an unorganised manner, the costs of cultivating social capital may outweigh its benefits.

From a managerial point of view, the results of the research speak for the importance of tuning the social capital of the firm to contextual requirements. Forging and maintaining social capital is costly, and furthermore, sometimes close and trustful relationships and common mindsets, both within the firm as well as in inter-firm collaboration, can in fact have negative consequences for organizational success. Therefore, it is necessary to integrate the management of intra-firm and inter-firm relations with the general strategic management and value creation logic of the company.

## REFERENCES

Adler, P. & Kwon, S.-W. (2000). Social capital: The good, the bad, and the ugly. In E. Lesser (ed.), *Knowledge and social capital: Foundations and applications.* Butterworth- Heinemann, Boston.

Adler, P. & Kwon, S.-W. (2002). Social capital: Prospects for a new concept. *Academy of Management Review*, **27**, 1, 17-40.

Blanchard, A. & Horan, T. (1998). Virtual communities and social capital. *Social Science Computer Review*, **16**, 3.

Blomqvist, K.-M. (2002). *Partnering in the Dynamic Environment: The Role of Trust in Asymmetric Technology Partnership Formation*. Acta Universitatis Lappeenrantaensis 122. Lappeenranta University of Technology.

Brown, J. and Duguid, P. (1991), Organizational Learning and Communities of Practice. *Organization Science*, **2**, 1, 40-57.

Burt, R. (1992). *Structural holes*. Harvard University Press, Cambridge.

Burt, R. (1997). The contingent value of social capital. *Administrative Science Quarterly*, **42**, 2, 339-365.

Cohen, W. & Levinthal, D. (1990). Absorptive capacity: A new perspective on learning and innovation. *Administrative Science Quarterly*, **35**, 128-152.

Cohen, D. & Prusak, L. (2001). In *good company: How social capital makes organizations work*. Harvard Business School Press, Boston.

Coleman, J. (1988). Social capital in the creation of human capital. *American Journal of Sociology*, **94**, 95-120.

Granovetter, M. (1973). The strength of weak ties. *American Journal of Sociology*, **78**, 1360-1380.

Granovetter, M. (1985). Economic action and social structure: The problem of embeddedness. *American Journal of Sociology*, **91**, 481-510.

Gargiulo, M. & Benassi, M. (2000). Trapped in your own net? Network cohesion, structural holes, and the adaptation of social capital. *Organization Science,* **11**, 2, 183-196.

Hansen, M. T. (1999). The search-transfer problem: The role of weak ties in sharing knowledge across organisation subunits. *Administrative Science Quarterly*, **44**, 1, 82-112.

Kogut, B. & Zander, U. (1992). Knowledge of the firm, combinative capabilities, and the replication of technology. *Organization Science*, **3**, 383-397.

Leana, C. & VanBuren, H. (1999). Organizational social capital and employment practices. *Academy of Management Review,* 24, **3**, 538-555.

Lesser, E. (2000). Leveraging social capital in organizations. In E. Lesser (ed.), *Knowledge and social capital: Foundations and applications*. Butterworth-Heinemann, Boston.

Lesser, E. & Prusak, L. (1999). Communities of Practice, Social Capital and Organizational Knowledge. *Information Systems Review*, **1**, 1, 3-9.

McElroy, M. (2002). Social Innovation Capital. *Journal of Intellectual Capital*, **3**, 1, 30-39.

Mishra, A. (1996). Organizational responses to crisis: The centrality of trust. In R. Kramer & T. Tyler (Eds.): *Trust in organizations: Frontiers of theory and research*. London, Sage.

Nahapiet, J. and Ghoshal, S. (1998). Social Capital, Intellectual Capital, and the Organizational Advantage. Academy *of Management Review*, **23**, 2, 242-266.

Nonaka, I. And Takeuchi, H. (1995), *The knowledge-creating company*. Oxford University Press, New York.

Putnam, R. (1993). The prosperous community: Social capital and public life. *The American Prospect*, **4**, 13.

Putnam, R. (1995). Bowling alone: America's declining social capital. *Journal of Democracy*, **6**, 1, 65-78.

Putnam, R. (2000). *Bowling Alone: The Collapse and Revival of American Community*. Simon & Schuster, New York.

Pöyhönen, A. (2004). *Modeling and measuring organizational renewal capability*. Acta Universitatis Lappeenrantaensis, 200. Lappeenranta University of Technology.

Reagans, R. & Zuckermann, E. (2001). Networks, diversity, and productivity: The social capital of corporate R&D teams. *Organization Science*, **12**, 4, 502-517.

Tsai, W. (2002). Social structure of "coopetition" within a multiunit organization: Coordination, competition, and intraorganizational knowledge sharing. *Organization Science*, **13**, 2, 179-190.

Tsai, W. & Ghoshal, S. (1998). Social capital and value creation: The role of intrafirm networks. *Academy of Management Journal*, **41**, 4, 464-476.

Uzzi, B. (1997). Social structure and competition in interfirm networks: The paradox of embeddedness. *Administrative Science Quarterly*, **42**, 35-67.

Walker, G., Kogut, B. & Shan, W. (1997). Social capital, structural holes and the formation of an industry network. *Organization Science*, **8**, 2.

Yli-Renko, H., Autio, E. & Sapienza, H. (2001). Social capital, knowledge acquisition, and knowledge exploitation in young technology-based firms. *Strategic Management Journal*, **22**, 587-613.

Yli-Renko, H., Autio, E. & Tontti, V. (2002). Social capital, knowledge, and the international growth of technology-based new firms. *International Business Review*, **11**, 279-304.

Zahra, S. & George, G. (2002). Absorptive capacity: A review, reconceptualization, and extension. *Academy of Management Review*, **27**, 2, 185-203.

Management of Technology: New Directions in Technology Management
M. Hashem Sherif and T.M. Khalil (Editors)



# 26

# SOCIAL IMPACT OF TECHNOLOGY: A PERSPECTIVE FROM DEVELOPING COUNTRIES*

*Mohamed Mamdouh Awny, Director of Technology Management Program,*
*College of Graduate Studies, Arabian Gulf University,*
*Kingdom of Bahrain, mohdma@agu.edu.bh*

## INTRODUCTION

The industrial Revolution gave way to the Information Revolution, which is leading to the Knowledge Age. Throughout this successive revolution, technology — as an abstraction of knowledge — has been applied to the creation of goods or the provisioning of services. And since the Renaissance, Western economies have perfected and fine-tuned their ability to translate scientific discoveries and then technical knowledge to fuel the wealth-creating engine. In this respect, Science and Technology have proven to be major engines of social changes. Because Western societies are the main consumer of the technologies that they have developed, there are strong interactions between the designers, developers and the consumers. On the other hand, developing countries are mainly importers of technologies. Therefore, if an imported technology is applied in a way that is not related to the local conditions, a conflict

* More focus will be put on Arab countries where some impacts are more noticeable. However, many effects impact developed countries as well.

may occur with the dominant ethical and spiritual values of the society that imported it, or may even pose a threat to what such a society considers valuable (cultural heritage, historical sites, environment, etc.). On the other hand, in some developing countries, the imported technology may be completely alien to the wants or needs of their societies at large. It may also stimulate unsustainable patterns of consumption, where profligate classes live side by side with abject poverty. Worst, a certain strata of a developing society may take advantage of the imported knowledge and technology for their own benefits and enhance their social domination and wealth.

Another perspective is that some advancement in technology may facilitate and produce double-edged phenomena that impact negatively both developed and developing societies. Examples are: Nobel's high sensitive explosive "nitroglycerine" which made wars disastrously destructive, and the drug "cyclosporine", which helps to control the rejection of the foreign human organ in a patient's body, but has made the illicit trade of human organ booming all over the world.

In this paper, the impact and interactions between societies and imported technologies are addressed with more focus on the majority of developing countries.

*Technology and the development of Societies* . There is no doubt that technology has been a source for improving and enriching the daily life of modern populations. Examples abound in health services, food production, education system, energy conversion, communication, financial services, and transportation. Yet, as the various reports of the United Nation Development Program (UNDP) have argued over the years, the real value of technology lies in its use to empower people and to expand the choices available to them in their daily lives (UNDP, 2001).

Ideally, technology development and acquisition should be done in a harmonious way, where each player in the society, has a distinct role. For example, governmental institutions would define strategies and policies at the national level, financial institutions would finance research and development education and training institutions would prepare human resources to work in the production and services sectors that adapt the technology to meet the needs of the society at large. In reality, the degree of interaction of societies with technology depends on the type of society and its technical maturity. In industrial societies, where most of the scientific and technology innovations take place, the large knowledge base encourages better utilization of the technology. And, since knowledge and technology —when properly utilized and exploited — are, nowadays, major sources of wealth, the result is more wealth as well as furthering additional technological development. We have then a self-fueled process that widens the gap between in industrial and developing countries.

On the other hand, many developing countries not only lack qualified manpower and social carriers of technology, but also suffer the absence of a technology culture, i.e., familiarization of the average individual with various technologies and their uses. As a consequence, these developing countries are unable to take advantages of many of the technology advancements (UNDP, 2003). The next section describes in more details how technology acquisition and its management could be enhanced by the transfer of knowledge associated with the technology.

*Knowledge Acquisition and Management of Technology in Developing Countries.* Advancements in Information and Communication technology offers the promise of faster and easier transfer of scientific knowledge to promote economic and social development. The World Conference on Science held in Budapest in 1999 called for increased international cooperation in the application of science and technology to enhance their benefits to develop and developing countries (Budapest Declaration, 1999).

Unfortunately, the different rates of advance in science and technology among different societies are frustrating this promise. Many developing countries sorely lack the capacity to be a full participant in the building of the knowledge society. In fact, the digital divide accentuates disparities in development by excluding entire social sectors and/or countries from the potential benefits of the new opportunities. Thus, a genuine global networking that permits all societies to share knowledge and its applications is not yet a reality. A tragic consequence is that, due to the lack of technological knowledge and savvy, the societies may develop a hostile attitude to scientific and technological innovations. A sense of insecurity and threat typical provokes ethical, social, economical, and environmental conflicts that may lead to the misuse of certain technologies or their rejection (Rooksby and Weckert, 2004; Sherif, 1986).

In this regard, it is worth noting many consider the Trade Related Intellectual Property Rights (TRIPS) agreement of the World Trade Organization to be an obstacle that prevents he developing countries from building their indigenous technological capabilities at affordable cost. This was emphasized as well in the World Trade Organization (WTO) round in Doha, in 2001. Shah (2002) reported that African ministers and civil societies organizations, as well as some other developing countries were opposing and resisting the declaration regarding the

TRIPS agreement as it could worsen the situation of the poorer countries rather than improve it. Oxfam (2004) also made important distinctions between reality and rhetoric and pointed out that TRIPS will "exacerbate the technological divide" between developed and developing countries.

## APPROPRIATE AND INAPPROPRIATE TECHNOLOGIES

Technologies developed in the industrial societies are typically capital intensive and depend on the availability of high technical capabilities. This is not the case in developing countries, where technical expertise is not indigenous, capital is scarce, and the labor force is unskilled. Many planners and technology consultants tend to overlook these differences with the hope that the imported technology will resolve magically the problems of underdevelopment, whether technological or social. Planners, sometimes, do not realize that the choice of technology is not only technical, but requires that the recipient society or organization is able of absorbing it.

Usually there are alternatives for each technology, and therefore the imported technology should be appropriate for the society, with regard to: its culture, technical capabilities, socio-economic conditions, and environmental constraints (Darrow, 1985).
A technology may be socially disruptive in one social context and incremental in another. The end products of a disruptive technology are normally, smaller, cheaper and/or simpler to use. Initially, the disruptive technology performs poorly as compared to the attributes of the existing technology in established markets. These disruptive products may enable the emergence of new market segments in the society in which customers have a different rank ordering of product attributes than those of established markets (e.g. cost, quality, etc.). Moreover, because these products are less costly, new strata of the society would be able to afford them, thereby affecting the socio economical patterns of consumption. Such a disruptive technology, once commercially established, will improve at rapid rates and displace established technologies in other markets (Christensen, 1999). The invention of the quartz movement disrupted the watch manufacturing in Switzerland, displacing mechanical devices that relied on precision engineering and manufacturing. During the early stages of diffusion of the quartz driven watches, the world market for Swiss watches dropped from 50% to 15%. Yet, although this new technology affected negatively some sectors in Switzerland, it was beneficial to developing countries because it made time-measurement devices affordable to

low-income people worldwide. Misa (1994) and MacKenzie (1958) illustrate a number of similar examples.

Another example that highlights the effects of technologies on developing countries is that of mechanization (or automation). While similar dislocations have also occurred in developed countries, their magnitudes are more severe in developing countries, because of the higher rates of population increases, the prevalence of poverty and a low skilled labor-force. More specifically, many developing countries rushed into mechanizing their agricultural and farming processes (Helbawi, 1992; Islam, 1994) without considering: (a) that most of their lands are divided into small pieces that are not suitable for mechanized agriculture, and, (b) that poor farmers owning these pieces of lands could not afford these machines. Moreover, farmers that could afford to rent the machinery would be renting them from rich intermediaries, thereby increasing the socio-economical inequalities in the countryside. Finally, and from a macroeconomic viewpoint, the importation of machinery enhanced the dependence on foreign expertise for maintenance and technical support. Hence, these developing countries ended by tying their national economy and strategic products, viz. food production, with the external world. However, a closer look to the technologies used in farming and agriculture in India, as an example of a developing country, reveals that India has succeeded in acquiring and adapting technologies appropriate to its own environment and socio-economic situation. In introducing new technology for producing sugar from sugar canes, the Government of India decided to allow for the importation of mini-sugar technology rather that more advanced large-scale sugar technology. The choice was based on socio-economic factors, not merely economic. Among other social benefits, mini sugar technology creates more job opportunities and enables the establishment of simpler industry in the rural areas (Garg, 1985).

Thus, introducing automation in certain activities, which may be beneficial wherever manpower is lacking, may be counterproductive, leading to increased unemployment, more poverty and social unrest in developing countries (Schumacher, 1985).

A different example of technology that may have reduced productivity is that of the penetration of satellite TV with long hours of broadcasting around the globe. Workers, especially in developing countries, may spend longer hours during the night watching TV programs. This affects, negatively, their productivity during daytime, particularly, wherever work ethics are not strong. This shows that some societies may be negatively affected by some technologies, leading to a rejection of the technology in question. This suggests that importation of technology should not be in the hands of technologists or entrepreneurs only, but that experts in social studies should also participate in the planning for their introduction. Here comes, as in the case of India above, the role of the governments. They need to raise the awareness of the societies to those negative effects and they are to engineer counter measures as possible.

## POLITICS AND TECHNOLOGY

Scholars have claimed that some technologies are by their very nature political (Winner, 1985), for example: military hardware and various space programs. A different example is the oil crisis of 1973 that stimulated energy conservation and less dependence on oil as the major source of energy. Therefore, research and development activities have been accelerated in order to develop new technologies that may reduce fuel consumption and to adopt other types of energy like nuclear, solar, wind, water waves and the like.

The adoption of a certain technology, or technical system, unavoidably brings with it conditions for human relationships, i.e., political goals (e.g., repressive or liberating, defensive or offensive, etc.). This argument is in-line with Mumford's view (1964) that two traditions of technology, one authoritarian, and other democratic, co-exist side by side. For example, many advocates of solar energy hold that, with regard to possible negative effect on environment and risk involved specially in less advanced countries, such technology is more compatible with democracy than, say, nuclear power.

Some technologies that are relatively flexible in design or application have very different effects and political consequences. A well-known example is the multiple uses of nitroglycerine invented by Alfred Nobel Prize towards the end of the nineteenth century.
Moreover, since technology itself has become a source of economic growth and wealth creation, it is one of the major sources of public power in modern societies. Decisions that affect the daily lives of the members of societies are being controlled largely by the enormous power wielded by masters of technical systems: corporate and military leaders, and professional association of groups such as physicians and engineers. To that effect, technology hegemony yields to social hegemony (Feenberg, 1995).

## IMPACT OF TECHNOLOGY ON THE SOCIAL STRUCTURE

In the past, when majority of citizen resided in villages, families used to be major production units, where members of the family had to work shoulder to shoulder and to nurture the young. Industrialization made a major change due to rural migration to urban centers. The technological revolution sharpens the change. In the end, the large traditional family structure was fragmented into smaller units losing many of its old characteristics. Technology, too, is changing the quality of women's lives (Doorly 1987). More specifically, the advancements in information and communication technologies have changed the role of business with respect to empowerment of women. The new communication methods and techniques such as telecommuting and home-based businesses, allow women to participate in the production and overcome restrictions on their movement imposed by some developing countries.

Clearly, the information wave is making deep changes in the culture of families and role of women. Whether the effect will be positive or negative, whether family relations and inter-generational links will be strengthened or weakened, or whether education and culture will improve or deteriorate, will vary according to the society.

The weakening of the family system, in developed countries, is also emphasized by a report issued by Population Reference Bureau, in Washington DC, which showed that the percentage of people who live alone in the USA is on rise. The number of adults between 25 and 44 years of age that have chosen to live alone independently have increased three folds in three decades (Population Reference Bureau 2002). The report also showed that, in highly developed countries, fewer people are marrying now than ever.

The above discussions point out some effects of the third wave technologies on the social life of both developed and developing societies. However, the effects are not the same in all societies due to the variable degree of resistance of traditions, and the preservation of their own heritage of cultural properties in each society

## TECHNOLOGY AND ETHICS

Advances in science and technology, while they may continue to improve the quality of life dramatically, have also the potential of sparking controversies as they affect human conduct and the proper courses of action for professionals. Professionals have to take decisions and make choices. These decisions will, materially affect, positively or negatively, the ability of one or more stakeholders (such as: employees, users, customers, etc.) to reach their goals. Ethics then have to play a major role in decision-making process. Ethical thinking about technology considers its ability to alter humankind, either to harm human beings, to demoralize them, or, alternatively, to enable them to more fully develop their talents and capabilities.

The role of ethics in science and technology has acquired many new dimensions of meanings and relevance. There are a great number of specific issues that raise fundamental and important ethical problems. One example of such issues is research experimentations that involve human beings, animals, and plants. Studies involving human subjects, in particular children, persons unable to give consent, pregnant women, or volunteers for clinical trials (whether paid or unpaid), raise serious ethical problems. This is also obvious in the use of human biological samples, human tissue banking, clinical research, genetic testing, and human stem cell research. Because they lack the sufficient technical knowledge, developing countries are more vulnerable to these threats. Advanced drug technology, viz. the "cyclosporine", which revolutionized organ transplants has stimulated the illegal traffic in human organs as well as crimes such as kidnapping of youth and children to steal their organs and sell them on the international markets.

Similar ethical issues arise when genetically modified organisms (GMO) are tested or sold in developing and/or under-developed countries; where citizens are poor, ignorant and neither aware of the possible risks involved, nor of their human rights. Another example of ethical violation that affects vulnerable people of a developing country is the dumping of environmental hazardous materials in their country.

In these countries, the ordinary citizen lacks proper education, information, and technical knowledge. This renders them more or less vulnerable and subject to be fooled or mislead by incorrect or incomplete information, for example, the possible risks of new technological products. Ethical and spiritual values of certain societies may also be shaken by particular technologies (Awny 2005). Ethical problems concern the inappropriateness of advertising and sales tactics, taking advantage of the relative lack of the prevailing general knowledge of the people in dealing with hazardous materials, e.g. anti-insect products, toxic chemicals, or the sales of near to expire products, etc.

## TECHNOLOGY AND THE ENVIRONMENT

There is strong relation and interactions between: the Bio-sphere (sphere where living creatures resides and get their living needs), the Techno-sphere (system created by man for his survival, leisure, etc.), and the Socio-sphere (social ethics, regulations, traditions, etc.). The techno-sphere is mastered by technology. So, if the technological processes, or its products, are harmful or risky, then it will affect the other spheres. Ozone destruction, due to the uses of different inert gases in industrial processes, results in the inability of upper atmosphere to absorb the gases at its rate of generation, causes warming effect to the earth as well as causing it to lose its ability to reflect harmful rays from the sun. Disasters like Chernobyl in the Ukraine or Bhopal in India are always possible to occur somewhere else.

Many developing countries are suffering from heavy pollution. One of the causes is the waste during the technological processes (gases, chemicals, etc.) or from the use of the technological products (engines exhaust, toxic liquids or gases, or solid materials). Measures against such pollution could be unaffordable and/or unknown to the people. On the other hand, in seeking larger profit, many of factory owners do not care much about possible harm of environment or their workers. And due to possible existing corruption in some developing countries, owners can get away avoiding governmental rules and regulation regarding pollution. Example of which is the cement and brick factories present all over these countries. Government policies may also discourage the rational use of products that have negative effects on the environment (e.g. power, irrigation water, insect killer sprays). For example some Gulf countries do not charge their citizen for home usage of electricity.

The exploitation of the vital resources that are not renewable (metals, charcoal, oil, etc.), or renewable at a slower rate (forests) that the rate of extraction, is another example of a hostile action to the environment. Large scale of wood extraction from the forests in many countries, (Ghana, for example), has caused severe land degradation, changing a rich soil into semi-arid or arid, thereby stimulating the irreversible process of desertification. That is why the government of Ghana put strict regulation to these activities.

## TECHNOLOGYY IMPACT ON EDUCATION

The nature, content and quality of education should help to develop knowledge, values, attitudes and skills necessary to ensure a high quality of life for all and specially needed by developing countries. Education is necessary to develop communities and societies rooted in principles of democracy, justice and respect for human rights. Such issues are strongly needed for developing and developed countries at the same footing.

In this respect, one of the crucial fields that technology has benefited is education. Technology has introduced various educational tools for self-paced education, e-learning, distance learning and similar techniques. . This can overcome the scarcity of qualified teachers, of schools, libraries and educational resources. Therefore, theoretically speaking, developing countries should be the most beneficiaries from introducing technology in the education process. However, practicality shows that availability of the technology at reasonable cost, that is a cost affordable by these developing countries, and the adequate training of both teachers and students are necessary conditions for the developing countries to benefit. Otherwise, educational gap between developing and developed countries will be even more sorely.

## CONCLUSIONS

Science and technology, morality and spirituality are intimately intertwined and they should not be viewed as antagonistic. Without science and technology, no civilization could have evolved; however, the survival of human race at the present critical juncture of human history will depend upon the respect of ethical and spiritual values while managing technology.
Technologies should, also, respond to society's needs, particularities, and expectations. Social phenomena and social needs lead to changes in traditional technologies and open vistas for the development of new technologies.

As technologies and societies interact together strongly, experience has shown that technologies may change the structures, habits and inherited local knowledge of societies. Therefore, impact of technologies on societies could be negative, as well as positive. Technology affects, to a great extend the economy of societies, education systems, and women empowerment. In the case of the developing countries under observation, the above-mentioned effects are more obvious and severe, since, in general, developing countries implement imported technologies that have, originally, been created and developed in a different socio-economic environment.

A technology typically is appropriate for the society for which it was developed, and in accordance with the objective function stated for its development. This implies that same technology may not be appropriate in a different time, surrounding (society), and/or if the objective function changes. For a technology not to have a negative impact on a specific society, that is different from the one in which it has been developed, its appropriateness should be considered. This includes- as mentioned above- the appropriateness with respect to this particular society's cultural and social status (e.g. unemployment, poverty, etc). Therefore, the choice of technology should be made in accordance with the development objectives and plans of the society with consideration to its cultural aspects. The licensing system covering foreign investment and imports of machinery and technology can be an effective instrument for preventing the adoption of technologies unsuitable to a country's development objectives and for promoting desirable ones.

The importance of traditional and local knowledge of societies is also to be emphasized as dynamic expressions of perceiving and understanding the world. Science must become a shared asset benefiting all people, in all societies, serving as a power resource for social and economic transformation and for understanding natural and social phenomena. This emphasizes, too, the importance of the exchange of knowledge, information and scholarship among governments and civic societies. And that public participation in technological decisions, even at grass-root levels, is vital.

Therefore, intensive programs for awareness, education, information dissemination, and knowledge transfer must be conducted not only in technical terms but also on a much broader basis in order to empower members of societies, at all levels, especially in relation to the applications of Science and Technology. When considering developing countries, developed and industrial societies have a vital role in helping developing societies in achieving these objectives.

## REFERENCES

Awny, M. M. (2005). Ethics, Spiritual Values, and Technology. In: *The Proceedings of the International 14$^{th}$ Conference of the International Association for Management of Technology* (IAMOT ), Vienna, Austria.

Budapest Declaration (1999). *World Conference on Science*. Budapest, Hungary. (www.iupesm.org/worldconfbudapest.html).

Christensen, C. M. (1999). The Evolution of Innovation. In: *Technology Management Handbook* (R. C. Dorf, ed.), Chap. 3.1. CRC/IEEE press, Florida, USA.

Darrow, K. and R. Pam (1985). What are Appropriate Technologies? In: *The AT Reader: Theory and practice of Appropriate Technology* (M. Carr, ed.), Chap. 1. Intermediate Technology Publications, U.K.

Doorly, M. (1987). A woman's place: Dolores Hayden on the 'grand domestic revolution.' In: *The Social Shaping of Technology* (D. MacKenzie and J. Wajcman, ed.), Part 3, pp. 202-219. Open University Press, Philadelphia, USA.

Feenberg, A. (1995). Subversive Rationalization: Technology, Power, and Democracy. In: *Technology and the Politics of Knowledge*, (A. Feenberg and A. Hannay ed.), pp. 3-22. Indiana University Press, place of publication, USA.

Gang, M. K. (1985). Mini Sugar Technology in India. In: *The AT Reader: Theory and practice of Appropriate Technology* (M. Carr, ed), Chap. 2, Intermediate Technology Publications, U.K.

Helbawi, Y. (1992). *Technology in the Arab World: Concept and Challenges*. Arab Union Study Center, Beirut, Lebanon. (in Arabic).

Islam M.N. and M.M. Haque (1994). *Technology Planning and Control*. Bangladesh University of Engineering, Bangladesh.

MacKenzie, D. and J. Wajcman, (ed.) (1987). *The Social Shaping of Technology*. University Press, Philadelphia, USA.

Misa, T. J. (1994). Retrieving Socio-technical Change from Technological Determinism. In: *Does Technology Drive History? The Dilemma of Technological Determinism*
(M. R. Smith and L. Marks, eds.), pp. 115-141. The MIT Press, Cambridge, London, UK.
Mumford, L. (1964). Authoritarian and Democratic Technics. In: Technology and Culture, Chap. 5, pp.1-8

Oxfam GB (2004). Oxfam condemns proposed trade deal for failing poor countries. (www.oxfam.org.uk/press/releases/wto_300704.htm).

Population Reference Bureau (2002). Washington D.C. 20009, USA.

Rooksby, E. and J. Weckert (2004). Digital Divides: Their Social and Ethical Implementations. In: *Social, Ethical, and Policy implications of Information Technology* (L. Brennan and V. E. Johnson, eds.), pp. 29-47. Information Science Publishing, London, UK.

Schumacher, E. F. (1985). In: *The AT Reader: Theory and practice of Appropriate Technology* (M. Carr, ed), Chap. 2. Intermediate Technology Publications, U.K.

Shah, A. (2002). Free Trade and Globalization, WTO meeting in Doha, Qatar, 2001. (www.globalissues.org/TradeRelated/FreeTrade/Doha.asp).

Sherif, M.N., (ed.) (1986). *Technology policy Formulation and Planning: A Reference Manual. Asian and Pacific Centre for Transfer of Technology (APCTT)*, Bangalore, India.

United Nation Development Program (UNDP), Human Development Report (2001). *Making New Technologies Work for Human Development*. UNDP, NY, USA.

United Nation Development Program (UNDP), *Arab Human Development Report (2003). Building a Knowledge Society*. UNDP, NY, USA.

Winner, L. (1985). Do artifacts have politics? In: *The Social Shaping of Technology*, (D. MacKenzie, and J. Wajcman, eds.), Part One, pp. 26-38. University Press, Philadelphia, USA.

# Section VI

## Innovation in Service

Management of Technology: New Directions in Technology Management
M. Hashem Sherif and T.M. Khalil (Editors)



# 27

# PROJECTS IN TELECOMMUNICATIONS SERVICES

*Mostafa Hashem Sherif, AT&T, Middletown, NJ 07748 USA*

## INTRODUCTION

Project management is the application of knowledge, skills, techniques and tools to align resources and achieve the objectives of the sponsors within specific constraints of cost, time and quality. Formal project management techniques have become important in telecommunication services because of several factors. Telecommunication services have been unbundled as a consequence of regulatory and technological changes as well as increased outsourcing. Thus, many independent entities need to cooperate despite opposing and conflicting agendas. Typically, the planning and development of infrastructure projects last several years and may involve up to several thousands persons from many suppliers. Finally, new services must fit within an environment defined by already existing technical and organization legacies. Thus, the introduction of new products is typically constrained by a diversity of factors such as legislation, standards, embedded customer base, interconnectivity agreements with other operators, etc.

Even though the contribution of the service sector is steadily growing and in many economies exceeds that of manufacturing, telecommunications is still treated in a generic manner, without making the distinction between projects that are associated with services and those that are related to equipment development. The purpose of this paper is to alert the readers, or better to convince them, that this fundamental distinction is essential for technological and financial success. First, we give define the scope of telecommunication services and give a few illustrative examples. Next, we present a set of characteristics to distinguish projects in telecommunication services from those related to equipment or product development. These differences are then summarized to support the conclusions that are given at the end of the paper.

## SCOPE OF TELECOMMUNICATION SERVICES

Offers of telecommunication services cover networking technologies in addition to operations support systems, methods and procedures applications and content. Figure 1 shows the components of telecommunication services. Accordingly, the scope of the telecommunication services projects includes aspects related to the design of the network and the networking technology, the architecture of the operations support systems and the management of resources for the procurement, testing, installation, operation, maintenance and billing of telecommunication services.

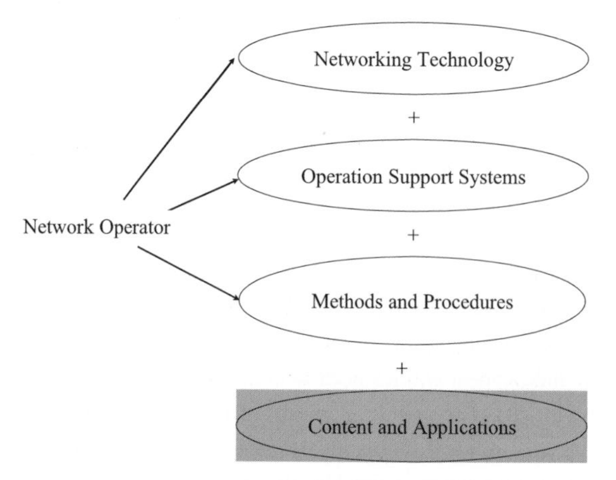


**Figure 1. Elements of telecommunication services**

The *networking technology* component relates to the physical infrastructure such as cables and transmission lines, the network elements such as switches as well as software enabled capabilities, such as messaging, call forwarding, and networked applications such as web hosting or storage networks. The equipment includes multiplexers, cross-connect, routing and switching equipment, power systems, and security systems such as intrusion detection systems. In some cases, such as managed services, customer premise equipment will be included.

The *operations support systems* component relates to the various network element management systems as well as systems used for provisioning, accounting, security, billing, etc. This component is essential for development, deployment and maintenance of high-quality network-based services using shared facilities, such as for public networks. They may be less important in the case of private and enterprise networks.

The *methods and procedures* cover the installation, engineering, operations, maintenance, repair and customer support aspects of the service. While some standardization and commonality exist among various service providers at the level of technology and support systems (because the equipment manufacturers offer similar equipment), the distinctive advantage of one service provider over the other resides in this component.

Finally, the *contents and applications* refer to content creation (e.g., customer relations management, disaster recovery, electronic data interchange, etc.) or content packaging (news, movies, voice mail, web hosting, weather reports or stock price, voice messaging, taxi services, catalogs and certificate management for electronic commerce, etc.). When content is essential for the growth of some services, the network or service operator use their direct relationship with the end-users to act as an intermediary for content providers as a distributor and to collect payments e.g., minitel, i-Mode or iTunes, etc.

## CATEGORIES OF PROJECTS IN TELECOMMUNICARION SERVICES

To illustrate the characteristics of telecommunication projects in the area of services, we divide them into three categories:

- Projects related to adding capabilities into an existing public network
- Projects related to establishing a specialized business network
- Projects related to the establishment and removal of a temporary network

It will be clear from the discussion that the relative importance of quality, cost and time varies for each category. More specifically, the main constraint on public services relates to quality; in enterprise environments, cost is the major concern while timeliness is the most important considerations in the case of temporary installations.

*Adding Capabilities to Public Networks.* This category of projects relate to the addition of new feature to an existing service in response to customer's demands or government regulations or the deployment of a new service. The challenge, of course, is to avoid or minimize any disruptions to the services offered because the changes are usually made in a live network. There are several reasons for these projects such as the introduction of new technologies, new regulations or the addition of capacity to meet growth in demand or the introduction of new services.

Replacements of obsolete technology are very common, e.g. analog equipment were gradually replaced with digital switches in the world-wide public switched telephone network. In public networks, these changes have to take place without affecting existing services. For example, during the 1990s, the 1A processor of all the 135 4ESS switches of the AT&T voice network were replaced the 1B process in the network without downtime nor service interruption (Golinski and Rutkowski, 1997).

As an example of the effect of new regulation, consider the case of local number portability, i.e., the capability to retain the customer telephone number, even when changing service providers. Examples related capacity increases include: 1) numbering changes such as the adding new area codes, 2) migration of existing traffic to different transmission facilities, for example, when a new undersea cable is introduce, 3) addition of dense wavelength division multiplexing (DWDM) equipment to augment bandwidth to long haul and metropolitan area networks without service disruption, etc. Examples related to operations support include the introduction of new billing systems or the improvement of existing billing systems. Finally, the introduction of new services is illustrated with the addition of toll-free (800) numbers, call forwarding, incoming call signaling, etc., to the existing capabilities of the basic telephone service.

*Establishing specialized networks.* Private networks are typically used by one enterprise or a government entity for its internal communication, such as air traffic control networks. A private network can also be used by a federation of enterprises, particularly when the industry is organized in a tiered fashion such as in banking or in the global automotive industry. For example, the Society for Worldwide Interbank Financial Telecommunications (SWIFT) — established in 1987 by 239 banks in 15 countries — has its own private network to relay the interbank messages related to international fund transfers. European automobile manufacturers have established a network called ODETTE for the exchange of information between suppliers and car manufacturers. Similarly, the Automotive Network eXchange

(ANX®) is the network of the Automotive Industry Action Group (AAIG) to link auto manufacturers with their suppliers in the U.S.

The notion of the "tipping of network coalition" due to Professor Eli Noam provides a good way to explain the relation between public and private networks. A telecommunication network is a cost-sharing arrangement among several users to meet their communication needs. Initially, external subsidies sustain the growth of the network until it becomes large enough to attract subscribers willing to join to benefit from the networking effect because the cost per subscriber decreases as their number increases. At a certain network size, however, some potential users will add more cost than their contribution to the value of the networking arrangement, because their specific requirements are not economic to meet (e.g., remote locations, peculiar security arrangements, etc.). When this happens, the network expansion stops and — provided that the technology is ready and the regulations are favorable — those who could not join will band together to form other networking associations (Noam, 1992, pp. 26–42). This explains why cost is the main consideration in private networks unless they transport mission-critical traffic, in which case quality remains the most valuable attribute.

*Temporary networks.* Temporary telecommunication installations consist of several networks for voice, data or video that are associated with specific events such as major United Nations conferences or global sports events (e.g., the World Cup for soccer, the Olympic Games) or in relief operations. These projects have an absolute end-date to be met at any cost (including sacrificing some functionalities). They have two main purposes: to provide timely information to the participants in the event in question (weather, press conferences, meetings, press information systems, etc.) through a variety of access points (fixed-wire, mobile, radio, TV, satellite, etc.) and to connect them to the outside world. Thus, the local networks must integrate gracefully with other national (emergency, hospital and police services) and international networks (e.g., broadcast).

The management of temporary installations covers planning, training, installation, deployment, operation and finally, dismantling. Such networks do not include only the transmission and switching equipment but also customer care and network care systems to accommodate fault reports or inquiries. The size of such networks can be very huge, such as during the Olympic Games, where the typical number of calls hovers around 12 million telephone calls. Furthermore, the calling pattern varies through out the event. For example, international conversations increase by about 20% with most of the increase after the opening ceremony (about 30%). It is similarly observed that the cellular phone usage is usually peaks during the opening ceremony. Traffic peaks to individual countries are random events that depend on gold medal performance and can be exceed 100% of the allocated capacity (Hunter, 2001).

## CHARACTERISTICS OF TELECOMMUNICATION SERVICE PROJECTS

From the previous examples, it is seen that telecommunication service projects consist of a portfolio of sub-projects. Their main characteristics the service projects are:

1. Complexity of the interfaces (internally and externally)
2. International orientation
3. Multidisciplinarity
4. No mass production
5. Diversity of user requirements
6. Relatively long planning stage (even for temporary installations)

*Complex Interfaces.* The interfaces with vendors, sponsors and customers are very complex. Additional complications arise when consultants act as intermediaries or when tasks are outsourced. To facilitate discussion, we consider two types of interfaces: external interfaces to other entities participating in the service delivery and internal interfaces among all systems.

*External interfaces.* For many services today, the service provider buys network services from a network provider and then resells them after adding some services such as Internet access, disaster recovery, international callback services, etc. The current architecture of telecommunication services is shown in Figure 2.

This representation shows how several providers contribute to the delivery of telecommunication services to the end-users. They are infrastructure providers, network providers, service provides and content providers. The infrastructure provider is responsible for the bandwidth (fiber cables, under sea cables, satellites, etc.). The network provider builds, operates and maintains the network elements and infrastructure. The content provider is responsible for content creation (news, movies, voice mail, web hosting, weather reports, stock quotations, taxi services, etc.). The content provider can also consolidate catalogs, store voice messages, provide answering services (call centers) or be a digital certification authority. The content manager has many functions such as managing customer relationship, packaging contents from several content providers, facilitating electronic payments, acting an exchange or a market place for electronic commerce, storing content, etc. Service providers can be viewed as virtual network operators to underline the fact that they have no physical assets and that they buy connectivity from network providers. In turn, they concentrate on the management of customer relations as well as supplier management. Service providers can be call-back operators, Internet Service Provider (ISP), providers disaster recovery, etc.

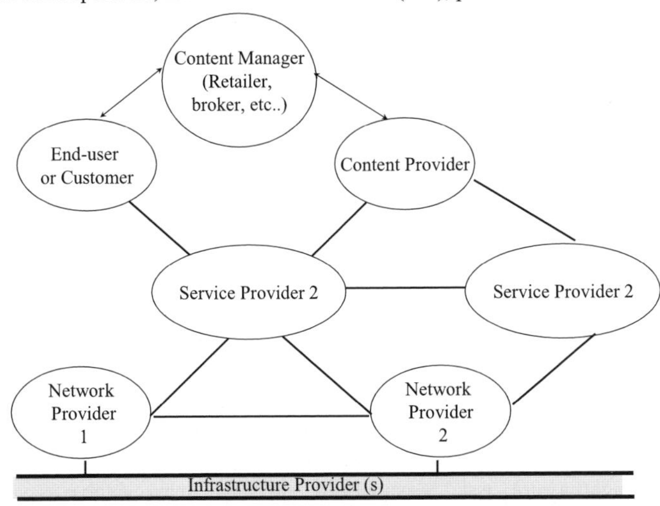


**Figure 2. Architecture of telecommunication services**

Cooperation among the operators can vary from interconnection agreements to allow transport and delivery of customer's traffic, to telehousing of equipment, to a full service agency. In this case, both operators participate in the pre-sales discussions, in the ordering and provisioning of the product infrastructure and in the deployment of the necessary network elements and management systems.

In the case of a disaster recovery service, the service provider offers facilities to recover from failures by replicating the customer's data centers and rents the necessary infrastructure from the network provider. The network provider, in turn, designs a network configuration with pre-assigned (but inactive) backup ports and access circuits for each customer's data center. The infrastructure provider may own the access circuits. However, it is the end-customer that designates which circuits will be activated to ensure that mission critical applications are minimally affected by the failure. Activation of the disaster recovery plan is triggered when the customer reports to the service provider a site failure and requests reconfiguration. The disaster recovery service provider, in turns, calls the infrastructure network provider to effect the change.

In the installation of undersea cables, teams from several companies collaborate on the specifications, selection of equipment vendors and in defining the network architecture. They establish the financial and accounting procedures among the various partners. They manage the purchasing, installation and testing of the submarine cable terminal equipment.

*Internal Interfaces*. The current architecture of OSS for public data networks, as shown in Figure 3 is very similar to that of traditional telephony (Rey, 1983, p. 374). In particular, systems for configuration management and for performance management, including alarm monitoring and maintenance systems, are only accessible by network operator. Performance management concerns the monitoring of network operation through the collection of data from the network devices and the analysis of traffic data. The interfaces among the network management systems and the various support systems for operations within a given network remain proprietary. They come from many vendors, which may be problematic as vendors merge, drop products or combine product lines. Furthermore, because of the lack of standardization, the element management systems are vendor- and equipment-specific. This makes the exchange of trouble tickets and accounting data among network providers and their customers not a straightforward task because this exchange may involve several administrative domains, particularly for global networks and on international links.

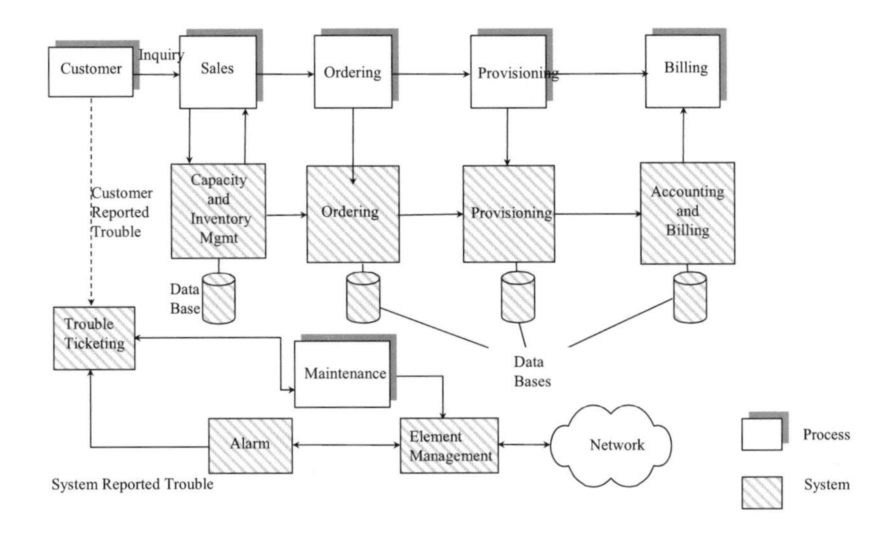


**Figure 3. The classical model of operation support systems**

It should be noted that the set of skills needed in each area are usually different. For example, configuration management and accounting management rely on different sets of tools and usually involved distinct departments. How are customers invoiced and, in cases of services spanning several countries which currency to use, depends on business policies. Furthermore, if electronic payments are used, the security of payments and the privacy of data must be ensured.

*International dimension.* Telecommunication services usually have an international component. International communications have gone through several technological generations from the telegraph, to the telephone, telex, facsimile and the Internet. From an organizational viewpoint, business globalization has stimulated attempts to form "global carriers," i.e., carriers with a variety of activities in different regions of the world to serve the telecommunications needs of multinational corporations. These services span several countries and mobilize various resources in different companies. However, service lead-time (i.e., the waiting period before the service is available) depends on the bandwidth and the location within the country as well as negotiation with the venues owners for access and installation of the necessary equipment and cabling. During operation, different operators may have different policies for trouble reports and may use different formats for trouble tickets. Finally help desk operations for customer contact may depend on the local holidays, vacations, time zone, work weeks, language, worker's rights, etc.

Some additional factors that should be taken into account are

1. Differences in licensing requirements, such as spectrum-management procedures, rules on the location of antennas or cell towers or the enforcement of service level agreements, the homologation of equipment or individual cards, etc.
2. Account settlement and payment with many different currencies. The global carriers will to identify cost components per country for taxation purposes and devise ways to split the overall bills into the correct local currency for each country.
3. Differences in legal systems concerning, rights and obligations of content ownership, right to privacy, encryption, etc
4. Regulatory constraints on voice communications (dial tone delay, connection to emergency services, communications available to the deaf, etc.) that vary from country to country.
5. Availability of services and their reliability depend on the country, for example number portability or subscriber identification and numbering (i.e., telephone number) regarding telephone operator or service provider.
6. Vendor support for the equipment is not the same in every country with respect to on-site maintenance, spares policy, board replacement service, etc.

In international projects, team members are quite dispersed among various countries and cultures, technical disciplines, many companies that may compete with each other. There is ample room for conflicts due to misunderstandings or opposing agendas. Dealing with local talent requires knowledge that goes beyond the technical aspects of the project as they affect cultural sensitivities to representations of power as well as the balance between power and knowledge. Working among different time zones gives a productivity advantage provided that there are no conflicts. Restrictions on travel for any reason such as cost or security make the coordination even more difficult because methods of remote communications (telephone, facsimile, web-based collaboration tools, etc.) have their limitations, even when they are well designed. Furthermore, cultural patterns of communications may favor different collaborative tools.

*Multidisciplinary Activities.* Projects to establish or run telecommunication services are multidisciplinary and cross functional. Implementation of telecommunication services involves several engineering disciplines (construction, physical design, mechanical, thermal, electrical, computer science, etc.) in addition to statisticians, marketing and legal professionals, etc. Many of these aspects with are intertwined due to regulations as well as the nature of the various technologies used. For example, the construction of buildings and the installation of antennas must be fire- and earthquake-resistant. Environmental regulations control the placement of transmission towers to protect the population for the radiation while the installation of satellite antennas must take into account resistance to wind. Cables must be rodent-resistant. There are also other legal obligations in procurement and contract management with various vendors or the use of frequency allocations, etc. Wireless transmissions have to meet specific health laws as well as esthetic standards. From a marketing aspect, there may be a need to offer different classes of service. This could translate into different types of licenses each of which is subject to specific terms that are subject to the laws and regulations of individual countries. Risk analysis and disaster recovery rely on a combination of engineering, financial and legal expertise. The operation and maintenance of the network require administrative skills for accounting, logistics, human resource management, etc.

These challenges can make telecommunication projects very rewarding because of the many possibilities of cross-education and the lack of monotony: the same project comprises many sub-projects that evolve at different speeds, using a wide variety of technologies and requiring many distinctive skills.

*No Mass Production.* Most telecommunication services are not dropped in a desert island. Therefore, they have to be adapted to a specific environment with existing procedures and technical constraints and meet the desired quality, reliability of service and cost control. Variations in telecommunication projects depend on several factors such as: 1) the type of network used (public, private, virtual private, etc.), 2) the target market (consumers, business, government, military, service resellers, etc.), 3) the nature of the installation (permanent or temporary) and, 4) the type of service (voice, video, high reliability data, etc.). Thus, each service project is different (different context, different user population, etc.), even though there can be significant learning from past experience.

One consequence of this characteristics, is that the boundary between the "end of the project" and the beginning of production and life-cycle management is less defined than in the case of equipment design and production, especially for in-house projects. In such a case, the project development team may be called for some field support in case of problems, particularly in the case of patch testing.

*Diverse user community.* Success of the service project depends on the level of customer satisfaction with what was delivered and how it was delivered. However, in most public telecommunication services, the user community is diverse and consists of various sub-groups each with different membership needs. In an enterprise, the success of a service depends of whether it has helped the functional organizations in improving their functions. Finally, in a temporary project for a conference or a sports event, the needs of the participants, for example, are very different from those of the media organizations or of the organizers themselves.

*A relatively long planning stage.* Planning for telecommunication services usually takes a long time. Network elements need to be tested and deployed. This process includes vendor selection and a thorough laboratory evaluation that can may last anywhere from 12 to 18 months. New network engineering rules have to be conceived and verified while the operation support systems are modified to accommodate the new services. Maintenance personnel need to be trained and sales people prepared to explain the offers to potential customers. In many cases, rights of way should be negotiated. Even temporary projects (e.g., disaster recovery contingencies) require a lot of planning and preparation (5 years in the case of the Olympics, for example). In addition to network planning and equipment testing, the planning includes aspects related to organizational arrangement, regulation, the logistics of installation and removing of the equipment (typically, more than 90% of the installed equipment for temporary projects) as well as the training of the personnel, whether permanent or temporary.

As a consequence, there is a considerable time lag proportional to the amount of effort expended for a new service to be generally available on a public network. The magnitude of the up-front investment explains why, once the service is up and running, operators prefer to exploit it as long as they can. Furthermore, unless there are substantial savings (e.g., 10 times) in terms of cost or quality, customers prefer to avoid the disruptions that are associated with service migration. Because of the evolution of systems, organizations and technologies are not necessarily synchronized, for any given technology, the market dynamics for network equipment may be considered a leading indicator for the evolution of network services. Similarly, the peak of the equipment revenues lags the peak of service sales by anywhere from 4 to 10 years (McCalla and Whitt, 2002; Sherif, 2003). The persistence of technologies in networks explains the long tail of service market penetration and revenues even after equipment sales have tapered off; this is shown in Figure 4.

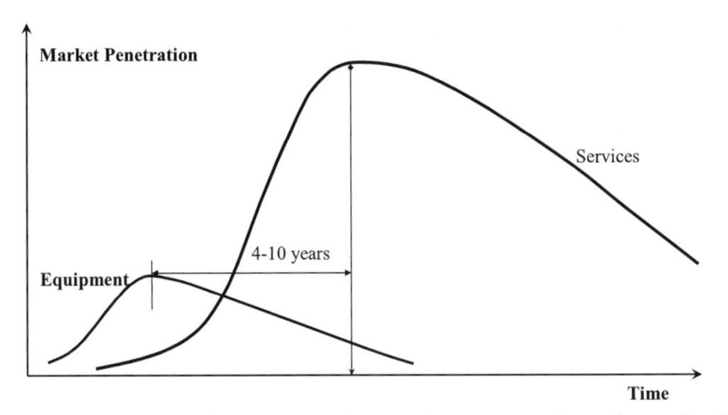


**Figure 4. Relationship between the market penetration of a technology in equipment and in services for telecommunications**

One obvious consequence is that, to cushion their revenues against the cyclical nature of equipment business, some manufacturers of equipment have signed off agreements with telephone operators to manage their networks (Munter and Odell, 2005).

## SUMMARY

A given technology cannot be treated the same way, whether it is used for service development or for equipment design. Table 1 summarizes the implications of these differences on the way projects are managed and the technology and its evolution are evaluated in terms of quality, cost and timeliness.

**Table 1. Implications of the differences among telecommunication projects in the areas of equipment manufacturing and service delivery**

| *Item* | *Telecommunication Equipment Manufacturer* | *Telecommunication Service Provider* |
|---|---|---|
| Stakeholders | Manufacturing, marketing, research and development, environmental | Administrative, legal, construction, quality assurance, marketing, environmental |
| Mass Production | Yes | No |
| Procurement | Individual components or subsystems | Equipment, bandwidth or support services, |
| Customer management | Distributors and end-users | Depends on the business model (customer or business) |
| Clear boundary between project termination and life cycle management | Yes | No, particularly for in-house development |
| International dimension | Optional — Mostly for marketing, regulatory aspects and compatibility through standards | Marketing, regulation, interconnectivity, account settlement, payment, troubles isolation and repair, vendor support, etc. |
| Quality criteria | Cost, size or footprint, power consumption, reliability, ease of repair, etc. | Cost, availability, reliability, billing accuracy, customer support, end-to-end quality, etc |

## REFERENCES

Golinski, S. and P. J. Rutkowski (1997). Flawless Execution: the 1B Process project: 1996 Project of the Year. *PM Network*, **11**(2), 19-29.

Hunter, J. (2001). Telecommunications delivery in the Sydney 2000 Olympic Games, *IEEE: Communications Magazine*, **39** (7): 86-92.

McCalla C. and W. Whitt (2002). A time-dependent queueing network model to describe the life-cycle dynamics of private-line telecommunication services. *Telecommunications Systems* **19**:9-38.

Munter, P. and M. Odell (2005). Upwardly mobile Svanberg. *Financial Times*, Dec. 19, 2005, p. 19.

Noam, E. (1992). *Telecommunications in Europe*, Oxford University Press, New York.

Rey, R. F, ed., (1983). *Engineering and Operations in the Bell System*, 2nd ed., AT&T Bell Laboratories.

Sherif, M. H. (2003). Technology substitution and standardization in telecommunications services, *Proceedings of 3rd IEEE Conference on Standardisation and Innovation in Information Technology* (SIIT 2003), Delft, The Netherlands, 22-24 October, pp. 241-252.

Management of Technology: New Directions in Technology Management
M. Hashem Sherif and T.M. Khalil (Editors)



# 28

# THE DEVELOPMENT OF A NOMOLOGICAL NETWORK TO DESCRIBE NEW AND EMERGING TECHNOLOGIES IN HEALTHCARE

*David George Vequist IV, Ph.D., H-E-B School of Business & Administration, University of the Incarnate Word, San Antonio, Texas, USA, 78209*
*Troy Dunn, M.A., H-E-B School of Business & Administration, University of the Incarnate Word, San Antonio, Texas, USA, 78209*

## INTRODUCTION

*"We think we know what we are doing. We have always thought so. We never seem to acknowledge that we have been wrong in the past, and so might be wrong in the future. Instead, each generation writes off earlier errors as the result of bad thinking by less able minds and then confidently embarks on fresh errors of its own.*
*Sometime in the twenty-first century, our self-deluded recklessness will collide with our growing technological power."* Crichton, M. (2003) Prey. HarperCollins Publishers, New York, New York

The forecasting of future technologies is quite possibly one of the most important tasks that should be improved in the early part of the twenty-first century, as Dr. Crichton points out in the introduction of his techno-drama. Not necessarily just because of the potential dangers that are frequently the antagonists in his books but also because it is important to understand what technologies are developing and why.

This art form (not quite a science yet), which is often the result of scenario planning (see Dearlove, 2002 for an interview with Schwartz) was given the term 'future studies' by Naisbitt in his landmark book Megatrends (1984). For fifty years experts, often called 'futurists' (e.g., see Toffler's books), have attempted to predict what technologies will arise and when, with much less success than Leonardo DaVinci had several centuries ago. According to futurist consultant and writer, Peter Schwartz, he believes the single most frequent failure in the history of forecasting has been the underestimating of the impact of new technologies (1996). Some could say that one of the difficulties with forecasting technologies has been the rapid evolutionary growth rate of technologies particularly over the last decade. [Note- it does seem as if Moore's Law is creating technological by-products at a geometrically increasing rate]. However, the authors believe it is still possible to create better scenarios that help in making more accurate forecasts about the operationalizations of technology.

This is particularly important in the field of healthcare where technological innovation is sweeping the world. It is becoming increasingly difficult to see the forest because of the number of 'new' trees cropping up. Because it is important to more accurately forecast these future technologies, the authors propose a new methodology to analyze past performance (i.e., recent technological developments in healthcare) to assist in forecasting future performance (i.e., future innovations in healthcare technologies). This methodology could enhance the scenario planning approach which is defined by Schwartz as a "methodology for contingency thinking, for thinking about different possibilities" and ultimately the ramifications (Dearlove, 2002).

In this paper, the authors develop a nomological network (Cronbach and Meehl, 1955) to describe new and emerging technologies in healthcare. The hope is that by understanding the theoretical constructs that are behind advances in technology (or the operationalizations of new technologies) that the error in forecasting of future technologies will be decreased. In this paper, new and emerging technologies in healthcare (both administration and delivery) are researched and then mapped using a concept mapping approach (Trochim, 2000) to form a logical network that represents the constructs that underlie the new and emerging technologies. These constructs, which are derived from the results of technological outcomes and observations of the impact of technologies, are mapped together to show the relationships (such as convergent or discriminant validity) that define this nomological network. This network is then evaluated to infer some nomologicals (basic rules or laws) to describe the themes that are currently underlying the development of the technologies.

## NOMOLOGICAL NETWORKS

In order to describe new and emerging technologies in healthcare the authors will use the concept of a nomological network which was developed by Lee Cronbach and Paul Meehl in 1955 (Cronbach, L. and Meehl, P., 1955). The nomological network was originally designed for the American Psychological Association as part of its efforts to develop standards for psychological testing. Trochim, in an online knowledge base about statistics, points out that the term 'nomological' is derived from the Greek word for 'lawful'; so the nomological network can be thought of as the 'lawful network'. The nomological network was Cronbach and Meehl's view of construct validity." (2000)

The nomological network is intended to represent the constructs that underlie the real-world applications (in this case, new and emerging healthcare technologies) of the measure. These constructs, which are derived from the results of outcomes and observations of the impact (again, in this case of new and emerging healthcare technologies), are mapped together to show the relationships (such as convergent or discriminant validity) that define this nomological network. This network is then evaluated to infer some nomologicals (basic rules or laws) to describe the themes that are currently underlying the development of the technologies.

Ultimately, a nomological network is supposed to imply construct validity which means that inferences can legitimately be made from the operationalizations in your study to the theoretical constructs on which those operationalizations were based (Trochim, 2000). In other words, you should be able to make sense of the observable manifestations and the interrelationships that you have measured and see the 'forest for the trees'.

In order to break down the various healthcare technologies or operationalizations of the technologies into a map, the concept mapping approach similar to what is suggested by Trochim (1998) was utilized. This is a methodology similar to brainstorming, brainwriting, nominal group techniques, focus groups, affinity mapping, mental mapping, Delphi techniques, facet theory, and qualitative text analysis.

The methodology suggested by Trochim (1998) uses groups of individuals and a structured approach. Because of the small group size (2 people) and the dynamic approach of the analysis, the methodology utilized was similar but the exact steps were different. The goals of the methodology stayed the same, which were to utilize a structured approach focused on a topic or construct of interest, involving input from one or more participants and to produce an interpretable pictorial view (concept map) of their ideas and concepts and how these are interrelated (Trochim, 1998).

The result of the concept mapping approach which is a grouping of similar constructs and their interrelationships was the desired outcome of this study. The resulting concept map could be used as a nomological network to infer what constructs were underlying new and emerging healthcare technologies and what the future may hold.

## HEALTHCARE AND TECHNOLOGY

In order to better understand the technological growth that is happening in the healthcare environment we should look at some of the writings by futurists in this area. One of the most famous futurists Alvin Toffler, the author of Future Shock and the Third Wave believes that there is going to be a revolution in healthcare due to the explosive growth of computers in the household. In a recent interview with the journal Canadian Healthcare Technology, Toffler is quoted as saying "There's a movement towards 'self-care' that's based on the vast amount of information available to patients" (Zeidenberg, 1999). He also suggests, in the interview, that consumers will be increasingly able to have their healthcare needs met from the comfort of their homes. He relates this to other trends such as at-home banking and shopping. Many of Toffler's beliefs are based on the macro-level writings of the Third Wave which suggests that we are in a society which is driven by data and information (1980). He believes that healthcare won't be able to stand apart from other industries because of the increasing availability of data and information (Zeidenberg, 1999). In a very thorough book, edited by David Ellis, entitled Technology and the Future of Health Care several authors outline some of the expected outcomes in healthcare technologies for the next 30 years (2000). Ellis and the other authors give examples of many of the new and upcoming technologies in healthcare such as:

- Intelligent subminiature drug and tissue manufacturing machine processes that can be implanted in the body to perform medical and surgical tasks
- Autonomous mobile robots driven by software and possessing more than human levels of intelligence, at least in specific domains of knowledge and expertise, as well as superhuman sensory perception and manipulative capabilities
- Workplaces, including doctors' offices and clinics, that exist only in virtual reality
- The interconnection of all these new artifacts through a vastly improved Internet, enabling them to remotely monitor, trouble-shoot, repair, augment, and improve one another, share information with one another and with us, gather and analyze data on a vast scale, and act on them (2000).

Ellis goes on to describe a model for the development of healthcare technologies and based on 20 key technologies that have been grouped together. From their analysis Ellis and the authors of this book identify 8 trends that they believe are visible trends of technological advancement in healthcare and other fields. These trends are:

1. Smart (e.g., Artificial Intelligence [AI] and expert/fuzzy systems) - makes decisions on its own
2. Small (e.g., PDA vs. a PC) – becomes smaller than initial versions
3. Mobile and dexterous (e.g., Robotics) – is able to perform tasks on its own
4. Aware (e.g., Sensing devices) – is able to collect data/information from the environment
5. Communicative (e.g., Wireless networks [WiFi]) – is able to communicate
6. Interconnected (e.g., Electronic Data Interface [EDI] and Bluetooth) – shares data/information with other machines
7. Autonomous (e.g., Agents) – operates without direct commands
8. Complex (e.g., saltation or emergent behaviors) – is more than its component parts (2000).

This list of key trends will be utilized further as the authors attempt to create a nomological network of constructs to describe new and emerging technologies in healthcare. These trends are supported by other futurists, like Toffler, who see a new wave of instruments and devices, powered by microchips and the telecommunications network (Zeidenberg, 1999). These tiny devices will undoubtedly be able to the collect more medical data (probably through wireless networks) from patients, which will lead to the increasing customization of treatment plans and cures. In support of this, Toffler in his interview states that "technology is ... making possible the customization of medical treatments, a shift away from the 'one-size-fits-all' medicine of the industrial era. For example, (in the future) using genetic screening and therapies, drug regimens could be tailored for specific individuals." (Zeidenberg, 1999).

## METHODS AND MATERIALS

The methodology utilized was the concept mapping approach described before. Research was performed on new and emerging technologies and a laundry list of these technologies was developed (Steps 1 & 2). The technologies or their operationalizations were randomly divided by the authors and were assigned to one or more pre-determined 'constructs' which were the Ellis' key trends in healthcare technologies (i.e., Smart, Small, Mobile, Aware, Communicative, Interconnected, Autonomous, Complex plus two were added: Interactive- is able to interact with humans, and Biological- is a biological or biotech application). This assigning was based on the perceived core purpose(s) of the technology or its operationalization (this is Step 3). [For example- the 3D touch system was considered to be Communicative (is able to communicate data/information) and Interactive (is able to interact with humans)] From there, the authors started to lay out a map of similar technologies based on these pre-determined constructs. Finally, linkages between constructs were drawn out for technologies that had more than 1 construct as part of its core purpose (this is Step 4).

Originally, the authors had a list of over 50 healthcare concepts and technologies from which to choose. They narrowed down the list to 38 that had specific operationalization usage in healthcare currently or in the immediate future. Using the concept mapping approach described earlier, the authors sat down with 38 new or emerging technologies (or operationalizations of technologies) and applied the concept mapping methodology to them to determine their linkages. From there the analysis produced 14 technologies that stayed in the map based on linkages to other technologies. The list of the 14 technologies can be found below:

T14. Intelligent Surface Technology (IST)- Designed for use in any product that comes into contact with the human body, including medical and athletic footwear, recliners, bedding and automobile seats
T15. Miniature Medical sensors- may be woven into the fabric of garments
T18. Bionic Senses (e.g., bionic nose and Light Detecting and Ranging [LIDAR])
T19. Intelligent Medical Robots
T20. Functional Magnetic Resonance Imaging (fMRI)
T22. Smart Agents- collect data/information to solve medical-related issues
T25. 3D Touch systems- gives haptic properties to graphic objects
T26. Medical Avatars- total body scanners (possibly VR)
T27. Parallel Processing to solve complex medical problems
T30. Medical/Clinical Data Warehouses
T31. Healthcare Smart Cards- keeps patient data and records on chip
T37. Automatic Speech Recognition (ASR)
T40. Automatic Language Translation & Interpretation (ALTI)
T51. Cybernetic technology and Super Health (being healthier than normal)

Another 11 technologies were concentrated under the Biological or Biotech category but did not have clear linkages to other 'constructs'. Another 11 were found to only fall under 1 category (Small, Smart, Mobile, Interactive, or Interconnected) with no clear linkages to other 'constructs'. In addition, two (2) were found to be too similar to other technologies and thus all of these technologies were not included in the analysis.

The result was a concept mapping matrix which shows the linkages between the constructs based on the technologies. Technologies 14, 19, 40 and 51 were particularly active in this model with each contributing at least four (4) or more linkages. The linkages are mapped out in Figure 1 below:

**Figure 1. Nomological Network for Healthcare Technologies**

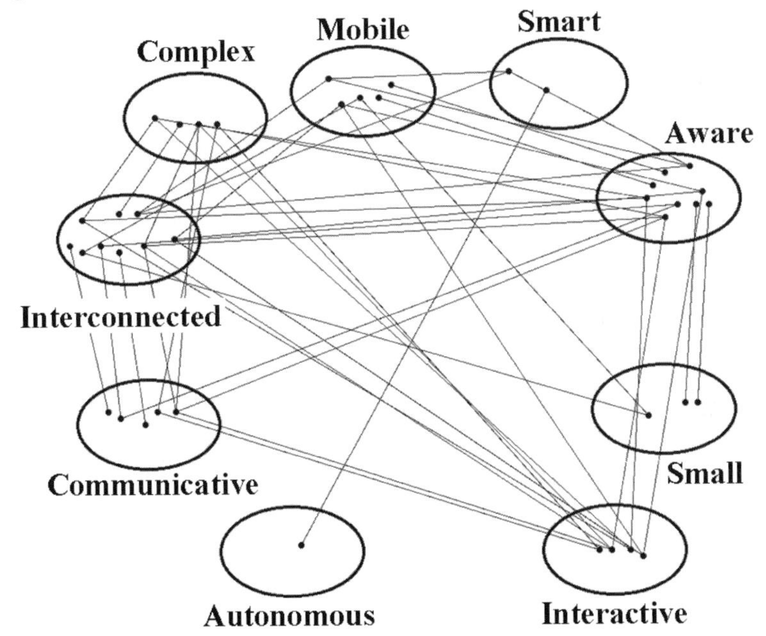


This map was now a nomological network that could be analyzed to determine what constructs were underlying new and emerging technologies.

## RESULTS

The authors then collected data on the nomological network and evaluated the meaning. The first analysis performed was the frequency count of technologies that had as their core purpose one of the nine (9) constructs that had clear linkages to other constructs (Note- these frequencies are based on the total number of linkages to other constructs. So, a technology that had several constructs associated with it would link each separate construct with the construct being measured.) The results are found in the table below (Table 1):

**Table 1. Linkage Frequencies from the Nomological Network**

| Linkage Frequencies | |
|---|---|
| **Construct Names** | **# of Linkages** |
| Autonomous | 1 |
| Aware | 18 |
| Complex | 9 |
| Communicative | 10 |
| Interactive | 12 |
| Interconnected | 20 |
| Mobile | 10 |
| Small | 4 |
| Smart | 4 |
| ***Totals:*** | ***88*** |

The most 'important' construct that was found in new and emerging healthcare technologies was Interconnected followed closely by Aware which makes perfect sense because in healthcare (as Toffler inferred) the most significant trend is the collection and sharing of medical/clinical data and information. In a second bunch, Interactive, Communicative and Mobile were found to be similarly important (12, 10 & 10 respectively). Again, to anyone involved in healthcare, this would come as no real surprise. An interesting aspect of the findings, that was somewhat unexpected, was that the strong frequencies counts (Interactive and Aware) were very rudimentary (after all, networking and data migration are somewhat mature fields and not at all bleeding edge) and that Autonomous, Small and Smart were not more significant trends in healthcare technologies.

The next analysis was to determine which linkage or linkages between constructs were most frequently found. The results are found in the table below (Table 2):

**Table 2. Linkage Frequencies from the Nomological Network**

| **Construct Linkage Frequencies** | | |
|---|---|---|
| **From Construct Names** | **# of Linkages** | **To Construct Names** |
| Autonomous | 1 | Smart |
| Aware | 5 | Interconnected |
| Complex | 3 | Interactive |
| Communicative | 4 | Interconnected |
| Interactive | 3 | Complex & Interconnected |
| Interconnected | 5 | Aware |
| Mobile | 4 | Aware |
| Small | 2 | Aware |
| Smart | 1 | *4 different constructs* |
| ***Totals:*** | ***28*** | ***Summary:*** ***Interconnected = 12, Aware = 11, The rest < 5*** |

The results were similar to what was found in the previous analysis; Interconnected and Aware were the major linkages for most of the other constructs. This could be inferred to mean they are the most important trend in new and emerging technologies in healthcare today.

## DISCUSSION

So, when this analysis is compared to the recent work of futurists what does it tell us? Author and consultant, Jeff Goldsmith suggested the following trends or vectors that were going to change healthcare (in 1986)- Scientific progress in biomedical research, technological innovations in diagnosis, treatment, and clinical information systems, changing clinical practice, institutional and managerial strategies that bring innovation to the patient.

He went on to suggest that by 2036 healthcare will see the advent of "bionic body" systems providing continuous medication to patients. Most likely, these will be cybernetic implants (perhaps nano-sized devices) which will become as prevalent (and most likely covered by insurance!) as prosthetics limbs, artificial joints/organs (e.g., metal hips, heart valves) and wearable pharmaceuticals (e.g., anti-smoking patches, implanted birth control solutions) are today. Because these systems will be 'networked', they will allow patients of the 21st century to be connected to their physicians or hospitals by webs of telemetry similar to those used in cellular communications. It is possible that the home or the residential community will reemerge as the primary site of clinical care (as also suggested in Zeidenberg,

1999). Also, he suggests there will be a maturation of artificial intelligence applications in medicine that may enhance, perhaps dramatically, the productivity of physicians and nurses; 'intelligent' clinical information systems will become the hospital's operating core interacting with physicians and nurses in diagnostic decision-making and patient management; and finally, physicians will use artificial intelligence systems to complement and to extend their diagnostic capabilities (Goldsmith, 1986).

In addition, he believed that referrals of patients to specialists or admitting patients to hospitals will be accompanied by machine-to-machine transmittal of clinical information that is necessary for therapy; clinical information systems will combine text and images in new storage and retrieval modes, such as the writable laser disc, that will replace paper medical records; and information transmittal will contain both high-resolution visual images of specimens or affected body parts as well as oral or written commentary from the consultant (Goldsmith, 1986). He also sees the structure of hospitals changing rapidly in future. Instead of a 'brick and mortar' building, he sees the hospital of the future being a high tech, critical care hub made up of a dispersed network of smaller clinical facilities, physician offices, and remote care sites linked together by 'intelligent' clinical information systems. He even suggests that "the economic boundaries of the system will be defined by the coverage of financing packages tied to the provision of care within the system"; it is possible that each metropolitan area might have multiple competing systems that stretch out many miles away from the core hub (Goldsmith, 1986).

This forecasting sounds accurate and makes sense compared to our analysis. However, the lesson learned from this study is that mature areas of technology (such as networking and data migration currently) are probably the areas that will yield the most value in application of new technologies in the future. The more exotic or advanced technologies that people like to forecast will probably not be commercialized as quickly as we would like and thus not have as much impact as some would believe.

An area that should be explored in more detail is the constructs that might be present within the biotechnological and biological technologies (11 of them identified by the authors) that were not analyzed in this study. This analysis may well yield more valuable research about the makeup of new and emerging technologies of tomorrow.

## REFERENCES

Cronbach, L. and Meehl, P. (1955). Construct validity in psychological tests. *Psychological Bulletin*, 52, 4, 281-302.

Brown, J. S. (2000). *Growing Up Digital*. Change 32, March, 10-20.

Ellis, D. (2000). *Technology and the Future of Health Care*. Jossey-Bass, San Francisco.

Goldsmith, J. (1986). 2036 A health care odyssey. *Hostpitals Magazine,* May, 69, 74-75.

Naisbitt, J. (1984). *Megatrends: Ten New Directions Transforming Our Lives*. Warner Books, New York.

National Research Council of the National Academies (2002), Preparing For the Revolution: Information Technology ad The Future Of The Research University, The National Academies Press, Washington, D.C. (Http://Books.Nap.Edu/Books/030908640x/Html)

Schwartz, P. (1996). *The Art of the Long View: Paths to Strategic Insight for Yourself and Your Company*. 166. Currency/Doubleday, New York.

Toffler, A. (1970). *Future Shock*. Random House, New York, NY.

Toffler, A. (1980). *The Third Wave*. Morrow, New York, NY.

Trochim, W.M.K. (1989). In: An introduction to concept mapping for planning and evaluation. (W.M.K. Trochim, ed.) *A Special Issue of Evaluation and Program Planning*, Vol. 12, pp. 1-16.

Trochim, W.M.K. (2000). *Research Methods Knowledge Base* (http://trochim.human.cornell.edu/kb/)

Zeidenberg, J. (1999) Toffler: Expect a move towards self-care and home-based healthcare. *Canadian Healthcare Technology*, Jan./Feb.

# SECTION VII

## EDUCATION

Management of Technology: New Directions in Technology Management
M. Hashem Sherif and T.M. Khalil (Editors)



# 29

# EXPANDING THE HORIZONS OF JAPANESE ENGINEERS

*Chie Sato, Biztech Inc., Tokyo, Japan*

*Satoshi Kumagai, Musashi Institute of Technology, Tokyo, Japan*

*Junsei Tsukuda, Musashi Institute of Technology, Tokyo, Japan*

*Jun Numata, Musashi Institute of Technology, Kanagawa, Japan*

## INTRODUCTION

This paper gives an overview of one of the core courses in the Management of Technology (MOT) program at the Musashi Institute of Technology (Musashi), Innovation Engineering. We have specially designed this course as a key tool to expand the horizons of Japanese engineers, who, more than ever in the history of our nation, are expected to make changes to our business environment to create a more stable and competitive position for Japan in the global economy. They are expected to achieve this even though they have been rather confined to their specialized engineering work and are not trained to connect their deep understanding of technology and engineering to business management. The core concept of the Innovation Engineering course is to devise an innovation-fostering environment through engineering approaches. The responses from experienced engineers who participated in our trial lectures were very positive, therefore, we are now convinced that we can advance the development further in MOT education.

In this paper, we will introduce Innovation Engineering, a novel concept in the academic world, and describe how this concept is implemented through our educational program and trial lectures, specially designed for engineers. Responses to the trial lecturers from the attendees, most of them seasoned engineers, are presented and analyzed, toward the further development of MOT education. The main author of this paper, as an expert in the education of engineers and business managers, has been involved in the program development from the outset, together with the other co-authors who all serve as professors in Musashi.
In this introductory section, we will describe the current situation surrounding engineers and universities in Japan, and our approach to providing education of fostering innovation. In Section 2, we describe the newly developed concept of Innovation Engineering, followed by the process of educational course development in Section 3. In Section 4, we describe how we planned and conducted the MOT trial seminars (intensive courses) and how the attendees responded. In the last section, Section 5, we describe the verified concept and remaining issues for further development.

*Engineers and Universities in Japan.*
Japanese industries and the engineers working there are facing many challenges today: increasing global competition, concerns about competitive edge after the mass-production and cost-reduction schemes, more innovative approaches to business, how to realize a nation based on scientific and technological creativity, and so on. Under such circumstances, engineers are required not only to keep up with rapidly evolving technologies, but also to become quick in responding to market and social needs by integrating technology and management toward innovation with marketing values. Also, middle-level managers are required to serve as a core of organizational knowledge and innovation creation, as Nonaka and Takeuchi (1996) indicated. Therefore, experienced engineers at the level of middle-level managers in technology-oriented companies are largely expected to contribute to innovation creation.

To face these challenges, the Japanese government introduced in 1996 the Basic Program for Science and Technology as a national initiative to establish Japan as a nation founded on scientific and technological creativity. This program implemented many practices to spur innovation through new national R&D schemes, regional clusters, academic-industrial alliances, and, especially in the second phase of the program (2001-2005), the practical involvement of universities in creating innovation has been stressed. Also, as a part of this program, the Ministry of Economy, Trade and Industry has enforced measures for encouraging engineers to be more venture-oriented, business-directed, and innovation-minded and has been continuously supporting universities and industries in developing and implementing MOT educational systems in Japan.

Meanwhile, though their circumstances are different from industry, universities in Japan have also been facing new challenges. Not only has the population of students of university enrollment age (about eighteen years old) been decreasing, but universities are also now forced to compete for resources, because the former national universities have become independent institutions since 2004, in the hope of bringing business efficiency into their management, with less government subsidies. In a sense, they are now about to be expelled from their ivory towers. On the other hand, seeking to gain a competitive edge in the presence of intensifying global competition, industries have expanded their reach for new technologies and innovation to outside resources, mainly to universities.

Under these circumstances, although universities have traditionally been reluctant to have contacts with industry in the past, and industry likewise expected little from universities, many universities have become active these days in strengthening academia-industry relationships in terms of education and research.

*Approaches to Fostering Innovation* .

As described above, innovation is an important keyword for Japanese industry these days, and universities are approaching innovation in various ways.

For example, the Institute of Innovation Research at Hitotsubashi University, whose approach to innovation is via the social processes involved, explains the reason for this importance on their website (http://www.iir.hit-u.ac.jp/aboutiir/aboutiir_e03.html):

". . . there is the historical fact that, . . (snip) . . it (Japan) has now advanced to the point where it must create its own innovations. Recognizing the urgency of this need, there have been calls recently to enrich basic research in the natural sciences. But that alone is not sufficient. Why has Great Britain, for example, which retains its excellence in fundamental research, had such a relatively poor record at industrial innovation for the past half a century? One can assume that the reason lies in the social processes, which fail to forge adequate links between basic research and industrial applications. . . . "

Their research, as we can see from this quotation, is supposed to give us a good top-down overview of how innovation is fostered in a society.

Another example is that of the Tokyo University of Science (SUT), a leading private science and engineering university. SUT recently established a graduate school specializing in the Management of Technology. The school's lectures are composed of three groups: Innovation,

Management, and Technology & Industries. The Innovation group includes many courses related both to technology and to business management, such as entrepreneurship, technology management, manufacturing management, project financing, business strategy, risk management, and so forth (SUT's website: http://www.sut.ac.jp ). In a relative sense with Hitotsubashi's approach based on social processes, SUT's approach to innovation seems to be a bottom-up one, because students are expected to obtain innovative capabilities by strengthening their knowledge of both technology and management.

The education of innovation, either to foster it or to understand it, is a vast area with many established theories. However, systematic educational programs, especially for engineers in business, are relatively new in Japan. When we look at some of these educational programs, however, we cannot help but wonder why aren't methodology-like approaches readily available for working engineers? Could new theoretical tools help those engineers in their business practices? Top-down overviews, as well as a deep understanding of the relationships among technology, business and innovation, such as we have just seen in the above examples, are of course needed. But isn't it possible to obtain some kind of guidance for engineers to foster innovation within their business activities?

The authors, based on years of experience working in various technology-related industries, have come to understand that innovation in business relies on the following principles:

- An environment for fostering innovation, though not the innovation itself, can be devised through engineering methods.
- An understanding of the evolving process of innovation in practical business environments, as well as of the variables to describe the dynamics involved, is essential for devising an innovation-fostering environment.
- The concept of devising innovation-fostering circumstances, once established, should be of great assistance to Japanese engineers.

Based on this understanding of innovation, as a part of the MOT education program, we have started the study of appropriate innovation education courses, under the concept of Innovation Engineering described later in Section 2.

*Musashi Institute of Technology.*

The Musashi Institute of Technology (Musashi) is a private institute of technology with a long and distinguished history. In three quarters of a century, it has produced more than 45,000 graduates from its undergraduate programs and about 4,000 graduates from its two graduate schools, in engineering and in the recently-established environmental information. These alumni work in many companies as leading engineers, supporting the backbone of Japanese industry. The size of Musashi, presently about 5,700 undergraduate and 600 graduate students, is rather small in comparison with Tokyo University (the top-level, nationally-funded university, with its 14,700 undergraduate and 6,300 graduate students) and SUT (12,000 undergraduate and 2,400 graduate students distributed among eight graduate schools). However, its focus on engineering, as well as its well-located campuses in the Tokyo metropolitan area, has enabled Musashi to establish a prestigious position in the engineering field. Because of this focus on practical engineering activities, Musashi has been conscious of practices much more than Tokyo University, which tends to educate policy makers and top leaders in government and industry. SUT's approach to education of innovation, on the other hand, is similar to Musashi's except that their coverage of innovation is rather comprehensive with no specific focus.

## CONCEPT OF INNOVATION ENGINEERING

*From Dynamics to Engineering.*

In 2002, we developed a course titled "Innovation Dynamics." As the title implies, the focus was on how innovations evolve in business, combining a basic understanding of innovation with case studies. The contents were structured based on a wide range of the precedent researches related to innovation, such as of Shumpeter (1926), Freeman and Soete (1997), Utterback (1994), Drucker (1993), Yoshikawa et al. (1997), and Christensen (1997). During the development of this course, we gradually realized that to understand innovation dynamics is only the first step toward innovation. To foster innovation, we realized that it is necessary to change some things within business environments based on the understanding of these dynamics. These changes may be as simple and as narrowly defined as business rules and materials to use in production, or they may be much wider concepts, such as how to gain the acceptance and empathy of society at large for our business activities.

Koen, in his publication "Discussion of the Method" (2003), states that there is no body of research that treats the engineering method as equivalently as Descartes does for the scientific method in *Discours de la Méthode.* He describes the engineering method as "the strategy for causing the best change in a poorly understood situation within the available resources." So, if there are some methodologies to foster innovation, they should be called

"Innovation Engineering", because in business practices we need to work toward innovation where no absolute and complete understanding of the environment, as well as the resources required, is available. Also, since our focus is to develop business tools for engineers and they are accustomed to an engineering way of thinking, we assume that this concept could make the best use of their capabilities.

The term "Innovation Management " is rather popularly used today. In order to give a clear definition of what we mean by Innovation Engineering, on the other hand, we temporarily define these two terms, in the context of business, as below:

"Innovation Management"

is to establish environments for innovation, i.e., to provide business environments required for fostering innovation. This approach to innovation is suitable for those who handle the whole innovation process and its environment. Therefore, to the eyes of someone inside the process, this is directed from the outside such as the upper management levels.

"Innovation Engineering"

is to devise schemes to foster innovation, implement those schemes, and evaluate them, with the business resources allocated by management. This approach is for those who are directly involved in the innovation process and environment and work on it from the inside, while involving the outside when necessary and possible.

We take it for granted that innovation itself cannot be "engineered", or intentionally planned. However, we believe that there may be optimum circumstances for fostering innovation, and that we can effect positive consequences by engineering some of the variables of such circumstances. Under the name Innovation Engineering, we focus on the business environment and try to identify a set of general frameworks that may be valuable in engineering activities to foster innovations.

We believe that this concept of Innovation Engineering should be of great assistance to Japanese engineers. At the same time, its uniqueness and practicality could distinguish the innovation-related classes in Musashi's MOT education program.

*Innovation Engineering study.*

Our study has been conducted with the approach shown in Figure 1. This approach is based on the following understandings:

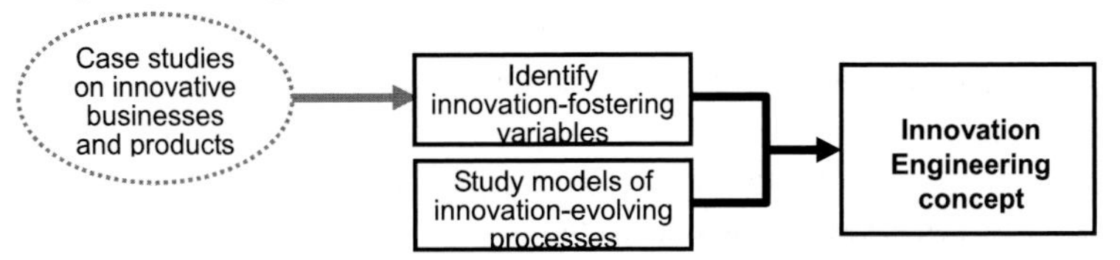


**Figure 1. Approach to Innovation Engineering Study**

1) The variables to foster an optimum innovative environment are to be identified, and once identified, the variables can be considered along two dimensions: whether they are controllable or uncontrollable, and whether they are inside or outside of the organization. With the variables identified through case studies on innovations in business, engineers can practically review their own business environments and consider how to work on them.

2) Existing models of innovation-evolving processes, e.g., the chained model of Klein (1990), are to be studied. With these studies, today's engineers can understand the variables identified above with a theoretical foundation for further application to their own business.

## COURSE DEVELOPMENT

*Structure of the course.*

To be counted as a credit for a degree, there should be at least twelve modules in the Innovation Engineering course, and we have categorized these twelve modules into three parts, as described below.

Four modules in Part 1, titled "Definition of innovation", address the basic understanding of innovation. The various definitions and meanings of innovation, such as of not only require some amount of time for lectures and interactive discussions, but also allow the students a good opportunity to start expanding their horizons. Part 2, "Innovation models", consists of three modules and is designed to teach innovation from the aspects of how the innovation process can be generalized into some models, and of what implications these models have for business. Well-known models of innovation in the management world are introduced and discussed, and students are guided to a more analytical and organized understanding of innovation. Part 3, "Innovation Engineering", consists of five modules. It provides lectures describing the concept, workshops for its application to practical cases, and individual presentations by students, in order to instill in the students the main concepts of Innovation Engineering.

The engineering method that Koen (2003) describes relies on heuristics and is the basis of the concept of Innovation Engineering that we use here. A heuristic is anything that provides a plausible aid or direction in the solution of a problem but is, in the final analysis, unjustified, incapable of justification, and potentially feasible. Therefore, in addition to the theoretical and deductive approaches based on the existing models of innovation, we also value case studies and workshops as a way to obtain some heuristics and at the same time to apply these heuristics to some situation. The structure of the entire course is shown in Table 1.

**Table 1. Structure of Innovation Engineering Course**

| Part & Module No. | Contents |
|---|---|
| <Part 1. Definition of Innovation> | |
| 1. What is innovation? | Discussion on innovation from various angles; its definitions, innovation and economy, Schumpeter's theory, impact on market, etc. |
| 2. Innovation, engineers, and business | Innovation in business from an experienced engineer's standpoint; how it evolved or failed, organizational or cultural issues, impacts on the market and society, etc. |
| 3. Case studies on innovative products | Studies of some innovative products; the destructive points, specific impacts on the market, society, and the company's business, etc. |
| 4. Workshop: evaluation of innovation's impact | Relative evaluation of the impact of innovation with hands-on cases; criteria for the evaluation, collection and analysis of related information, etc. |
| <Part 2. Innovation Models> | |
| 5. Innovation models (1) | Existing models of innovation, e.g., linear and chain-linked models, their adaptability to business, and possibility of new models, etc. |
| 6. Innovation models (2) | |
| 7. Case study and workshop | Adaptation of the innovation models; case studies based on the models mentioned above, with discussion on the value of those models in business. |
| <Part 3. Innovation Engineering> | |
| 8. Concept of Innovation Engineering | Introduction to Innovation Engineering; the concept and framework, its application in business, its significance in education, etc. |

| 9. Objectives and innovation | Hands-on work with the objectives sheet, a tool to understand the approach of the engineering method; case studies with student's own topic and environments |
|---|---|
| 10.Workshop: Innovation-fostering variables | Hands-on work for identifying and applying the innovation-fostering variables in business; their analysis and meaning in Innovation Engineering, especially focusing on the two dimensions described in 2.2 above. |
| 11.Workshop: Application of the variables | |
| 12.Presentation: Objectives | Completed objective sheets are to be presented by all students, followed by a wrap-up discussion on innovation engineering. |

*Target students and schedule.*

This course has been designed mainly for experienced engineers who have some business knowledge but are anxious to expand their horizons to be more business-directed and innovation-minded in rapidly changing business environments. This profile of the target student matches well with Musashi alumni, as mentioned in 1.3. We plan to offer this course, combined with other courses, first as a series of professional MOT seminars and finally as a professional graduate school of MOT in a few years. In either form, we plan to hold classes on weekday evenings and on Saturdays, for the convenience of working professionals.

In order to design these courses realistically, we offered trial MOT seminars to the public in the autumn of 2003. We will describe these trial seminars in the next section.

## TRIAL MOT SEMINARS

*Seminar settings.*

These MOT seminars were held mainly to test the concept and content of our MOT education program through feedback from industry and to publicize Musashi's MOT activities. The seminars consisted of four courses: IT usage in technology-oriented businesses, Technology development and society, Technology as business resources, and Innovation Engineering. Each course had only four classes and were therefore arranged as intensive courses.

**Table 2. Intensive Course for Trial MOT Seminars**

| Class 1. What is innovation? |
|---|
| "Innovation" is discussed from various perspectives, as in module 1 of the full course (Table 1) and some case studies are also provided.<br>*Lecturer: Overall understanding of innovation studies, research on business development, and years of experience in product development and marketing at a highly innovative company. |
| Class 2. Innovation models |
| Existing models of innovation, their adaptability to business, and possibility of new models for innovation are discussed, as in modules 5 and 6 of the full course.<br>*Lecturer: Research in management engineering and system engineering areas, with understanding of innovation studies and business activities. |
| Class 3. Innovation, Engineers, and Enterprises |
| Innovation in real business settings, from engineers' standpoint, are discussed, and some tools, such as objective setting sheets, are presented, as in modules 5 and 6 of the full course.<br>*Lecturer: Years of experience in corporate management, management engineering, and innovation studies. |
| Class 4. Concept of Innovation Engineering |
| Concepts and framework of innovation engineering studies, such as the two dimensions described in 2.2, are introduced, and their application to business as well as their significance in MOT education is provided, as a combination of modules 8, 10, and 11 of the full course.<br>*Lecturer: Same as Class 1 above. |

For the intensive course for Innovation Engineering, the four classes were arranged as shown in Table 2. Classes 1, 2 and 4 were arranged as abstracted versions of Parts 1, 2 and 3, respectively, of the planned course shown in Table 1, and Class 3 was added to give a feeling of real cases and practices within the limited time of the intensive course. The contents of these abstracted four classes were arranged to get sufficient implications to syllabus development of the regular course in later stages. The lecturers, as their qualifications are described in Table 2, were also arranged from the university and from industry, in consideration of the contents and their expertise and experiences.

These classes were held on three consecutive Friday evenings. The number of attendees was around fifty, most of whom were experienced engineers. However, they varied widely in their responsibilities, ranging from business planning and sales to research and product development; some of them were presidents and CEOs, and others were rank-and-file engineers.

*Attendees' Appraisal of the Intensive Course of Innovation Engineering.*

After providing the course, we passed around questionnaires among the attendees asking them to comment on the value of the course and their satisfaction with it.

The results were very positive: around 90% of the attendees gave mostly good appraisals regarding the course contents, materials, and lectures, as well as overall satisfaction level and positive engagement in the class, as shown in Figure 2. As for the unsatisfactory appraisals given by about 10% of the attendees, we looked into the comments attached to each appraisal

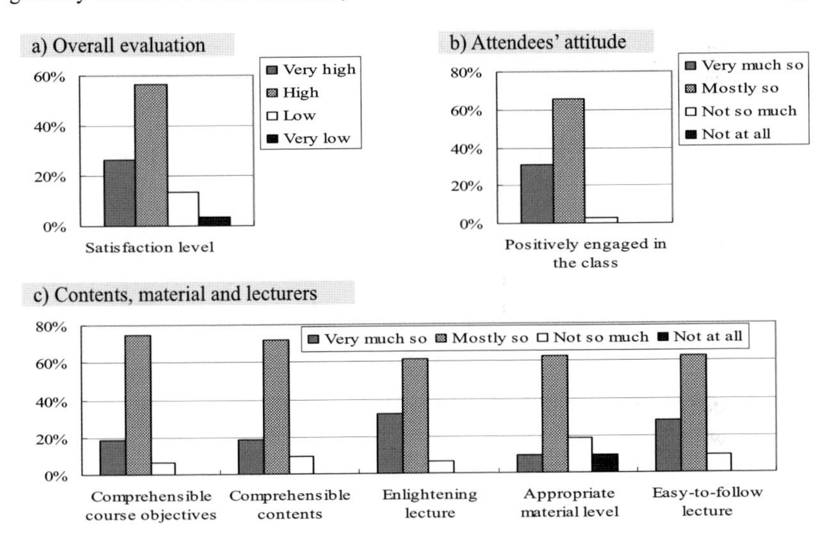


**Figure 2. Appraisal of the Intensive Course**

and found that the main reasons were not-well-organized materials and lectures, as well as slightly confusing context.

We found that, in general, the topic of Innovation Engineering was very enlightening to the attendees, while our material preparation still had some room for improvements. Very keen attention to Innovation Engineering was also seen in the attendees' positive attitudes to the course, as shown in Figure 2 b).

In Table 3, excerpts of attendees' comments are categorized into four types: favorable comments on the course and/or its contents; comments of good understanding of the Innovation Engineering concept; comments based on some misunderstanding of the concept; and comments of dissatisfaction with the concept. As shown, though there were some misunderstandings and dissatisfaction, as a whole we received very positive appraisals for the concept of Innovation Engineering as well as the intensive course based on the concept, with strong expectations for the concept's further development. In particular, many comments recognized the practical applicability of the concept of Innovation Engineering, especially the two dimensions described in section 2.2.1, in their businesses.

**Table 3. Attendees' Comments on the Intensive Course (Excerpts)**

| GROUP-A: FAVORABLE FOR THE COURSE AND CONTENTS |
|---|
| • This course is excellent, combining examples and theoretical concepts.<br>• Very practical and interesting course.<br>• The framework (two dimensions in section 2.2) seems a very practically useful tool.<br>• The course supplemented what I have been thinking in my own business.<br>• I will make a trial of applying the two dimensions to my own business activities.<br>• Attractive lectures. Very interested in how Innovation Engineering concept goes from here.<br>• If this course came first in my study of innovation, I would have got the whole picture of innovation better.<br>(15 comments in total) |
| GROUP-B: GOOD UNDERSTANDING OF THE INNOVATION ENGINEERING CONCEPT |
| • To look at innovation from an engineering viewpoint seems unique, and the relationship between innovation and stable/unstable environments was intriguing.<br>• I think that the essence of Innovation Engineering resides in studying the eventuality of innovation.<br>• Want to apply the framework to my own business, to verify its usability and to think about the applications of the two dimensions in my own company.<br>• Interested in how Innovation Engineering concept can explain the case of a successful company in "Innovation's Dilemma" which cannot create innovation in a certain area of business.<br>(6 comments in total) |
| GROUP-C: MISUNDERSTOOD THE CONCEPT |
| • The concept of Innovation Engineering should be good to evaluate and analyze what has happened in the past, but I doubt whether it is meaningful to create new innovation.<br>• Compliance to guidelines is essential in manufacturing a product, but innovation creation is much more than compliance to guidelines, and also smaller companies may not be able to spare extra |

| personnel for innovation.<br>(2 comments in total) |
|---|
| GROUP-D: NOT SATISFIED WITH, OR SUSPICIOUS ABOUT THE CONCEPT |
| • Something seems missing here in this Innovation Engineering concept.<br>• Concept of Innovation Engineering may be applicable to larger companies, but for smaller companies like my own, the meaning of the concept, including the frameworks, seems unclear.<br>(3 comments in total) |

As for the style of education for the Innovation Engineering course, we found that most of the attendees, about 70% of them, preferred to take the course as part-time course (i.e., in evenings and on weekends) over several weeks to months, and smaller groups preferred intensive course over a few consecutive days (10%+) or studying in an e-Learning environment (10%-). Full-time courses such as conventional graduate school programs were not favored.

## INNOVATION ENGINEERING AND ROLE OF ENGINEERS IN JAPAN

*Results and issues in the course development.*

We have introduced the novel concept of Innovation Engineering and have developed an educational course for teaching this concept to engineers in business. Though we are still developing this concept, we have obtained several useful results and issues to address from industry:

- The concept of Innovation Engineering, as a more practice-oriented and methodology-like approach to innovation fostering in business environments, has been very well accepted and recognized.
- This concept is enlightening to experienced engineers, and their expectations to use this concept in business are rather high.
- However, the way to offer this concept as an MOT education course, both in terms of material and lectures, should be reviewed and elaborated.
- Also, since the target students, i.e., experienced engineers, expect to apply this concept in their business, not only case studies but also hands-on style exercises, such as project work for real business situations experienced by the students, should be extensively incorporated into the course.

- Offering this concept in a conventional graduate school framework (i.e., full-time program for two years) seems impractical for the market. Therefore, some new approaches of the educational system should be established for the Innovation Engineering course, and finally for Musashi's MOT program.

*Next steps to expand the horizons of Japanese engineers.*

In the hope that engineers will take leading roles in the new technology-intensive Japan in the 21st century, they are required to be more innovative and have a more business-directed mind. Since they have trained and worked as engineers, they should be very experienced in understanding and applying structured methodologies to the real world. In this sense, a methodological approaches like the Innovation Engineering concept could be a good first step for them to understand and expand organizational and managerial aspects in an organization.

We are continuously refining the concept of Innovation Engineering by conducting various activities, such as the ones described below, in collaboration with professionals from the industrial world as well as from the academic one.

*Application of the modified Innovation Engineering framework in education.* The intensive course introduced the framework of the two dimensions, for variables that are controllable/uncontrollable and for those inside and outside of the organization. Since then, we have refined this framework further, introducing two new terms: a Business Practice Unit to define the inside/outside of the organization in a more flexible manner, and Six Generic Factors as an alternative categorization to the controllable/uncontrollable variables. The effectiveness of this modified framework for the education of engineers in business should be verified.

*Case studies with the Innovation Engineering concept.* To verify the applicability of the concept, and refine it when necessary, we need to conduct more case studies. In conducting these studies, interviews with persons who have been involved in the process of innovative product development are essential because our approach to innovation is of those who are directly involved in the innovation process and work on it from the inside. Also, the differences among industrial sectors should be considered because the business process in an organization depends to a large extent on the sector; therefore, we assume that the process of innovation should be similar.

*Further investigation of relevant studies of innovation.* We believe that those who are interested in innovation in business are becoming increasingly aware of the value of practical approaches and tools. More specifically, approaches based on the engineering method, i.e., approaches without a completely worked out theoretical foundation, but with some heuristics, seem to be gaining in popularity. For example, J. Tidd et al. (2001) indicate the importance of activity patterns in business practices, while Lester and Piore (2004) stress the necessity of interpreting changes in the flow and environment of business practices to improve the understanding of innovation gained through a conventional analytical approach. Thus, by studying the relevant research on innovation and incorporating its results, we can strengthen the value of education programs on MOT and Innovation Engineering.

## REFERENCES

Christensen, C.M. (1997; 2001 in Japanese). *The Innovator's Dilemma.* Shoueisha, Japan

Drucker, P.F. (1993;1997 in Japanese). *Innovation and Entrepreneurship.* Diamond, Japan

Freeman, C. and L. Soete (1997). *The Economics of Industrial Innovation - 3rd Edition.* MIT Press, USA

Kline, S. (1990). *Innovation Systems in Japan and the United States: Cultural Bases; Implications for Competitiveness,* Stanford University Press

Koen, B.V. (2003). *Discussion of the Method : Conducting the Engineer's Approach to Problem Solving.* Oxford University Press, USA

Lester, R.K. and M. J. Pior (2004). *Innovation--The Missing Dimension.* Harvard University Press

Nonaka, I. and H. Takeuchi (1996). *The Knowledge-Creating Company.* Tokyo Keizai Shinpo, Japan

Schumpeter, J.A. (1926;1977 in Japanese). Theorie der Wirtschaftlichen Entwicklung, Iwanami Bunko

Tidd, J., J. Bessant and K. Pavitt (2001). *Managing Innovation.* John Wiley & Sons, Ltd.

Utterback, J.M. (1994). *Mastering the Dynamics of Innovation.* Yuuhikaku, Japan

Yoshikawa, H (Editor) (1997). *New Engineering Intelligence Series 1, 2 & 3.* University of Tokyo Press, Japan

# SECTION VIII

# TECHNOLOGY FORECASTING

Management of Technology: New Directions in Technology Management
M. Hashem Sherif and T.M. Khalil (Editors)



# 30

# NEW METHODS FOR TECHNOLOGY FUTURES ANALYSES

*Alan L. Porter, Search Technology, Inc., Norcross, GA, and Georgia Tech, Atlanta, GA, USA*

## FUTURE-ORIENTED TECHNOLOGY ANALYSES

Analyses of emerging technologies are vital to management of technology (MOT). Decisions to be informed concern: prioritizing R&D efforts; managing the risks of technological innovation; exploiting intellectual property; and enhancing the technological competitiveness of products, processes, and services. Such analyses inform critical choices from the organizational (e.g., company) to international (e.g., European Community) levels.

Recent years have seen a rejuvenation of **future-oriented technology analyses (FTA)** to meet these demands. Today they form a set of partly overlapping fields of practice, including: competitive technical intelligence, technology foresight, tech forecasting, technology roadmapping, and technology assessment. This multiplicity in forms of FTA is made more diverse by differences in purpose of the analysis (e.g., corporate technology planning, public policy formulation), availability of source information, scope (geographic scale and time horizon), relationship to decision making, and extent of participation..

The conduct of FTA is challenged by a lack of attention to methodological development. There has been little systematic attention to conceptual development, research on improved methods, methodological selection, or integration of analytical and stakeholder engagement processes. Yet, demand for technology analyses is rising sharply over the past decade, especially in Europe. In response to these needs, an initiative to address new FTA methods came to fruition as an EU-US Seminar in Seville in 2004. This paper draws heavily on that seminar to put forth a range of candidate new FTA methods.

*Background of the FTA Initiative.* The FTA initiative aims to advance the *methods* and the *methodology* (effective performance) of technology foresight, including technology forecasting and assessment. Three stimuli for this initiative are that 1) FTA lacks an established meeting at which methodological innovators and practitioners can share and germinate ideas; 2) FTA lacks funding to promote methodological advance; and 3) application of FTA to inform management of technology needs attention to fulfill its potential.

In 2001, seven of us collaborated in writing a perspective on where the field of FTA could and should be heading (Coates et al., 2001). We observed that FTA had emerged from an extended dormancy with an upsurge in new forms and incipient new tools in the 1990's. We perceived several potent changes and challenges for FTA:

1. Changes in the nature of "technological change" with increasingly *science-based innovation*
2. Shift in the prime drivers of technological innovation from the more narrowly technical concerns of Soviet-American Cold War military systems to *industrial competitiveness* concerns requiring inclusion of socio-economic contextual influences
3. Renewed attention to *societal outcomes* (and sustainability)
4. Opportunities to *exploit electronic information resources* to enrich FTA
5. Better capabilities to *address complexity* in technological innovation

These changes all imply the need to adapt classical tech forecasting methods to address these challenges of informing technology management effectively. Based on later interchanges, I would augment this list of changing challenges to include:

6. Recognition of essential technological innovation process uncertainties that mandate adaptive *risk management* responses
7. Interest in discontinuous advances in science and technology, pointing toward *radical innovation*
8. Suitably engaging multiple stakeholders in *participatory FTA processes* to assure distributed understanding.

Through 2001, an informal group (primarily American) continued to exchange ideas on how to move the field forward. In December, 2001, The European Commission released a report on *Strategic Policy Intelligence* that assessed the state of the art and roles of technology forecasting, technology assessment, and technology foresight. We made contacts in the European FTA community and gained momentum toward new activities to bolster professional interchange.

By 2003, a number of us were informally collaborating to formulate ideas on the state of the art and where it should be heading. In addition to working to find a sponsor and host for a seminar, we worked to advance the conceptual foundations for FTA. The abstract of our co-authored paper conveys the thrust (Technology Futures Analysis Methods Working Group, 2004). [That earlier acronym, TFA, corresponds to the current "FTA."]

> Many forms of analyzing future technology and its consequences co-exist, for example, technology intelligence, forecasting, roadmapping, assessment, and foresight. All of these techniques fit into a field we call technology futures analysis (TFA). These methods have matured rather separately, with little interchange and sharing of information on methods and processes. There is a range of experience in the use of all of these, but changes in the technologies in which these methods are used -- from industrial to information and molecular – make it necessary to reconsider the TFA methods. New methods need to be explored to take advantage of information resources and new approaches to complex systems. Examination of the processes sheds light on ways to improve the usefulness of TFA to a variety of potential users, from corporate managers to national policy-makers. Sharing perspectives among the several TFA forms and introducing new approaches from other fields should advance TFA methods and processes to better inform technology management as well as science and research policy.

*The FTA Seminar.* In 2002, the Institute for Prospective Technology Studies (IPTS) agreed to lead the effort to convene a diverse group with intersecting interests in FTA. Over an extended period, details and support were worked out to enable the EU-US Seminar to be set for May, 2004. With funding from the European Commission Directorate General for Research, IPTS organized and hosted the seminar.

One of the challenges in organizing the seminar was terminology. Many in the public and private sectors are concerned with changing technology. Accordingly, they perform a variety of analyses, including technology forecasting and assessment. However, interaction among the various contingents of methodologists and practitioners is relatively weak. The seminar strove to bring together those engaged in pubic sector technology foresight with those pursuing private sector competitive technological intelligence. Bridging European emphases (e.g., participatory processes) and American strengths (e.g., technology roadmapping) added another mix of perspectives.

The EU-US Seminar on FTA was framed to address the following six issues:

1. Which FTA methods should be used, when? In particular, the interplay of multiple methods is critical given the inherent uncertainties in addressing the future of rapidly advancing technologies.
2. At a "meta" level, how can such methods be combined to generate effective study results compatible with policy and management decision processes?
3. Tensions arise between highly quantitative and qualitative methodological approaches; how can these be effectively integrated?
4. How can practitioners best balance validity and utility considerations?
5. What's new? We sought to identify new approaches to FTA and share ideas for cross-fertilization.
6. What approaches from other fields can contribute novel methodological elements to FTA?

Some 120 papers were proposed for presentation at the Seminar. Acceptance was selective, with main papers augmented by poster presentations. Despite outreach efforts, fewer than 10% of the applicants came from the U.S. Despite this initiative starting in the U.S., we had a hard time interesting more than a handful of participants. In various discussions, the sense is that the U.S. now lags severely in engaging technology foresight activities and in undertaking technology assessment. The strongest American FTA efforts seem to be in technology intelligence and roadmapping, especially in the private sector.

The Conference Proceedings is available from The Institute for Prospective Technological Studies (IPTS, 2004; www.jrc.es). In addition, separate papers from the Seminar and a special issue of the leading journal in the field, *Technological Forecasting & Social Change,* are to appear.

## NEW FTA METHODS

This treatment of new methods for FTA draws primarily on the presentations and discussions at the EU-US FTA Seminar. It is also colored by my personal experiences and preferences. So, in reading this give credit to those contributors; I will not reference each contribution separately, but instead point to the Seminar Proceedings (IPTS, 2004). I treat only selective ideas from the Seminar and a few from elsewhere. Any distortions and biases are my fault.

Before posing "new" methods, I note that there are many "old" methods still worthy of attention. Indeed, a fundamental premise it that quality FTA requires MULTIPLE methods. This reflects the underlying complexity and uncertainty in gauging advances in science & technology (S&T) and interpreting their implications. Valid FTA conclusions draw upon three key ingredients:

- constructs -- conceptualizations or models of what factors matter for technology innovation to take place, and of its impacts upon its socio-economic context
- data – the information upon which FTA draws; this includes both S&T information (e.g., R&D funding, research literature, patents) and contextual information (e.g., social preferences and concerns, standards & regulations, competitive setting, policies)
- methods

Vagaries in constructs, data, and methods preclude the application of single methods being sufficient to generate accurate and credible FTA findings.

A number of textbooks address technology forecasting and assessment (c.f., Martino, 1993). Heavily colored by our own work on technology assessment (Porter et al., 1980), tech forecasting (Porter et al., 1991) and competitive technical intelligence (Porter and Cunningham, 2005), I suggest these six as base FTA methods:

- Monitoring
- Creativity methods
- Trend analyses
- Simulation and modeling
- Expert opinion
- Scenarios

Many of the new methods reflect variations on these base methods. I will take the liberty of using these six to organize consideration of a number of novel approaches. In some cases, my categorization is pretty arbitrary. And, obviously, I have neither the expertise nor the space here to detail each new method. The intent is rather to introduce these ideas and encourage you to explore particular ones of interest further, beginning with the FTA Proceedings (IPST, 2004).

*Monitoring.* This family of methods includes many variants, such as environmental scanning, technology alerts, and competitive technical intelligence. All share the basic approach of perusing a body of information (often, but certainly not exclusively, R&D publication and patent abstract sets), digesting pertinent messages for an organization's interests, and interpreting the implications. What's new here consists, first, of the increasing availability of S&T information in handy, electronic form. As Bill Gates put it, we now have incredible "information at our fingertips." This includes the major R&D databases, such as *Web of Knowledge* (including *Science Citation Index* and *Social Science Citation Index*), *EI Village* (with access to the two leading engineering databases, *EI Compendex* and *INSPEC*), *MEDLINE* (covering biomedical research), and the world patent databases (e.g., *Derwent World Patent Index, Micropatent*), and many others (e.g., *RaDiUS* covering U.S. Federal research projects or NSF's Awards Database). Beyond these are business, popular press, venture capital, standards, and other contextual information resources. And, of course, the Internet offers access to a wealth of individual research-oriented websites plus fascinating compilations. So, why use the databases? They scan multiple sources (e.g., thousands of journals and/or conferences), filter, format, and index the raw information. They also provide search & retrieval capabilities otherwise lacking. That is, in a minute or so, one can locate and download thousands of well-structured abstract records. For instance, if you were analyzing a particular agent-organ-disease combination, a search in MEDLINE's collection of 12,000,000 or so world bio-medical article abstracts could provide excellent, first-order coverage of years of research results.

Established bibliometric approaches track R&D activity patterns. New methods incorporate "text mining" to discern trends and relationships. These allow comprehension of entire research domains via "research profiling" (Porter et al., 2002). More generally they allow the analyst to answer "who, what, where, and when" questions about research activity – i.e., to generate technical intelligence (c.f., Porter and Cunningham, 2005). Kevin Boyack's paper (NOTE that papers mentioned without a date reference are from the EU-US Seminar;

see IPST, 2004) addressed the vital step beyond analysis – illustrating interactive information visualization possibilities.

*Creativity method.* This diverse family of methods seeks fresh ideas for technologies, their fusion, and new applications. TRIZ is an important approach, deriving from Russian patent analyses, to draw upon analogous problem solutions from other domains. Using typologies of technical changes and challenges, one abstracts the problem at hand so as to recognize analogous solutions that may offer new perspectives to try out. TRIZ applications are reaching into MOT, not just technical issues (c.f., Mohrle, 2000).

A standby creativity approach is brainstorming. Van Notten presented a new approach of staggered brainwriting. An important way to enrich new product development is to move from "technology push" to "societal pull" considerations. Josephine Green described how a major company effectively takes into account social drivers in the design process in the form of "cultural creatives."

*Trend analyses.* Trends (time series data) lend themselves to growth modeling and extrapolation (trend projection). The S-shaped growth curves (e.g., logistic growth patterns showing an essentially exponential growth phase tapering into an asymptotic approach to a limit) are prevalent in tech forecasting. Technology or product families often witness successions of such S-curves.

Linstone and others point to the increasing extent of chaotic, transition regimes interspersed with smooth growth regimes. On the one hand, these imply intrinsic limits to forecasting – this suggests that rapid analyses and adaptive MOT are increasingly necessary. On the other, it lends importance to new methods to address the chaotic regimes (see next segment).

*Simulation and modeling.* This family of methods encompasses a wide range of approaches. The FTA Seminar treated both quantitative and qualitative modeling. Indeed, modeling in one form or another is incorporated into a good number of the new methods noted under the other headings as well.

Complex adaptive systems (CAS) modeling reaches out, for instance, to use genetic algorithms in treating technological innovation processes. Devesas presented evolutionary process modeling, using interactive growth modeling (Lotka-Volterra). He highlights the theoretical affinities among biological, cultural, and technological change processes.

Du Jouvenal presented a modern cross-impact approach. By crossing technological "push" attributes with social "pull" in the form of values, needs, and objectives, one can adjust a developing technology in its formative stage. Looking downstream, Pals and colleagues described how to operationalize consideration of the behavioral factors attendant to adoption of a technological innovation. They have a matrix of 26 product characteristics crossed against 14 personality traits of target groups to assess fit.

Interactive simulation, or gaming, offers a fresh tool for FTA. Gaming approaches are reaching beyond war games to address competitive interplay among technologies and products. At the seminar, Ahti Salo introduced gaming in the context of climate change.

"Lock-in" was noted as an essential consideration in anticipating technology "winners." This is not a new method per se, but rather a feature to consider in modeling innovation processes. The classic example of VHS vs. Beta VHR systems is well known. VHS, by gaining the initial success locked out Beta to a large extent. Another example is the long run of semiconductor innovations building on the silicon platform. So much capital investment and experiential learning make it very difficult for alternative technologies (in this case, gallium arsenide semiconductors) to catch on. Fleischer and co-authors presented lock-in as a factor in considering alternative development pathways and likelihoods of successful innovation for nanotechnologies.

"Roadmapping" (i.e., planning stepwise through a series of interrelated technologies and, often, products) might well be considered as a separate form of FTA. But, let's mention it here. Multiple papers at the Seminar addressed variations on technology roadmapping (c.f., Summers). De Laat provided a meta-analysis of 80 roadmapping exercises to identify conditions for success. Moving toward new versions, Green described how roadmapping can be adapted to a product design setting. Fiedeler discussed a "cross-form" application – namely, use of roadmapping for technology assessment (specifically, impact assessment for nanotechnology). Lizaso crossed methods in relating scenario-based roadmapping.

*Expert opinion.* The inclusion of some form of expert knowledge is virtually a given in FTA. Scapolo compared alternative ways to gather expert inputs. Ferola discussed another methodological combination – expert opinion with formal analyses.

Participatory issues are prominent in technology foresight. Berloznik offered another form of combined methodology. He described the use of consensus-building games to enhance participation.

*Scenarios.* This family of methods is widely practiced in many forms (Mietzner overviewed). The Seminar was rich in variations. Again, the theme of methodological cross-fertilization was well-represented. Fontella devised scenarios based on probabilistic cross-impact analyses. Barre also worked with a quantitative, input/output-based scenario approach. Elsewhere, Lempert (2002) has written about agent-based modeling that can yield a million alternative scenarios with ways to reduce these to effective policy options.

An often neglected consideration regarding methods is their suitability to generate results that FTA users find compelling. Gabner and Steinmuller showed the potential benefits of a story-telling scenario option.

Another intersection came between one of the eight changes/challenges – namely the importance of discontinuous advances in S&T – and this method. Van Notten compared alternative approaches for scenario development concentrated on discontinuous change.

## LOOKING FORWARD

This catalogue of new FTA methods offers rich prospects. Of course, new methods need to be carefully considered and vetted. Organizations should try out methodological elements that appear promising in light of their technology information norms and needs. Adaptation is obviously in order. I would hope that those trying and modifying these (and other) approaches would share their experiences with the professional community.

Several themes arise in reflecting on this sharing of methodological ideas. FTA incorporates both quantitative and qualitative methods. A number of new approaches consist of deliberate integration of particular forms of each. Note the important role of cross-fertilization. New methods often emerge at intersections. Many of the new methods entail a combination of two distinct methods. Others reflect specialization. One could array the eight changes/challenges as a matrix against the six methodological families and come up with possibly better suited methodological modifications. For instance, van Notten adapted scenarios to radical change situations.

Turning to a quite different issue, as an American recruiting for the EU-US FTA seminar, it was distressingly difficult to identify and engage U.S. practitioners. The roots of FTA, particularly in methodological development are heavily based in the United States. The needs for FTA to inform MOT are clear. Where have we gone wrong? Active programs in U.S. universities engaging future-oriented technology analyses (FTA) in any form have dwindled. One is hard-pressed to locate programs offering technology foresight training, technology assessment, futures research (the Houston- Clear Lake program is shutting down), or technology forecasting. I would recommend that FTA components be incorporated into MOT education. For a decade I taught "analysis of emerging technologies" in both the Georgia Tech and National Technological University executive masters in MOT programs. I'd be glad to share that content with anyone interested.

Research support can generate miraculous flowering of academic interest. In the early 1970's, the U.S. National Science Foundation had a small technology assessment (TA) research program. That few million dollars in research support, along with the prominence of the newly formed Congressional Office of Technology Assessment, contributed to the inception of many TA courses and programs in American universities. As a consequence, faculty and students learned about, wrote about, and went forth with knowledge about how to perform TA. I note at least some European funding of academic research to advance tech foresight methods (Dutch NSF); I don't know of any in the U.S. I would heartily recommend creation of a small FTA methods research program in NSF. A major stimulus for new FTA methods is the emergence of science-based technologies as increasingly important commercially; that could make for a nice program focus. Such support would reinforce topically oriented efforts, such as the newly created Centers for Nanotechnology in Society.

U.S. FTA activity appears strongest in industry. Americans do not undertake overall national technology foresight activities to anywhere near the degree that others do (Porter and Ashton, to appear). On the other hand, we have a robust, broad R&D enterprise that responds quickly to emerging science and technology opportunities. U.S. practitioners conduct many versions of FTA, most typically of a proprietary nature for use within organizations. Sharing of experiences through conferences such as PICMET and IAMOT has been organized at times. I would encourage renewed attention to providing a venue for interchanges among FTA methodologists and practitioners. Moreover, it is vital that FTA capabilities be brought to the attention of technology managers.

To close on an upbeat note, I am pleased that IPTS is organizing a second FTA methods seminar. This conforms to the initial vision that an ongoing interaction would be highly valuable. Previously there has not been a regular venue at which methods developers and those applying such methods could come together to interchange ideas. To track future FTA workshop scheduling, check the IPTS website (http://www.jrc.es/home/index.htm).

## REFERENCES

Coates, V., Faroque, M., Klavins, R., Lapid, K., Linstone, H.A., Pistorius, C., and Porter, A.L. (2001). On The Future of Technological Forecasting, *Technological Forecasting and Social Change*, Vol.67, No. 1, p. 1-17.

IPTS (Institute for Prospective Technological Studies) (2004). New Horizons and Challenges for Future-oriented Technology Analyses (FTA), Proceedings of the EU-US Scientific Seminar: New Technology Foresight, Forecasting and Assessment Methods, JRC-IPTS - Seville, 13-14 May 2004.

Lempert, R.J. (2002). Agent-based Modeling as Organizational and Public Policy Simulators, *Proceedings of the National Academy of Sciences (PNAS),* Vol. 99, Sup. 3, 7195-7196.

Martino, J. P. (1993). *Technological Forecasting for Decision Making*, third edition, McGraw-Hill, New York..

Mohrle, M.G. (2000). TRIZ-based Competitor Analyses, Ninth International Conference on Management of Technology, *International Association for Management of Technology (IAMOT*), Miami, Feb. 20-25.

Porter, A.L., and Ashton, W.B. (to appear). United States Case Study, in *International Handbook on Foresight and Science Policy: Theory and Practice* (L. Georghiou, J. Harper, M. Kennan, and I. Miles, eds.), Edward Elgar Publishers.

Porter, A.L., and Cunningham, S.W. (2005). *Tech Mining: Exploiting New Technologies for Competitive Advantage*, Wiley, New York.

Porter, A.L., Kongthon, A., Lu, J-C. (2002). Research Profiling: Improving the Literature Review, *Scientometrics*, Vol. 53, p. 351-370.

Porter, A.L., Roper, A.T., Mason, T.W., Rossini, F.A., and Banks, J. (1991). *Forecasting and Management of Technology*, John Wiley, New York.

Porter, A.L., Rossini, F.A., Carpenter, S.R. and Roper, A.T. (1980). *A Guidebook for Technology Assessment and Impact Analysis,* North Holland, New York.

Technology Futures Analysis Methods Working Group [Alan L. Porter (U.S.), Brad Ashton (U.S.), Guenter Clar (EC & Germany ), Joseph F. Coates U.S.), Kerstin Cuhls (Germany), Scott W. Cunningham (U.S. & Netherlands), Ken Ducatel (Spain), Patrick van der Duin (Netherlands), Luke Georghiou (UK), Ted Gordon, Hal Linstone, Vincent Marchau (The Netherlands), Gilda Massari (Brazil), Ian Miles (UK), Mary Mogee (U.S.), Ahti Salo (Finland), Fabiana

Scapolo (Spain), Ruud Smits (Netherlands), and Wil Thissen (Netherlands)] (2004). Technology Futures Analysis: Toward Integration of the Field and New Methods, *Technological Forecasting and Social Change,* Vol. 71, 287-303.

Management of Technology: New Directions in Technology Management
M. Hashem Sherif and T.M. Khalil (Editors)



# 31

# MANAGERIAL RESPONSES TO COGNITIVE DISSONANCE: CAUSES OF THE MISMANAGEMENT OF DISCONTINUOUS TECHNOLOGICAL INNOVATIONS

*Dr. Andrew White, Cranfield School of Management, Cranfield University, Bedford, UK*
*Professor John Bessant, Imperial College, London, UK*

## INTRODUCTION

Discontinuous technologies have been shown to affect a wide variety of industries, and the evolution of different types of technologies. Technologies evolve within paradigms, and along trajectories (Dosi, 1982). For most of the time, their evolution is of a continuous nature i.e. increases in the performance of the technology, in which the direction of this progress is an extrapolation of historical trends. However, a type of evolution that is referred to as discontinuous, periodically punctuates this continuous evolution.

There is a considerable body of research that shows that established organizations struggle to manage this type of technological evolution successfully. Utilizing a technology after the period of its market attractiveness has passed, misreading signals concerning customers needs and intentions, wrongly defining competitors and allowing inertia to prevent change in the business model operated, are all responses, by incumbent organizations, that have been identified. Whilst the current body of knowledge contains a level of understanding of how organizations mismanage discontinuous technologies, it struggles to give a comprehensive description and analysis as to why these factors occur. This paper will seek to address this omission by presenting a theoretical argument, which will use theory from the social psychology domain, to develop propositions that explain the mismanagement of discontinuous technologies by managers in incumbent organizations. This approach has been referred to as "multiparadigm perspectives" (Gioia and Pitre, 1990) and "metatriangulation" (Lewis and Grimes, 1999). This work will build on recent attempts to examine this empirically by Kaplan *et al*, (2003) and Tripsas and Gavetti, (2000). These authors studied the management of discontinuities in biotechnology and digital imaging respectively. It will seek to address a weakness in the literature on the management of discontinuous technology, which *"in general, (this body of literature) has not focused attention on management's cognitive processes"* (Kaplan *et al*., 2003). Moreover, this paper will seek to explain how the collective cognitive maps held by members of the upper echelons of an organization, concerning the value and role of a technology, can be in a state of dissonance with the reality of a technologies direction of evolution. Due to the psychological discomfort of the presence of this dissonance, the managers will be caused to misread signals coming from the market/industry that they are operating in, and consequently make strategic decisions that can have a detrimental effect on the performance of their organizations. Start-up organizations, or established organizations, who are not incumbents within a given market or industry, may not possess such cognitive maps, which cause them to misread these signals, and therefore may gain competitive advantage, and improved levels of performance over the incumbent organizations.

This paper will not seek to explain how the cognitive maps are developed, other than through a brief overview of the literature, or why they have evolved into a specific format. This will be addressed in further papers to be written by the authors.

## DISCONTINUOUS INNOVATIONS

Several authors have identified the presence of discontinuities. Foster (1986) defines them as being when one competitor is reaching the limits of what can be achieved with a technology, while another (or sometimes an incumbent), often less experienced, is exploring alternatives. Christensen (1997) develops the understanding of this phenomenon by observing that:

1. In the short term, they are often worse performers than the incumbent technology.
2. These technologies often have features that attract new customers and, often, are cheaper, or more convenient to use.

Henderson and Clark (1990) described incremental innovation as; relatively minor changes to existing designs that exploit the potential of the established design, and often reinforce the dominance of established organizations. By contrast, radical innovation is based on a different set of engineering ideas, opening up whole new markets, and they can create great difficulties for established organizations. Dosi (1982) identifies technological paradigms and trajectories, where paradigms are the context (e.g. internal combustion engines, magnetic tape recording and gas turbine aerospace engines) in which technology progress is made, and trajectories the direction in which developments progress. Tushman and Anderson (1986) develop this concept in the identification of competence-enhancing and competence-destroying discontinuities. Competence-enhancing discontinuities are described as significant improvements in terms of price and/or performance of a technology, which builds on an organization's current knowledge base. Competence-destroying discontinuities require the mastery of a new technology, which fundamentally alters the competencies required within a product class. Anderson and Tushman (1990) and Utterback (1996) both identify the presence of dominant designs. Anderson and Tushman (1990) describe dominant designs as being the consequence of periods of ferment followed by order, and Utterback (1996) as the design that organizations wishing to innovate, must adhere to e.g. the VHS standard for videocassette recorders. In summary, technology progress appears to follow a pattern characterised by an initial period of chaos, out of which new dominant-designs or paradigms emerge. Organizations competing within this paradigm innovate, incrementally or radically in nature, along a given trajectory. This innovation is constrained by the dominant-design. Over time, a new paradigm emerges that is founded upon a new technological architectural knowledge base, which causes a period of chaos. Out of this chaos new organizations, serving new customers, often emerge along with the new dominant design.

Discontinuities do not just happen in the process of the evolution of technologies, but also the evolution of businesses (Markides, 1998 and Hamel, 2000). Markides (1998) defines this as strategic innovation where "a fundamental re-conceptualisation of what the business is all about that, in turn, leads to a dramatically different way of playing the game in an existing business." And Hamel (2000) suggests the idea of business concept innovation that can be defined as "the capacity to reconceive existing business models in ways that create new value for customers, rude surprises for competitors, and new wealth for competitors. Foster and Kaplan (2001) found that most1 organizations that operate with an assumption of continuity concerning the nature of their operations, are unable to deliver above average levels of shareholder value.

In summary, technologies are not the only source of discontinuity. Figure 1 presents some of the other sources; markets, political, regulatory etc. These discontinuities are located externally to the organization, and can, under some circumstances, become disruptive to the incumbent organizations, which are competing in a market or industry. The nature of these disruptions is described later in this paper. It is when discontinuous technological innovations have a high disruptive potential that this paper will propose the

---

1 Out of the original 500 S&P (1957) companies only 74 were still in operation in 1997. Out of these 74, only 16% outperformed the S&P 500 index in this year.

mitigating effect of cognitive dissonance will be greater.

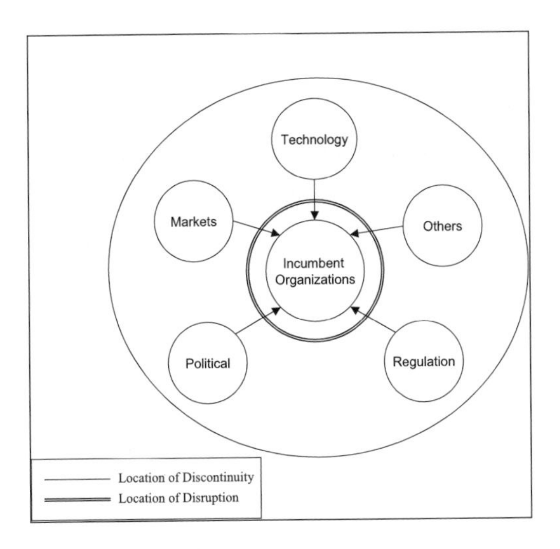


**Figure 1. The sources and location of discontinuities and disruptions**

Given the discontinuous nature of the evolution of technology and businesses, what impact does this have on organizations? A number of authors have identified that they have struggled to manage discontinuous technologies and business models successfully (Utterback, 1996; Barr, *et al*, 1992; Christensen, 1997; Tushman and Anderson, 1986). The consequence of this has been:

1. Corporate bankruptcy.
2. Loss of market share.
3. Stock (material) write off's.
4. Stock (equity) price reduction.
5. Financial losses.
6. Redundancy of staff.

This demonstrates that research into this subject is of benefit to a diverse set of stakeholders. The principal group is shareholders, who are at risk of seeing their investments eroded as a consequence of the mismanagement of discontinuous innovations. In addition to this, there are employees and managers whose personal finances and reputations may be negatively impacted, and governments who will have to suffer the consequences of possible increased numbers of unemployed people. These policy and practice implications are in addition to the case that has been made for the benefit of this theoretical contribution to innovation and technology management researchers.

## MANAGERIAL RESPONSES TO DISCONTINUOUS INNOVATIONS

Many authors have suggested reasons why companies fall victim to these disruptions. One of these reasons is the mismanagement of competencies (Hamel and Prahalad 1990, Andersen and Tushman, 1991 and Modis 1998). Discontinuous innovations are responsible for an organization tending to loose its core competencies, and, no longer being able to compete. Leonard (1995) referred to the entities that core competencies turn into as core rigidities. Anderson and Tushman (1991) showed that competence-destroying discontinuities advance the technological frontier of knowledge with skills in a way that that is inconsistent with prior know-how. Other reasons include the factors, which the management of organizations look to, to act as guides concerning the strategic decisions they make. Christensen (1997) found that it was the principles, traditionally practised by good managers, which cause them to falter in the face of discontinuous technologies:

1. Companies depend on customers and investors. Customers often do not want discontinuous technologies when they first see them because often they perform at a lower level, initially, then existing products, but with greater limits of performance. When customers do want discontinuous technologies, incumbent companies cannot respond quickly enough. As investors take a similar attitude to managers, that of

listening to customers, managers have neither the motivation, nor resource, to develop discontinuous technologies.

2. Small markets do not solve the growth needs of large companies. Many large companies wait until markets look interesting, in terms of sales volume, before entering. This strategy leaves time for competitors to establish themselves in the market.

Foster (1986) identified a pattern of customers telling companies what they wanted, only to change their minds when an alternative, discontinuous innovation had been produced, offering greater performance at a lower cost. Several authors identified a pattern of becoming comfortable with the status quo. Leonard (1995) found that the history, or past of a company had a negative effect in defining its future, in terms of placing limits on its problem solving abilities along with, what was referred to as "overshooting the target". Markedis (1998) found that the inertia of success acted as a barrier to companies developing discontinuous innovation. Foster (1986) found that companies thought they would have ample warning about a discontinuity, and an evolutionary approach to technology would be enough.

However, if we consider the case of Polaroid (Tripsas and Gravetti, 2000) who went into Chapter 11 bankruptcy on the 12$^{th}$ of October 2001, we find that they were doing many of the things that previous research on the successful management of discontinuous technologies suggests that organizations should do. They invested in, and developed new competencies in digital technologies, as well as instant print technology. They reorganizing the business, and hired people from digital camera technology companies. However, they failed to recognize that the market for cameras had completely changed, and still believed that customers wanted a physical print, something that had underpinned their remarkable commercial and technological success for the past fifty years. The authors suggest the reasons for this imminent, and correctly predicted failure on their part, was due to

Polaroid's difficulties in adapting to digital imaging and *"were mainly determined by the cognitive inertia of its corporate executives. As we have documented, managers directly involved with digital imaging developed a highly adaptive representation of the emerging competitive landscape. We speculate that the cognitive dissonance between senior management and digital imaging managers may have been exacerbated by the difference in signals that the two groups were receiving about the market."* Bihide (2000) and Christensen (1997) support this view. Both found that employees at incumbent companies often generated the ideas that went on to form the basis of the discontinuous technologies. However, these were exploited and developed by competitors, or new organizations, and consequently adversely affected the incumbent. Hence, organizations facing discontinuous technologies often do not lack innovative ideas or strategies, but in some circumstances, seam unable to develop them successfully.

## THE DEVELOPMENT OF COGNITIVE MAPS

During periods of technical stability, when innovation evolves in a continuous form, the individual (Fiol and Huff, 1992) and collective (Langfield-Smith, 1992) cognitive maps of senior managers, of technologically successful organizations, concerning the perceived value of a technology critical to their organization, are highly correlated with the actual value of this technology to their organizations. Senior managers exert influence over the strategy and operations of their organizations (Hambrick and Mason, 1984), through a process that can be referred to as *"sensemaking"* and *"sensegiving"* (Gioia and Chittipeddi, 1991). When technologies evolve in a discontinuous form (Anderson and Tushman, 1990; Christensen, 1997; Utterback, 1996), dissonance can occur between senior managers cognitive maps concerning the perceived value of a critical technology to their organization, and the actual value of this technology. This can result in them mismanaging the discontinuity. This actual value is referred to in Figure 2 as *"external unmitigated reality."* This is defined as when reality is interpreted either by a) persons who do not have a vested interest in the success of the incumbent organization, and who are external to the organization, and/or b) the emergence of empirical evidence which possesses a low potential for subjective interpretation i.e. growth in sales figures for a particular product. The presence of this dissonance has been identified in other areas of organizational change, such as TQM initiatives (Reger *et al.*, 1994). The cause of this can be attributed to a number of factors. The first of these will be role of the individual cognitive maps of senior managers. These can be understood through the utilization of personal construct theory (Kelly, 1963). It states that individuals organize, interpret and draw meaning from the data that they encounter, and this data is developed into *"systems of meaning"* or schemas about their environment, which consequently determine their actions (Reger *et al.*, 1994). The limitations of these schemas can be referred to as *"absorptive capacity"* (Cohen and Levinthal, 1990), which is defined as an individual needing *"prior related knowledge to assimilate and use new knowledge."*

The second cause of dissonance occurs at the level of the organization. Organizational identity theory and related concepts are possible factors here. For example, Walsh and Ungerson (1991) present the concept of organizational memory, and propose, *"decision choices framed within the context of an organizations history are less likely to be met with resistance than those not so framed,"* and Ciborra and Lanzara (1994) suggest that formative contexts, and the cognitive imageries that result from them, impact on the practical and reasoning routines in organizations, and thus organizations abilities to successfully adopt innovative technologies. Hogg and Terry (2000) discuss the concepts of social identify and self categorisation, and proposed that when groups are faced with subjective uncertainty they may *"produce a prototypically cohesive and homogenous organization with which members identify strongly."* These ideas point towards the tendency for organizations to gravitate towards homogeneity in some form. When the factors that this homogeneity consists of are dissonant, with respect to the technology that is under threat of a discontinuous type of innovation, it is possible that that the organization will be at risk of mismanaging its response this innovation.

Other factors that could affect the inability of an organization to perceive this dissonance is the presence of confirmatory (of its historical cognitive maps) information that is communicated by the communities of practice that it belongs too (Swan *et al.,* (2002), and the tight coupling that is required for high performance teams (London and London, 1996). This discussion is presented as a model (Figure 2), and will be further developed and discussed in future papers by the authors.

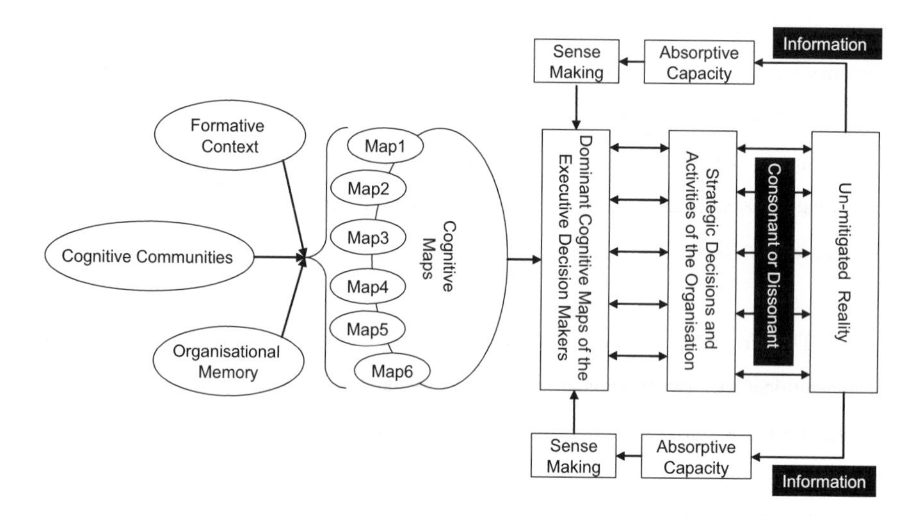


**Figure 2. The development of the cognitive maps of the dominant upper echelons of an organization, and their role in causing dissonance with the externally unmitigated reality of an organizations environment.**

## Cognitive Dissonance and the Management of Discontinuous Innovation

Cognitive dissonance is a theory from social psychology presented by Festinger (1957). Harmon-Jones and Mills (1999) define it by suggesting:

*"Pairs of cognitions (elements of knowledge) can be relevant or irrelevant to one another. If two cognitions are relevant to one another, they are either consonant or dissonant. Two cognitions are consonant if one follows from the other, and they are dissonant if the obverse (opposite) of one cognition follows from the other. The existence of dissonance, being psychologically uncomfortable, motivates the person to reduce the dissonance and leads to avoidance of information likely to increase the dissonance. The greater the magnitude of the dissonance, the greater is the pressure to reduce dissonance".*

This theory is presented as Figure 3, and shows how inconsistency between cognitions leads to the creation of dissonance. This can create the need for a reduction strategy to be implemented, and consequently the dissonance alleviated.

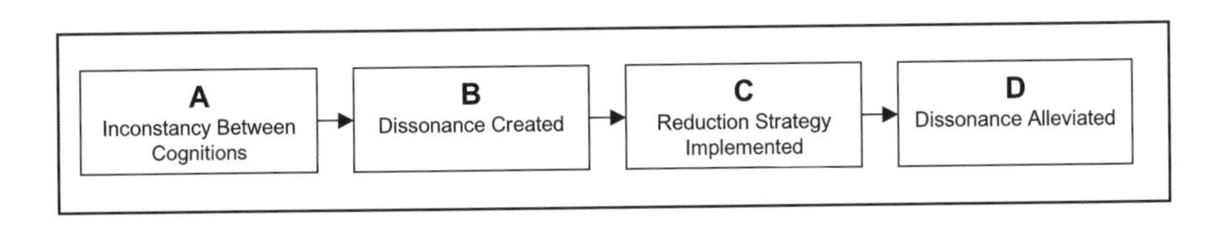


**Figure 3. A Model of Cognitive Dissonance (Devine *et al,* 1999)**

Mills and Ford (1995) found that the greater the difference between the alternative options a person has, when deliberating in private, and the more important a personal choice is to an individual, the greater efforts they will go to, to reduce the dissonance that would occur after a choice was made. Moreover, they also found that the more important an issue is to a person, the greater the difference between the alternative options will be when deliberating in private than in public. Festinger (1957) suggested that this reluctance to deliberate between alternative options with a high degree of difference is based upon an individuals fear of dissonance, and thus to commit themselves. In later work Festinger (1964) stated that *"if a person anticipates dissonance as a consequence of making a decision, he would be expected to react by attempting to minimize, or avoid completely, the anticipated dissonance."* Aronson (1999) suggests that the concept of the self is a critical factor in determining whether or not dissonance occurs. So when an important element of the self is threatened, e.g. competency, morality or ability to predict their behavior, people endeavor to maintain a sense of self that is both consistent and positive. This phenomenon is described as self-affirmation theory.

Other authors have further developed understanding of this phenomenon in terms of suggesting how people might respond when experiencing cognitive dissonance. The first of these responses is referred to as the **spreading of alternatives** (Brehm, 1956; Shultz and Lepper, 1996). This is where persons experiencing cognitive dissonance seek to reduce the discomfort experienced, through removing negative aspects of the chosen alternative, or positive aspects of the rejected alternative. In the context of the mismanagement of discontinuous technologies, this reaction to cognitive dissonance could involve managers either disregarding negative aspects of a strategic option or information concerning factors such as customer needs, or positive aspects of the rejected alternative.

*Proposition 1: Due to their experiencing of cognitive dissonance, managers may seek to remove as being valid evidence that suggests that their current technologies or business models may no longer offer the highest return on capital employed and/or possess the most competitive advantage.*

The second response is the **belief – disconfirmation paradigm** (Festinger, 1956; Burris et al, 1997). This occurs when people are presented with information that is inconsistent with their beliefs, and they don't change their beliefs as a result of this information, this can lead to misperception or misinterpretation of the information, rejection or refutation of the information, and seeking support from others who agree with one's belief. The belief – disconfirmation paradigm suggests that managers who are presented with information and data, which suggests that their current technologies or business models may no longer offer the highest return on capital employed and/or the competitive advantage in the marketplace, may go on to dismiss this information, misinterpret it and/or persuade others within the organization to do the same.

*Proposition 2: Due to their experiencing of cognitive dissonance, managers may dismiss or misinterpret information if it does not fit their understanding of what strategies will generate the highest levels of returns on investments made, and influence others to do the same*

The third response is the **effort – justification paradigm** (Aronson and Mills, 1959; Beauvois and Joule, 1996). This suggests that the more effort people have to put into an activity, because of the relatively higher level of dissonance experienced, the more they will seek means to exaggerate the desirability of the outcome of this activity.

*Proposition 3: Due to their experiencing of cognitive dissonance, managers who may have invested a lot of personal effort and economic capital in a project, business model, or developing a specific knowledge base, may seek out evidence that validates this effort, at the expense of another project, business model or knowledge base, which might offer greater competitive advantage and returns on capital employed.*

The fourth response to cognitive dissonance is the **induced – compliance paradigm** (Festinger and Carlsmith, 1959); Linder *et al,* 1967), which suggests that people who are given a small reward to engage in a counter-attitudinal behavior, are more positive about the behavior, then those are paid a larger reward. This paradigm was developed further by findings that indicated the opposite of this occurs when people are not given a choice i.e. the greater the reward the more positive the attitude towards the behavior. This paradigm suggests that rewards offered by organizations, explicit (financial incentives, promotions etc) or implicit (sense of belonging, self actualization etc.) cause people to disregard information and evidence that suggests that the organization's current technologies or business models may no longer offer the highest return on capital employed and competitive advantage.

*Proposition 4: Managers will seek to reduce the dissonance caused by opposing cognitions because of their desire to receive the rewards on offer, and thus disregard any cognition that would position them as being opposed to the dominant thinking within the organization, which may exclude them from any such rewards.*

This section has presented a set of proposition that could explain why senior managers, also referred to as members of the upper echelons of an organization, mismanage discontinuous technologies. It has linked this to the managerial responses to discontinuous technologies because of the presence of cognitive dissonance. It has generated four propositions that use the responses to cognitive dissonance, as a basis for interpreting the reasons why senior managers mismanage discontinuous technologies. Several reasons are presented as to why mangers mismanage discontinuous technologies in a previous section of this paper, such as inertia of success (Markedis, 1998) misunderstanding the timing of the entrance of discontinuous technology (Foster, 1986), the power of a companies past on its problem solving capabilities (Leonard, 1995) and a failure to understand the evolution of customer segments and markets (Christensen, 1997). This research does not go to the level of detail required to understand the cognitive process responsible for why these factors occur. This is clearly a weakness in the literature that is discussed in more detail in the conclusion section of this paper.

## CONCLUSIONS

This paper has sought open up a new area of research that examines the relationship between the mismanagement of discontinuous technologies and theory from the field of social psychology. Through using cognitive dissonance to understand the mismanagement of discontinuous technologies, it has established that there is a need for greater understanding of this mismanagement, with respect to the role of management cognition. Specifically, it has shown that the current body of knowledge in this area does not pay enough attention to the cognitive process undertaken by senior managers when faced with such technologies. It suggests that the reasons why managers from incumbent organizations often respond to the entrance of a discontinuous technology, in a way that causes them to mismanage the discontinuous technology, can be caused by the presence of cognitive dissonance. Through the analysis undertaken, it is apparent that there is a need for further theoretical and empirical work into the detail of how managers process information, in areas such as; customer needs, technology strategy and inter-organizational relationships. There is also a need to understand empirically whether or not cognitive dissonance is actually present, and is a contributing factor to the mismanagement of discontinuous technologies by senior managers. This will require new inter-disciplinary research to be undertaken by technology management researchers and social psychologists.

This paper is divergent, rather than convergent in nature, and seeks to open up a new area of enquiry. It does not claim to be precise in terms of its *comprehensiveness* or *parsimony* (Whetten, 1989), in covering all the relevant factors that should be considered, with respect to this relationship between the mismanagement of discontinuous technologies and cognitive dissonance. It has made an attempt to bring to the attention of scholars and practitioners, that existing knowledge from another domain, that of social psychology, could be used to understand why managers in incumbent organizations struggle with the mismanagement of discontinuous technologies. Further empirical work could also lead to development of theory, which would help explain the presence and role of collective dissonance among senior managers when faced with a discontinuous technology, and how cognitive maps are constructed, and can be changed. This would build the propositions presented in this paper, to advance to a stronger theoretical and empirical level of understanding.

The end point of such a collective research endeavour should be the assistance of these incumbent managers in correctly managing such technology change successfully. In addition to this, any future studies into this area should consider focusing on the following variables, and how they might either encourage, or mitigate against the presence of cognitive dissonance. Firstly, the diversity of the senior management team must be a consideration. This could be considered in a number of ways, such as length of time employed by the organization or working in the industry, psychological profile (for example see Kirton's (1976) and (1984) concept of innovators – adaptors), technology specialism, functional experience and specialism, and national culture. The second variable that should be investigated is the role of industry structure. It would seam a reasonable hypothesis that companies such as Polaroid will be more susceptible to cognitive dissonance, due to their reliance on narrow group of technologies to underpin their products, than companies such as 3M, who employ hundreds of different technologies. The number of technologies employed could have a linear relationship with the number of cognitive maps in the organization. Thus a greater amount of maps could mean that each individual one was diluted in terms of its over all impact. Moreover, should any one of the technologies undergo a discontinuous period of change, then the impact of this on the overall company would be diluted, if the presence of cognitive dissonance caused the technology to be mismanaged. The role of the existing culture, processes and organizational structure of an organization should also be considered as factors. Cultures that tolerate a higher level of ambiguity (Markides, 1998), the development of formal processes that encourage and facilitate risk and exploration (Veryzer, 1998), and innovative organizational structures (Tushman and O'Reilly, 1996), such as corporate venturing units (Sorrentino and Williams, 1996 and Thornhill and Amit, 2000), could all play a role However it must be noted that Tripsas and Gavetti (2000) noted similar practices were employed by Polaroid, who still suffered from the presence and effect of dissonance, with severe commercial consequences. Consideration should also be given to the inter-organizational relationships that an organization has, and its role and purpose within a value chain. This has been shown to make an organization more rigid in the face of disruptions (Christensen, 1997 and Hill and Rothaermel, 2003).

Finally, any research endeavour in this area must ultimately be focused on assisting the art of practice in the successful management of discontinuous technologies. Hence there is the need for interventions that can assist with the diagnosis, and facilitation of an increase in self-awareness, of senior managers, of the construct of their own cognitive maps. Moreover, to help them overcome the role that dissonance between these maps and the external environment, in which their organization operates in, might play in mismanaging discontinuous technologies.

## REFERENCES

Anderson, P. and M. Tushman (1990). Technological discontinuities and dominant designs: a cyclical model of technological change. *Administrative Science Quarterly*, **35**, 604-633.

Anderson, P. and M. Tushman (1991). Managing through cycles of technological change. *Research Technology Management*, **34**, 26-31.

Aronson, E. and J. Mills (1959). The effect of severity of initiation on liking for a group. *Journal of Abnormal and Social Psychology*, **59**, 177-181.

Barr, P.S., J. L. Stimpert and A. S. Huff (1992). Cognitive change, strategic action and organizational renewal. *Strategic Management Journal*, **13**, 15-36.

Beauvois, J.-L. and R.-V. Joule (1996). *A radical dissonance theory*. Taylor & Francis, London.

Bhide, A.V. (2000). *The origin and evolution of new businesses*. Oxford University Press, UK.

Brehm, J. W. (1956). Post-decision changes in the desirability of alternatives. *Journal of Abnormal and Social Psychology*, **52**, 384-389.

Burris, C. T., E. Harmon-Jones and W. R. Tarpley (1997). "By faith alone": religious agitation and cognitive dissonance. *Basic and Applied Social Psychology*, **19**, 17-31.

Christensen (1997). *The innovators dilemma*. Harvard Business School Press, USA:

Ciborra, C. U. and G. F. Lanzara (1994). Formative contexts and information technology: Understanding the dynamics of innovation in organizations, *Accounting Management and Information Technologies*, **4**,61-86.

Cohen, W. M. and D. A. Levinthal (1990). Absorptive capacity: A new perspective on learning and innovation, *Administrative Science Quarterly*, **35**, 128-152.

Dosi, G. (1982). Technological paradigms and trajectories. *Research Policy*, **11**, 147-162.

Festinger, L. (1957). *A theory of cognitive dissonance*. Row, Peterson, USA.

Festinger, L. and J. M. Carlsmith (1959). Cognitive consequences of forced compliance. *Journal of Abnormal and Social Psychology*, **58**, 203-210.

Fiol, C. M. and A. S. Huff (1992). Maps for managers: where are we? Where do we go from here? *The Journal of Management Studies*, **29**, 267-286.

Foster, R. (1986). *Innovation: the attackers advantage*. Simon & Schuster, USA.

Foster, R. and S. Kaplan (2001). *Creative destruction: why companies that are built to last under-perform the market and how to successfully transform them*. Doubleday, USA.

Gioia, D. A. and K. Chittipeddi (1991). Sensemaking and sensegiving in strategic change initiation, *Strategic Management Journal*, **12**, 433-449.

Gioia, D. A. and E. Pitre (1990). Multiparadigm perspectives on theory building, *Academy of Management Review*, **15**, 584-602.

Hambrick, D. C. and P. A. Mason (1984). Upper echelons: The organization as a reflection of it's senior managers, *Academy of Management Review*, **9**, 193-206.

Hamel, G and C. Prahalad (1990). The core competence of the corporation. *Harvard Business Review*, May/June. 79-90.

Hamel, G. (2000). *Leading the revolution*. Harvard Business School Press, USA.

Harmon-Jones, E. and J. Mills (1999). *Cognitive dissonance: progress on a pivotal theory in social psychology*. American Psychological Society, USA.

Henderson, R and K. Clark (1990). Architectural innovation: the reconfiguration of existing product technologies and the failure of established organizations. *Administrative Science Quarterly*, **35**, 9-30.

Hill, C. W. L. and F. T. Rothaermel (2003). The performance of incumbent organizations in the face of radical technological innovation, *Academy of Management Review*, **28**, 257-274.

Hogg, M. A. and D. J. Terry (2000). Social identity and self-categorisation processes in organizational contexts, *Academy of Management Review*, **25**, 121-140.

Kaplan, S., F. Murray and R. Henderson (2003). Discontinuities and senior management: Assessing the role of recognition in pharmaceutical organization response to biotechnology, *Industrial and Corporate Change*, **12**, 203-233.

Kelly, G. A. (1963). *A theory of personality: The psychology of personal constructs*, *The Norton*, New York.

Kirton, M. (1976). Adapters and innovators: a description and measure, *Journal of Applied Psychology*, **61**, -629.

Kirton, M. (1984). Adapters and innovators: why new initiatives get blocked, *Long Range Planning*, **17**, 137–143.

Langfield-Smith, K. (1992). Exploring the need for a shared cognitive map, *The Journal of Management Studies*, **29**, 349-369.

Leonard, D. (1995). *Wellsprings of knowledge: building and sustaining the sources of innovation*. Harvard Business School Press, USA.

Lewis, M. W. and A. J. Grimes (1999). Metatriangulation: building theory from multiple paradigms, *Academy of Management Review*, **24**, 672-690.

Linder, D. E., J. Cooper and E. E. Jones (1967). Decision freedom as a determinant of the role of incentive magnitude in attitude change. *Journal of Personality and Social Psychology*, **6**, 245-254.

London, M. and M. M. London (1996). Tight coupling in high performance teams, *Human Resource Management Review*, **6**, 1-24.

Markides, C. (1998). Strategic innovation in established companies. *Sloan Management Review*, **39**, 31-42.

Mills, J. and T. E. Ford (1995). Effects of importance of a prospective choice upon private and public evaluations of alternatives, *Personality and Social Psychology Bulletin*, **21**, 256-266.

Modis, T. (1998). *Conquering uncertainty*. McGraw-Hill, USA.

Reger, R. K. and A. S. Huff (1993). Strategic groups: A cognitive perspective, *Strategic Management Journal*, **14**, 103-124.

Reger, R. K., L. T. Gustafson, S. M. Demarie and J. V. Mullvane (1994). Reframing the organization: why implementing total quality is easier said than done, *Academy of Management Review*, **19**, 565-584.

Shultz, T. R. and M. R. Lepper (1996). Cognitive dissonance reduction as constraint satisfaction. *Psychological Review*, **103**, 219-240.

Sorrentino, M. and M. L. Williams (1995). Relatedness and corporate venturing: does it really matter? *Journal of Business Venturing*, **10**, 59-73.

Swan, J., H. Scarborough and M. Robertson (2002). The construction of "communities of Practice" in the management of innovation". *Management Learning*, **33**, 447-496.

Thornhill, S. and R. Amit (2000). A dynamic perspective of internal fit in corporate venturing, *Journal of Business Venturing*, **16**, 25-60.

Tripsas, M. and G. Gavetti (2000). Capabilities, cognition and inertia: evidence from digital imaging. *Strategic Management Journal*, **21**, 1147-1161.

Tushman, M. and P. Anderson (1986). Technological discontinuities and organizational environments. *Administrative Science Quarterly*, **31**, 439-465.

Utterback, J. (1996). *Mastering the dynamics of innovation*. Harvard Business School Press, USA.

Veryzer, R. W. (1998). Discontinuous innovation and the new product development process, *Journal of Product Innovation Management*, **15**, 304-321.

Walsh, J. P. and G. R. Ungson (1991). Organizational memory, *Academy of Management Review*, **16**, 57-91.

Whetten, D. (1989). What constitutes a good theoretical contribution? *Academy of Management Review*, **14**, 490-495.